K.S. Karol was born in Poland. From 1955 to 1970, he was the foreign correspondent of the *New Statesman*. He now lives in Paris and is senior editor of the influential weekly, *Le Nouvel Observateur*. His previous books include *China: The Other Revolution*, *Visa for Poland*, *The Second Chinese Revolution* and *Guerillas in Power* (on Cuba). *Solik* is the first volume of his autobiography.

K. S. Karol

Solik

Life in the Soviet Union 1939–1946

Translated from the French by Eamonn McArdle

Pluto Press

First published in 1983 by Librairie Arthème Fayard,
75 rue des Saints-Pères, Paris 6
This translation first published in 1986 by Pluto Press Limited,
The Works, 105a Torriano Avenue, London NW5 2RX
and Pluto Press Australia Limited, PO Box 199, Leichhardt,
New South Wales 2040, Australia. Also Pluto Press, 27 South Main Stree
Wolfeboro, New Hampshire 03894-2069 USA

7   6   5   4   3   2   1

90   89   88   87   86

Cover designed by Chris Millett

Phototypeset by AKM Associates (UK) Ltd,
Ajmal House, Hayes Road, Southall, London

Printed in Great Britain by Guernsey Press Co. Ltd.
Guernsey, C.I.

British Library Cataloguing in Publication Data
Karol, K.S.
   Solik: Life in the Soviet Union, 1936–1946.
   1. Soviet Union —— History —— 1939–1945
   I. Title
   947.084′2′0924   DK273

ISBN 0 7453 0063 4

Contents

Solik

1. The schoolboy from afar

At the lycée in Rostov-on-the-Don they called me Solik, diminutive of the Russian word for salt, but I no longer recall why. That was, it is true, 40 years ago, and it is idle of me to protest my good memory; it sometimes lets me down. As early as this school year of 1940–1, however, I knew that I would one day have to tell Solik's story. This idea never left me in the seven years that I spent in the Soviet Union, in the Red Army, in prison, in a camp, then once again in Rostov, at university and at work. Like a good reporter I noted everything, but only in my head, trusting exclusively in what it would retain. It was not a propitious time to keep a journal, even in Polish – which would, theoretically, have protected it from indiscreet glances – in this town where only Russian was spoken. But I couldn't have foreseen that I would write this story 40 years later and in French into the bargain; this language of aristocrats that colours the pages of Tolstoy, obliged me in Rostov to look for the translation of certain words at the foot of the page or in the appendices.

My school in Rostov is situated in a street parallel to the River Don and parallel also to the city's longest and most famous avenue, which bears the name Friedrich Engels but which even young people, born after the Revolution, continue to call by its former name, the Sadovaia, 'avenue of the garden', doubtless on account of the tall trees that border its wide pavements. The *diesiatiletka* (school for 10-year-olds plus), having been founded under the Soviet regime, has no former name: it is designated only by a number, 44. To get there, you have to go down at right angles from the Sadovaia in the direction of the Don. I remember it very well because of the glacial wind that blows in winter from the river towards the slopes, forcing us to walk backwards to protect our faces. The nose is very vulnerable to the cold, and also the eyes, because this wind carries a great deal of dust in addition to snow. After this descent along an avenue which bears the name Voroshilov, but which used to be called simply Bolshoi Prospekt ('grand perspective'), you experience, as soon as you cross the school threshold, a sensation of relief and well-being: my *diesiatiletka* is very well heated.

Otherwise, to my Polish eyes, it is a very poor school. In my home town, Lodz, I attended an altogether more elegant lycée, endowed with laboratories, large theatres, gymnastic halls and sports fields. However, during this long and cold winter of 1940–1, remarkable for the unleashing of the wind from the Don, the warm school No. 44 is a place that I like very much. Unfortunately you spend only five hours a day there. My *diesiatiletka*, like a factory, does three shifts: the morning shift from eight o'clock to one, the afternoon from two o'clock to seven, and the evening, two or three times a week – perhaps even more – when it lends its premises to nightclasses for adults enrolled in the Moscow Institute of General Construction Engineers. Our classrooms are therefore utilized to the full and, for this reason I presume, energetically heated day and night, but cleaned only at long intervals, which gives them this slightly dilapidated air, at least to my eyes. In my lycée in Lodz, which was a private establishment, we walked on parquet floors and, in order not to dirty them, we had to put on slippers of a prescribed style as soon as we arrived. We also wore made-to-measure uniforms with distinctive badges attesting to our membership of a 'superior' educational establishment. In Rostov there are neither slippers nor uniforms and the cloakroom, where you leave only overcoats, is always disorderly; sometimes even fights break out. Here the cloakroom is a nondescript sort of room, without spaces allocated to different classes, without lockers for shoes or personal effects. There is no cloakroom attendant and the students hang up their coats in any old way, less carefully, needless to say, than did the relevant, paid personnel in my lycée in Poland.

2

For Solik, in the hierarchy of his discoveries, the greatest of all is to attend a mixed school for the first time, to share a class with girls who are almost young women, because he is in the upper sixth form. It is one of these girls, Vera – it is coming back to me bit by bit – who gave Solik his nickname. In Russian, Karol means king and, according to her, it is hardly decent to be called such a name in the country of progress, which has broken once and for all with monarchy and everything connected with it.

There are several Veras in my class, at least three, perhaps even four. I had read, in my time at the 'superior' lycée in Lodz, that forenames had been imposed in the USSR, 'Octiabrina', for example, in honour of the October Revolution, or 'Marlen', a condensing of Marx and Lenin, or again 'Josipina', to perpetuate the glory of Josip Vissarionovitch Stalin. But at school No. 44 no girls are so called, while the Veras, Nadezhdas and Lioubovs – Faith, Hope and Charity, the three Christian virtues – are legion. And the Veras are the most numerous. It is in their honour that we sixth formers sing, at breaktime, a very old student song, rather daring for the Rostov of 1940: *Vera tchoudnaia moia, Vera liache, tra-la-la* (my marvellous Vera, Vera come to bed, tra-la-la). In the chorus the archangel Gavril (Gabriel) is punished for not having understood the mores of student life, to the great joy of the 'marvellous Vera' who makes fun of him. In 1940, however, the Veras, like the Nadias and the Lioubas, remain faithful to the archangel's prescriptions and are very chaste – at least in my experience. Between me and the Vera who baptized me Solik, thereby manifesting a certain interest in my person, there is not even a flirtation; nor is there with Klava, a young Cossack who sat next to me. I picture Klava as beautiful and smiling, but she is even more timid than I am. I do not remember the other girls in my class. In my memory, however, the image of Clarissa remains engraved because of her unusual forename and demeanour. Throughout this cold winter of 1940 I nourish a secret passion for her without mentioning a word of it to my closest friends. They do not know her anyway, for the good reason that she doesn't attend our school, nor does she stroll with us along the

3

Sadovaia at the close of the day. Clarissa pays not the slightest attention to me, however, absolutely none. She isn't even interested by the prestige, the exotic quality, which attaches to my status as a foreigner.

My position in Rostov-on-the-Don is unique. I am the only student in this city to have lived abroad and to have been born in Poland, far away from the imposing banks of the Don. Poland has just collapsed, but until then it was a capitalist country, linked to the old imperial powers, France and Great Britain. There is no question therefore that I should ever speak positively of anything Polish to my friends here, to Micha or to Kola (but didn't Kola, a central character of my Soviet past, perhaps appear on my horizon only later, in 1941 in the Red Army?). In any case I cannot explain to them that I owe my good class marks, and later the title *otlitchnik* – first in my class – not to any particular diligence on my part, but to the baggage of learning that I brought with me. And it isn't the only secret that I cannot confide to them. I have another, more important and more dangerous.

Contrary to what I tell one and all, and contrary to what everyone believes, I did not come to Rostov direct from Lvov, which was annexed by the Soviets after the partition of Poland in 1939. My itinerary was altogether longer and more perilous. Before ending up in the capital of the Don, I passed through that same Western Siberia which would later supply the USSR with the bulk of its oil (40 years ago it wasn't event dreamt of). I didn't go there as a tourist either. I was deported there with more than a million other Poles but, not having greatly appreciated the large forest that extends between Tioumen and Omsk, I decided to run away and succeeded in getting as far as Rostov, taking in Moscow en route. At school No. 44, nobody, I'll bet, has had such an adventure.

My new friends of that year are not great travellers. The most adventurous among them, Kola – it hardly matters at what moment he appeared in my life – has only taken the shuttle between Mietchotka, his native village, and Rostov. Micha admits to me that he would like to see the world but so far he has gone no further than Nakitchevagne, an area not too distant from the town centre, starting immediately beyond the square in front of the large theatre which, curiously, was built in the shape of a tank. Even among our teachers, those who have been to Moscow are the exception, and foreign countries exist for them only in the atlas. I could, therefore, have boasted about my travels, but the instinct of self-preservation obliges me to keep silent and to pretend hypocritically that I would so like to go to Moscow and see Red Square, when in fact I have already walked the length and breadth of it.

Nevertheless I feel good at school No. 44. I am flattered by my good marks and my status as *otlitchnik*, and my interest has been aroused by the novelty of my position and by the incessant discovery of the peculiarities of Soviet daily life. My own secrets do not weigh heavily on me, perhaps because I am insouciant by nature and live from day to day, forgetful of dangers already encountered and those which still lie in wait. Sometimes I feel guilty about keeping secrets from those who surround me because this shows that I remain on guard, that I have no confidence in them. But do the others tell me everything? Don't they too have their secrets?

Clarissa, for example. I meet her at the home of Matvei – Motia to his intimates – a young mathematics teacher at the university whom a stroke of luck put my way. His home, a handsome room with a balcony, in a communal apartment, is always open, although Motia has a lot of work to do and his wife, Tima, a student, is often working for examinations. One day, in private, I ask Motia: 'How is it that Clarissa is always so well dressed? She is more carefully made-up than other girls of her age.' I take care not to admit, even to Motia, that I also find her very pretty, because it would be ridiculous to admit such a feeling for a girl who pays no attention whatever to me. But, without giving myself away, I can reasonably ask him about Clarissa, whose appearance is exceptional in a poor and relatively egalitarian country like the USSR. Here, in contrast to the situation in Poland, a woman's elegance cannot be explained by her wealth. I add that I notice that Clarissa, without appearing obviously very sad by nature, talks very little and rarely becomes

5

involved in our conversations.

'She is an orphan like you,' Matvei replies laconically. In 1940, although alone in Rostov, I am not for all that an orphan, having by no means lost hope of retracing my parents, who stayed on in Lodz when it came under German occupation. What is it with Clarissa? Is she, like me, provisionally an 'orphan', waiting to see again the parents with whom for the moment she is unable to communicate? Is this the secret that weighs on her and renders her so little inclined to be talkative?

Now, 40 years later, after all the revelations on the Gulag – the existence of which was no mystery to me, having been through the forest of Western Siberia myself – I tend to believe that Motia, whose answer had in no way replied to my question about Clarissa's strange appearance, had intended to put me on the track of certain secrets that a number of people in Rostov shared. That wouldn't have been so surprising: historically, this Cossack town, one of the 'White Guard' capitals, had experienced waves of severe repression unmatched elsewhere. At the time, however, his reply simply appeared to me to be evasive.

In this school year 1940–1 all that I know is that Matvei, himself an orphan, has a lot of friends, for the most part mathematicians like himself (Boris R. for example), and that I enjoy a great deal of his Russian hospitality. What attracts me to his home, in addition to the solidarity between orphans, is its studious atmosphere, the cleanliness, the parquet floors, just like my lycée in Poland.

I have taken for myself a miniscule room for a small rent at the home of a militiaman, a decent sort whose wife totally ignores him and is outrageously unfaithful to him. When he is on duty she hardly bothers to disguise the visits from her lover, a shady character. Lost in their frolics they forget that my little room doesn't even have a door, only a curtain. After the well-heated lycée and a few hours spent at the Karl Marx municipal library, if I don't go to Micha's house, which is quite a way off, I turn up sooner or later at Motia's. No matter what the time Tima ritually asks me 'Have you eaten yet?' but, nine times out of ten, I do not take advantage of her offer. This is partly because, this year at least, I am well fed – from this point of view it will be my best year in the USSR – and also because I don't come to Matvei's home to eat, but to enjoy the company.

Matvei reciprocates this sentiment in calling me *Solik chouh-kharnoi paren* – Solik, the funny kid. I make him laugh a lot, often unintentionally, by telling him my impressions of school No. 44, of the Karl Marx library or of Rostov life in general. He would like me to become a mathematician – 'It's the best career for you, believe me' – and that bothers me a little: I trust his judgement but I feel no vocation whatever for science. To overcome my reservations Motia sometimes takes me to his own evening classes for correspondence students enrolled in another Moscow Institute. The relaxed atmosphere of this class pleases me enormously. Ignoring all the usual academic formalities, it is rather more like a group of friends, a sort of working meeting between people of roughly similar age. Motia, although already well qualified, is only 26 years old and appears even younger. With his robust, athletic build he doesn't resemble at all the popular caricatures of mathematicians, figures with their heads in the clouds or forever in chase of butterflies. After the class, the students – there are a dozen – accompany us, with Boris R., who also teaches here, and the discussion continues in the street despite the cold. In Rostov, buried under snow, where the rule is early-to-bed, we are the only nocturnal pedestrians, almost sleep-walkers. We don't quite manage to take leave of one another. I follow the very technical conversation only with difficulty, but this is no reason to leave it for my bed in the cuckold militiaman's house. In fact, I am the last to go home; with Motia and Boris R. I feel more adult, a student already, better protected also.

Matvei is not interested solely in mathematics. He is a great poetry enthusiast and particularly admires Alexander Blok. He knows Blok's poems by heart and his talent in reciting them is really worthy of an actor. With 'his' Blok, Motia could have staged a theatrical production instead of contenting himself with enlivening our evenings in the course of this Rostovian winter. And he doesn't recite merely *The Twelve* or *The Scythians* – the standard sixth form fare: 'his' Blok is especially that of *Nieznakomka*, 'The Unknown One,' attired in splendid silk at once beautiful and ephemeral, woman and mirage. This *Nieznakomka*, to tell the truth, doesn't really inspire me, and Matvei's recitations would have wearied me had there not been in 'his' Blok a very Western melody which struck a distinctive chord in me, recalling my past, my origins, my sense of belonging to another world. I have been a Soviet citizen for only one year after all, and there is nothing surprising in the fact that, for me, *Nieznakomka* is merely an exotic lady, on a par with Greta Garbo or Marlene Dietrich for example, both of whom remained fresh in my memory from the cinemas in Lodz. Be that as it may, I start to think very seriously about enrolling in the faculty of mathematics at the University of Rostov in order to become a real student of Motia's – and I promise myself to read Alexander Blok.

Some months later, I shall no longer be faced with a choice: the war is here and decides for us all. I was not to return to Rostov until April 1944, having lost all contact with my friends of 1940. The town was disfigured: the war front had passed through it three times, sparing nothing, not the Sadovaia, nor the university, nor the large tank-shaped theatre. Motia's house, however, had remained intact amid the ruins. Tima welcomed me, but there was no more Matvei: as an artillery officer he had been killed, according to witnesses, at Sevastopol in 1942. The news was unconfirmed, because the army had still not sent any formal notification, so there was nothing for it but to wait and hope along with so many other families in Rostov. I went back again on one other occasion, much later, to ask for any news of him. This time Tima didn't show me in: she seemed to have just got out of bed and it was clear that, in the large room with the balcony, there was another man to whom she didn't care to introduce me.

As for Clarissa, she died of typhus in Rostov in 1942, during the German occupation. I shall never know whether she really was an orphan, nor for what reason she crossed our world so elegantly, almost in silence, on tiptoe.

*

It wasn't chance which brought me to Rostov-on-the-Don after having fled Western Siberia. It seemed to me that I already knew the avenues of this town, especially the Sadovaia; they had been lovingly described to me by my family, who had lived for a long time on the banks of the Don before settling in Lodz. Nostalgia for this past, which had been shattered by the Bolshevik Revolution, was demonstrated by a tenacious linguistic loyalty: at home, I spoke only Russian. Even today, after so many years, my brothers Alexander and Boris still write to me from Poland in this language, as though to carry on the family tradition. It is no longer anything more than a fanciful indulgence because, through lack of practice, all three of us get confused by the Cyrillic characters. At the time though it was otherwise: I was proud of being bilingual, of knowing the works of Pushkin and Lermontov, Chekhov and Tolstoy, not to mention Maxim Gorky and Vladimir Mayakovsky with his *March to the Left*. It was as if I had already had some inkling that, thanks to them, in Rostov Solik would astound his teachers by his capacity to catch up and overtake the other pupils, even in the field of Russian and Soviet literature.

In Lodz I was careful not to flaunt these interests too much for fear of being taken for a *moskal*, or Russky, the common pejorative given to Russians. I felt myself to be Polish; I didn't set myself apart in any way from my schoolfriends and I took part in their entertainments and amusements. But the feeling of belonging to another world, vaster than the confined framework of a single country, did not suddenly come to me in Rostov. I had experienced it already in Lodz, certainly in a less acute fashion, but sufficiently to render me immune to the anti-Russian rhetoric of Poland under the colonels. In vain did my lycée teachers praise to the skies the Polish Nobel laureates Sinkiewicz and Raymond: I knew that Tolstoy and Dostoyevsky had been immeasurably greater.

As consistent atheists my parents had had to expend a great deal of energy to get themselves registered in the category of those 'without a faith'. They had decided, nevertheless, to send me to a private Catholic lycée, contenting themselves with securing for me

9

an exemption from all religious teaching. Every morning however, I had to attend morning prayer, dedicated to the 'Very Holy Mother of God'. I wasn't permitted exemption from this routine, so as not to appear unduly privileged in arriving a quarter of an hour later than everyone else. Present but mute, I took part daily in a rite which, for me, was deprived of all meaning, under the mistrustful eye of the priest who sometimes made me recite the prayer, alleging that I was exempted only from the obligation to say 'amen'. To make matters worse, my lycée was named after Ignacy Skorupka, the 'martyr priest', who perished, we were told, on the Vistula front in 1920, after having repulsed the Bolshevik hordes by making signs of the cross. In the ceremonies devoted to his glory each year, the stories we were told would have sent you straight to sleep. They were tall tales that would have scandalized any serious theologian, yet I was supposed to learn them conscientiously. 'It's a good school and you should take advantage of it, without concerning yourself with these priests' tall stories,' my mother would say imperturbably.

On this point – it was practically the only one – my father agreed with her. In other respects my parents didn't form a very harmonious couple, either in terms of age – my father was 25 years older than my mother – or in terms of cultural interests. If I have trouble in retracing their respective itineraries it is not from a want of memory; there are too many things in their lives that I never knew about or understood. My father must have been 50 years old when I was born in 1924. He had been a wealthy man in Rostov-on-the-Don but was so no longer in Lodz, where, materially speaking, he was dependent on his young wife, a lawyer, an intellectual and a socialist. On coming home from school I would find this already elderly man boasting without any great conviction of his former riches and in fact thinking only of the imagined or real infidelities of his pretty and active spouse. Having witnessed these scenes, I and my sister Alicja, two years my senior, had genuine difficulty in understanding what could have brought our parents together in Rostov. Money, perhaps? But our mother, in our eyes, was the most disinterested of people, the least calculating kind of person that one could imagine.

10

In order to solve this mystery we would have had to have known our father during his heyday in Rostov. There, in this far off town, he had furnished proof of talent as an entrepreneur. He had succeeded in leaving a province designated 'open' to Jews, to become a banker, a property owner, and to receive a residence permit in Rostov – a town in theory 'closed' to Jews – made out in the rank of 'Merchant of the First Guild', which, for a bourgeois in czarist Russia, was the highest of social distinctions. Married, the father of three sons – my stepbrothers – he had fallen head over heels in love during the First World War with a young student – my mother – at that time in Rostov with the University of Warsaw, which had been evacuated there. The timely death of his first wife – suicide was mentioned – allowed him to remarry, with an ostentation befitting his rank, and to organize a sumptuous honeymoon voyage with friends, aboard a cruiser on the River Volga, then at Yalta. Only one of my stepbrothers, Eugene – a student by then – was allowed to join in these almost legendary festivities. Boris and Alexander, being still too young, stayed at home under the strict authority of their French governess, Mlle Lily.

When the era of cruises on the Volga came to an end as a result of October 1917, Genia – diminutive of Eugene – accompanied the family as far as Lodz in 1921. But he left there soon after to move to London where, after completing his studies, he found a place in a large import-export company, S. Behr and Matthiews, and became in the course of time a loyal subject of His Gracious Majesty. He came back to visit us only at holidays, for Christmas, sometimes at Easter, loaded with presents but hardly at all inclined to become involved in my parents' domestic scenes, and still less inclined to talk with a youngster like myself about the reasons for their marriage. Papa would have preferred him to remain at home with us but, having established from experience that Lodz was no place for a 'real businessman', he didn't insist.

He had still possessed the means to send his other two sons to study abroad – Boris in France, Alexander in Austria – but his 'sacrifices' were poorly rewarded. Having returned to Lodz at the

11

height of the 1930s' depression neither of them found a job worthy of their education and consequently didn't help the family at all. At the University of Bordeaux, Boris had learned to play cards and he became one of the pioneers of bridge in Poland. This obliged him to lead a nocturnal life criticized all the more by the family in view of his uncertain income. With Alexander the situation was worse still: having witnessed the lost battle of the Schutzbund in Vienna, he veered towards the far left and declared himself a communist. Even for my mother it was too much; as for Papa he often baited him with defiant taunts: 'Help yourself to the fresh cream, go on. When your Bolshevik friends come that will be an end of it, just as in Rostov.'

I had become, within the family, the sole interlocutor of Chourka – Russian diminutive of Alexander – whose Polish friends called him Olek. He took charge of my political education and had me read some Marxist works, beginning with Bukharin and Preobrajenski's *ABC of Communism*. Sometimes, on Sundays, he took me to the park where, as if by accident, we would always meet his friends (those for whom he was Olek) and they would talk earnestly about the 'fascist Pilsudski regime'. I could hardly contribute to these discussions, but I learned a lot of things from them. I heard about these 'useless men', landless peasants and the unemployed, forced into exile in the West to work at only the harshest and most menial jobs; about the poverty of the eastern provinces where, to economize, people were reduced to 'cutting each matchstick in four'; about the persecution of national minorities; about the Bereza-Kartuska concentration camp. 'You have a fine forename,' one of Olek's comrades said to me one day, 'just like Marx and Liebknecht.' This made me blush with pleasure.

I was 12 years and one month old when, in September 1936, Olek was arrested somewhere in the eastern provinces, the 'Polish Ukraine', for clandestine activities. My mother, with the help of her socialist lawyer friends, managed to get him out of prison but wouldn't forgive him for having 'tarnished the family's good name'. Olek then set up home in Gdynia on the Baltic coast, married Zosia, a young worker, and showed his face at our home only for holidays.

He didn't enjoy the same preferential treatment as my British brother, but it was Chourka whom I preferred. His presence always sparked off impassioned political discussions and, even though they both represented the 'left wing' of the family, it was always my mother the social democrat and my communist brother who confronted each other. My mother expressed herself better: it was her job and, good jurist that she was, she knew how to expose, for example, all the lies of the Moscow Show Trials which, in her view, had demonstrated the degeneration of socialism in the USSR. On this topic Chourka replied only with defensive quips as if he too remained unconvinced by the confessions of this same Bukharin whom he had made me read at the age of 10. But he retorted that it was nevertheless over there that 'the future was being built', and not in our society which was rotten to the core with injustice. Alone against everyone he even went so far as to state that 'we would have done better to stay in Rostov'. I hadn't the courage to come to his aid: I knew little enough about Rostov, and my mother's accounts of the situation in the Soviet Union worried me.

Chourka regained stature in my eyes when he spoke about the ineffectiveness of the opposition Polish Socialist Party (PPS), which the regime tolerated merely in order to maintain a facade of democracy, or when he evoked the Nazi monster that he had seen with his own eyes, 'back home, in Austria'. He knew everything there was to know on the origin of Hitlerian barbarism: it was nothing but big capital's war machine against the workers' movement and against the USSR. In his view 'Stalin and his loyal comrades' – an expression engraved on my memory ever since – were alone in fighting the Nazi threat consistently and were the only ones capable of ridding the world of it. Without the USSR, he predicted, Poland would be the first to be submerged, because its French and British allies were playing a double game and pushing Hitler towards the east.

My mother, clearly, didn't share this viewpoint; nor did Genia, or even Boris, the least politicized of my brothers who nevertheless had learned 'back home, in France' to trust in the Republic. However in

13

1938, after Munich, events proved Chourka singularly right, at least in my view. At Eastertime in 1939, Genia arrived from Prague where he had had business to settle for S. Behr and Matthiews; he had seen for himself the Nazi monster at work. He had never brought us so many presents, as if he knew that it amounted to a final goodbye. He was so surprised to see me almost as tall as himself that he left me a suit he had had made to measure from Herman Horovitz, the best tailor in Prague. Little did he imagine that, a few months later, this present would open for me the road to his native Rostov. Not that I had any hint myself of my future Siberian wanderings; in fact I felt reassured by what he told us concerning Churchill. Genia reported that Churchill's arrival in power was imminent and that he was resolved upon cutting short Hitler's career once and for all. Chourka smiled ironically: he wasn't looking for a fight but observed simply that the veteran of Munich was still prime minister and that the so-called 'providential Churchill' had rightly criticized him for the slow pace of the negotiations with the USSR. In the course of a recent Commons debate this distinguished Conservative 'semi-rebel' had cited the exemplary power of the Soviet airforce and armoured divisions. Chourka spoke to us about it as though he were concluding an argument, reminding us discreetly that he had been right all along: without the help of the USSR it would be impossible to crush Hitler's Reich.

My mother was the most preoccupied of all: the participation of the Polish colonels' regime in the dismemberment of Czechoslovakia after the Munich Accords had sapped her morale. She was forced to admit that the socialist opposition, tolerated by the colonels, had shown its complete impotence on this occasion, which she regarded as a sinister omen. Her long-standing advocacy of a 'class struggle without hatred' – the favourite theme of her epic debates with Chourka – henceforward gave way to a more violent language against Warsaw's ruling class, now acting as Hitler's unwitting accomplice. But an alliance with Stalin's Russia appeared to her to be impracticable and dangerous; the 'guarantee' that Britain had accorded Poland didn't reassure her either, and she couldn't forgive the French for having brought down Leon Blum's government. At the end of the day, in her view, only the awakening of the Polish people could be counted upon, to produce the heroic feats of which they had always shown themselves capable in times of danger, on several occasions in their history.

I took up the thread of Chourka's argument, contesting even more radically than he had done, without a trace of bad faith, the analysis made by my mother, and accused her of having succumbed to a *weilkomocarstwowy* state of mind (favouring a Greater Poland). I admit I wasn't taking any great risks: as her only son I was mollycoddled and favoured. Instead of reproaching me for the provocative style of my arguments, my mother, who normally got easily excited, became very sad and was on the verge of tears. I remember the strange silence which then descended upon this last family reunion. To bring it to an end my mother uttered only one sentence in a strangled voice: 'You haven't understood anything at all: at this stage it is certain that no one will save us.' There was something definitive in her prophecy, which was neither polemical nor conducive to discussion, which came to an abrupt halt.

It was because of football, however, that my relations with my mother became soured for good shortly afterwards. Thinking of myself as gifted at this game that was rarely played at the lycée, I had succeeded after no little trouble, in getting myself accepted into the junior section of the LKS (Lodz Sports Club). Two afternoons a week I practised diligently and with enthusiasm in the position of outside right, obtaining only relative success because although I had good acceleration I still had poor ball control. My schoolwork was hardly affected by it and in any case as the spring term came to a close I already knew I was assured of a place in the upper sixth. In principle, the management of this good school oughtn't to have concerned itself with my hobby, still less so since in the words of the old slogan appropriated by Poland under the colonels, 'a healthy body guarantees a healthy spirit'. However, one fine day I was ordered never to set foot in the LKS again. My mother was asked for a written undertaking that I wouldn't disobey this ban. Ever since then I have remained a frustrated outside right: in my dreams I control the ball magnificently, make finely judged passes and occasionally score some very good goals, as if the 1939 ban had remained inscribed for life in a corner of my brain. At the time, however, it was the straw that breaks the camel's back. The lycée in my view wanted to stop me from attending the LKS just to keep me away from ordinary young people, the better to keep me in the ghetto of an indoctrinated elite.

This political context to my little football drama was understood perfectly well by Stefan Wegner, my liberal-progressive drawing and practical arts teacher, and he expressed his solidarity with me without, however, being able to intervene in any way. My mother on the other hand accepted the lycée dictat without batting an eyelid, saying that in her opinion the LKS was full of hooligans. She insisted that I avoid any conflict with the lycée, so that I should not be prevented from sitting for the baccalauréat the following year on the pretext that I was too young. Her attitude saddened me. It recalled to me some of Chourka's quips against this social democracy which, in order to avoid future dangers, accepted any present humiliation. But there was nothing to be done: my rebellion didn't go as far as preferring football to everything else and besides, conscious of my poor ball control, I already suffered doubts in my more lucid moments about my future as an outside right.

The incident had at least the advantage of bringing me close to Stefan Wegner. He was not only a teacher and a radical. As a gifted painter he was linked to the group of avant-garde artists around Strzeminski and his wife Kobro, and he was to me the incarnation of intelligence and kindness. His convictions concerning art had led him to a radical critique of society and to a practical non-conformism in his own life. At that time, the teaching staff were expected not to entertain informal relations with their pupils. Wegner nevertheless invited me to his home with two of his other 'favourites', Jurek B. and Rysiek D., both the sons of printers linked to the opposition. We went with Wegner, not to the park where I used to go with my communist brother, but to the museum, and sometimes to Strzeminski's home. This was not in order to become better acquainted with painting (in Wegner's view everyone ought to have their own key to understand it) but rather to talk about the movement of anti-fascist intellectuals in the West and about the great international battle of 'Reason' against obscurantism and barbarism. None of them belonged to the Communist Party; Strzeminski was even a veteran of the anti-Bolshevik war of 1920. But their political and cultural positions seemed to me to be very close to those of my brother Alexander. The enemy to be defeated was Nazism, and the USSR could only be an ally in this battle since it was threatened just as we were and belonged in the final analysis to the Left.

I came to the conclusion that my mother's warnings against 'Stalin and his loyal comrades' in fact reflected the anti-Bolshevik rancour of her husband, who had been ruined by the October Revolution, and that they were explicable in terms of the peculiar history of my family rather than by History with a capital H. Now, too, that I had reached 1.76 metres, and that I was admitted into Wegner's circle of radical intellectuals, I could no longer remain a 'Mama's boy'. I made a defiant display of my political emancipation by sneering at *Robotnik* (*The Worker*), the Socialist Party newspaper which exalted the flag of the PPS 'covered in blood and glory' but which didn't propose anything – in part, in any case, as a result of the censorship, because it often appeared with blank pages. But what really separated us, even if I hardly ever spoke about it, was the fact that my heart was beating more and more in unison with the USSR. Over there there was surely less meanness, and the future was not choked off as it was in our country under the colonels' regime.

On 1 September 1939, the upper-sixth form students of Skorupka lycée were in Wlodzimierzow on the Pilica. We had just spent a month there, in a military training camp, a boring time but all things considered almost like a holiday. The course was compulsory for candidates of the baccalauréat. We were due to return to Lodz

17

that day; but it was also the day that the Germans chose to attack Poland – and to launch the Second World War. Since the conclusion of the German–Soviet pact eight days earlier, the event had been in the air but since no news of it had arrived in our camp we knew nothing about it. The camp's commander, *pan porucznik* – a lieutenant – did not meddle in politics, or else he didn't want to speak to us about Poland's isolation. But perhaps my own memory has eliminated from that period any recollection of the all too famous handshake between Stalin and Ribbentrop.

Whatever be the truth of the matter, I remember that we were taken by surprise by the war and indignant, but certain of victory for Poland. While waiting to know what our destiny had in store, we hurried to buy notebooks and pencils, apparently thinking only of our future essays. I had another anxiety also: that *pan porucznik*, discovering that I was two years younger than the rest of my class, would send me home. But my dossier didn't interest him and besides he didn't force anyone to follow him. He announced on the contrary that the war would be a long one and that we would have the opportunity of enrolling when we reached 18, or even 21 years of age. He only wanted some volunteers to make up a detachment of auxiliaries whose task would be the protection of public buildings, perhaps in Warsaw. This would release a company of the regular army for duty on the front. We all volunteered, and all took a step forward. I imagine that we resembled closely those lycéens of the Kaiser's Germany, described superbly by Erich Maria Remarque in *All Quiet on the Western Front*. Our eyes, too, blazed with patriotic ardour. In the cases of Jurek, Rysiek and myself – Stefan Wegner's three protégés – it was above all an anti-fascist fervour. In addition, I promised myself that in the hour of victory, after crushing the Germans, I would direct my gun at the oppressor regime in Poland. Protecting public buildings would suit me very well meanwhile: our army at the front had to have its rearguard well secured.

However, in this war the front was everywhere, beginning with the road which we took to reach Warsaw. In undisputed command of the air, the Luftwaffe pounded and bombarded everything that moved, at least in western Poland. To start with we were terrified. During the first raid, Sergeant-major Bartczak, a stupid and cruel man, even ordered a peasant woman to strangle her baby so that it should not expose us to risk with its crying (our fallback position was a gully on the edge of a potato field). Fortunately the brave *baba* decided not to obey. Bit by bit we became used to the Luftwaffe; it had claimed no victims from among our little troop, which comprised 100 auxiliary soldiers and 10 or so regular soldiers who flanked us. The real problems were our slow progress and the perceptible lowering of morale, the fear that perhaps we weren't after all on the side destined to conquer.

Where were our planes anyway? Did Poland have any planes? Some took comfort in pretending that our airforce was active on the front, unlike the Luftwaffe which was being used against civilians, women and children. But this explanation, based on trust in the moral superiority of our pilots, collapsed when we reached the suburbs of Warsaw. Muffled rumblings of artillery fire convinced us that the front couldn't be very far away; and, alas, there wasn't a Polish aeroplane in sight. Worse still, nourished by the myth of the combined might of France and Great Britain, we half expected to see their squadrons fly above our country. Instead they were conspicuous by their absence.

Things were going really badly, much worse than even the most pessimistic forecasts. During the first days of the march our lieutenant, confident in his knowledge of military history, had explained to us that at the start of each war German armies rushed forward but that they were then always forced to beat a retreat. In the suburbs of Warsaw he no longer made this point and tried simply to establish contact with his superior officers. Until now he had led us without regular communication with any sort of general staff; for all we knew he might have invented all of this story about auxiliaries guarding public buildings. Now, his weary eyes betrayed fatigue and disarray: in Warsaw they hadn't any need of us and it was too late to send us back to Lodz, which was now occupied by the Germans. The lieutenant recovered his verve after meeting a group of officers among whom was a major, who agreed to help him and us. I remember that after their conversation they separated on a perky note: 'See you again, after another miracle on the Vistula . . .' 'All they're short of is a new Skorupka,' commented Jurek, the most sarcastic among the three of us. I myself wasn't shocked by the bravado of our officers, imagining, like them, that the Polish Army still had the capacity to wage a victorious battle on the outskirts of the capital. Hadn't my mother told me that in the hour of danger our people were capable of surpassing themselves, of revealing unsuspected reserves of heroism?

Our small troop, however, was not supposed to contribute to this exploit. Our leader, the lieutenant, having assembled our supplies and received his instructions, ordered us to march towards Lublin – and to sing en route! In our song even the trees were supposed to salute us, because it was for our Poland that we were going into combat. In reality neither man nor beast paid us any respect, and we didn't have the opportunity to fire a single shot. The enemy always came from the air and, even when they flew very low they were still beyond the range of our old Mausers. The war rapidly became monotonous; day after day we saw the same scenes: civilians running to save themselves from aerial raids, convoys dispersing, lorries or carts on fire. The smell along the road was unchanging too: it was the smell of dead horses which no one had bothered to bury and which stank to high heaven. We moved only at night and we learned to sleepwalk while marching. Smoking was forbidden, as though the light of a cigarette could bring down on us the might of the all-powerful Luftwaffe.

That September of 1939 was a marvellous month, mild, sunny, worthy of an Italian end of summer. On the other hand we were cruelly short of information. Where were the allied armies? Were they advancing on the heart of Germany, forcing young Wehrmacht auxiliaries like ourselves on night marches towards the east? Hardly. Our lieutenant would have told us because despite the blackout he still heard some news from the 'Centre'. 'The war on the western front is non-existent, just like our airforce,' Jurek proclaimed, with his usual decisiveness. 'But why would they have betrayed us?' I objected without, it must be said, much conviction. 'And why did they make a present of Czechoslovakia to Hitler?' Rysiek took Jurek's side and my explanations about Churchill, based on Genia's 'revelations', had no effect. 'Neville Chamberlain is still prime minister of Great Britain,' he replied, just as my brother Alexander used to do.

Then one morning, choking with rage at having a gun and being unable to use it, Rysiek, who was a born troublemaker, started firing into the air, just so that he could enter this first burst of gunfire into his diary of our journey. The ferocious sergeant-major, unable to put him under arrest, chose to take revenge by confiscating his watch – in order to time the pace of our march. It was downright scandalous, because there really was nothing to time since we weren't aiming to keep any appointment in our trek across a blitzed and martyred Poland. Rysiek decided to complain to our lieutenant and we went to see him as a delegation, though without much hope: a regular army officer never disavows a subordinate officer, especially not a sergeant-major, his right-hand man. In fact our lieutenant merely frowned and gave no response, as if these little details of the life of his adolescent regiment hardly concerned him. The same evening, however, Sergeant-major Bartczak returned my friend's watch to him, saying nothing more about measuring anything whatever.

Two weeks after our departure from Warsaw, when we had already gone well beyond Lublin, our lieutenant suddenly ordered us to make an about-turn. We were going back towards the west, towards Chelm. What had happened? Had the miracle on the Vistula materialized? Were we finally going to protect the public buildings in Warsaw? Orders, in an army, are never explained, and the Polish Army was no exception to the rule. But, along the roads, day or night, we were never alone: other soldiers and civilians were also on the march and, thanks to what is called in the West the 'arab telephone' and in the USSR 'Radio Yerevan', we learned that no miracle had taken place. We were heading towards the west because the Soviets were arriving from the east; and they were not coming to our aid, to fight 'in a consistent manner against the Nazis', as my communist brother's old formula had it. 'Stalin and his loyal comrades' were coming to take their share of Poland.

We three accomplices were seized with consternation. If the Bolsheviks had become friends with the Nazis, then there really were no longer any principles anywhere in the world, there was no longer any hope for our poor Poland. On the other hand, why should we go to meet the Germans, who had attacked us first, rather than towards the Soviets who, as far as one could tell, were neither bombing nor destroying everything in their way. Ought we to try to repeat our exploit with the watch, and go to see the lieutenant to discuss his decision with him? Such a step would certainly have yielded nothing and would have marked us out as communist sympathizers, which, in Poland, even at this moment of total disarray, could only lead to unfortunate results. What then if all three of us took off to try and join up with the Russians? But this solution didn't have much to recommend it either. The atmosphere in our little troop was good, our lieutenant had won our respect and he was surely more knowledgeable than we were about how to move around in wartime. If there were a way out of the trap which enclosed us, it was still our commander who had some hope of finding it. We followed him to the end, therefore, but we were bitter and disappointed at having been betrayed by all sides, by the Western powers, by the Soviets and by our own government, which had already fled to Romania.

While still marching I began to sleep more and more deeply, to such an extent that I ended up dreaming as though I were in bed. Thus it was that one night I saw the sky fill with countless Soviet squadrons which opened up the road to their powerful armoured divisions, the importance of which Churchill himself had recognized. They were coming to deliver us from the Nazis and our lieutenant thanked them very courteously for it, as a comrade-in-arms who knows how to appreciate fraternal bravery and help. Even Sergeant-major Bartczak, that vitriolic anti-Bolshevik who never missed an opportunity to curse the reds, ignoring the fact that it was the

Germans who had attacked us, even he embraced the Russian tank-drivers and cried out: "We are all part of the same family, three Slav brothers.' And our Soviet liberators also had an enormous tank of fresh cream, which they were generously distributing in order to show just how wrong my father had been to think that there wasn't any to be had under the Bolshevik regime . . .

'Are you crazy or what?' Jurek pulled me towards a gulley to get me off the road as quickly as possible. That night some Luftwaffe pilots were amusing themselves by flying above our heads. According to Jurek, I replied that they were Soviet squadrons but I don't remember anything about it: all I know is that ever since this rudely interrupted dream on the great Polish–Soviet anti-fascist reconciliation, I talk in my sleep and even reply, it appears, to questions, just as if I were awake.

We went round in circles for one week more. Warsaw surrendered on 27 September but we continued our march until 5 October, the day on which we found ourselves encircled, with some detachments of the regular army, by the Germans, near the village of Krzywda ('Injustice'). The Wehrmacht, for its own amusement or to encourage us to surrender, sprayed us with bursts of machine-gun fire and with an abundant stream of grenades. I received something in the eye almost without noticing it, and without feeling any pain. My right eye simply closed and I could no longer open it except with the help of my fingers. I didn't make a fuss about it, believing that it would pass, and I took part in all of the farewell ceremonies. A high ranking officer, a colonel or perhaps even a general, had been authorized to make a speech to us in which he said that the war was not over, that the Polish Army, under the command of General Sikorski, fought on in France, that our powerful Western allies were more than ever at our side. Our lieutenant also came to say goodbye, because the Germans were separating the officers from the NCOs and the ranks. He gave us to understand that we would soon receive orders on the best way of pursuing the war; then he shook hands with each of us, showing particular warmth towards Rysiek, Jurek and myself. It was as though he thought that after the arrival in power of the opposition general, Sikorksi, we ought to take over the leadership of his little troop.

In Demblin Fortress on the Vistula, however, where we were taken, there were no leaders among the prisoners, at least not during the ten days that I spent there. It wasn't a camp like the one in Renoir's *La Grande Illusion*, with barracks, beds and even a theatre. In Demblin we were shut up in a depot full of racks for arms and we were allowed out only to queue up, in the rain, in front of an improvised open-air kitchen. At night we arranged bunks as best we could with boards torn from the partitions and placed on the racks because, without them, there wouldn't have been enough space for everyone on the ground. Our bunks, however, had an unfortunate tendency to collapse, which often provoked a good deal of stumbling, swearing and jostling in the darkness. The Germans would arrive hurling abuse and insults, the wealth and variety of which far exceeded anything I had learned at Skorupka lycée. Blows struck with rifle butts landed here and there on the heads of these 'Polish dogs' but I was lucky enough to avoid them. We were waiting for them to take a census of their prisoners in order to explain our peculiar situation as auxiliaries, but they didn't seem to be in any hurry. On the other hand, I remember that in the course of one rainy morning one of the Wehrmacht loudmouths came into our depot screaming: '*Alles was Jude ist, aufstehen*' (Anyone who is Jewish, stand up'). 'These savages don't even know how to speak German,' remarked Jurek, who was 100 per cent Aryan but who was even more afraid than I was, because he had a bronze tint to his skin and a flattish nose which had earned him the nickname 'golliwog' at the lycée.

At the St Casimir Hospital in Radom where I was sent to have my eye attended to, the groans of the wounded seemed restful to my ears after the screams of Demblin. The atmosphere of this hospital was very special: tense, a little surrealistic. The Germans had taken charge of everything, from surgery to administration, but they had let the nuns continue nursing. They were excellent nurses, and strong Polish patriots, conspirators even. The sister who looked after me had a German-sounding first name, Kunegunda, but she would rather have had her tongue torn out than have to pronounce a word in this language. As with all the other nurses the occupiers had to speak to her through the intermediary of an interpreter. The military doctors were above talking to the wounded. I only found out about my operation from Sister Kunegunda. In her view, the procedure followed by 'normal people' was to remove a splinter of grenade shrapnel from the eye by means of a magnet (it was such a splinter that had pierced my eye), whereas these Teutons, these butchers, had proceeded directly to enucleate my eye, without a general anaesthetic. Today, I know that it was too late to save my eye at Radom: it might have been saved if the operation had been performed on the same day that the injury occurred, but not 10 days later – the 10 days that I spent in Demblin Fortress. At the time, however, I was convinced that I had been intentionally mutilated by the barbarian Germans.

Sister Kunegunda was very good to me, perhaps in the hope of bringing me to religion, or more simply because of my youth. She did all she could to keep up my morale, sometimes brought me sweets and promised to contact my family through the intermediary of another sister who happened to be travelling to Lodz. I wrote a long letter, as amusing as I could possibly make it, with the aim of minimizing the drama of my adventure for my parents, but also informing them of my irrevocable decision to move to the provinces incorporated in the USSR, beyond the River Bug.

Days passed, snow fell on Radom, but no reply arrived from Lodz. Despairing ideas crept up on me: did my parents no longer want to hear from me, in order to show me their disapproval, as often happens in certain American films? Or had they died during the awful blitz? Sister Kunegunda prolonged my stay in hospital by spinning yarns to the Germans. She urged me to be patient, arguing that 'under the Teuton regime it isn't easy to write or to travel about'. If it came to the worst, she said, she would find me some civilian clothes and get me out of there to enable me to avoid returning to the infernal Demblin Fortress.

Then one morning the doctor announced to me the arrival of '*eine dame*', my mother. This was one of the rare occasions on which he consented to say a few words to me, but it was obvious that he had eyes only for Mama, this young woman wearing a pretty hat and veil, which hid her face and gave her eyes a mysterious look. Having complimented her on her command of German he assured her, very courteously, that thanks to replacement parts 'made in the Reich', one would hardly even notice that I had lost an eye. Still pursuing this almost sociable conversation, he sent someone off to look for the 'replacement part'. While waiting for it he deplored aloud this useless war, stupidly provoked by England. Then, as the demonstration drew to a close, he expressed surprise that a woman so young should have a son in the army. 'He is only 15 years old,' my mother replied, whereupon the chivalrous German ophthalmic surgeon raised his arms in the air as if to say that, really, these Poles were even more bellicose than the English. He left us alone for a moment, then returned to announce to my mother that she could take me home, suggesting that he himself had issued the requisite authorization. In fact, though I found out only later, all my comrades from the lycée detachments had been released from Demblin at roughly the same time.

At the home of some friends of Sister Kunegunda in Radom, my mother gave me a suitcase with all my things carefully arranged, and directions on the best way to cross the Bug. Once we were alone together my mother's poise, which she had maintained admirably at the hospital in the presence of the Germans, began to fail her, and showed the extent of her fatigue and despair. Resting on her elbows on the table, she supported her head in her hands and repeated, 'It is far worse in Lodz than anything you can imagine.' She wasn't going to try to keep me at home and wanted me to avoid seeing the situation there at first hand. I suggested that she come with me to the USSR, despite her political apprehensions, but it was out of the question. My father, compelled to wear the yellow star, was completely shattered and no longer able to travel. She didn't intend to leave him in Lodz: marriage, even if not very harmonious, is for life. My sister and her fiancé would help her, she added, as if to reassure me. She also gave me an envelope from Papa containing 12 pounds sterling and the addresses of his two sisters, one of whom lived in Rostov, the other in Moscow. In accompanying me to the station my mother pulled herself together. She kept back her tears and whispered in my ears: 'I'll not see you again, ever.'

On 30 November, at nightfall, I cross with 10 others a vast, melancholy-white landscape under the direction of a guide. We walk across the Bug frontier river, which has already been frozen over for at least two weeks; a deep layer of fresh snow hinders our steps. The sheets which serve us as camouflage keep slipping from our shoulders; we stumble repeatedly. If a patrol were to pass by, it would spot us without difficulty. Then the guide murmurs some directions to us and leaves us to it; he returns to his village on the German side. It is up to us to find his Soviet opposite number. We carry on in silence, uncertain of going in the right direction. In the mist of this moonless night you can't see any light or any sign of an inhabited place. 'Siberia must be like this,' I tell myself, 'the snow, the cold, and not a soul for a hundred miles around.' Suddenly we hear voices: someone is approaching, apparently without nervousness. Everything turns on whether he will cry 'halte' or 'stoi', whether he is German or Russian. This waiting seems to us to last an eternity because the stranger, or strangers, like us are unable to clear a path in the snow. But gradually, as they approach, my apprehensions dissolve: these newcomers swear in an inimitable Russian.

I am certain about this date, 30 November 1939, the day of my entry into Soviet life, because it was on this day that my personal white magic performed a good turn for me. Having been brought up without religion and not being accustomed to praying to God, I had constructed for myself a whole system of oracles and portents, a sort of personal method of divining the directions of destiny and of formulating my own fancies and desires. The signs, which seemed addressed to me by some occult power, were narrowly linked to political or sporting events, or suggested to me by Maria, our housekeeper in Lodz. If, for example, both the Krakow and LKS football teams played well on the Sunday – I gambled on both of them in order to increase my chances – I was going to be very successful at school all week. The same was true if the number four turned up in the national lottery, or, better still, the number 24 (the year of my birth). On top of this, my own successes were supposed somehow to carry on in the external world, and I believed myself authorized, in these instances, to formulate certain wishes. During the icy-cold period of waiting on the Bug I gave myself over to this game of omens: if I got out of this scrape it would signify that something very positive would soon happen on a global scale, for example that the USSR would break off its pact with Hitler, liberate Lodz and that I would be reunited with my mother and the rest of my family.

The crossing of the Bug ended better than I could have hoped for. The Soviet frontier guards were not in the least bit unfriendly. On the contrary, they brought us to a warm shelter, gave us tea and, having discovered that I spoke Russian, positively warmed to me. They even found me space on a lorry that was leaving the next day for Lvov. Their manner of addressing me – *'Eh ty Rousskii'* ('You there, the Russian') – made me a little uncomfortable, because Sister Kunegunda's last piece of advice still rang in my ears: *'Badz Polakiem'* ('Be Polish'), with the unspoken afterthought, 'Fight for Poland'. But I learned the most worrying news only upon arriving in Lvov: on 30 November the USSR had indeed gone to war – not against the Third Reich, but against little Finland.

My system of portents was to function badly in the USSR, under this materialistic regime which is so hostile to superstitions. I was furnished the proof of this seven months later, on the occasion of my deportation to Siberia. These seven months were both baffling and distressing for me. Lvov was a far more beautiful town than Lodz and in fact far more Polish.* In vain was it proclaimed the capital of

---

*Turn by turn Russian, Polish, Austrian (from 1772 to 1918), once again Polish after the First World War, the town had been taken in 1939 by the Germans, who then ceded it to the Soviets on 22 September. Lvov had been 'Soviet' for only two months when I arrived there.

the Western Socialist Ukraine, to no avail were its walls covered with posters in the Siberian language: its majority Polish population remained more than ever attached to the pre-war nationalist ideology. The Soviet attack against Finland and the reactions it provoked in the West could only reinforce their convictions. The world appeared to them to be divided into two camps, the Western democracies on one side, pledged to defend small countries such as ours and Finland, and, on the other side, the totalitarian regimes, in the front ranks of which figured the Third Reich and the USSR. The Western powers were certainly disappointing with their 'phoney war': however, though democracies are always slow to mobilize, this doesn't prevent them from deploying, in the end, an irresistible force.

I felt ill at ease with these amalgamations. How was it possible to put the USSR and Hitler's Germany on the same level, the one with its prestigious history, its aspirations, its struggle for the future, the other with its primitive obscurantism? My experience told me that these totalitarian regimes were different in nature. There was a world of difference, as I had been able to see for myself, between the Wehrmacht soldiers in Demblin and those of the Red Army on the Bug. Besides, if my anti-communist mother had advised me to go to Lvov rather than return to Lodz, she must have had good reasons for doing so, reasons which were at odds with the Manichean vision of our compatriots. But I had no other friends than them, having no contacts with the Ukrainians and still less with the Soviet soldiers of the Red Army.

I found a modest job in a chemistry laboratory where I washed test-tubes, and even more modest lodgings (a commode, in a kitchen, on which I stretched out at night, my feet half dangling in the air) at the home of a retired Polish lady who, if I remember rightly, was an acquaintance of Sister Kunegunda. The snow, which fell abundantly that year, was also my ally: the authorities decreed that all citizens had to clean the streets and this resulted in those with status getting young people like myself to substitute for them. The few roubles a day that I earned at this were essential. For lack of time, however, I no longer studied anything, nor did I go to any public entertainments, or even read newspapers: the *Ukraine Pravda* would have discouraged anyone from taking the slightest interest in politics.

Nevertheless, I decided to enrol in the Komsomol. It was in reaction to an anti-Soviet evening at the home of one of my landlady's friends. Everyone there gloated over these shabbily dressed Russians and their ragged army which had been held in check by Finland; when all was said and done, the Germans were a deal more serious and respectable. My landlady, by way of proof, related how the wives of Russian officers had bought up all the nightdresses from the shops in Lvov, thinking that they were buying evening dresses. 'That's the way your communist ladies dress to go to the opera.' And the poor woman burst out laughing even though she herself hadn't a stitch to put on her back, and never frequented the theatre. Feeling myself under an obligation, and having no one there who shared my views, I hadn't the courage to preach solidarity between the dispossessed, nor to argue against the 'old ideas', but I felt that I would have to go to the communists and discover what they were really saying among themselves, outside their official speeches, whose stupidity doubtless derived from tactical considerations.

My expedition to the Komsomol was a humiliating failure. I had written and learned by heart a text of adherence that declared my support for the goals of the Komsomol, avoided thorny subjects such as the pact with Hitler and the war in Finland, and insisted instead on my overall intention of contributing to the construction of socialism and, in particular, to better communication with the Polish population. I delivered my speech in front of a man of about 40 who listened to me without the least interest and gratified me only with a sentence which left me stupefied: 'Lenin's Komsomol (*leninskii komsomol*) is not a public house where anyone can enter whenever they wish. To become part of the Komsomol you have to be chosen.' He didn't condescend to note my name, convinced that I would never be 'chosen'. (He was mistaken.)

Having thus established that I was not wanted for the 'process of transition to socialism in the Western Ukraine' I remembered that I had the addresses of my two aunts in Rostov and in Moscow. What I really hoped was for them to invite me to join them in the 'real Russia', but travelling around in the USSR was an even more reckless project than wanting to join the Komsomol. We belonged to the same republic, administratively speaking, but not in terms of railway communications. My Rostov aunt didn't reply to my letter, while my aunt in Moscow declared herself delighted to learn that her brother had a grown boy like me, but asked that I please not write to her too often, because the big bad dog in the courtyard of her block frightened the postman . . . There wasn't a great deal to be expected from her either, it seemed.

However, my oracles were becoming more and more favourable. Following a whole series of successes – I forget which – I felt myself clearly permitted to express a wish and, this time, unwilling to trust in the might of the Red Army – I made a local wish: departure for the 'real Russia'. Sure enough, some days later, I found myself in a convoy travelling to Western Siberia.

Today I am very proud of having made this great journey and of having spent some time in the country of 'fabulous riches'. If I allow myself to insist on this point it is because I see myself as Western Siberia's honorary consul in Paris. When I read for example in Leonid Brezhnev's report to the Twenty-sixth Congress of the CPSU, that 'my' region alone will produce 390 million tons of oil and 370 billion, I repeat, billion cubic metres of gas in 1985, I am overcome with a vertiginous pride. Even less sensational news items make me react, like the reportage in *Newsweek* and *Business Week* on the Siberian mosquito. American experts called in as consultants to the oilfields of Tioumen have discovered that the mosquitoes of 'my' region are totally immune to all US insect-repellents. I was jubilant on reading this, since it would finally enable me to convince my sceptical French friends that these insects, about whose invincibility I had often boasted, were no figment of my imagination.

At the time, before being forcibly taken there, I knew of Western

Siberia only from Polish films whose heroes were patriots deported by the czars. I had drawn from them the impression that it consisted of an interminable, snow-covered steppe swept by a polar wind, an open-air prison where the temperature was permanently 40 degrees below zero. Animated by hatred of the czarist regime, our patriots generally succeeded in returning to their fiancées, played by the most beautiful actresses, after an escape on foot or on a sleigh across the infernal Siberian landscape. But these mediocre films had succeeded only in inspiring me with a holy terror of everything which touched upon Siberia. In Lvov, after my unhappy experience of the frozen Bug, I wouldn't have agreed to any expedition across the snow, even if the patriotic fiancée who awaited my return had been Greta Garbo.

However, my stay in Siberia bore no resemblance at all to the Polish films. In fact, this massive deportation of Poles to the country of future 'fabulous riches' in my opinion belongs among the great ironies or ambivalences of history. It was without a doubt the greatest police operation that Europe (outside the USSR) had ever seen and it could also have been one of the most destructive. Yet, thanks to a strange reversal, this episode eventually proved favourable to those who, at its outset, had been its victims. The People's Republic of Poland and, paradoxically, the new state of Israel ended up as its beneficiaries, which would tend to show that, in this business at least, Stalin's system of predictions worked even less well than mine.

In Lvov, people were disappearing. A selective but systematic repression struck the former propertied classes as well as left-wing militants. One of the first targets was the communist poet Wladyslaw Broniewski who, in a famous poem, had evoked 'the red flag flying over liberated Warsaw'. Now, according to the German–Soviet pact, Poland ought never to exist again. If the new regime showed its claws in this manner it was because it nowhere found support; it had no 'social base'. The Ukrainians and Byelorussians, peasants for the greater part, who were supposed to have called for this regime from the grassroots, in no way wanted a Soviet-style collectivization. Among the Polish population the Communist Party (KPP) could perhaps have played a role, but Stalin had dissolved it in 1938: the leaders and the best cadres, summoned to Moscow, were exterminated in the course of a Soviet St Bartholomew's night, concerning which we still don't even know the exact date. There remained in Lvov only a small group of intellectuals around Wanda Wasilewska, who had insufficient influence to reassure a public opinion that was either apprehensive or hostile. The whole of Europe was living in a provisional frame of mind, as if in parenthesis. The war was spreading and it seemed reasonable to think that the USSR, after its semi-victory over Finland in March 1940, would choose to act according to the old British motto: 'Wait and see.'

Moscow, on the contrary, decided to strike a major blow in what had formerly been eastern Poland. At the beginning of June 1940, these provinces with their 15 million or more inhabitants were suddenly cut off from the outside world; all means of transport and communication were blocked, towards west and east alike. It was almost like a state of siege except that, in the daytime, nothing happened. It was only at night that the men in the blue peak caps of the NKVD, the Cheka, moved into action. In house after house, in cities like Lvov and also in the towns and villages, they pulled people from their beds and forced them to show their Soviet passports.

What were they looking for? Did they have lists of those suspected of trying to organize an armed Polish resistance? Not at all; they were apprehending all those who had no passport, to whom one had been refused on the grounds that they were not originally from the region. For these people no appeal was available: convoys awaited them at the nearest station.

Among those arrested, Jews who had come from the German zone were a clear majority. Persecuted by the Nazis and forced to flee, they had hoped to find a safe refuge in the zone controlled by the

USSR. There were also many Poles, originally from the western provinces, who hadn't asked for a Soviet passport because they thought of themselves as 'in transit', and were hoping to emigrate to other continents or to join up with General Sikorski's army in France. Yet others still, of various origins and faiths, had sinned by negligence, in underestimating the fastidious susceptibilities of the Soviet administration. In my own case, I had no passport for the simple reason that I hadn't yet reached the age (16) when one would be issued to me.

My birth certificate and a bundle of documents from Skorupka lycée ought to have sufficed to throw light on my case, but the three men in blue peak caps were not disposed to read them; what's more it is possible that they didn't even know how to read the Latin alphabet. My landlady, outraged by this contempt for the written word, offered her testimony: she pretended to have been present at my birth. But obliged to carry out an exact order, the Chekists remained coldly impassive: passport or convoy. A neighbour who had survived the ordeal, being in possession of his passport, came to ask them, 'What are you going to do with this youngster? Why are you insisting on throwing him overboard from society?' Although something of an intellectual this neighbour spoke a very approximate Russian, and his phrase sounded bizarre. It is for this reason that the expression left an indelible impression, and came back to me some years later, at a critical moment of my life in the USSR. In the panic of departure I didn't understand the inner meaning of it and thought simply that there would be time enough for me to learn to swim once I was overboard. The trio from the NKVD reassured my friend: 'He has nothing to worry about, he will be given a good job in our country, far from the frontier provinces.'

The next three days were an ordeal. It isn't easy suddenly to find oneself enclosed in a *tieplouchka* with 50 or so strangers. The *tieplouchka* is a freight-car fitted with rudimentary bunks (bare boards arranged on three tiers) and provided with an iron stove for heating and cooking. The name, which derives from the word *tieplo* (warm, lukewarm) was familiar to me from my early childhood days: it was in a *tieplouchka* that my parents had left the USSR in 1921. Here was I, in 1940, taking the same route, but in the opposite direction, moving away from Poland, lost among these strangers who made up a representative sample of the totality of deportees.

The Jewish colony, which formed the majority in my *tieplouchka*, comprised very different groups. On the one hand there were some very orthodox families, of the hassidic faith (though they no longer wore their traditional clothes). They huddled together, communicated very little with the others and seemed unconcerned with the outside world. On the other hand, the less religious families or non-believers spoke better Polish and discussed their opinions openly. All Jewish political tendencies were also represented, from left Zionists to ultra-conservatives. The spread of the Catholic colony was more difficult to pinpoint because those concerned preferred not to discuss either religion or their activities. Several of those aboard belonged to the liberal professions, but there was also a Renault foreman who had come to spend the month of August on holiday with his Polish family, and there was even a veteran of the International Brigade who had fought in Spain.

No one knew where we were being taken but, according to the initial rumours at any rate, we were going to Donbass, the homeland of Alexei Stakhanov, the most productive miner in the history of coal-mining. At the end of three days, just as we thought we were nearing our destination, a man in a blue peak cap, a Chekist, came to announce a 'liberal reform': our *tieplouchka* would henceforward be opened during prolonged stoppages near stations and a delegate from each wagon could go and make purchases.

In retrospect, the origin of this 'liberalization' is not hard to understand: the Soviet authorities were well equipped to apprehend individuals found to be without the proper papers, but they were less well equipped to transport them over long distances. Some thousands of enormous convoys carrying more than one-and-a-half million people, proved too much for the USSR railway network, the Achilles heel of its economy. In order to facilitate their uninterrupted passage it would have been necessary to bring all passenger and freight traffic to a halt, which clearly wasn't desirable. Therefore we were often parked on secondary lines while awaiting the green light for a further phase of the journey. Chekist guards knew that at this pace, the rations they had received for us wouldn't be sufficient for the journey. Fortunately, near each station in the USSR, there is a kolkhoz mini-market where a little bit of everything is on sale, even cooked dishes. Not wanting to let us out of their sight, they had found this democratic formula whereby we had to elect delegates who would then go and do the shopping, each one for their little collective. It was thanks to this reform that I began to discover the 'real Russia', in my capacity as the delegate of *tieplouchka* No. 27.

The sad and monotonous appearance of the mini-markets didn't surprise me. They usually consisted only of stalls supplied with the needs of travellers, and I knew in any case that the USSR was not a land of plenty. But I was struck by the fact that the peasant women stallholders much preferred barter to commerce in roubles. The news of the passage of Poles had spread to all the stations, probably because of convoys which had preceded us. The dealers, who seemed to know in advance what we had in our *tieplouchki*, presented their lists of requests in an imperative fashion: everything was included, clothes, household goods, bedding, as though we were a mobile Woolworths. 'But I have roubles,' I said to one of them who had prepared a whole mountain of *pierojki*. 'So have I,' she replied, and she begged me to go off quickly and find a better currency of exchange before her dish got cold and lost all its flavour. I shuttled back and forth, advised by companions who were more expert in this kind of commerce – the kolkhoz *babas* never wanted to accompany me as far as our convoy. Was it the custom to stay away as far as possible from the blue peak caps, or weren't our exchanges totally above board?

This trading encouraged the emergence of a new social hierarchy within the wagon, favouring the richest families, or at least those who had brought a lot of baggage with them. In my *tieplouchka*, for example, a shoe manufacturer from Lublin, at first very self-effacing and a little ashamed of his social origin, began to play a predominant role, and he did not hesitate to invite the guards to his sumptuous meals. His offspring – three boys and four girls – were offered the best places for the night, and the other passengers who, at the beginning, had deplored their poor upbringing, now found that these 'charming children' brightened up our journey. We settled into this way of life of railroad people and no longer seemed in a hurry to arrive at our journey's end.

We crossed all of central and eastern Russia in this fashion, then one early afternoon at the end of June, our convoy came to a halt on a secondary line at Sverdlovsk, capital of the Urals. It seemed just another stop. We completed our purchases, ate, and most of us settled down for the night. It must have been quite late in the evening when I saw a really big train go by: Vladivostok–Moscow, the famous Trans-Siberian line. Then our convoy moved off, slowly as usual, and took the same track, but towards the east. From this moment on it was no longer possible to doubt our destination: we were entering Western Siberia. We were about to become the new generation of Siberian deportees. I felt as though we ought to have been doing something, deliberating, adopting measures, protesting before the worst came to pass. But the unofficial leader of the *tieplouchka* refused to hear me out, while the others slept on peaceably. In front of the half-open door, alone and too excited to sleep, I waited to see the steppe appear and hear the Siberian wind. But the landscape became more and more wooded, and, to my surprise, it was actually quite warm.

The climate in Siberia is better understood nowadays. The USSR and its allies in the course of the 1960s did indeed have to buy steel tubes from Federal Germany in order to pipe oil and gas from Tioumen all the way to Bratislava. Although technically capable of producing steel adapted to the cold, they are unable to produce the kind which is resistant to large variations in temperature ranging from minus 50 degrees to plus 40 degrees. And, ever since this massive importation of West German piping, which contributed to Comecon's heavy foreign trade deficit, it is known that, in the region of Tioumen, it commonly reaches 40 degrees in summer. In my time there, the world was unaware of it; in the pre-war films in Poland, no deportee ever suffered from the summer heatwaves in Siberia.

My second surprise is difficult to express. We had been brought to a place that, for want of a better term, is called a forest. But can the enormous wooded extent which stretches between Tioumen and Omsk, and which is three-quarters the size of France, be included in the category 'forest'? Oughtn't there to be another word which communicates the awesome character of this infinite space and the impossibility of escaping its tentacles, of crossing it without getting lost?

After a journey by lorry and a long march we arrived exhausted in a clearing, where some Chekists were waiting to receive us. 'This place,' says their chief, 'is called Liebiedovka. There is only one exit and it is closely guarded. So get used to the idea that you are here for good and think only about organizing your life accordingly. *Mastiera* (specialists) will teach you how to cut wood and this will be your main task. But all initiatives are encouraged and there will be plenty of work for you to do. Wages will be paid at the full rate, according to the scales in operation in our socialist fatherland, because you are not prisoners but *pereselentzy* (displaced persons). You will earn a good wage if you work hard, and productivity bonuses are paid in accordance with the principle, "From each according to their capacities; to each according to their labour." With what you earn you will be able to buy yourselves anything that will be of use to you in your life here – even a cow.'

He would have liked to say more, to describe to us in detail this great Siberian destiny that had been decided for us, but his last sentence, mistakenly interpreted as, 'A single cow is the most wealth you can aspire to', provoked the nervous collapse of those listening. Collective lamentations rose up on all sides: the women cried, imitated by their children, the men screamed out, swore or prayed. The men in blue peak caps who had escorted other prisoners and who must have observed other deportees on their arrival, appeared baffled by this collective outcry and didn't even attempt to re-

38

establish silence. The scene took place at sunset however, and a swarm of mosquitoes took charge of quietening down and dispersing the assembly. There is no way to avoid these insects which bite deep, except to be locked up in the barracks.

I spent the whole of the summer of 1940 at Liebiedovka and it was there that I got to know my first 'real Russian'. I am slightly embarrassed not to be able to remember his name, but I believe that we called him simply *mastier*. He was a highly experienced man, a real expert on tree-felling, and he liked a job well done. In contrast to the other *mastiera* he quickly realized that Russian is not a universal language and that, to make himself understood, he had to have his instructions translated into Polish. He chose me as interpreter, a position for which there was no official provision. He got around this obstacle by inventing a fictive well paid function for me, which created between us, in addition to a mutual liking, something like complicity.

My *mastier* was about 30 years old, perhaps more, but he didn't like to talk about himself or about those who had occupied the already ancient barracks of Liebiedovka before us. Today I am inclined to believe that he was the son of a deportee or a former deportee himself, who had been released some years before. But at the time, observing his reticence, I didn't ask him any questions. He often questioned me, however, about life in Poland and would even have liked to learn Polish. He had me describe to him a dozen times the story of my departure from Lvov, and, at the end of each of my narratives, he shook his head with compassion and astonishment: '*Nie poviezlo*' ('really bad luck'). When one of his colleagues set off on official business or for medical treatment in Zavodooukovsk, the nearest railway centre, he invited me to sleep in the vacant bed in his barracks, which were more spacious and comfortable than ours. Thus it was that the idea came to me of going legally to Zavodooukovsk myself, on a one-way ticket, on the pretext of consulting a doctor to discover whether my (imaginary) migraines were linked to my eye injury. The first part of my plan to leave the forest through the guarded route, was well conceived, but everything else was left to chance and, retrospectively, it still appears to me to have been extremely reckless. It could only be realized with the help of my *mastier*, or at least by exploiting his trust. To allow me to be examined by an eye specialist in Zavodooukovsk, he had to get the Cheka's permission.

I seriously hesitated: it was my first Soviet case of conscience. On the one hand with his '*nie poviezlo*', the *mastier* seemed to be insisting not on my past bad luck but on that which awaited me in Liebiedovka, and so, quite unintentionally, incited me to take off. On the other hand, nothing indicated that he would accept the role of accomplice in an undertaking which risked backfiring on him if he were found guilty of an 'administrative irregularity'. I decided therefore to make him believe that I really was suffering from headache, and he took the necessary steps without suspecting anything of my project. Even at the moment of my departure he suspected nothing: he offered to look after my suitcase for me to save me the bother of carrying it until I got a lift. However, I declined his kind offer and set off with my suitcase.

My gamble having succeeded, I never again returned to the land of 'fabulous riches' and, at the time, I couldn't know if my friend had had problems because of me.

It was only 16 years later, at the time of the 'Polish spring' of October 1956, that I received the inkling of an answer. I was in Warsaw reporting for *L'Express* when a man in a leather coat approached me in the hairdressing salon of the Bristol Hotel and said: 'Don't you recognize me?' I am a little suspicious of this style of approach, especially when the face of the person who so addresses me isn't at all familiar. Also, I was in the very precarious situation of a Polish political refugee travelling in Poland. But the man in the leather coat was neither a provocateur nor a policeman: he had been deported, like me, to Liebiedovka, and he offered me sufficient proof of it to dissipate my fears. We spent the evening amicably at the Bristol Hotel, in front of a *bigos* and a bottle of vodka, reminiscing over what other people call 'the good old days'. He had become since then a senior functionary in the People's Republic but, contrary to what one might think, we talked neither of Gomulka nor of Kruschev, but of a Siberian *mastier* without a name.

'He was transferred to the sawmill sector,' this witness told me, 'and everything that you had earned as interpreter was deducted from his wages. This was to discourage the other *mastiera* from doing us any favours, in order to reduce their contacts with us to what was strictly necessary. Your *mastier* for a time spoke to us only through gestures, but he later recovered the use of speech, for he was a decent man and he understood that, without his help, the Siberian cold would end up crippling all of us.'

Here he paused to explain a little known scientific problem to me, one about which he had definite ideas, indeed a whole theory: 'You must realize that this kind of cold has a special quality, and it is dangerous because of its anaesthetizing effects. You go out into a temperature of 40 degrees below zero and you tell yourself "Huh! It's not so bad. You suffer from it less than you do at home in 10 degrees below zero." After this you spend hours outside, and you attach no importance to the fact that, for example, your nose tickles you a little. But when you return to the warmth, suddenly, bang! your nose falls off like a dead branch. At the first sign, you should have rubbed it with all your strength to make the blood circulate because afterwards it is too late, there is nothing to be done.'

My drinking partner had plenty of other things to tell: 'You remember the shoe manufacturer from Lublin with his seven children? On his way to work one day he wandered off the path and the snow penetrated his *valenka*; as you know these felt boots are warm but large, and the snow easily gets inside. He realized that it was dangerous because, even in Lublin, if you get snow in your shoes you might catch cold. But he was robust and, still not having understood the difference with Lublin, he went to work with his leg wet. The same evening it was completely black. He had to be taken to hospital and his leg was amputated.'

An inexhaustible mine of information on his two winters spent in Liebiedovka, he could have taught me everything about the peculiarities of the Siberian cold – due, among other things, to the absence of any polar wind – if I hadn't then committed a blunder. We journalists, as soon as we hear surprising facts which might interest our readers, are in the habit of asking to have an article written about them, or asking that we be allowed to quote them. This proposition that I put to him, ready to back it with a generous payment from my magazine, spoiled everything. Suddenly it was he who had the impression of having fallen into a trap: 'You don't imagine, do you, that a man in my position would take part in the anti-Soviet campaign in the West?' 'You wouldn't need to sign it,' I insisted naively. 'Besides, any such paper from you would be published under a rubric dealing exclusively with scientific and natural questions.' 'My past is my own affair,' he replied gravely, and he sent for his leather coat to be brought to him. He left without suggesting another meeting or leaving me his address.

Since then, things have changed a tiny bit in Warsaw, but really very little. No testimony on the 'Siberian years' has yet appeared in Poland, even though the entire population is thoroughly convinced that in 1940 the Soviets executed the majority of Polish Army officers in Katyn and deported a large number of civilians to Siberia. Unofficially, they joke about it within the leading circles of the regime, and say that if this deportation were a claim to fame, the majority of the leaders of the Unified Workers' Party and of the government would qualify. Officially though, with the exception of the KPP leaders rehabilitated posthumously in 1956, there isn't any question of referring to this past, which is dismissed as belonging to the private life of those concerned.

Let's take for example, Wojciech Jaruzelski. This general, who has pulled off the first ever military coup d'état in the entire history of the Soviet bloc, prides himself in his official biography on having been trained in the USSR. But his unofficial spokespersons – confident that the news will get back to the population on Western radio, listened to by everyone – discreetly tell foreign correspondents that before going to Riazan Infantry School in 1943, Jaruzelski had been deported with his whole family 'somewhere in the USSR'. This 'somewhere' could well have been far away from Zavodooukovsk and there is of course Eastern Siberia, itself very rich and situated, as its name indicates, much further to the east. I am sure therefore that this ex-companion in misfortune, my junior by one year, would have a lot of things to tell about the *tieplouchki*, the giant trees of Siberia, or the mosquitoes, and that in telling them he would perhaps lessen a little the hostility of the population who detest his dictatorial features, complete with dark glasses. It would also allow him perhaps to get rid of the handicap of his execrable reputation as a *moskal*, a simple agent of the Russians.

I would even be able to help him make public his Siberian past without disturbing too much the men of the Kremlin who are extremely vigilant in relation to all forms of Polish anti-Sovietism. It would mean placing the great deportation in its historical context, and making an objective assessment of it. I talked about it in Geneva on 14 August 1980 – I remember the date because that afternoon I had learned of the strike in the Gdansk shipyards, which was to give birth to Solidarity – with Bronislaw Baczko, Professor in the history of ideas. He is, with Leszek Kolakowski (a former pupil of Skorupka lycée), the pride of the University of Warsaw, from which he and many others were hunted in 1968 simply on the orders of semi-literate and reactionary policemen. But Bronek Baczko is not merely a friend and an enlightened thinker: he himself narrowly avoided becoming my companion aboard a *tieplouchka* in 1940.

On the night of the great identity check in Lvov, he hadn't reached the legal age of 16 years and found himself in exactly the same position as myself; but the Cheka after long hesitation left him alone. Throughout the two following nights, Bronek, in spite of his sympathies for the USSR, slept in a stable in order to avoid further identity checks. After these three agitated nights everything returned to normal in Lvov and there was no more talk of identity checks or inspections.

However, one year later, in June 1941, it was the Germans' turn to go through Lvov with a fine comb in order to 'liberate' the town of Jews and Poles. For Bronek and a great many other Poles this exodus was much worse than that of 1940, because the Wehrmacht had begun a war of extermination in the eastern zones, seeking allies only among the Ukrainian extreme right. For the very numerous Jewish community in the region this was the end of the road, the 'final solution', but there was also a settling of accounts with the Poles, a sort of 'war within the war' which claimed innumerable victims. Bronek's future wife, Rela, came very close to death from multiple stab wounds inflicted by a member of the 'Banderovcy', followers of Bandiera, the Ukrainian independence leader, and future recruits of the notorious SS Vilna Ukraina (Free Ukraine) division. My landlady from Lvov, whom chance once again put in my way after the war, told me that nearly all her friends, starting with the intellectual who had intervened on my behalf, had disappeared or had been killed during the first six months of the German occupation.

At around the same time, at the end of 1941, following General Sikorski's visit to Moscow which finalized an accord between his government exiled in London, and that of Stalin, the *pereselentzy* and the other Polish deportees began to leave their forests. It took some time because the Soviet state apparently had some difficulty recovering them from the Godforsaken sites where it had stowed them away 'for good'. It was for this reason that the Liebiedovka barracks were emptied only in the spring of 1942. This Polish diaspora was sufficiently large to permit General Anders first of all to recruit an army from it – which went to fight at Tobruk and Monte Cassino – then to allow the Committee of Patriots, of communist persuasion, to form another two divisions which saw combat alongside the Red Army from Lenino to Berlin.

It would be tempting, in the light of this outcome, to attribute Stalin's action in June 1940 to his clairvoyance; to suggest that he had organized this gigantic round-up in order to have a reserve army of Poles at his disposal, well stored in the Siberian refrigerator, to draw upon later for combat against the Germans. Since the Twentieth Congress of the CPSU however, one avoids, even in Moscow, placing the words 'Stalin' and 'clairvoyance' together. Despite the active help of my friend Bronek Baczko, I still haven't found any solution to the enigma which has bothered me for more than 40 years: why, at a single stroke and at such great cost, was such a large number of people, of all ages and professions, sent off to this oven/freezer that is Siberia? Why these people in particular? In order to do what? Couldn't their skills have been used in a more rational manner, in making them work far from the frontier regions, but at least in more familiar surroundings than those of the country of 'fabulous riches'? One day, when the archives of the Kremlin have been opened, there is a study to be made of all these questions. It would be interesting also to find out how many of these deportees and their children later became leaders of People's Poland, and how many, after having been in transit in 1945–6, went on to Israel and helped set up the new State.

In Moscow a mock tribunal composed of eight people, one of whom was a Red Army general, formally concluded after examining my documents that the Chekists in Lvov had committed an error. The members of this improvised court had no power to correct past wrongs, however, for the good reason that they were only my cousins brought together in haste by my Aunt Lisa soon after my impromptu arrival in Moscow. The image that I had of my Moscow aunt proved to be wholly inaccurate. I had imagined her small, stooped and timorous when in fact she was tall, thin, straight as a die and not a bit irresolute. The ridiculous story of the wicked dog which prowled around the courtyard must have been invented by some member of her family who wished to keep me at a safe distance – Aunt Lisa would willingly have taken me into her home. It was to discuss this very possibility that she had summoned her sons to come and join her after work. Certainly in announcing that a Polish cousin who had escaped from Western Siberia had just arrived at the house, she gave an imperative character to her convocation: at the other end of the line strangled voices asked her not to prolong the conversation and, at seven o'clock sharp, her seven sons had arrived to keep the rendezvous. My first family reunion in the 'real Russia' was about to begin.

It wasn't a particularly cheerful affair. Aunt Lisa, seated beside me, tried to plead my case, but my cousins with the exception of Stepan, the general – and the only single man among them – swept away her arguments with objections like: 'Mama, I have a family too, and children of his age.' In order not to frighten her they avoided emphasizing the extent of the danger I represented to them and their offspring, but the gloomy tone of their voices and their tense faces showed clearly that even a successful Soviet citizen cannot allow himself to have relations abroad, much less to put one of them up – especially in the aggravating circumstance of his having come from Western Siberia.

How was it that my Aunt Lisa hadn't understood this herself, with her long experience of life in the 'real Russia'? She was already in her seventies and lived very much on her own: her daughter Maria lived with her only from a sense of duty and seldom kept her company. Maria hadn't the beauty of the proud heroine of Pushkin's *Poltava*, but that didn't prevent her from having just as complicated a love life as her namesake. During my stay in Moscow I often saw her linger in front of the mirror, doing or undoing her bun or her plait as if uncertain as to how to show her chestnut-brown hair to its best advantage. Then off she went like a shot, in too much of a hurry to say when she would be back. On the day of my arrival her presence had been vainly awaited at the family council.

My Aunt Lisa was very forthcoming on the achievements of her sons but not on those of her only daughter. 'Maria gets by too, she teaches in a *diesiatiletka*,' she said, or again, 'In my day she would have been married by now, but the women today don't know how to live their lives, they behave like fools.' She didn't reproach her son Stepan, however, for having stayed single; on the contrary he was her favourite and, not having any family of his own, he came to see her more often than the others.

She wanted for nothing. Her apartment was at the bottom of the courtyard, in a building in the rustic Russian style – the ground floor in brick and the first floor in wood. It was spacious – about 40 square metres – and was certainly proof that Aunt Lisa hadn't exaggerated on the subject of her sons. Only Soviet citizens who had succeeded in life could give to their mother such comfortable accommodation in the heart of Moscow, in the Arbat, a stone's throw from the underground railway. In the dining-room – where Maria had her bed – even nine of us were not cramped and, the meeting having been a long one, some of my cousins paced up and down to stretch their legs or to calm their nerves. Apart from Stepan's, I remember neither the names nor faces of my cousins; it seems to me that I saw them only this once, on the evening of my arrival. In the course of this meeting, however, they submitted me to a lengthy interrogation. It was as though they were taking part in a commission of inquiry that was punctilious in respect of each detail, capable of detecting the slightest lie.

I had no reason to lie about my flight from Western Siberia: for once I was very lucky. On arrival in Zavodooukovsk I had presented myself at the Kolkhozians' Centre, the only hotel in the place. By a neat coincidence my dormitory neighbour was a railway worker. That very evening, without having seen an eye specialist, to whom in any case I would have had nothing to say, I had proposed a swap to my neighbour: the suit that my brother Genia had given me, or the Omega watch that my parents had bought me for my fifteenth birthday, for a ticket to Moscow. The railway worker, who was evidently interested in the exchange, went off to check things out with his friends but brought back a negative answer: it would be possible to get on the Trans-Siberian only if a passenger got off at Zavodooukovsk, which alas happened but once every two months or so. Neither the stationmaster nor even the Jaloutorovsk regional railway director could do anything, so full was this damned train. Impressed nevertheless by the suit from the best tailor in Prague, the railwayman wasn't ready to give up on it so easily. (The Omega had less success, Western Siberia having still not entered the age of the watch.) 'Come to Tioumen with me,' he said. 'After two or three days there I'm sure I can fix you up with a train for Moscow.' 'I haven't got a permit to go there,' I replied. 'There is no inspection on this trip, and in Tioumen you shall stay with me and sample some of my wife's bortsch.' Faced with such convincing arguments I didn't hesitate for very long.

At this point in my story one of my cousins exclaimed, 'You must have been mad. This con-man wanted to drop you en route after having stolen both the suit and the watch from you.' General Stepan put him in his place: 'The fact that he is here proves your objection to be invalid; moreover I would ask you to put a little more trust in our working man.' From this moment on I felt that I had found an ally in this dry-humoured general, whether because he wanted to please his mother or because he had taken a shine to me. He signalled me to continue.

The railway worker lived in an isolated wooden shed, not far from Tioumen station. We arrived there at night. No one saw us, just as I myself saw nothing of this future oil capital. My host and his wife set out for work early in the morning leaving me alone. I listened to the radio or read their few books, among which, in the place of honour, was the *History of the CPSU (Bolsheviks)*. In the evenings the railwayman's wife did indeed prepare a good bortsch and sometimes a stew, which she served out, pronouncing Stalin's famous phrase: 'Life has become better, life has become more gay.' No news came about a ticket for Moscow: it seemed clear that the Trans-Siberian passengers did not get off at Tioumen in large numbers either. At last, the railwayman found a solution: I would take the Novossibirsk–Leningrad train as far as Boui, and after a 10-hour wait I could continue on to Moscow – no longer very far away – on an express that would have plenty of free bunks. As proof of his good will he gave me, as well as a ticket, some used Soviet clothes which would assure me of a trip without incident.

Another cousin pulled a face: 'To cover three-quarters of the Soviet Union without falling upon an identity check appears to me to be improbable.' My Aunt Lisa flew to my aid, recalling a long journey that she had made some years earlier, without being importuned either by the railway militia or by any other inspection.

'You have a short memory,' the other replied, 'for I was with you and our passports were checked at least three times!' 'Not at all!' 'Yes they were Mama, – it was I who was carrying them.' Stepan had to intervene once more to allow me to continue. 'Carry on, young fellow; tell us if there is still some proletarian vigilance left on the railways in the land of Soviets.'

'It never relaxes for a moment,' I resumed, trying to imitate the ironical tone of my cousin Stepan, 'but I managed to foil it by passive resistance.' On the Novossibirsk–Leningrad train an odd incident occurred: an important passenger who was due to get off the train at Sverdlovsk had his boots stolen. It was the middle of the night and, in the penumbra of the poorly-lit 'hard'* carriages there was a generalized shambles. The militia made a thorough search, checking not only passports but also all the baggage. I could see no way out; panic prevented me from even thinking of any sort of ruse. I remained immobile on my bunk close to the ceiling, my head pressed against my case, my eyes closed, mortified at the thought that I hadn't even succeeded in crossing the West Siberian frontier. This momentary paralysis saved me: a woman passenger, convinced that if I could sleep through such a racket I must have had a few, said to the militia, 'He is *podpivchyi* and, since he hasn't budged since Tioumen he certainly hasn't stolen the boots.' This argument was decisive.

'She chose just the right word for it!' the general declared well satisfied. 'A *podpivchyi*, here, is even favourably regarded, as someone who maintains reasonable, measured relations with vodka. If this woman had said on the other hand that you were loaded to the gills they would have made you get down straightaway because drunkards are a permanent source of problems on our railways and don't deserve the right to the indulgence of our militias.' No one laughed, and my cousin's attempt to enliven the evening, while simultaneously initiating me into the subtleties of Soviet life, fell flat.

---

*The 'hard' carriages (second and third class) are fitted with wooden bunks, the 'soft' carriages (first class), with bunks with mattresses.

The Tioumen railwayman hadn't told me the whole truth about the train connection at Boui station. Instead of telling me about the 10-hour wait I had to expect he ought to have warned me that in order to board the other train, it would be necessary to have the ticket stamped and show one's passport. On learning of this I thought first of contacting a railway worker in Boui, but circumstances didn't lend themselves to a new bartering deal. I took my place in the queue for Moscow-bound passengers, resigned and without any definite plans. As the hours went by this queue got longer and longer, becoming nearly a kilometre in length. Other trains were unloading more passengers bound for Moscow into Boui station. And the only counter position for this crowd remained closed: the regulations did not permit it to open until 30 minutes before the departure of the fast train for Moscow (which on that day was five hours late). During this long wait the passengers had time to get organized to allocate numbers to themselves and, obviously, to discuss their respective chances of having their tickets stamped and their passports checked during such a short period of time. Finding myself almost at the head of this interminable queue of passengers, I had received several offers: some wanted to buy my place in the queue – this didn't interest me at all – and some asked me to show several tickets alongside my own, in return for a more modest reward. Thus, when the counter position finally opened, I had five passports and six tickets (mine was the extra ticket, of course). Pressed for time, the counter clerk didn't ask me for any explanation of this group journey and, without counting either the passports or tickets, duly stamped them.

Silence. My cousins, having satisfied their curiosity, seemed plunged into a deep meditation. All of them were heavy smokers and they filled the dining-room with a cloud of tobacco smoke so thick that you would have thought yourself inside a second-class carriage. My aunt, having protested and even threatened to forbid cigarettes, appeared resigned, although half-asphyxiated. Finally a cousin sitting at the end of the table took on the task of summarizing the essentials of the situation. From a legal point of view my position was indefensible: I ought to have taken the steps necessary to correct the mistake made in Lvov while I was still in Siberia and not to have fled like a thief into the night. On the other hand, even if I had pursued the proper channels and been vindicated in Jaloutorovsk or in Omsk (my forest came under their jurisdiction), my chances of obtaining a Moscow residence permit would have been zero – and he made a figure O with two fingers to dissipate any misunderstanding – because the capital fiercely defended itself against any influx from the provinces.

Another cousin, having approved of this analysis, was anxious lest I had mentioned the existence of my relations in Moscow in the questionnaires that I might have completed in Lvov or Siberia. My reply in the negative – I had been asked nothing in Lvov, even when I had been put aboard the *tieplouchka* – provoked a sigh of general relief; even the affable general Stepan seemed reassured. 'That will give us time to reflect,' he said.

There gradually emerged from the ensuing thinking-aloud, this Muscovite 'brain-storming', the idea of sending me back to Lvov. The purchase of a rail ticket didn't pose an insurmountable obstacle as it happened – they had much better contacts in the train stations in Moscow than my railway worker in Tioumen – but, as one of my cousins said, 'Lvov counts as abroad.' The checks on this line were going to be altogether more rigorous than in the Novossibirsk–Leningrad train. According to Stepan, though he was probably joking, it would have been easier to send me to Istanbul than to the Western Ukraine. As my opinion was not sought, I was slowly overtaken by somnolence – the previous night, spent in Boui station, I hadn't slept a wink – and, following the habit that I had acquired during the 1939 campaign, I began to dream in this semi-waking state. My mother sits near me, makes some remarks to me touching upon minor details of my life in Siberia, then turns towards the tribunal composed of my cousins and pleads in favour of the right of everyone to choose their own place of residence; she protests against a bureaucracy devoid of soul or reason which only hinders the development of humanity. Suddenly she abandons her advocate's robe to dress up as on 1 May, with flowers in her hand. She recites a text of Lermontov against the police, followed by a line of Pushkin's exalting the men of noble sentiments, those who, even in the darkest hour, know how to defend freedom. My mother is very beautiful with her impassioned air and her flowers, and her smile gives me to understand that things are not as bad as they seem, that everything will work out. . . .

What drew me out of this comfortable doze was a screaming match between my cousins. Having lost hold of the thread of their discussion, I was unaware of the origin of these acerbic exchanges. I had the impression that my cousins were divided on the prudence of taking steps to help me in Moscow. According to Stepan and a second cousin, probably supported by my Aunt Lisa, something had to be tried, even if it were only to have me sent back to Lvov. The others found this attitude 'suicidal', arguing that it might compromise the family; they wished that I would undertake the journey at my own risk. In the absence of a democratic tradition in Russia they didn't consider resolving the matter by a vote – which would have gone against me – and they continued to shout at each other.

'We must speak with Michka,' the general said forcefully, and I discovered later that he meant Mikhail Kalinin, the president of the Republic. 'Why not with Stalin while you're about it?' the chief of the opposing faction burst out. 'Because I haven't access to him,' Stepan retorted. 'Whereas you can invite Michka, of course, to call at mama's for tea with our Polish cousin?' Sorely tried by it all Aunt Lisa reacted forcefully: 'You have made me very angry. All of you leave now, straightaway.' Incredible as it may seem, they immediately obeyed her without arranging a time for a further meeting. None of them seemed concerned to find out who, finally, would take a decision about their compromising relation. It was clear that a mother in the 'real Russia' enjoyed more authority than in Poland, more than mine in particular.

Our memory doesn't 'latch onto' the little everyday things, it retains only what appears to us as unexpected, those things about which we ask ourselves questions. Concerning my Aunt Lisa, for example, I recall especially what in her behaviour had baffled me, what seemed to me to be bizarre, inexplicable. The same applies in relation to General Stepan Vladimirovitch who was an important engineer in the armaments industry: his character remains engraved in my mind because of certain enigmatic, ironical quips or asides, because of his relations with his mother or his sister – because of everything I didn't understand. It was thanks to them, however, that during the two weeks of September 1940 that I spent in Moscow, I learned to 'do as the Soviets do', to behave like everyone else in public places, to read the papers, to learn the pecking order of the members of the Politbureau, and a thousand other things without which I would surely have had much less chance of getting accepted at school No. 44 in Rostov, of finding friends there, of becoming Solik.

Try as I might I don't really remember when or where Aunt Lisa sent me out for the first time to do some shopping for her in the Arbat. I know that she described the route to me with great precision, and that she explained to me, in detail, the way I ought to behave towards the shop assistants. On the other hand the places have disappeared from my memory; it is useless my trying to recall them. Certainly I could invent a 'Gosmag' and transplant it to the Arbat, all the more easily since this old neighbourhood no longer exists; it has been rebuilt from top to bottom in the American style, and Muscovites today call it 'our denture' to underline its artificial character. But there is little point in inserting in this framework details which one no longer remembers.

I remember on the other hand as though it were yesterday the morning that Aunt Lisa said to me: 'It's a fine day, let's go and see the kolkhoz exhibition.' We took the underground train and she explained to me the history of each station name, finishing on an almost authoritarian note: 'You really must visit Moscow, I assure you it is a very beautiful city.' Once inside the great exhibition park, built in the Stalinist style, where the agricultural exploits of each republic are on display in separate pavilions, she appeared to tire quickly. 'You are young, you can carry on without me,' she said to me after we had covered the Russian pavilion, and she went off mumbling something to herself, forgetting to arrange with me a time to come home. In the following days this scenario repeated itself. We always left in a hurry, even though Aunt Lisa, unlike her daughter, wasted no time in front of the mirror; she tucked her white hair under a Russian style neckerchief, patted her sombre dress which was too hot for the time of year, and off we went. Once we had arrived somewhere, after we had visited the first room, she would say the same thing: 'You are young, you can carry on without me,' and I was free for the day. This didn't altogether displease me; in fact I preferred to go on these visits alone. However, given my uncertain legal position I couldn't help worrying and even having suspicions. Was Aunt Lisa bringing me into town to get me out of the way so she could discuss my fate with her sons behind my back? Sometimes, losing all sense of proportion, I went so far as to imagine that she banked on my making a false step and was relying on the vigilant militia to deliver her family from the encumbrance which my presence constituted. It was foolish and ungrateful of me for in the event of a slip-up Aunt Lisa and my cousins would have had more worries than I. After all, I was young and impoverished, an escaper from Siberia who, as the Russians put it, 'couldn't be sent back any further'.

I visited Red Square and the sight of Lenin's mausoleum had a powerful effect on me. The large panel proclaiming 'Class brothers, prisoners of capitalism, receive our ardent proletarian greetings' no longer ornamented the Goum facade but I saw it through the photo my brother Alexander had shown to me in Lodz. These places symbolized the hopes born of the October Revolution, and its adversaries abroad, like its partisans, had never stopped talking about it. One side dragged the Revolution through the mud as the 'leadership of subversion' and the other exalted it in the name of a 'better future'. I was very happy to be there and quite taken with the beauty of the place for, political considerations aside, Moscow was a more imposing city than either Lodz or Lvov. But even there my stupid obsessions came back to me: why, when she thought I was incapable of finding my way around the Arbat, hadn't Aunt Lisa asked me at what time I planned to arrive home, and where I was going to have lunch?

On my return she didn't ask a lot of questions about how I'd spent the day, and confined herself instead to commenting on the weather, asking me for example if I hadn't been too warm. Although her sense of family loyalty was obvious and fully repaid my gamble on coming to Moscow, she seemed hardly curious at all to know how we lived in Lodz, nor preoccupied by the fate of her brother under the Nazi occupation. When I spoke to her about it she raised her arms in the air as though to say 'what an awful world we live in', and then she would produce one of those phrases which I had already heard in September 1939, of the genre, 'At the start of every war the Germans win some victories but they are always beaten in the end.' From the Vistula to the Urals, the 1914 defeat on the Marne had tarnished the reputation of the German Army, and its victory in France in 1940 hadn't been enough to redeem it.

Although she subscribed to *Pravda, Izvestia* and the majority of periodicals, Aunt Lisa had in fact only one source of news: her son Stepan. The general always called at the house in civilian clothes, during the day and in the evenings alike. He replied to his mother's thousand questions about the war with an angelic patience, generally repeating in a more lively manner the news from the official dailies. Each time she questioned him she did so as if she hadn't seen him for months. In fact he was coming from the Sklifassovski Clinic nearby, where he was attending sessions of physiotherapy for his right leg which had been fractured the previous winter. Plump, always good humoured, often bringing cakes that he ate for the most part himself, Stepan was in my view an accomplished liar. Knowing full well that his mother was against the Germans – and which Jew was not? – he very clearly favoured in his reports the British and their American allies (who still hadn't entered the war). Reassured by these, Aunt Lisa nevertheless pointed to my testimony on the strength of the Wehrmacht, and he then replied that, in the eyes of a mouse, a cat appeared to be the most frightening animal in the world. The general didn't tell the truth about his private life either, and in this case I thought he lied without apparent reason.

One evening he took me to the opera to see *Rigoletto*, having announced to his mother that he would take advantage of the occasion to introduce me to a useful friend. The friend in reality proved to be a very pretty young woman with short, fair hair, who had a harsh look about her and a slightly martial bearing. Her whole presence had a decidedly more military air to it than had Stepan's, which had something irremediably civilian-like in its gestures and expressions. Not only was he plump, he also accompanied his jokes with facial contortions ill-befitting the solemn rank of general. 'What a mess!' he said to the fair-haired woman. 'We came especially to see Lemiechev and it isn't him after all who is playing the role of the Duke of Mantua. What a pity, eh?' 'Yes,' she replied stiffly, 'he's our favourite tenor and he's the best in the show.' They left the box soon afterwards, leaving me alone. Their story was obviously a ploy of some kind.

Three days later we returned to the same box; this time Lemiechev was to sing for sure, but once again they left. The same thing happened a third time and I became a habitué of *Rigoletto*, almost certainly judged as a fervent music student by the usherettes. I didn't mind. I observed the stage, the hall, the Soviet theatrical costumes; I noted the popular character of this public, very different from that which frequented the theatrical entertainments in Lodz, where there was no opera. But I was puzzled by the behaviour of my cousin, and my reflections on him took an obsessional turn. Why did he need to close me up in this box – always the same one, and always for *Rigoletto* – when in fact he was free to go where he liked with this young blonde-haired woman? After all, unlike his sister Maria, he wasn't answerable to his mother since he didn't live in the Arbat. No doubt he had had a reason for wanting to introduce me to the woman but I didn't discover it then, and I still don't know it today. Fortunately on my return from each *Rigoletto* performance, Aunt

Lisa didn't ask me what I had seen, but asked me questions only about the audience, what people were wearing, the weather.

To top everything, this mysterious cousin, when he was with his sister Maria, teased her continually about her love life – egged on in this by his mother. Since Aunt Lisa had become a little forgetful it was Maria who assumed the main responsibility for the house-keeping. She did the shopping or made a note of what was needed for the house, and most of the time she also did the cooking. She spent some hours at the house each day reading, correcting homework or preparing lessons. Very well read in the field of Marxism–Leninism, she got me to read chapter four of the *History of the CPSU (Bolsheviks)* on *diamat* and *histmat* (dialectical materialism and historical materialism), personally drafted by Stalin, and her commentaries later proved very useful to me. But occasionally Maria showed the strains of her responsibilities and could be short-tempered, to the extent that the least quip from her joker of a brother about her amorous tribulations or about her cooking sent her into a rage: 'You are very welcome to go and eat in the Kremlin, they have better cooks there!' Even to my Aunt Lisa she would sometimes reply harshly: 'Mama, I am 37 years old and I don't need your advice any more.' On more than one occasion this bickering provoked anger which left me feeling ill at ease. I sympathized with Maria, however, for I considered that in an advanced society liberated from the domination of the Church, free love oughtn't to be considered a sin any longer. I was careful, none the less, not to broadcast my views in front of Aunt Lisa, and anyway I didn't know the exact nature of the problems in Maria's love life.

If my sojourn in Moscow had been longer I would surely have got to know my aunt and my cousins better, so that the 'mysteries' which are stamped in my memory would have been resolved. Barely two weeks after my arrival, though, General Stepan cordially but firmly invited me to leave – not, however, in search of the adventure that his timorous brothers would have liked to send me. He advised me to go to Rostov, to present myself to a certain Ivanov in the local NKVD leadership, and to tell him that I had come from Lvov, without the proper papers, but moved by the irresistible desire to get to know my family's home town. I was to give as my new domicile the address of my other aunt, who was even older than Aunt Lisa and without means – she had three daughters, none of whom had succeeded in life – but I wasn't to worry about means of support. Each month I would receive poste restante a money order for 150 roubles sent anonymously from Moscow. In my dealings with Ivanov of the NKVD, I was not to cite any name nor offer referees for testimonials; in particular I was to avoid all mention of either Moscow or Siberia. The general didn't explain to me why I had to go and see precisely this Ivanov, but he suggested to me that in my new life I should ask fewer questions and listen a bit more to official talk and opinions. In his view my future hinged on whether or not the authorities of Western Siberia had judged it necessary to send out a search warrant for me. If they had done, neither Ivanov, nor any other NKVD leader, could do anything about it and I would be sent back to my forest of origin. This being unlikely, Ivanov would have two options: he could either send me back to Lvov – which wouldn't be such a disaster after all – or accord me residence in Rostov. In the latter case the departmental Committee of National Education would come to my aid. I could take it or leave it, or rather only take it since I wasn't asked for my opinion in the matter.

When the time came for me to leave it emerged that my suitcase had disappeared: Aunt Lisa pointed the finger at her daughter, accusing her of having taken it in order to go and spend the night elsewhere, but Maria swore that she hadn't touched it. In my opinion it was General Stepan who had carried it off, not for his own rendezvous with the pretty fair-haired woman, but in order to save me carting around an object of Polish origin. You can't be too careful when you travel without papers even if, this time, I was going to enjoy a bunk in a 'soft' carriage, under the protection of an attendant who would receive a handsome tip. Having no suitcase, I set out on my journey with my possessions in a bundle made out of one of Aunt Lisa's old sheets.

The plan dreamed up by my cousin Stepan, doubtless with the

help of his brothers, worked with marvellous precision. For the 10 months which followed, until the declaration of war, I received a money order poste restante each month. I never saw Aunt Lisa again however; she died on the eve of the evacuation of Moscow, during the winter of 1941. Her first-floor neighbours gave me the news in 1944, but they didn't have the address of Maria, who was a refugee somewhere in central Asia, nor that of General Stepan Vladi-mirovitch, who was off at the front.

The match between the NKVD and I finished in September 1940 with a draw: one all. The Cheka had scored a goal in Lvov by shoving me inside a *tieplouchka*, but I succeeded in equalizing in Rostov, by palming off on them the version of this great journey suggested by cousin Stepan. Given the renown of my adversaries and the fact that I had been playing on their home ground, far from my Lodz supporters, this result was more than honourable. Every match, however, generates commentaries. Couldn't I have avoided conceding this goal in Lvov by hiding myself in a stable as Bronek Baczko did? On the other hand, hadn't Ivanov, the NKVD goalkeeper in Rostov, been a little absent-minded, perhaps even bribed, the way it happens with soccer games in Italy?

Seated on the same bench as the timid Klava at school No. 44, I obviously can't confide to her my uncertainties. We went to the big theatre in Rostov on Sunday 30 November 1940, to see *Anna Karenina* together. I remember it because it was the first anniversary of my arrival in the USSR. In the last act, Anna's suicide beneath a noisy train upsets Klava and she presses herself closely to me. While accompanying her home, to the other end of the Sadovaia, I imagine I can detect in her glances an invitation to confide in her, to tell her everything, but the image of the debonair General Stepan, a finger to his lips, rises up before me: 'Not a word, don't speak of this to anyone.' It is only four years later, during the summer of 1944, that I shall come to understand that I could have told everything to Klava, because she was already the tenderest and most loyal of my Soviet girlfriends.

Having failed to confide in her I am left on my own to puzzle about Ivanov. The man to whom General Stepan had so imperatively sent me was only a captain in the NKVD, a fair-haired man of about 30, who didn't seem well disposed towards me. When I told him that I had come secretly from Lvov to Rostov purely out of love for this town, he gave me a grim look which could well have signified: 'This guy is completely crazy.' As he went out of his office, his threatening air seemed to say: 'You will leave here this very day my boy, and I'll teach you once and for all never again to break the laws of the Soviet Union.' I expected to see him return with an escort which would take me back again either to Western Siberia or to Lvov.

In fact he came back after two or three hours, accompanied by a certain Vlassov, a civilian from the Oblono (Department of National Education). He was a former student of the University of Warsaw and he was able to translate my Polish documents for Ivanov. Ivanov began to relax a little and spoke to me without further hostility, as if he had come to understand in the interval the noble sentiments which had brought me to Rostov. Able to relax in my turn, I noticed then that he bore a slight resemblance to the young blonde-haired woman who on three occasions had accompanied General Stepan to *Rigoletto*. Here is the key, I concluded, to the mystery of the opera box in Moscow. To find out if this wasn't pure fantasy on my part, however, it would have been necessary to ask: 'By the way, Comrade Captain, have you a sister who is a great admirer of Lemiechev who knows General Stepan Vladimirovitch in Moscow?' Of course the rules of the game precluded any such question, and I wasn't willing to take such a risk in order to satisfy a mere curiosity (even an obsessive one).

Ivanov brought me back into the small office soon afterwards to get me to write out my curriculum vitae and to complete the administrative forms. 'Take your time, there is no hurry,' he advised me, as if he sensed that at 16 years and one month, I already had a biography that was difficult to summarize. It didn't conform closely to Soviet criteria: my parents were not proletarians, and my education was very suspect as the Lodz lycée bore the name of a priest who had fought against the Bolsheviks. Finally, what could I say about my participation in 1939 in the defence of Poland, against the Third Reich, the ally of the USSR? From another point of view though, what did this Ivanov know about the Polish careers of my parents, or Skorupka's death on the Vistula? For all he knew, I could have been born into a workers' family and have attended a school dedicated to the memory of a heretic who had been excommunicated by the Roman Catholic Church. . . .

So, I make my parents office workers or clerks, belonging to the class of the exploited who, under the hegemony of the proletariat, play a positive role in the anti-capitalist struggle. Next, while admitting to the Catholic character of the Skorupka lycée and deploring it, I emphasize strongly the intransigent atheism of all my family, myself included. Finally I say that I lost my right eye in the course of a bombing raid in 1939 and, having given details of neither the place nor date, I wasn't actually lying: the village of 'Injustice' where I was wounded had been bombarded by mortar and artillery fire. Ivanov read my form with interest, and passed it to Vlassov from the Oblono, who decided it was very well written. Neither of them asked me for the least extra detail, and I heard the resounding applause of an imaginary public. 'Look. Envy me, I am a citizen of the Soviet Union!' as Vladimir Mayakovsky had put it. The passport that Ivanov issued to me had not, however, the same qualities as those of the poet, but of this fact I was going to become aware only much later.

The second match began soon afterwards. It was against Oblono, a much weaker opponent than the NKVD. Before awarding me a grant they wanted to be satisfied that I was capable of following sixth form classes and making up lost ground in Russian literature and the history of the USSR in particular. Vlassov, on the basis of my Skorupka lycée experience, accepted only that I be given a 'trial run' at school No. 44 in Rostov. Now, one month later, I was already doing so well that the rest of the class had difficulty in keeping up with me.

Am I at least satisfied and proud to be the best in all disciplines, Russian literature included? Having been an idler in Lodz, threatened more than once with having to resit examinations, I informed myself thoroughly on the careers of other idlers who, like Adam Mickiewicz, the Polish national poet, later became famous. On the other hand I knew nothing about those who came first in their class. I had also observed that swots are appreciated by their teachers but are rarely liked by their school peers: in Rostov I almost feel guilty each time I find the correct answer while the others dry up. In my defence, I must say that I became a 'professional' in my studies because in Rostov I have nothing else to do: no family obligation, practically no sporting activity and, alas, no political life.

It is for want of protagonists that political discussions have disappeared from my life. The thread was broken, immediately after my forced departure from Lvov. Western Siberia is far away, very far away, too far to allow oneself any interest in the rest of the country, let alone the rest of the world. If I am to believe a recent Soviet film, *The Siberiad*, crowned with awards at Cannes, in certain Siberian localities the people learned of the German attack on the USSR only several weeks after the fact. That explains why, in the immense wooded region between Tioumen and Omsk, we were totally unaware of the Battle of Britain and of other matters which were unfolding in faraway Europe. Later, in Moscow, I managed to fill in these gaps when I sat in on General Stepan's briefing sessions at Aunt Lisa's, but their conversation never went very far, and didn't touch upon any fundamental question.

It is not much better in Rostov from this point of view. None of my friends, beginning with the mathematician Motia, is troubled by the catastrophic turn taken by the war. 'As long as it doesn't reach as far as us,' is their sole thought, so they give their genuine approval to the policy of 'neutrality' chosen by Stalin. However, in the *kinekroniki*, the newsreels shown before the films, the Secretary of the Communist Party of the Ukraine, Nikita Kruschev, could be seen on a friendly visit to the gauleiter Frank in Krakow, and Viatcheslav Molotov could be seen in Berlin, but one never saw any

Soviet leader in London or Washington. There would have been an interesting subject for discussion among friends in all this, and I am surprised that cultivated people such as Motia's colleagues never make any allusion to it. Neither the 'finest hour' of British history, nor Churchill, who is alone in confronting Hitler, really concerns them.

During my Siberian summer the USSR annexed in turn the Baltic countries of Estonia, Latvia and Lithuania in June, and in August, Bessarabia and Bukovina, which belonged to Romania. In Rostov each of these events was registered and approved but, in the September after my arrival, those who still recall them are the exception. Micha, my best friend – the one who would like to travel around the world – is of the opinion that 'Stalin has advanced our frontiers' the better to parry an eventual surprise attack by the capitalist powers. Micha's father, a supervisor at Rosselmach, a large agricultural machinery factory, has supplied him with this unofficial version of events. But when I eat with Micha's very hospitable family, his father only repeats the editorials from *Molot* (*The Hammer*), the Party newspaper in Rostov. 'Nicolai-Stepano-vitch, do you think there is a danger of war?' I asked him to try to get him to commit himself. 'You must always be prepared,' he replied, breaking into a few bars of a song then in fashion: 'If war should come tomorrow, be ready from today.'

I am satisfied with Micha's hypothesis. In this region the USSR can feel threatened only by the Third Reich; if it is taking measures against this danger it is because it doesn't believe in the solidity of the pact with Hitler. Reading *Molot*, however, never fails to bring me disagreeable surprises: it argues for example that the war undertaken by Britain in Europe is only a continuation of the previous conflict between imperialists, a kind of extension of the First World War. I would really like to write a letter to the editor to re-establish the truth about the facts of September 1939, and to protest against this putting of democratic Great Britain on a par with Hitler. The instinct of self-preservation carries the day however, and I refrain from revealing the truth as

I see it to the readers of *Molot*.

Although I feel concerned by the world situation I recognize that my schoolfriends have other legitimate worries in their everyday life. As a rule, both their parents work and delegate to them a large part of the household work, including care of the youngest children. It is for this reason, it seems to me, that school No. 44's programme is much less onerous than at Lodz, and that we are given very little homework. Even Russian literature is studied here only in anthologies of selected pieces and not in the original works. In my parents' library I had had the opportunity to read all the books listed in the syllabus and many more besides – from those by Dostoyevsky to those by Bounin. As for the Soviet political indoctrination which was talked about so much in Poland, I am obliged to note that none of Marx's writings circulates in school No. 44, not even *The Eighteenth Brumaire*, *The Civil War in France* or other generally accessible works. All that we ever do is regurgitate in all its forms the *History of the CPSU (Bolsheviks)* to learn Marxism–Leninism and the history of the USSR.

It is in January 1941, at the end of term, that I am awarded the title of *otlitchnik*, best pupil of the upper sixth form. A *lińeika* is organized – a sort of general school assembly – and the head teacher, accompanied by the secretary of the Party organization, praises me as a shining example, with eulogies that would have turned my head were it not for the fact that I understood that circumstances alone had made a model pupil of me. I obviously accept, however, the responsibility of helping those who have fallen behind and work with them in the evenings. Klava is one of these.

In my view Klava is the most attractive girl in the class, with her even-featured face lit up by lovely green eyes. However, she is not as tall and physically mature as some of her classmates – in fact she has the air of a young girl, which doesn't incite a young lad's thoughts to courtship. I suppose that the form-master has put me on the same bench as her to show me that in Rostov the sixth form girls may be pretty but they are also very serious. He chose the one on whom he could rely not to distract me from my duty. Whatever be the truth of it, recalling the numerous Western films that I saw in Lodz, I associate Klava with Rosemary, a 'flower of the scented prairies', but, unlike the disconcerting Jeanette Macdonald, she inspires only the chastest of dreams.

She lives in an isolated, wooden maisonette, near the station, similar to but larger than that of the Tioumen railway worker. Klava has her own room but she receives me in the dining-room in the presence of her parents, Emilian and Maria, who remain patient and silent throughout our reading and discussions of texts. They are very courteous towards me and always thank me for helping their only daughter (she is the baby of the family, her three brothers having already left school) but they do not seem willing to leave me alone with her, even to study the utopias of Vera Pavlovna, the protagonist of Chernyshevsky's *What is to be Done?*

Curiously the prohibition on our being alone together applies only in her house, for in other circumstances Klava often comes with me as far as the tramway and we sometimes go to the cinema or theatre together. What then is the meaning of this partial system of surveillance? Klava thinks she can explain everything with a single phrase: '*Ja Cosatchka*' ('I am a Cossack'). She seems neither proud nor ashamed of this fact, but she thinks that I ought to understand what it signifies since my parents, in their time, lived in the 'region of the army of the Don'. Originally nomadic horsemen, the Cossacks were given an entire territory which became famous for its autonomy, its chiefs who resided in Novotcherkask, and for its very specific customs. That was a long time ago however, and the storm of the October Revolution ought not only to have swept away the privileges and the artificial status of this former czarist praetorian guard, but also to have changed their way of thinking. Why should a young girl like Klava feel herself to be different in a society which has overturned everything and which has been constructing the future for the past quarter of a century?

I can't criticize her on this subject: she doesn't claim anything, merely alerts me to a fact. Certain Cossacks in my class on the other hand, Arkadii and Alexander in particular, have already drummed into me their theories concerning the Cossacks' superiority over the Russians, and still more over the Ukrainians, whose inferiority has been generally acknowledged since the dawn of time. At the beginning I couldn't believe that they were being serious, because the Cossacks satisfied none of the criteria elaborated by Stalin in *The National Question* to define a nation. Didn't they speak the same language as the Russians? Didn't they, like them, belong historically to the same culture and to the same territory? But when I ask politely of Arkadii: 'O.K., you are the strongest, but tell me, how do you tell yourselves apart from others?' he replies proudly: 'Simple. Any fucker off the streets can become a Russian, but to be a Cossack of the Don, you have to be born one.'

I encounter the myth of privileges inherited at birth not just among the Cossacks – my own family in Rostov has some similar surprises in store for me. Aunt Lisa's sister, Raia, is older than her, more corpulent, and has an even poorer memory. Her husband, David, who is also retired, is short and bald. Neither of them recalls having received a letter from me sent from Lvov. It is not important now since, according to General Stepan, they have simply to supply me with an address for Ivanov of the NKVD. They live frugally and have few resources – their daughters have married men of modest means – they can neither put me up nor help me financially. In any case they should not find out about how I have come to Rostov, nor that I receive poste restante a monthly money order from family in Moscow.

If he has a short memory in respect of the mail, my Uncle David still remembers an old score he has to settle with my father. You would even think that he has been awaiting my arrival for a quarter of a century to get it off his chest. So he attacks me on the theme: 'Your father is not a good Jew.' He accuses him straight off of having sold his soul to the 'goyim' of Finland (for whose stationery industry he had apparently acted as the representative in South Russia). My father had thus betrayed the mission that God had confided to the Jewish people. If you were to believe Uncle David on the matter, my father's present misfortunes in Lodz, like his earlier loss of wealth, were the direct rewards of treason, and proof that God didn't easily forgive.

This 'chosen people' seems to me a mythology as strange as that of the Cossacks, but it is absolutely impossible to argue with Uncle David. This pious little man places himself on a transcendental, biblical terrain and doesn't want to understand that real Jews, those of Lodz or Liebiedowka, divided between thousands of spiritual families and political tendencies, cannot accomplish together a single and identical mission ordained by their God.

After this dialogue of the deaf I decide to speak with his daughter Genia who works at the Karl Marx Library and who is always extremely kind to me: she even bends the rules a little to allow me to take books home with me. When I press her to comment on the zealous religiosity and excessive Judaism of her parents, she has, like the Cossacks, no other argument than that of birth: 'You can't understand these things for you were born into a family of atheists.'

The problem of my origins acquires a fresh relevance when I see Pudovkin's film on Souvorov. When the czarist hangman Souvorov, in this B-movie, is acclaimed by his troops to the cry of '*Slava, slava, slava Warszawa, slava, slava, slava Ismail*' (Glory, glory, glory for Warsaw, glory, glory, glory for Ismail'), I can't take it. Let him glorify this butcher for other victories – though it is a shame that Pudovkin does it at all – but surely not for having crushed the rising of a people fighting for its freedom from the czars! And suddenly, despite my internationalist and Russophile education, I say to myself: 'These Russians are right bastards to make films like this.' The same night, it is not my mother but Sister Kunegunda who comes and repeats to me in my dream: '*Badz Polakiem*' ('be Polish!'), '*Badz Polakiem, Badz Polakiem*!' On waking, I am filled with an infinite sadness. How is it that the old rivalries persist in this society where there are no longer either capitalists or landowners; Russians against Cossacks, Jews against Poles, each with their own mission, the result of which is always to denigrate, always to despise the others? I am in the throes of a crisis of national identity when the cuckold militiaman, in whose house I am living, interrupts my reflections by commenting brusquely that I cry out too much in Polish during the night. I like it better that way: if I shouted in Russian, he would have a fine report to make on my negative attitude towards the 'great Souvorov'.

Joining the Komsomol was the key event of my year in Rostov. It played a determining role in my future career in the Red Army, and even in my first loves. I have never underestimated nor forgotten what the *Komsomolski billet* brought me, this membership card whose name curiously evokes the title of a voyage. On the other hand, I can recall little of my state of mind at the time and the reactions of those around me to my membership. In particular I no longer recall the opinion of Motia, the adult figure to whom I listened most, nor that of Klava, who was then still only a schoolmate but who, because she was my desk-companion, had her word to say on everything which happened in my life. The story of this episode therefore, although it is of crucial importance, involves certain lacunae, and everything combines to persuade me that I did indeed enter the Komsomol as I might have a 'public house'.

At the beginning of February 1941, in the middle of a German lesson, Borissov, the Party Secretary, sends for me with an urgent message. Borissov is a man of considerable importance and he has an office of his own that is larger than the teachers' staffroom. Loyal to tradition, he always wears, in the Bolshevik style, a *cosovorotka* – a long shirt worn over the trousers with a belt – and army boots. To understand the importance of his role you need only meditate on the slogan on the town walls: 'Let us close ranks around the glorious Bolshevik Party, the steely nucleus of the Soviet people.' The Partorg (Party Secretary) is a particle of this nucleus, illuminated by Stalin, 'our sun', around which the planets of the NKVD or Komsomol gravitate.

Confident from such authority, the Partorg can send for whomsoever he wishes whenever he likes. He deigns nevertheless to explain to me that having followed my school career very closely he knows that I can skip a German lesson without difficulty (the Wehrmacht camp hadn't been entirely useless). Then, he talks about my excellent school marks and informs me that usually after having obtained the title, the *otlitchniki* join the Komsomol. He understands, however, that I am still unfamiliar with the customs, and doesn't interpret unfavourably the lack of zeal I have shown to follow their example. According to him, the enthusiasm that I show in my studies sufficiently demonstrates that I am animated by a noble ideal, that I aspire to serve the socialist fatherland and the great Stalin in person. In no doubt at all that my place is firmly in the Komsomol, he has already arranged everything so that I can join it with a minimum of fuss. Every candidate needs two sponsors and he hands me an application for membership countersigned by himself and by the Komsorg (secretary of the Komsomol), Sobourov, nicknamed 'the Blond'. It only remains for me to thank him because, if the procedure now appears to me to be somewhat expeditious I was nevertheless flattered by the eulogies heaped on me by this member of the 'steely nucleus' and by the confidence that he shows in me. I tell myself that perhaps he is right after all and that my good school marks must have a political significance which I had overlooked because of my ideological immaturity. In any case, I am still not mature enough for reflection upon the mode of recruitment to the Komsomol and to the party; it is only a quarter of a century afterwards, in Mao's China, that someone will say to me, sensibly enough, that productivism is not necessarily an indication of the 'correct political thought', and that the Soviets, using wrong criteria, had selected a depoliticized soul-less elite, which ended up leading the country down the revisionist road and made it 'change colour'. In 1941, however, the Chinese themselves didn't yet know this.

While escorting me back to my class, the Partorg gives me some advice: I am to read attentively the regulations of the Komsomol, and to follow national and international affairs very closely, because my application for membership, once approved by the relevant committee, has to be ratified by the assembly of all the Komsomol members in our school, and, on this occasion, the candidate is often asked difficult questions in order to check the level of his ideological preparedness. Convinced that I shall pass this test he announces to me that by the Red Army holiday on 23 February, I will surely be marching in the ranks of the Komsomols but, since he is my proposer, he alerts me to possible obstacles. Only 10 days remain before the test of the general assembly.

The worst of idlers wouldn't have needed more than half a day to assimilate the little book entitled *Oustav* (Statutes) explaining the rights and duties of a young communist. During this month of February 1941 I can devote myself entirely to a more attentive reading of the Soviet press, which is the only means of following the news. Now *Molot* as well as *Pravda* contain agreeable surprises: from them I learn on one hand that the German air raids over England are drawing to a close, fewer and fewer towns are being bombed while Luftwaffe losses are on the increase; and on the other hand, that in Africa, it is the British who are making clear progress in Cyrenaica – a name that doesn't mean anything to me – and especially in Abyssinia.* It happens that I am very attached to this country, because I cut my political teeth, as it were, on the demonstrations organized in my home town against the invasion of Haile Selassie's empire by fascist Italy. The entire left, for once, was unanimous in condemning this act of aggression: my social democratic mother, my communist brother, my dear geography teacher at Skorupka lycée. The latter, Tadeusz Greiber, was so impassioned by this theme that he would drop whatever he was supposed to be teaching in order to talk to us at length of this proud African country attacked in such cowardly fashion by the fascists and abandoned by the European Pontius Pilates.

In 1941 the British finally make amends for their crimes of default in 1935, when the League of Nations had voted sanctions against Italy in Geneva, without ever succeeding in having them

*The name employed by the Italians for the Ethiopian Empire, which allowed them to speak of the Abyssinians as of a people without either a history or a right to independent existence.

enforced. Better still, a short dispatch on the inside back page of *Molot* announces that the British troops are being actively aided by Abyssinian partisans in their march on Addis-Ababa – underlining in my eyes the value of this just anti-fascist revenge. On the other hand I am not blind to the historical misdeeds of Great Britain in Africa, to a colonial past which could allow one to interpret its landing in Ethopia as a struggle between imperialists for the division of the colonies. Something tells me, I don't know what, that it is on this point that I am going to be questioned and so, considering that the subject is at once delicate and symbolic, I draft a very personal and emotionally charged exposé of the situation.

The candidate members – there are 20 or so of us – are not admitted to the plenary session straightaway. We have to wait in the antechamber until the meeting goes through its agenda and comes to 'any other business'. Only then are we summoned one by one and those who are accepted as members remain in the hall. I am among the first to be called and I walk with a firm step to the platform where, beside some Komsomols from my school, several representatives of the Gorkom (Urban Committee) are seated. Among those present I recognize many of the faces, some of them very young – you join the Komsomol starting at 14 – who look at me with a certain respect. Wishing to leave as much time as possible for the discussion on Abyssinia or whatever other theme is chosen by my examiners, I reduce my declaration of adherence to a strict minimum. The problem of Abyssinia in fact interests no one, and I am asked only two elementary questions concerning the number of medals which have been awarded to the Komsomol. Then, a show of raised hands decides in favour of my membership. In less than five minutes I have become a member of the Leninist Communist Youth of the Soviet Union. The other candidates are also speedily dealt with – some of them go through it even more quickly than I do – and, in the space of an hour, the Komsomol has been enlarged by 20 new members. The next day *Molot* honours us with a report: its columns explain that the tremendous vitality of Soviet youth, just at the very time of the forthcoming Red Army holiday, pushes the best of them to rally to the ranks of communist youth.

On the eve of the five kilometre march in homage to our army, the wind from the Don stops blowing and there is a thaw, unusual at this time of year. Thus we set out in snow transformed into a kind of muddy soup, in rows of four, singing 'If war should come tomorrow . . .', but after half an hour of it our shoes are completely soaked in the melted snow and, here and there, you can see gaps in our columns; Komsomols or not, certain comrades cut their losses and take French leave. Despite wanting to show my mettle, I manage with great difficulty to get just beyond the tank-shaped theatre. I don't feel I have the strength to go as far as Rosselmach, the factory at which the march is supposed to finish. I have a bad conscience about giving up but it is not a sports club that I have just joined, and this march could not in any way be seen as the test of my worth to the Komsomol. Anyway, how many stayed until the end? *Molot* the next day publishes only a photo of the march as we are about to set off, when we are still very numerous. Klava believes she can recognize me in this crowd and thinks that I ought to keep the poor quality newspaper photo as a souvenir.

In fact I am a very good Komsomol because I like to hang around in the Gorkom premises, where, after classes, you meet pupils from other schools and even young workers, all of them *oudarniki*, 'the workers' vanguard'; thus do I enlarge my circle of acquaintances. I refuse no task, I spend time at the House of Pioneers – a large palace at the centre of the Sadovaia. I work at organizing cultural activities, such as film shows for our school, or outings to the theatre. I am quickly promoted, and I become a member of various committees, at school first, then in the neighbourhood, and I am well-liked at the Gorkom. Obviously the Komsomol Secretary in a large town like Rostov is too busy to chat with a young man like me, but I am sure that without my knowing of it, he follows my work closely, just as the Partorg at school No. 44 had done before I was promoted to the position of *otlitchnik*.

Admittedly I owe this progress to the free time I enjoy as much as to my capacities as an organizer, but it is possible that it has an

72

ideological significance which, for the moment, still eludes me. What worries me, however, is that Motia seems to suspect me of being some sort of careerist. Not that he says anything to offend me, on the contrary; my attempts to discipline the 'pioneers', youngsters of less than 14 years, make him laugh, and even the beautiful but silent Clarissa joked once or twice on this subject. Motia however insists that I ought to give priority to the sciences. 'It's the best career for you,' he repeats, as if he were afraid of seeing me become an official of the Komsomol.

At the end of the school year, the problem of each person's vocation urgently presents itself. In the USSR all the *vouz* (higher education establishments) do not enjoy the same status. The rate of maintenance grant varies, and the quality of the refectories and student accommodation provided ranges from one extreme to another. In certain *vouz*, the *otlitchniks* are accepted without examination; in others, the mere fact of being an *otlitchnik* and even of having the *caracteriska* – a recommendation – from the Komsomol, is not sufficient. At the 'Mifli' or the 'Lifli' for example, competition is obligatory, even after a preliminary selection. Russians have a mania for abridging the names of their institutions and the titles of their functionaries which sometimes baffles the novice, but the Komsorg explained to me that the 'Mifli' (the Moscow Institute of Philosophy, Literature and History), and its Leningrad homologue, the 'Lifli', are formidable universities: when you have succeeded in getting into them you have it made for life. I continue to promise to my protector, Motia, that I shall go to his faculty of sciences at Rostov, but the name 'Mifli' rings in my ears. Moreover, if I were to pass the entrance examination to the 'Mifli' I could go back to my Aunt Lisa's in the Arbat. I would like to see then the expression on the face of this cousin who had made the figure zero with his fingers to show in peremptory fashion what little chance I had of obtaining a residence permit for Moscow!

Today on thinking back to these plans, which occupied my mind during the last spring of peacetime in Rostov, I realize that no one was really expecting this war that was imminent. It is singular that a country so seriously threatened as the USSR had done nothing to prepare its people for such an eventuality. We were led to believe to the very last that the conflict which was then raging in Europe, Africa and Asia (in China), didn't concern us, as though we were certain to remain mere spectators. In my own case, having counted on a speedy end to the war to be able to rejoin my family, I had been affected by this soothing atmosphere. I decided that first of all I would bring my studies to a brilliant conclusion at the 'Mifli' or in Rostov, and only then would I search for my mother. But how? In the midst of my euphoria I imagined that she would be proud of my diplomas. My main worry, in all this collective myopia, was that my mother, firm anti-communist that I knew her to be, would not be very pleased to learn that I was now in the Komsomol.

For Alexander Blok, the greatest Russian poet of this century (according to Motia), Russia is a land of *taina* – secrets or mystery – now a sphinx of many faces, now a world hidden behind 'its maze of rivers and encircled by its forests'. On this day, 22 June 1941, upon hearing Viatcheslav Molotov announce the news of the German attack, the USSR gives the impression of a giant transfixed by fear. You might say that even its rivers stop flowing for a time, that nothing moves in its forests and that the only perceptible trickling sound is that of the tears which flow down the cheeks of Blok's imaginary sphinx. Having lived through the outbreak of war in Poland two years earlier, I find the atmosphere in Rostov a striking contrast. True, in Poland, I was in a paramilitary camp and the Poles in general are rather inclined to boasting, but that is not sufficient to account for the difference. The people of the USSR were living as if anaesthetized (since the signing of the pact with Hitler's Reich), put to sleep by their own leaders who repeated to them only 10 days before the start of hostilities that the Germans would respect their treaty commitment to refrain from any aggression. The other capitalist powers had other problems of course, and were failing to deal with their chief one for the moment:

Nazi Germany. All the songs in fashion – 'If tomorrow war should come,' for example – were to the Soviet mind jolly but rather vacuous themes, without any relevance to the way the war was going, and didn't in any way herald immediate fighting.

Yet here is Viatcheslav Molotov suddenly speaking about a real war, and denouncing Hitler because he didn't declare it in good and due form and because, without warning, he has had 50 of our towns and cities bombed. Next, in order to explain our troops' retreat, he informs us, in his dreary official's voice, that the Germans have concentrated 170 of their best divisions along our frontiers, and that their all-powerful airforce controls our air space. And our leaders? How is it that they haven't acted in time to prevent the arrival of this monstrous army at our doors? Klim Voroshilov, our commander-in-chief, is supposed to lead us to victory with his 'iron hand' according to the song. Hasn't he foreseen any of this, and if he hasn't reacted until now, is it for want of formal notification that the combat has begun? And Stalin? Too many questions assail our minds for Molotov's final promise – 'the enemy will be crushed, our cause is just and we shall conquer' – to be credible. People who, like me, heard this speech broadcast in the street, disperse without comment, without offering each other a single word of hope. Convinced for a long time of the ineluctable defeat of Hitler, I hear, behind the sound of the 'Internationale', the voice of Blok's 'Archangel' as recited by Motia: 'Is the fire or the mist before us? Are we going to perish? Are we going to die?' Fear is contagious, decidedly.

In the days following, the decrees multiply and the men are called up: there is a general mobilization, all wireless sets are confiscated (they are to be handed in to the militia within 24 hours), a war directorate presided over by Stalin is formed in Moscow, and 'Sovinformbureau' is established with the task of relaying the communiqués of our military high command. Motia is one of the first to leave and, at the station, I witness the heart-rending lamentations of women who are seeing off their nearest and dearest, as if they were never to meet again. 'No you mustn't! Get hold of yourselves; they'll be back; bring flowers for them. I've seen other departures for the front in American films in Poland, and they are joyous and patriotic!' I want to say this to them; but I am not authorized to do so and no one else does. Perhaps Russia already has a presentiment, in these first days of the German invasion, that she will obtain victory only at the price of 20 million dead; so she weeps for them in advance.

Finally, 3 July 1941 arrives and Stalin speaks. He addresses us as 'brothers and sisters'. It is the most remarkable speech of his career, the only one which reaches straight to the heart. Later, at the time of the Twentieth Congress of the CPSU, Nikita Krushchev will claim that since he was the only one able to speak, Stalin did no better than expected. It is a mistake though to judge people as either all black or all white. I have never written anything in praise of Stalin, but I maintain without hesitation that his speech of 3 July was a masterpiece, even better than Churchill's 'blood and tears' speech. I saw with my own eyes how it raised the morale of a whole country; and mine in particular.

Some who heard it on powerful radios will allege, again during the Kruschev era, that Stalin was so terrified that at times you could hear his teeth chattering. In a country that is prey to a formidable fear, it isn't such a bad thing to know that the supreme commander-in-chief shares your sentiments; it renders him more human and brings him closer to his people. It was the technique used by F.D. Roosevelt in his fireside chats: in order to be understood you have to penetrate the homes of your listeners, sit at their table, be one of them. If Stalin's teeth chattered during his speech of 3 July, it was in order the better to convince us that he was one of us. And the speech worked: from 3 July onwards, the whole of the USSR unites to make war.

What did he say in substance, to reassure us, to reassure me? Nothing very original. He explained, arguing from history, that there is no such thing as an invincible army, and that Hitler's army, like that of Napoleon's in another era, would be beaten. The parallel between these two conflicts emerges didactically, but discreetly, and we are left to deduce from it ourselves that the more the Wehrmacht penetrates into the immense Soviet space, the more thoroughly it will be crushed. At the end he also found some apt expressions to show how this time it was not a matter of an ordinary war between two countries and two armies, but a trial of strength between two visions of the world, and how therefore the Red Army fought not only to defend its own soil, but for the freedom of all peoples who 'groaned under the yoke of German fascism'. Ever since my crossing of the frozen Bug, I had been waiting to hear exactly that, no more, no less. 'Shall we revive?' Blok's poem asks; in my mind, from July 3rd the USSR is already beginning to revive.

Towards the end of July I leave with a brigade of Komsomols to help with the harvest in a kolkhoz in the Salsk region, six hours by train from Rostov, in the steppes of the Don region. It is halfway through the night when the train is ready to leave the station, all the lights are switched off and my comrades daren't sing or even talk aloud for fear the noise might draw German bombers down on us. It is an absurd fear, but I don't blame my companions; hadn't I, in 1939, seen a professional soldier order a peasant woman to strangle her child to keep it quiet? We leave Rostov in a blacked-out train in silence, like conspirators, and by the next morning we have already started work in one of the richest agricultural regions of the country.

There is only one older person among us, Gricha Voronov. His title in the Gorkom of the Komsomol – Zamzavkomprop, assistant to the President of the Propaganda Committee – is too cumbersome for everyday usage. Between ourselves we call him 'Senior', and we address him with the respect due a superior. I am one of his four assistants, representing those taking exams at school No. 44; we are more than a third of the brigade. My closest friends unfortunately haven't come with us: Micha has gone to work in a factory, Klava has stayed at home with her parents who have been badly shaken by the departure of their three sons. I would have preferred to go off with them myself, but the military committee, overwhelmed by its tasks – it has to mobilize all of those eligible who were born between the years 1905 and 1918 – refuses volunteers. Being too young in any case, my only chance of getting enlisted is through the Komsomol, in which my work is highly regarded. At the Gorkom, I have even been promised that my case will be examined on my return from the kolkhoz when I shall at least have celebrated my seventeenth birthday (4 August) and given proof of my political capacities. Resolved upon conducting myself like a man of steel, as a fit compatriot of Felix Dzerjinski, within a week I am obliged to admit that I am not of this stamp of men. It is a young literature student, Olga Alexeievna Spodina who, by her sudden and agreeable eruption into my life shows me that it is illusory to make great plans in the USSR without taking account of the dictates of love.

Some might find Olga peasant-like, especially as she always runs about barefoot, without worrying much about the details of her clothes. She has a snub nose, *cournosyi*, which can often displease; 'an acquired taste' as my snub nosed friend Kola will say to me later. Finally her laugh is almost embarrassingly loud. Despite all this, there is not a fellow in the brigade or among the kolkozians who, when she appears, doesn't look up. And Olga doesn't lower her eyes before their stares. She seems on the contrary very sure of herself, and capable of holding her own in any circumstances.

One evening, 'Senior' summoned her in front of the executive committee in order to talk to her both about her lack of enthusiasm at work and her occasional absenteeism. 'Senior' isn't really a bad sort: he is 30 years old, a graduate of an obscure history institute; he knows how to involve us in taking decisions, but he is tiresome and complicates matters by ornamenting his already long sentences with well-known quotations from Stalin. Instead of saying 'Right, Olia (the diminutive of Olga), what's going on?' he addresses her ceremoniously as 'Comrade Olga Alexeievna Spodina', and goes on to quote a whole passage of Stalin's on the need to abandon the insouciance of peacetime and to organize one's work in a military fashion. 'I am not insouciant,' she replies with aplomb. 'I am unwell. I was badly sunburned yesterday and it has left me feeling terrible.'

'Senior' launches, without acrimony, into an interminable speech on the war, the enemy's atrocities, the duties of Komsomols and a string of truths which have no connection at all with sunburn. Olga listens, calm and distant. The gaze of her blue eyes wanders across our faces. Then she takes us all by surprise: 'If the comrades of the committee don't want to believe me, they have only to look.' Quickly, she removes the bodice of her dress. 'Touch my back,' she says to me, 'it's on fire.'

We are all well accustomed to seeing women in their bras, because it is very hot at this time of year and many comrades, for want of bathing suits, work with their blouses off. There is no plausible reason therefore to explain the overwhelming effect that Olga's gesture has on me: even before touching her shoulders, I have the impression of being on fire myself. 'Obviously she can't work in the sun in this state. Go on home, Olga, and when you are better you shall return to the fields.' I said this with an air of authority even though I have no authority to take such a decision. No one contradicts me though, and Olga readjusts her bodice and says goodbye to each of us. In shaking my hand she smiles the merest hint of gratitude, which makes me even more aroused. I experience an irresistible desire to go with her to try my luck. But you don't leave a meeting like that, especially given my situation, when my military future depends on my good leadership record.

The rest of the meeting is all the more trying. 'Senior' lectures another comrade who is supposed to have tormented some bulls by prodding them with a pitchfork in order to get them to run, and is even said to have organized a cart race, to the great indignation of the kolkhozians. The accused defends himself badly, claims that he has to service scattered work sites, which in this enormous kolkhoz are often very far apart. He claims he has done no harm to these stupid animals, which understand perfectly well when the kolkhozians order them to move left or right, but which remain deaf to our orders, except when you prod them gently in the backside. Who could possibly be interested in this interminable discussion on bovine intelligence when he thinks he has a semi-rendezvous with the fair-haired Olga?

Towards midnight we finally go our separate ways. Olga doesn't live at the school but, like nearly all the women, with a private family. In Polish villages each farm is clearly recognizable: the enclosures are never identical, the stables and granaries vary in shape and size. In short there are plenty of markers to help you find your way around. Here, the same bare cottage, without either granary or stable, is followed by another similar cottage 100 metres further on and there are no streets. I walk randomly in the silence of Zhdanov Kolkhoz, convinced that even if by some miracle I manage to find where Olga was staying, she will surely be fast asleep, exhausted from sunstroke.

Not at all: Olga emerges from the darkness, and slips her arm under mine. 'I knew you'd come. No, this way. Let's get away from the village.' Olga takes the initiatives. When finally the time comes to talk, she manages to make me a flattering reproach: 'Is that how you get to know each other in Poland?' I play my part and explain that it is not Polish habit but rather her exceptional attraction, her beauty, her frankness which have moved me to act, and which explain why I feel happy in her arms. Then I admit to her my astonishment at having gained her favours so rapidly. Is it to thank me for my decision at the meeting that she has given herself to me, or is it because I am a member of the committee? She sweeps all of this aside as so much nonsense. 'I like you because you aren't like the others. Our men are thick brutes (*groubyié*), drunkards as well; whereas you are different, subtle.'

The next day, on an ox-cart, forgetting the comrades who surround me and even forgetting the war, I can't refrain from an immense smile of satisfaction: 'I have the most beautiful girl in the brigade!' Astonished, the others ask me what has happened, and I hide behind the first excuse that comes to mind.

At the end of three or four days the entire brigade knows the truth. It is partly the drawback of group life, perhaps also partly a result of Olga's free and easy manner: she pretends still to be ill and I can't resist the temptation to worry about (and to ask after) her health. In fact Olga likes to sew and she does a lot of small jobs for her friends, repairing clothes they have torn, for they are unused to working in the fields and often tear skirts and bodices. It is obvious that she prefers to work at home and it suits everyone – except 'Senior'. However that might be, I hear the others sing behind my back the well known air from a Tchaikovsky opera: 'I love you Olga! I love you Olga!' or again *Za Rodinu, za Spodinu* ('to the fight for the fatherland, to the fight for Spodina' – whereas, in the song, the words are 'to the fight for Stalin'). I feel that my authority is clearly waning although 'Senior' has said nothing and I omit none of my duties. It is true that I no longer think of anything but Olga. Not only am I infatuated but she thoroughly fascinates me. She is lively, observant, and talks easily and well: 'The Komsomol is not a monastery; it is not written in our rules that we are a religious order,' she says to me, when I confide to her my fears about having problems because of our relationship. 'Don't let yourself be affected by these hypocrites who pretend to live only for the party; my father is one of them. If I had had a *tchervonietz* (10 roubles) for every time that he was unfaithful to my mother, I would be a millionaire in the land of the Soviets.' Her parents, it seemed, didn't form a very harmonious couple.

Suddenly everything comes to a head. 'Senior' calls a general assembly early in the morning to tell us that our work will be remunerated, even though we are volunteers. He puts me in charge of a commission which, with the help of the kolkhoz accountant, will determine the rewards of each person and the method of payment in agricultural products. Everyone cheers: in these times flour, corn and eggs will be a valuable and unexpected present for the families in Rostov. Olga applauds too, delighted with the rest, but then her enthusiasm is dampened: 'Senior' by way of a postscript adds in a deadpan voice a few words on loafers, Comrade Spodina for example, who thinks she is on holiday, etc. All eyes turn towards her as if expecting protests, but Olga refuses to get riled. 'Have me summoned to the committee this evening,' she whispers to me before we separate for the day.

A little disoriented in the middle of this conflict I turn for help to 'the Blond', because I haven't the courage to confront 'Senior' alone; and I also lack authority to summon Olga to the meeting of our committee. 'The Blond' is not a friend; but as one of my sponsors at the time I joined the Komsomol, his interest in my good conduct coincides with mine. I find him near one of those giant machines made at Rosselmach, which reap the corn magnificently while creating a great cloud of dust, but which just as often break down. We sit down at the edge of the field. I tell him about my liaison with Olga, and ask for his help to summon her the same evening.

'Listen,' he says finally, 'you have adapted yourself well among us, you are already one of us. But with us, nothing is ever guaranteed. The least false step can compromise everything. I advise you to drop Olga since she will only create problems for you. She is an individualist and pig-headed. She thinks that she has the right to choose whichever man she wants. With us, things don't happen like that. The last thing you want to do is join with her in a battle with "Senior". Especially not you!'

It is a harsh recall to reality and no doubt timely. 'The Blond' is right perhaps to think of me as not quite like the others, but after what Olga has told me of the hypocrisy of party members, I don't consider for a moment modelling my behaviour on theirs. It is not a question of love but of dignity; besides Olga and I have not made any great declarations or promises to each other. I believe I already know that she has a man in her life who is in the army, and we are aware of the ephemeral character of our encounter.

'Please, I beg you. Summon her,' I say.

He shrugs his shoulders: 'OK, but watch out, or women will be the end of you.'

'The Blond' tosses off this bitter prediction without any malice, but the future will show that he is no more of a prophet than was the functionary in Lvov who announced to me that I would never join the Komsomol. My Russian lovers, far from leading me to my ruin, were more than once to give me a helping hand in the difficult times ahead.

After a meeting that was as tedious as the one about oxen, Olga enters the little room occupied by the brigade committee. She looks pleased with herself, almost gay. She greets us and chatters away about the weather. I note that she has dressed to effect this evening, and has even put on high-heeled shoes in order not to appear in a position of inferiority before this all-male tribunal. What is she up to?

In fact she says to 'Senior', as if in passing, 'You reprimanded me this morning in a full assembly. Yet didn't you agree, the other day, that I shouldn't have to work for a few days? You will kindly give me the satisfaction of removing this extract from the minutes of the assembly, because I refuse to accept an undeserved reprimand in my dossier.'

On this occasion, 'Senior' pauses even longer between each word. There is a war going on, entire regions of our country are devastated, and Stalin has alerted us against carelessness at work or work carried out without enthusiasm.

Olga listens, smiling, as if amused. 'You haven't answered my question, Comrade Zamzavkomprop Grigorii Vassilievitch Voronov. Yes or no, did you exempt me from work for a few days?'

This time 'Senior' replies more rapidly: 'I am not answerable to you.'

'Ah! I see,' she says laughing. 'You are directly answerable only to Moscow. To whom then, tell me if you please, to Stalin or to Mikhailov (Secretary General of the Komsomol)? So you don't condescend to discuss the matter with the simple comrades at the base, is that right? We shall see, we shall soon see about that when we get back to Rostov.'

Olga is strong, there's no doubt about it, but I tell myself that she must have something up her sleeve and that her father probably occupies an important position in the party.

I rush to Olga's aid, ready to witness that her back is peeling like a baked apple and that by sewing at home she performs a much greater service to the brigade than by sorting out grain in the sun; but 'the Blond' intervenes:

'Come now. Let's not fight between friends. Our country is at war. Go back to work from tomorrow, Olga, even if you aren't completely cured, and everything will be forgotten. If you agree, the comments by Gricha will not figure in the minutes of the assembly, and there will be no reprimand.'

We adopt this suggestion almost without discussion and all of us leave together, good friends. And to put an end to any secretiveness, Olga takes me by the arm and leads me quietly away: 'It was terrific of you to get me called this evening. In fact I don't give a hoot about their reprimand, but I don't like their digs below the belt. Don't let them walk over you, ever – that's my principle.'

Our precarious idyll will continue until the end of the stay on the farm. Olga works in the kitchen and, in the evening, she makes my old trousers into a bag in which to carry provisions. Since I have no family she will take double rations to her parents. However, during the final general assembly, 'Senior' 'suggests' to us that we contribute our earnings to the Red Army supply stocks. 'It's decided unanimously then,' he announces, without having consulted anyone, not even the committee. These Soviets definitely haven't got many democratic habits and their manner of imposing decisions is stupid, for it removes all motivation from people. After all, the majority in this Komsomol brigade would have supported a patriotic resolution, and wouldn't be left with this bitter impression of having been fooled by false promises. Olga laughs at my disappointment: 'We've ruined your trousers for nothing, but you will receive a diploma of merit and you have got to know our habits and customs a little better.' I don't find it funny at all.

Once we get back to Rostov we hardly see each other because she lives at the other end of town. It is out of the question for me to go to her home or for her to come to my room in the militiaman's house.

The Gorkom of the Komsomol is as good as its word and obtains a post for me in the political branch of the airforce. The date of my departure is not yet fixed however, and I experience a period of tension.

I remember Olga well because of an episode which took place

after victory in 1945. Deported to Germany during the occupation of Rostov in 1942, she was placed on her return in a 'verification of identity camp' near Novotcherkask and although it was really quite close, she hadn't the right to come to town. One of her friends, a former member of our brigade, contacted me to ask me to go and see her, without specifying the reason. Knowing that Olga had been deported and hadn't gone to Germany as a volunteer, I told myself that she would be released any day and that we would have the opportunity to clear up her problem on the spot, in Rostov. In fact I didn't think any more about it.

Once I had gone to the West, I discovered that the 'verification camps' had been a point of transit for the majority of former deportees or POWs before their deportation to the Gulag. Olga's message obviously took on another meaning in my eyes. Perhaps she wanted to ask me to help her to escape this tragedy that she was alone in anticipating. I don't know if I would have been able to help her, nor if she too was indeed a victim of the great wave of Stalinist deportations of the postwar period; I do know that I ought to have gone to see her in this 'verification camp', if only in memory of the happiness she had given me in the Andrei Zhdanov Kolkhoz.

2. Nievka

Well before the invention of the video-camera I used to project mentally scenes of life from wartime Russia, and to describe them to my friends in the style of clips from coming attractions, to whet their appetite for the film's eventual appearance on the screen. My listeners were sometimes well-known figures and their favourable reactions impressed me, but I don't want here to indulge in 'name dropping'. I shall mention only Aneurin Bevan, the leader of the left wing of the Labour Party who, on the occasion of the twentieth anniversary of his death, was eulogized by the British press. In his lifetime, however, it had nothing but hatred for him because he was a tribune of the people, a 'Welsh miner MP', who talked in the language of his class. Everyone knows that the class struggle is a reality, but the propertied classes prefer not to talk about it – at least not in public. Nye played a role for me in the West similar to that played by Motia in Rostov: like my Russian friend, he encouraged and protected me without any particular motive, in a totally disinterested manner. Although this book is devoted only to my years in Russia, I should like to express my gratitude to Nye. In 1959, he had the courage to take me with him to the Kremlin and thereby force the hand of the authorities, then on to Leningrad. His meetings with the leaders of the USSR attracted daily coverage in *Pravda*, and, to add a comic note, I was referred to in the plural as 'the persons accompanying' the Labour Party leader.

In Leningrad, the most beautiful city in the whole of Russia, Nye and I gave our official guides the slip one morning in order to visit the city on our own. I took him everywhere, to Peterhof and to the

'Venetian' districts where the Nievka joins the Nieva, to form the majestic river so frequently evoked in the literary classics. Since I had never set foot in these places before I referred necessarily to the person who had spoken of them to me with such enthusiasm, a woman from Leningrad. She, curiously, was called Nievka, and was my first great love in Russia, in Kislovodsk in 1941 and 1942, at the height of the war. In order to place her better I had also, for Nye's benefit, to sketch the portraits of my commissar, Bielokonienko, and of my friend Kola, a trainee pilot with Marshal Anatol Golovanov's Eighteenth Airforce. I related several anecdotes about our life in the airforce, and finally about the drama that ensued when the Wehrmacht succeeded in penetrating to the heart of the Caucasus. I can say without boasting that Nye Bevan seemed to enjoy my stories even more than Peterhof, which hasn't an awful lot to dazzle the eyes of a Westerner, and he urged me in a peremptory fashion: 'Write that down, you lazy oaf, and you would have a film to smash the box office records.'

My reluctance to apply myself to the task wasn't due to laziness: the real problem is that the film lacks probability, its scenario is incoherent, there are gaps that I can't manage to complete even today. For, after having been a spruce and chubby young man in a handsome, blue airman's uniform, I find myself one and a half years later marching on the frozen Volga, following perhaps the same route as my parents on their honeymoon cruise, and I am in the pitiable state of a vagabond who weighs 46 kilos, roughly the weight of a sheep. Such a reversal of fortune already runs the risk of astonishing my hypothetical spectators. To render the film credible I would have to explain to them in detail in what circumstances and for what reasons I was arrested one fine December morning in 1942, in Yerevan, Armenia, and then deported to a camp on the Volga. Someone had denounced me in an underhand manner to the NKVD, and two Chekist captains, having heaped on me a series of accusations too improbable to be taken seriously, had then sent me to the very depths of the Gulag. In a sense my fate bore some resemblance to that of Edmond Dantès, the hero of *The Count of*

Monte Cristo by Alexander Dumas, except that he had succeeded in cornering one of the jailers and discovering the origin of his misfortune, but not me; in Yerevan, in any case, to assault a jailer would have been a suicidal act.

I didn't succeed in escaping and I didn't even need to: I was freed from the Gulag as abruptly as I had been arrested, without further explanation. At this point, in order to give a measure of credibility to the scenario, which involves 180° reversals, I would have had to find Andrei Bielokonienko, my commissar during my untroubled stay at Kislovodsk, but this prime witness had been killed at Korsoun Chevtchenkovski, in his native Ukraine, during the final stages of the war. My friend Kola managed to come up with a plausible hypotheis according to which the airforce had intervened on my behalf, at Bielokonienko's request, and that its wartime prestige was such that the NKVD had been obliged to release me. If I am to believe that it really happened in this way, I might also interpret the facts in a more pessimistic fashion and conclude that, even in wartime, the airforce had taken 13 months and three days to extricate me from the Gulag!

There again my scenario could give rise to complications, because the Soviet authorities, well known for their sensitivity in such matters, might dispute my story. They could claim firstly, that I had never been in a camp – it doesn't in fact show up in my dossier – and secondly, that I had suffered concussion on the Caucasian front – they have all the certificates to prove it – which had transformed me into an irredeemable anti-Soviet slanderer. The fact is that not only have I no proof that I was arrested by the NKVD, but, to complicate matters, before leaving the camp I accepted a mutually beneficial arrangement, thanks to which my official papers certified that I had not left the Red Army since September 1941. In fact, because of this, after my demobilization and return to Rostov in the spring of 1944, I was welcomed everywhere as a war hero and given the freedom of choice in my work and my studies. One word more on the subject of my concussion: I was twice wounded, in Poland in 1939 and in Nalchik in 1942, but without losing a single drop of blood. At the village of Krzywda, it was my Polish companions Rysiek and Jurek who asked me: 'Why are you keeping your right eye closed?' whereas, without a mirror, I didn't even know that I could no longer open my eyelid. At Nalchik it was a similar story: my platoon comrade, Boris, was convinced that my last hour had come whereas I seem to remember that I was more frightened than in pain. Hardly the stuff of which movies are made: a wounded soldier should bleed, groan, suffer, arouse the pity of the nurses, and not get the business over with in a few seconds.

The final section of my scenario is disjointed and fits badly in any logical whole. The war still hasn't come to an end when I return to Rostov: the USSR still endures martyrdom, loses its men, goes hungry, but for me the entire world dissolves into the background and I have eyes only for Klava, 'the flower of the scented prairies' of the Don. That doesn't ring true, spectators would say, reaching for their coats; he ought to be overcome with bitterness after what he has lived through in the Gulag. What's more, he has described his school bench companion to us as a timid youngster and now here he is presenting her as an irresistible woman. But the incoherence in my story is limitless: I married this Cosatchka knowing full well that she wouldn't be able to come with me to Poland after victory since it was against the law – it would be a fine thing indeed for the USSR if any Pole had the right to carry off with him a daughter of the Don! The hero of a well-constructed film would have organized a spectacular escape in order to take his wife with him to the West, and thus provide a happy ending. I didn't know how to, and that is one of the reasons for my prolonged hesitation before deciding to write this narrative.

If I project this impossible film in my head so often, it is because I have never lost the hope of understanding the reasons for my different changes of fortune. Even if sheer luck played a part in it, I need to return to the details and try to disentangle the threads of an intrigue which developed bit by bit without my knowing it. My 13 months in the Gulag formed only a tiny drop in the unpredictable torrent of Stalinist repression, but it continues to interest me; I still ask myself about its possible origins. The same is true of my marriage to Klava, and of our life among a circle of friends in Rostov, which greatly affected me, although obviously in an altogether different way. So, while thinking that Nye Bevan was mistaken about the value of this scenario, I ended up convincing myself that I should write it even if, as is so often the case with true stories, it didn't respect the rules.

At the time of my return from the kolkhoz in September 1941, there is no threat officially hanging over Rostov. According to the Sovinformbureau communiqués, the Germans are stumbling about the far away Ukraine and will be forced to revise their plans on account of the unexpected resistance of the Red Army. Our city begins to empty surreptitiously, however, and shamefully, without any official control over the exodus. The authorities help only the factories, administrative organizations and sometimes even certain individuals to leave. My own departure for military service is still delayed by surprising traffic jams among the transport convoys heading south. In principle I have no great worries, but this strange atmosphere, reminiscent of the end of a reign, completely saps my morale. The evacuation which is under way is sufficient to persuade us that Rostov is going to fall, and that the Red Army has abandoned the idea of halting the Germans' advance along the Don, one of the most imposing, natural frontier defences in the country. Where then will it stop them? On the Volga? On the Ural?

The people in the town, although visibly sad, don't talk openly about their fears. Defeatist talk is forbidden and wouldn't help them one bit. Discussions centre rather on the problems of food supply – an inevitable subject. Supplies pose insoluble problems because the rations bureau is proving incapable of distributing the available products fairly. Some people manage to get their provisions almost entirely from the state shops, but many others, in spite of having queued for hours at a stretch, leave empty-handed. For these unfortunates, the only recourse is the kolkhoz market where prices defy imagination: a kilo of bread costs as much as a skilled worker earns in a week, and the prices are spiralling upwards. After three months of war, the USSR settles into a dual economy (which still persists): the official one is fairly inexpensive but marked by a penury of goods; the other, parallel to the first, is better supplied, free of restrictions as to how much you can buy, but characterized by galloping inflation.

It isn't the only novelty to emerge. In the shadow of this secret exodus, trafficking of all kinds thrives, looking after Number One becomes the general rule. Thus, for example, Olga's father is evacuated along with his organization – and his latest mistress – while his wife and daughter remain behind, 'for the moment'. The kolkhoz market and the fleamarket experience considerable growth, creating an outlet for a great many repressed entrepreneurial talents. Small dealers buy at low prices the goods of those in a hurry to leave, and calmly resell them at a large mark-up to those who stay behind. You would have to be blind not to see that there is something suspicious in these deals, to say the least, but the authorities close their eyes to them. Preoccupied with their impotence when faced with the problems of supplies, they appear to encourage them.

Rostov by night even in normal times offers nothing to write home about; in this wartime September its nightlife is practically extinct. From nightfall the city plunges into darkness and silence, and its avenues call to mind the streets of the Middle Ages emptied by epidemics. In theory though, everything is normal: there are no restrictions placed on moving around, and the cinemas, like the theatres, remain open. But people stay in their homes, fearing to go out into the darkness, or to stray far from their homes in case of air raid alerts. Despite this I carry on going to the cinema where the *kinekroniki*, the filmed newsreels, are incredibly mediocre; sometimes they even appear to have been shot in studios, far away from the real theatre of war. My nocturnal homecomings across this deserted town inspire me with defeatist reveries: I am leaving with my mother to join my brother Genia in England and I carry on with the war from there . . . For my unconscious, the

91

Battle of Russia is apparently already lost.

Silence has also fallen on the militiaman's apartment. In the room that a curtain separates from mine all bustle has ceased. The militiaman and his rival are no longer there, having been impartially mobilized by the army on the same day. Their wife and lover, Maria Pavlovna, known as Moussia, spends her days out of doors. She has decided to make a career in the parallel market. In the evenings, at a loss as to how to spend her time, she was restless at first but gradually regained control of her own solitude in a kind of oriental meditation, almost without moving. One day, she remembers my presence and, putting her head around the curtain, she asks me whether I have eaten. She then has the idea of providing me with half-board; in exchange she asks for only a trifling additional contribution based on pre-war prices. How can one refuse such a godsend? In accepting, however, I am filled with the fear that this agitated woman has inspired in me from the beginning. Finding myself alone with her each evening promises to be an unnerving experience.

Moussia shows her discernment in declaring from the outset that I am a 'timid young fellow', and limits herself over the first two or three meals to asking my opinion of her cooking, which is excellent, by the way. Then bit by bit she begins to tell me about herself in a terribly intimate manner. In the course of these chats she will reveal to me nothing less than the joys and miseries of an honest Russian woman who has been far too much in demand with men, constantly obliged to avoid the traps set for her by those who only want her for her body. According to her, men have been running after her like madmen since she was but a girl, even men in 'high places' and the 'well educated'. All of them swear that they are ready to do anything for the love of her green eyes. If most of them were liars, she has known real passion with some of them, combining break-ups, reconciliations, suffering and moments of exaltation. In short, her life has been one long chain of amorous entanglements – some painful, some happy – eclipsing all the rest, notably her material difficulties and, obviously, politics.

I am somewhat taken aback, but the spontaneous confidences of this Soviet woman interest me. Moussia, it must be said, presents love as though it were a boxing match, but without a referee to penalize the opponents for any punches struck below the belt. She had barely turned 15 when a supervisor in her factory cornered her on a nearby wasteground where, being ignorant of the rules of the game, she let herself be abused. Since then, being better armed and having learned to counter-attack, she had learned how to 'neutralize' far more imposing adversaries. In her husband, the militiaman, she recognized a loyal combatant, someone who was really attached to her. The same went for her current lover, a good man who, without her, would have foundered in misfortune and vodka. In this three-cornered match, however, it is she who runs the show, dealing as best she can with each of her men.

All of these stories, punctuated by assorted stillbirths and abortions that she tells me about so matter-of-factly, leave me a little bemused.

From here she goes on to a theme that is dear to her: that what is most intolerable about war is precisely the unnatural separation of the two sexes; all the men are on one side, all the women on the other. It is 'against nature'. She thinks that it is completely stupid and inefficient – even from a military point of view. If a certain equilibrium were maintained among the population in this respect, it would raise the morale of the troops considerably. I don't count in this connection. She places me in a sort of sexual no man's land: certainly I cannot be counted as a woman but I am too young to be treated as a man. Moussia remains evasive about her own age but that doesn't prevent me from making my own calculations: she must be at least 30. Nothing therefore can happen between us; and, after each dinner, I withdraw sagely behind the curtain.

It was only much later, when she was far away, that I began to think that Moussia had treated me in this way in order to give me the courage to behave with her 'as a man'. Certain of her gestures and words came back to me, confirming this sensation of a missed opportunity. I often dreamt of Moussia and of our beds separated by a simple curtain, while Olga, with whom I had had a passionate idyll, practically never appeared in them. From afar, Moussia punished me in this way for having doubted that men could desire her so much.

In September 1941, however, during our period of chaste companionship, the big problem is the career that she pursues on the black market. For the first time in the USSR I am living under the same roof as someone who is breaking the law, albeit in a minor way. The bulk of Moussia's income derives from profit made on the sale of food-ration cards that one of her former suitors gives her each week. The loyalty of her supplier consoles her: she can always count on those who, at some stage, have been in love with her. It is flagrantly obvious, however, that their joint venture constitutes a clear offence; and each time that Moussia speaks to me about it, I half picture a swarm of Siberian mosquitoes buzzing around her curly, chestnut-brown hair. (At the time I still believed that Western Siberia was the worst of punishment centres.) To persuade her to give up a form of commerce I think is dangerous, I appeal to her conscience. Is she unaware of the plight of her fellow citizens who, armed with official food-ration cards and unable to find anything in the shops, haven't enough money to purchase provisions at the kolkhoz market? Or of the fact that the more surplus cards are put into circulation, the more the people in Rostov suffer? Moussia lets me have my say; a light smile forms little wrinkles on the left side of her nose. Certainly she feels sorry for the unfortunates who cannot obtain their rations, but she calmly points out that all of this is a long standing practice. In Russia, the people have been familiar with rationing since time immemorial. With the exception of newcomers like me, people know very well from experience that a ticket represents the hope of a food ration, but that it doesn't in any way guarantee it. Thus the food-ration cards represent a kind of supplementary currency that one uses at will. Citizens short of roubles have never hesitated to sell their monthly card knowing they are perfectly at liberty, some days later, to buy another. Sometimes they make a small profit from it since the price of cards is subject to fluctuation. Now, Moussia argues, the surplus cards that she puts on to the market tend to lower the prices. And when her supplier – who might be pressed for money – brings her a larger packet than usual, she even goes as far as flooding the market with cards at giveaway prices, thereby provoking a temporary collapse in the price, from which all buyers gain a profit. She performs a genuine service therefore. In any case, she adds, her customers come from all walks of life – even men in uniform – and her conscience is easy.

Defeated on this ground I next express surprise that she forgets her position as the wife of a militiaman, the representative of order. At this she laughs openly and the wrinkles appear on both sides of her nose. Firstly, she retorts, she married a man, not the militia; secondly, the members of the militia are just like everyone else. They don't hesitate to sell their ration cards, which, she remarks in passing, are not among those most sought after. 'Here, we are all in the same boat, and that means you too. Everything in this dinner we have just eaten came from the black market. You knew that and yet it didn't affect your appetite. Live like us, and you'll get by like the rest of us.' She says it without any aggressiveness but she makes it very clear that whatever I may think of it, she sees more of the black market in my future. I don't reply. She has more determination than I have for dealing with cases of conscience.

In any case our conversations come to an end. The Komsourd has finally obtained a place on the Transcaucasian for me, while Moussia, deaf to the danger, has decided not to move. There is no way to make her change her mind. When I warn her that she is running the risk of suffering atrocities at the hands of the Germans, she replies very patriotically that the Russians are the strongest precisely because they know how to suffer. When I return I shall be pleased to find her still there. I have the impression that, in her mind's eye, the idea of an heroic popular festival in a liberated Rostov has already taken shape. But perhaps I am crediting her with some of my own fantasies? Dear Moussia! At the time of my departure she refused what I owed her in rent for the month of September and without my knowing it placed some newly-pressed underwear in my suitcase.

We saw each other again in 1944. At Rostov market – where else? Her house had been destroyed so she couldn't invite me, but she was now selling bortsch instead of tickets and more than once she treated me to some. We chatted about this and that and promised to arrange a proper evening together, at the earliest opportunity, to talk at greater length about our war years. The opportunity never arose. I only know that Moussia was up in arms against the Red Army because it hadn't granted a single furlough to either of her men. Both of them were still living and burned with the desire to see her again.

My adjustment to the armed forces was rather like my dinners with Moussia: first apprehension, then, relaxation and contentment, and finally a certain frustration.

It is futile to dwell on my apprehension; everyone feels it at a time when their life is going through a major upheaval. I needn't have worried: everything went very well for me at Kislovodsk; agreeable company, decent food, indifferent but tolerable accommodation (in a mineral water depot). In short, it could have been a lot worse, especially given that my tasks in the political service came under the heading of cultural activities and recreation rather than surveillance or indoctrination. I was in with young people hardly older than I was, and excited by the prospect of their future as pilots. For a 'politico' such as I was, there could be no question of flying, whence my unacknowledged frustration.

Everything started with my meeting with Bielokonienko, my commissar and benefactor-to-be. This 40-odd year old Ukrainian, a former worker from Zaporojié, from the first gave me the feeling that my life in Kislovodsk would hold surprises but not an excessive amount of military rigour. He was taller than me, a robust, fair-haired man, greying at the temples. He read through my eulogistic recommendations from the Komsomol without betraying the slightest interest, and limited himself to murmuring by way of welcome: 'You will tell everyone here that you are 20 years old; we are not running a kindergarten.' Then he shut his eyes, as if afflicted by the sight of me, or as if he were seized by an irresistible somnolence. After some long minutes he said abruptly, 'Let's go to the park, I have to speak with you,' and, doubtless to make up for lost time, he hastily seized his peak cap, hurried down the staircase and broke into a kind of jog. In fact I had difficulty keeping up with him. Later I was to adapt myself to his walking pace and would even develop a life-long habit of walking quickly; but, at the time of this first outing, I listened to him while trailing a good metre behind.

It didn't bother him. He spoke, apparently, for himself, and said some unexpected things about the trees and about Lermontov, situating, with a precision which is absent from the text, the action of the protagonists of *A Hero of Our Time*. What could all this mean? Malicious tongues in the first squadron would tell me later that because he was self-taught he liked to pass himself off as erudite, and that his strolls in the park were a Ukrainian way of coping with hangovers. I didn't find this very convincing. In my view our commissar's taste for Kislovodsk Park was perfectly justified: it is an incomparable spot, one of the marvels of the Soviet Union, a splendid sample of mountainous forest with waterfalls and even a river, preserved in the middle of a town. People are misled by the emphasis placed in the tourist guidebooks on the thermal springs, which are of only secondary interest: the real attraction of Kislovodsk lies in the beauty of its park. From the first day it took my breath away. To move at a stroke from the sad, wartime atmosphere of Rostov to this 'pearl of the northern Caucasus', and to have this singular military chief as a guide, added up to a marvellous experience. It was thanks to this striking setting that Bielokonienko's words immediately proved salutary in their effect on my spirits.

He explained to me that we, as members of the political service, belonged to a separate vertical structure, operating throughout the armed forces, but that we had to identify with the branch to which we were attached and to share its esprit de corps. Clearly, though we were not pilots, we were supposed to defend the honour of the airforce. The commissar wasn't a specialist on planes, but he did communicate to me some little revelation about our sector of the war effort. Its effect on me was immediate. My morale, which had been vacillating at Rostov, suddenly became extremely buoyant; it went from an unacknowledged defeatism to an excessive optimism.

What could Andrei Bielokonienko have said to me that day about the Armed Air Forces (the VVS)? Since I am unable to recall exactly what he told me I shall limit myself to recounting what I know today about the airforce then.

During the first three months of the war each of our armies at the front exercised control over its air support, its armoured divisions and its artillery. With this system we lost a lot of planes without striking a serious blow at the enemy. In the month of September 1941 the Stavka – the GHQ – which Bielokonienko sometimes called the 'Armed Forces Politbureau', had decided to entrust the unified command of all air forces to the air staff. Having thus conquered or reconquered their autonomy, the latter wanted to give a special status to long-range aviation straightaway, foreseeing a key role for it in the second phase of the war.

Let us recognize that a decision of this sort, taken at the very moment that the Wehrmacht, having passed Smolensk, was making straight for Moscow, showed that these technicians were lacking in neither sang-froid nor foresight. The founder of this special force was Lieutenant-General Anatole Golovanov, promoted later to the rank of Air Marshal (one grade below that of Marshal of the Soviet Union). A former airline pilot, he could well appreciate that long-distance flying required special and detailed preparation.

A certain number of training schools were therefore created – that of Kislovodsk bore the number 11, but I imagine that there were at least 30 of them – to train over the next two years the future strategic airstaff (for that in fact is what it was). In 1944, however, some reaction is thought to have taken place within the airforce general staff against this 'separatism', and particularly against the real or imagined privileges enjoyed by this special section, and it was renamed Marshal Golovanov's Eighteenth Airforce.

Among the former Kislovodsk trainees, the curious belief grew that, from the beginning, from 1941, they had belonged to the prestigious Marshal Golovanov's Eighteenth, the crème de la crème. The 17 other sections comprised only very ordinary tactical aviation outfits. In reality, however, at Kislovodsk, we were simply called the 'eleventh school of the VVS'.

I doubt if Commissar Bielokonienko would have been able to talk to me about Marshal Gologanov at the time of this first conversation. He certainly did tell me about how our trainee pilots, in two or three years' time, would go and bomb 'the German beast in his own lair'. It is this capacity to plan for the war in the long term, to prepare in advance for its second phase, which made a striking impression on me. After all, in Poland in 1939, or in France in 1940, it would have been unthinkable to 'programme' at the height of the German offensive what was going to happen in two or three years' time. The USSR, I told myself in meditating on these precedents, despite appearances, wasn't in the process of collapsing. A brief calculation confirmed this conviction: our school was training 450 pilots; as there were in my opinion at least 30 such schools, that meant some 15,000 trainees, not counting the teaching personnel. In short, a whole élite was being put in reserve – in spite of the urgent exigencies of war – in order to inflict decisive blows later on against the Nazis. Decidedly the Soviets were not short of breath; and I found myself swelling with pride in thinking about it.

It was at this precise moment – according to impartial historians – that the USSR really was on the brink of defeat! The Soviet command openly sent out distress signals. To cite only one episode about which much is written nowadays, on 16 October 1941, seeing their government – and Stalin himself apparently – fall back upon Kuybyshev, the people of Moscow crowded into the railway stations in a rush to leave and many people were killed in the resulting crush. It is possible that my Aunt Lisa was one of the victims. (She died at this time though she had been healthy enough a year before.) Four days later, in an appeal for the defence of the capital, the High Command strongly advised against 'any panic'. This phrase ought to have aroused my suspicion. In the course of a war panic is never mentioned unless it be in reference to the enemy camp. The Allied powers, though they didn't hide their defeats, strictly observed this procedure. Terrible things must have happened in Moscow on this fatal day, therefore, to prompt the Soviets to refer to panic on their own side.

On the other hand, everyone knows that the Soviet Union is a big country where news is slow to spread. The events in Moscow of 16 October wouldn't have been known about in Kislovodsk until at least two months later, and then only through the reports of the wounded from the front. Meanwhile, back in the capital, Stalin had celebrated the anniversary of the October Revolution in full public view, and presided over a military parade from Lenin's mausoleum on 7 November. (We now know that the troops left Red Square for the front, a few kilometres away, directly afterwards.) Our army finally went on the counter-offensive on 6 December, inflicting on the Germans their first great defeat of the Second World War.

News of this victory spread rapidly and again reinforced my tendency to optimism. All things considered I had had a lucky break in being sent to the 'pearl of the northern Caucasus', the sunniest spa-town of the region, which never suffered even the least aerial alert. Kislovodsk enjoyed other advantages too: it was given priority in food supplies as well as in entertainment, for its sanatoria and hotels had been converted into hospitals where friendly and charming nurses tended the wounded. The great tragedy of the autumn unfolded far away from us; we certainly perceived the echoes of it but we didn't live it in the first person. For 11 months we were sheltered, and it was a piece of good fortune that we were able to appreciate properly only after it had run out.

Among the changes wrought by the war, a celebrated title, born with the Revolution and the Red Army, is going to undergo a difficult metamorphosis: the political commissar will henceforward merely be a *zampolit*, an abbreviation of the Russian expression meaning 'substitute for political affairs'. The well known commissars' deputies, the *politrouks*, will be even less well favoured: they are to be designated by the ridiculous and very unmartial *pompolit*, 'political assistants'. You have only to pronounce the word to savour its soft, culinary resonance.

The great reorganization takes place in October 1942, during the critical phase of the Battle of Stalingrad. A decree proclaims that the political consciousness of commanders has reached a level such that they no longer need commissars to give them lessons in politics. The latter survive only with the title of *zampolits*, and only 'where they might be needed' (a use can always be found for advisors). By a reverse process the Red Army 'commanders' are to become 'officers' once more, a style of rank banished after the Revolution, and in doing so are going to don magnificent uniforms gleaming with epaulettes, closely resembling those of the Imperial Czarist Army. Let us note, in fairness, that the politicos, the *zampolits* and the *pompolits*, still enjoy the same sartorial privileges, thus enabling us to admire in certain photographs today the martial bearing of Nikita Krushchev or Leonid Brezhnev.

This decree of October 1942 (which in the West hasn't received the attention it deserves) offers, however, somewhat perfidious explanations for these reversals of 'protocol' in the Red Army, for this absolute priority accorded officers.

This revolution – or counter-revolution if you prefer – was allegedly necessary to 'reinforce discipline', and to strengthen the patriotic motivation of the combat troops. One could suppose that the commissars had, until then, sapped discipline and put a brake on the ardour of the troops.

Of course the decree does not formulate conclusions in this way; but a good advocate, before an impartial tribunal, would have had no difficulty in demonstrating its defamatory character. My share of the damages thus awarded the political services of the Red Army would doubtless have been a meagre sum, consistent with my minor importance, or even the slight ambiguity of my role in Kislovodsk. What in fact is the situation in 'training school No. 11', the 'eleventh' of the Armed Air Forces, at the end of 1941?

The 'eleventh' is composed of three squadrons, each divided into five *zveno* (chains) of 30 men; it is provided with one commissar assisted by three *pompolits*, all of them seasoned members of the CPSU, and lecturers in Marxism–Leninism and other serious matters. At the base, however, there are in each squadron simple 'political workers' such as myself, sent by the Komsomol to take charge of subordinate, routine daily tasks. Without wishing to prejudice the reputation of the *politrouks-pompolits*, I think it can safely be said that they serve no practical function, whereas the ungraded ones like myself are very useful; even when, as in my case, they don't contribute to reinforcing discipline.

The *politrouks* tirelessly give the courses based on the *History of the CPSU (Bolsheviks)*, which all of the trainee pilots have already learned at school. What's more, since the beginning of the war this line no longer corresponds to the actual doctrine of the country, which puts the struggle of the Slavs to the forefront – with Russians at their head – and relegates that of the proletarians to the shadows. In the USSR, today still, the ritual counts even more than the content. When something is inscribed in the programme it isn't changed; that would be wholly incongruous. The ritual lessons in Marxism–Leninism are very popular in Kislovodsk anyway; they allow the trainees to rest and to doze in the heat, no exam is planned, and it is clearly more sensible to rest comfortably in the shade than to trail along in the mud or dust under the orders of a sergeant-major with sadistic tendencies.

My work, in contrast, doesn't deal with indoctrination (to employ the expression so dear to Westerners). I have to take part with everyone else in military training not directly connected with training in aviation – there is far too much of it for my taste – and busy myself with the cultural life of my companions. I put on film shows for them at least once a week, arranging for the films to come from Stavropol, the nearest large city. I also obtain reading matter for them on request, by searching through the town library, and convene meetings of Komsomols (*zveno* by *zveno*, in little groups) in order to read *Pravda* with them or the daily paper from Stavropol. To be honest, my recreational programme meets with only limited success: most of the members of the first squadron organize their own favourite sport – chasing after nurses. These future pilots illustrate right down to the finest detail Moussia's description of the behaviour of Russian males as 'frantic skirt-chasers'. As for the nurses, they appear to behave just as Moussia herself did, in the days before she had learned to keep her distance. However, this sport can only develop thanks to other politico-cultural activities; it is rarely the practice in the army to leave you with the pastime of your choice. In our case, after dinner – served early in the evening between five-thirty and seven o'clock – we all have to return quickly to our depot dormitories at the other end of the town, in order to think about aviation or service our firearms. Only those who take part in my properly scheduled meetings are allowed to stay behind in the large, centrally situated building which houses the school. Now the duration of these meetings is unspecified and so, unless a *politrouk* announces that he is going to come along, which is extremely rare, we can cut short our reading of *Pravda*. In this way we gain the time to make a detour, returning to barracks via the Piatatchok, where, despite the darkness, nurses are strolling outside.

Personally, I am a mediocre predator (no doubt I lack conviction and self-confidence), but I don't wish to hinder the success of more gifted friends who find prey on each occasion, and afterwards recount exploits that are stupefying, given the shortness of the time and the precariousness of the places available. We came to the following arrangement: the trainees to whom I am attached turn out in large numbers to my recreational evenings, thus convincing the commanders of their deep interest in everything that I organize. Other meetings, on the other hand, last for only a minimum length of time – as long as it takes the last NCO to clear off. This clearly makes me an accomplice to a violation of the regulations, but who could condemn me for it? As Moussia would argue, sex is good for the morale of the troops, and strong morale is all the more important for us to keep defeatism at bay during the autumn of retreats and the difficult winter of 1941.

None of this interests Commissar Bielokonienko or his *politrouks*. The surveillance of comings and goings at barracks is the exclusive responsibility of (usually stupid and spiteful) career NCOs. Their chief, in the first squadron, Sergeant-major Orlov, understands nothing about the manoeuvre which allows us in turn to frequent the Piatatchok; he is convinced that we climb over the wall of the barracks. So he reinforces the guard and organizes patrols in the surrounding area. Sometimes he goes as far as sacrificing his sleep in order slyly to await the return of latecomers, whereupon he immediately inflicts punishment duties on them. And fatigues here are not merely minor duties around barracks: we are sent in groups as far as Min. Vody, the railway centre on the Moscow–Yerevan Transcaucasian line, to dig anti-tank trenches, or standing in for mobilized workers, we load and unload trains.

Orlov can only let off steam with me during exercises, and he doesn't spare himself. All my efforts to flatter him, to persuade him to stop considering me as his biggest enemy, fail completely. I am fascinated by his resemblance to Sergeant-major Bartczak of the Polish Army, particularly in their use of language. Like him, he screams automatically at the sight of an unbuttoned collar: 'What sort of farce is this?' Now, in Polish, as in Russian there are at least 10 more accurate expressions to signify 'untidy'. Overall, however, the similarity of their vocabulary seems to me to be explained by a linguistic phenomenon, whose existence I would never have suspected. In these two languages that have become as different from each other as French from Spanish, the words designating the sexual organs have remained the same. Now it goes without saying that Orlov's expressions, like those of Bartczak, are heavily garnished with these; and I often have the impression of finding myself two years back in time, in front of a Polish sergeant-major who has just changed his accent a little.

At Kislovodsk however, I belong to the separate political hierarchy, and the scurvy Orlov is powerless to impose fatigues on me. Because he has no control over my timetable he is forced, in order to punish me, to go through Bielokonienko, the sole figure next to God with authority over his service. So Orlov takes me along to the commissar's office, stiffens in the *smirno* position (attention), clicks the heels of his boots and, to underline the gravity of his indictment, delivers it in such clipped tones that it is difficult to follow him. Bielokonienko, though, feigns to have understood everything. He knits his eyebrows in a frown as if he were really outraged and ready to have me shot, then pronounces a single word: '*besobrazie*', which, in the language then current, expresses the strongest indignation. It is '*besobrazie*', all right, but that's all. Orlov, for his part, daren't say: 'It is not enough to say "*besobrazie*", he ought to be put on fatigue.' A sergeant-major, fanatically respectful of the hierarchy, cannot permit himself to suggest anything whatever to someone who wears the insignia of a colonel, even if it is primarily a political title. After three or four fruitless attempts, my persecutor gives up on his sinister plot to have me dig anti-tank trenches at Min. Vody. And I no longer risk very much by going for a walk along the Piatatchok, or even, later, when the *sanitarka* Nievka has arrived in Kislovodsk, by actually sleeping away from my depot barracks.

I still haven't explained what the Piatatchok is exactly, and the problem that the name presents from the socialist internationalist point of view. In Rostov, as I have already said, the main avenue, straight as a die, bore the name of Frederick Engels; but for the population and even for we Komsomols, it was the Sadovaia, from the word '*sad*', meaning garden. In Kislovodsk, the avenue that descends abruptly from the station and then traces a semi-circle before dividing up into several boulevards, bears the name Karl Marx. The slightly unusual shape of this avenue resembles the figure 5, which is '*piat*' in Russian, whence the general tendency to refer to the '*Piatatchok*', the little five, and for the prestigious name Karl Marx to vanish altogether. The centrally-located building which houses the 'eleventh school' of the airforce is close by, situated in a street giving on to Lenin Boulevard which itself opens onto the Piatatchok. Certainly this admirably placed street must bear a famous name, probably linked to the workers' movement. I shall always remain ignorant of it though for want of having paid due attention, and because we called it 'Green Alley', in honour of its trees.

Today I am struck by this curious coincidence: in the two towns where I lived, Rostov and Kislovodsk, the most popular places were dedicated to Marx and Engels, but in practice they were referred to by quite different names, because the Russians have always preferred the visual – trees, shapes or colours – to the abstraction of great names.

One day the commissar orders me to keep an eye on Kola P. Why him? What has he done? 'Nothing. Don't ask stupid questions. I am not asking you to set a trap for him, nor to put him away. We are not the military police,' this *tchoudak* (bizarre man) Bielokonienko replies. Much later Kola will attach a special importance to these remarks in order to fashion his hypothesis on the benevolent role played by the commissar in my mysterious misadventure. What is certain is that, thanks to this order to keep an eye on him, Kola P. is going to become my best friend for the rest of my stay in the USSR.

He is called the 'Herring'. This nickname has nothing prestigious about it and, in Russian, it is even a bit ungracious. Kola is admittedly very thin and of a very ordinary appearance. He doesn't distinguish himself in any way from the average trainee-pilot, and hasn't any great ambition. He is neither very agile during exercises nor very gifted in theoretical matters. Yet this 'Herring', inexplicably, is a remarkable leader of men. He has established himself as leader in the first squadron, and that is what worries Andrei Tarassovitch Bielokonienko.

In fact, in my view, these two men would have got on very well together in other circumstances. My commissar is one of the rare Soviet citizens to remind me of the communists or left-wing socialists in Poland. Neither the dogmas of the *History of the CPSU (Bolsheviks)* nor the vicissitudes of life have crushed in him the need to think about the future society, real communism (or the great utopia as they call it today in the West). These things interest Kola too, in spite of his disabused airs and his overall tendency to concentrate on day-to-day survival. Both of them in addition share an aversion to the nationalist prejudices which play havoc in the 'eleventh school' of the airforce.

Kola's merits in this domain are far superior to those of the commissar. He is a Cossack in fact, like the great majority of the first squadron; he even descends, it appears, from an illustrious family of the former 'special region of the army of the Don'. Bielokonienko comes from the Ukraine. Now the Ukrainians are held in open contempt by the Cossacks who describe them as *khokols* – a specific and untranslatable term – at the best of times, and as *gady*, or serpents. In declaring that these prejudices don't mean anything to him Kola deliberately goes against the herd and, incidentally, lends a hand to the commissar, who, as things stand, is rather poorly equipped to fight on this terrain.

It has to be said too that since 22 June 1941 the Cossacks have once again found a place of honour in the USSR. As soon as war broke out giant posters were put up in Rostov showing these fierce cavalrymen in their uniform of yesteryear, sabres held high, galloping to the front under the slogan: 'Cossacks of the peaceful Don, crush the German invaders as your ancestors crushed Napoleon!' These posters at first sent shivers down my spine: in the Polish films I saw as a child it was this cavalry in these same uniforms who hunted our compatriots and smashed strikes. For me they were savages, the czarist praetorian guard. A Soviet communist could also feel the same alarm by recalling that the Cossacks' brave ancestors had not only crushed Napoleon but had also come close to inflicting the same fate on Lenin and the Bolsheviks. Hadn't their leader, Krasnov, struck at the gates of Leningrad with the declared intention of hanging all the Reds?

In the 'eleventh school' of the airforce, the Cossacks, to be truthful, ask only to have their national identity recognized; they simply want to be considered differently from the Russians – as I have already been able to see for myself at the peaceful school No. 44 in Rostov. They don't seem to know how to assert their identity except by showing their contempt for others (in our own day there are more or less similar cases among the minorities of countries which are more developed than was the USSR at that time, which render the phenomenon, and also the limits of nationalism in general, more easily comprehensible). In our military college, nobody dreams of ruffling the pride of the Cossacks, given the general political line, but they cannot be given commanders drawn from Cossack personnel. It is impossible for the simple reason that there aren't any: until the 1936 Constitution, the Cossacks were '*lichentsy*', citizens shorn of certain rights, particularly the right to make a career in the army. Nothing can be done therefore; the commander of the 'eleventh' is a Russian, terribly Russian in fact. He is Colonel Leonid Vassilievitch Ganachek, commonly called Lionka Swiste, 'little whistling Leonid,' because of the pitch of his voice. The chief instructor, Colonel Gerch Yakovlevitch Zlotnikov, is Jewish, and it will readily be guessed that he is generally referred to as a 'dirty Yid'. As for the commissar, I have already said that he comes from Zaporojié; he is therefore a *gad*, a serpent, like all Ukrainians.

It is in this context that Kola's originality must be appreciated. He declares against allcomers that he cares as much about being Cossack as he does about his first pair of trousers, that all things considered he would prefer to be Polish or Jewish – and why not? These people, in his view, travel more, have broader horizons. And when Kola says something, 'herring' or no, it counts. It counts first of all for his three loyal clan followers from Mietchotka, a Cossack *stanitsa*, where they were born and spent a harsh childhood together. Now these three are endowed with nicknames which leave no doubt as to each one's importance. Vassia S. is *Slon* or 'Elephant', and in the squadron there is neither a 'lion' nor 'tiger' to contest his prowess. Next comes Volodia, the 'Singer', and when one becomes aware of the privileged place the song occupies in the real or supposed identity of the Cossacks, all further commentary becomes superfluous. Lastly, Kostia, the closest to Kola, is a solid cheerful type, but shrewd as a monkey. Because of his slightly projecting cheekbones he is called the 'Khan'; an Asiatic certainly, one of those who for centuries have dominated the whole of Russia. Certainly the Mietchotka clan has neither the pretension nor the power to put an end to the Cossacks' anti-semitism and anti-Ukrainianism; but Kola and his friends succeed in moderating their effects, and this simplifies the lives of the non-Cossack trainee pilots, not to mention that of the commanding personnel, the commissar included.

It isn't easy for me to speak about this to Bielokonienko. The barrier of hierarchy separates us, despite the understanding that he seems to show towards me. He is also of another generation, if I am to judge of it by his tired blue eyes, that of a man who has lived through much and who fears that everything he has built might collapse with the war. In the nationalistic gossip of the barracks, he sees merely the survival of the old world, which was supposed gradually to disappear with the progress of industrialization, after the completion of three or four five-year plans. Now it is as if this scheme is suspended for some time at least; instead of the work of construction, everything in the Ukraine, in Russia, is being destroyed; and when the Germans haven't done it, we have had to do it ourselves, in the name of the 'scorched earth' tactic, more discreetly described as 'active, in-depth defence'. My commissar has plenty to worry about therefore and these Cossack legends are merely an extra nuisance for him. In contrast to the *politrouks* who deliver their lessons without any qualms of conscience, he worries about his. He was more at ease when the driving force of history was the class struggle, rather than this 'great, patriotic Russian people'. After all he has been a worker himself and isn't even a Russian anyway but a Ukrainian.

He would prefer me to be a Russian, however, and even decrees that 'culturally and consciously', I am one. The intrigue at the origin of my 'mysterious misadventure', in Kola's version of events, starts with this fortuitous discovery of Bielokonienko's, and on this point at least it is not merely an hypothesis. Overall, however, Kola does not reproach this *tchoudak* Ukrainian, who persists in designating him as the 'mischievous spirit' of the first squadron; he is actually rather fond of him. In his eyes, our commissar possesses, among his innumerable eccentricities, a quality that redeems all of them: he is not in the least bit repressive. And, Kola adds, it is not from either weakness or stupidity; on the contrary, it is the attribute of an intelligence which has never let itself be drowned in vodka. In fact Bielokonienko drinks a lot and so too does Kola; it is another point they have in common. At the time, for that matter, I manage to keep up with them without too much difficulty.

In the month of December, at the time of the Soviet victory at Moscow, Nievka arrives in Kislovodsk. Her real name is Natalia, for in Russia girls do not take their forenames from the names of rivers. Natalia, however, who was born 23 years earlier in the quasi-Venetian part of Leningrad, had pronounced the word 'Nievka' even before 'Mama' or 'Papa'. To her parents therefore Natalia became Nievka, and she grew into the habit of introducing herself thus – even though her real forename is very nice in my view, and pleases me enormously.

According to those who are familiar with Leningrad, all of this implies a certain snobbery. In practice only the families of important communists live in her area of the city, heirs in this respect of the former aristocracy. Natalia Trofimovna, what's more, makes no secret of it. She makes no attempt to conceal the fact that her father is a man of consequence: he is sufficiently friendly with Andrei Zhdanov for the latter to have approved personally, it seems, of her nickname Nievka, and for Zhdanov to have taken her on his knee more than once when she was a child. It was thanks to him – or so it seems – that she was one of the very few to be evacuated from an encircled Leningrad. She is not proud of this fact, and she enlisted in the army as a simple *sanitarka* (nurse) whereas she could have, as a third year medical student, taken quiet refuge in a good faculty to take her diplomas in peace.

Nievka's evacuation from Leningrad seems to have been something of a miracle. At the time, she explains, the last access to the town was across Lake Ladoga, but the flotilla of ferry boats which usually served the lake was practically out of action and the lake was swept by German artillery fire. As soon as it froze up, however – and the winter of 1941 was both premature and severely cold – Andrei Zhdanov had a 'lifeline' cut across it. Lorries carrying vital supplies began to arrive at night; on their return trips they evacuated mainly children and the sick. In the lorry that escorted Nievka, children were packed tightly together under a tarpaulin to try and keep them warm. During the night Nievka and another student, Rosa, clung to each other in the cabin, frozen by the cold wind that blew at 30 degrees below zero. To avoid artillery fire the convoy had had to leave the track and make an interminable detour before ending up at a military post where, of course, there was no one waiting for them. It must have been an awful journey.

I didn't meet Nievka on the Piatatchok but at the hospital where she was working, in the former 'fortress' sanatorium. The latter is situated in the upper quarters of the town, near the ruins of the fortress built by the Russians to combat the Ciscaucasians (or by the latter to fight the Russians, I am no longer very sure). When I go along there it is on an errand for Bielokonienko who uses me as his Man Friday – it is the general lot of the youngest in the service – now secretary, now message boy. He needs some information concerning a wounded man who comes from Zaporojié. Nievka knows nothing about him; she has just arrived. She asks a junior nurse to go off and find out what she can, and in the meantime asks me about Kislovodosk and about my handsome uniform; she didn't know that there were airmen here. Then, by a second miracle, this stylish classy young woman, having still not located the dossier I need, offers to bring it to me in town the next day. It is only a business rendezvous but it is a rendezvous all the same. We arrange to meet near the columns of the main entrance to the park in the early afternoon. At that time of day there is almost no one there.

The next day Nievka arrives for our meeting with an almost

military punctuality, attractively wrapped in an infantry commander's cape. She also wears a discreet military cap – but in fur, finely matching her short black hair – and a pair of boots of supple leather. On my side I have mobilized all my sartorial resources; I have even put on dress boots belonging to Kostia, the 'Khan'. A business meeting doesn't perhaps require such an effort at style but, in any case, there was no longer any business matter to see to. The dossier concerning the man from Zaporojié had been sent a long time before to the hospital administration of the Caucasian military region, which is on Green Alley, 25 metres from my *tchoudak* of a commissar's office. So we go for a stroll in the park and Nievka, with a perfect naturalness, takes me by the arm. I play the role of guide, repeating word for word Bielokonienko's commentaries on the splendours of the place, and in this way we arrive at the large waterfall, a favourite spot according to my commissar, for ladies and gentlemen of good society in the previous century. The sun is setting after a clear December day and the place is bathed in a mild, romantic light fit to inspire poets and to bring young souls together. After enjoying the view in silence Nievka stiffens suddenly and, tears in her eyes, presses herself against me; but it is her Leningrad that she talks about, not the Lermontovian phantoms.

'You don't realize what is happening there. It's awful. It's worse than awful, it's a nightmare.' I wipe away her tears by covering her with timid and affectionate kisses, appropriate to this refined setting, and to an upbringing inherited from former times.

Our innocent scene is interrupted by a group of patients in pyjamas, wandering away from the hospital. They are wrapped up in blankets, which gives them the appearance of down-and-outs, and they begin to hurl vulgar taunts at us, as if the indecency were on our part and not on theirs. In Mikhail Lermontov's day I would surely have challenged them to a duel, but we leave without saying a word. We are forced sadly to admit that in 1941 the 'heroes of our time' wear pyjamas and are as indifferent to fine language as they are to courtesy. Nievka, in all innocence, invites me to have tea with her at her home. If she is not exactly privileged, she has at least been very lucky: she has been allocated a beautiful room with independent access, on the ground floor of a building surrounded by a small garden, to the south of the town, in the sunniest part. She shares it with Rosa, her companion from Leningrad. It isn't very far from the centre; nothing is very far for that matter in a town of only 50,000 inhabitants.

The room is furnished in a way both spartan and bizarre: two iron beds stand at opposite walls and between them, a large Persian carpet covers the floor. There is only one chair and a battered old armchair. We sit on the carpet. Nievka, however, keeps her distance: she is more prudent than Moussia. We then enter a stream of conversation which will flow all night; among other things there will be much talk between us of a strong and sincere love, through which we can help each other surmount the trials of war . . . a love inspired by the classics of romantic Russian literature. We shall always look back upon this night, during which we dreamt aloud, with a hint of nostalgia, as we would upon a wonderful, shared secret.

Although news circulates very slowly in Russia viewed as a whole it spreads at an astonishing speed within Kislovodsk itself. In relation to my night with Nievka it is hardly a surprise. Kola's bunk or *nary*, these planks of wood placed side by side on two tiers and covered by straw mattresses, is next to mine. He is delighted to see that I have spent the night away. The 'four musketeers' of Mietchotka have already given up the chase for more stable relationships: it was high time that I did the same. My principal enemy, Sergeant-major Orlov, has inevitably noted my absence too, because of his obsessive hobbyhorse: the ban that he places on my singing (out of pure malice and in order to humiliate me). For we play the part of the joyous morning reveille in Kislovodsk; at seven o'clock we cross the town, from the barracks to Green Alley, singing at the tops of our voices the official war song: 'Stand up, enormous country / Stand up for a fight to the death.' And each time he gives the order, 'Col-umn –

Sing!', Orlov takes two steps backwards, points a finger at me and with the other hand signals me to be silent. The regulations allow him to do this since being barred from singing doesn't interfere with the timetable of a member of the political service. The fact is that I have always sung out of tune, but I can hardly be the only one. The 450 future pilots were not recruited on the strength of their vocal performances.

Having noted my absence Orlov leads me off around midday to the commissar's office. This time, however, Bielokonienko listens to him with barely disguised impatience. There is not even so much as a '*besobrazie*' on this occasion, but merely '*ladno*' an ambiguous word which can mean either 'I shall straighten this out' or 'It's already straightened out for me.' In this case the second interpretation is the correct one: my commissar, discounting my absenteeism, asks me for suggestions for the New Year celebrations. In his view things are going well in the international arena. After Pearl Harbour the United States is determined to enter the fray, and on 1 January next under its aegis, 26 countries, including the USSR, are due to sign in Washington a declaration of total war on the Axis powers, and principally Nazi Germany. It is important therefore to celebrate the event and the New Year by organizing something better than a film show – even though, in my view, a good American film would be entirely appropriate – a concert for example, a theatrical evening, or even a dance. Obviously he reserves for himself the job of delivering a lengthy, in-depth speech for the occasion.

His friend, Captain Pietia Danilov, the *zavkhoze*, or senior figure in the quarter-master's department, and a native of Zaporojié himself, arrives in the meantime and becomes involved in discussing America, this powerful America, the famous engine manufacturer. It is a little upsetting for an Anglophile like myself, but these Russians – in fact, Ukrainians in this case – really have an extraordinary liking for the United States. They are fascinated by this country which is similar in size to their own and is not (yet) classified as imperialist because it hasn't officially any colony. Stalin, moreover, in the course of his speech on the anniversary of the

Revolution came out with this peremptory statement: 'The war of today is a war of engines, and it will be won by whoever has a crushing superiority in engines,' and this made a powerful impression on my commissar and his friend Captain Danilov. It is obvious that they associate the United States with the automobile industry. Bielokonienko, who has time to play with, goes as far as calculating on the basis of approximate statistics, the combined level of steel production of the 26 countries in the anti-Axis coalition which are to sign the declaration in Washington on New Year's Day. (Today I wonder just what Mao's reaction must have been in Yennan, on hearing of Stalin's speech on the primacy of engines; his Red Republic wasn't producing any, but he was convinced that he would succeed, thanks to the human factor, in simultaneously defeating the Japanese and the nationalist army of Chiang Kai Shek.) In Kislovodsk of course this problem doesn't even enter my head, and little do I imagine that it could have its importance in the two different interpretations of Marxism which will clash in the great schism of the 1960s. While maintaining a personal preference for Churchill, who was one of the first and most resolute of Hitler's adversaries in the West, I gladly drink a bumper measure of vodka to the health of Franklin D. Roosevelt, while paying tribute to the political perspicacity of the commissar and of Captain Danilov. The idea of a New Year's Eve party with internationalist overtones, dedicated to these 26 countries, pleases me a lot too.

More immediately however I have to confront a more private party: one organized by the Mietchotka four, who have evolved from the stage of nomadic life to the historically more advanced sedentary life. The first to give up the chase was Vassia, *Slon*; he fell for a local nurse, Raia, who has a room in a communal apartment to which she can invite as many people as she likes. Raia has a pronounced Mediterranean personality, enhanced by amazingly bright eyes. She has a cheerful disposition, enjoys singing and launches into magnificent duos with our Volodia. Later, towards the end of the war, she will claim that she had a child by Vassia, but in fact the dates makes this mathematically impossible. In Kis-

115

lovodsk, of course, we have no inkling of the future behaviour of the beautiful and hospitable Raia. She was the first to organize an evening for us, at her place, and she gave us the taste for more intimate and more domestic pleasures.

Shortly after, Kola met Maroussia, a local schoolteacher, who also has a room. Maroussia is as accomplished a hustler as is our 'Herring'. They discover together, from experience, that in Kislovodsk the men in uniform are given priority over other customers in the foodstores. Although we are lodged and fed by the airforce, extra food is very helpful for our collective dinners; so, the food-ration cards which are quite cheap on the black market – because of the risks of disappointment involved in queuing in front of the shops – acquire their full value when we use them. Thanks to our military uniform they allow us to buy at low prices most of the products needed for good Russian cuisine, and the cost of each private meal becomes extremely reasonable. Kola and Maroussia don't confine themselves simply to the role of providers however; they also see to more ethereal pleasures by reciting for us a large repertoire of poetry ranging from the classics to more recent works. They provide the backing support to Raia and Volodia whose vocal duo remains the principal attraction of our evenings.

Next, Volodia the 'Singer' links up with Tania, who has nothing of the prima donna about her. Volodia had been hoping to meet a nurse but in fact met someone much better placed: Tania works in a vodka factory. It is a wholly unexpected stroke of luck, even though the kindly Tania, because of searches at the factory exit, takes a lot of risks to earn her title of 'honorary supplier'. She too is from the town and has a two-roomed flat – her parents' flat – but only on Wednesdays, because once a week they go to Min. Vody for 24 hours. Finally Kostia, the 'Khan', began to date Vera, a fair-haired nurse from Rostov, who is very Russian-looking with her braided plaits, but she says she is half-Cossack. She lives in a dormitory and cannot contribute anything on the logistical front, and frets a little because of it, the more so because at 24 years old she is the oldest of our group. Vera compensates with her culinary skills; she makes an excellent salad with a base of marinated cabbage, and a mushroom *pirog* worthy of a de luxe restaurant. She tries to find a nurse for me – I am still the only one who is not yet 'fixed up' – but in vain; I don't suit her friends nor do they suit me.

Then comes the news that I have slept away from barracks, and I am expected to bring my 'girlfriend' to our next evening get-together. No one has any doubt as to the nature of my relationship with her; what else could we have done throughout the whole night? My 'wedding' celebration coincides with Kostia's twentieth birthday, and so the evening acquires great importance. Nievka joyfully accepts the invitation and even finds a present for Kostia, a belt which comes from Leningrad. However, I am ill at ease because of my not-so-matrimonial situation. And then I have an even vaguer presentiment.

With ten of us in Raia's room we really are a little bit crowded. The lads remain perched on the bed so as not to get in the way, while the girls, including Nievka, busy themselves with the cooking. Then the fatal moment arrives: as soon as they have sat down they all help themselves to a vodka, except Nievka, who, undaunted, fills her glass with mineral water. Consternation. What kind of provocation is this? So Leningrad is no longer in Russia? They haven't heard of vodka there? Nievka, in her lovely north-Russian accent, soft and almost singing, relates the story of her trip across Lake Ladoga and adds to it a final episode. In the military post where there had been no one waiting for them, there was nothing to help her warm up, so someone massaged her legs with some eau de cologne and made her drink the rest of the bottle. Something had twisted her insides and, ever since, the least taste of alcohol makes her sick. Silence falls, and incredulity follows. A long debate develops on the difference between eau de cologne and vodka. The nurse from the north doesn't change her mind; she merely smiles and informs us that she never prevents others from drinking, especially not on a birthday. Honestly. Thanks all the same.

The party mood is shattered. Relations between those who drink mineral water and vodka enthusiasts have always called to mind the class struggle. Amiable arrangements do not serve any great purpose: you can't get quietly pissed under the allegedly indulgent gaze of the abstemious. To save what I take to be our common honour, I try to drink for the two of us, until Nievka pulls me forcefully by the arm and orders me to take her home immediately. Once we are out in the street she lectures me as though I were personally responsible for the generalized consumption of the 'prokliataia vodka' (damnable vodka) in her country. Back at her place, however, she allows me to stretch out on the Persian carpet, makes some tea and, good nurse that she is, calmly explains to me that vodka is no good for 'people like us'. This plural reassures me as to the state of our relations. I remain more reserved as to the possibility of the 'eleventh school' of the airforce giving the stuff up.

With the Mietchotka clan things have taken a more serious turn for the worse: these fine connoisseurs of women didn't appreciate my Nievka because she has small breasts. To them she was 'flat-chested', didn't drink, and put on airs. Vassia's line was: 'What do you hold in your hand when you're screwing?' Kola himself said sulkily: 'Frankly, you can do better.'

No way. I chose Nievka and left Kola's clan. We redivided possessions that we had shared and cut in half several towels whose ownership was in doubt. Everything was over between us. Two days later I took Nievka to the theatre to see La Dame aux Camélias, with permission from the commissar to get back late. Nievka, who knew nothing about my row with the clan, perhaps noticed my distress. When we got back she no longer kept her distance from me on the Persian carpet. It is possible that the play by Alexander Dumas fils had something to do with this: in it, love is rather less spiritual than it is in romantic Russian literature.

'There will be nothing for the New Year. A short assembly, a speech and then everyone will go back to barracks, in good order and without exception.' Bielokonienko raises himself from the table to announce this to me in the manner of a judge delivering a verdict.

And all this simply because of some *galouchki*, those little balls of flour which float in our soup. The evening before, a few trainees had the bright idea of using them as projectiles to bombard some NCOs for the hell of it. For the commissar it is going too far. And yet it was hardly worth getting upset about: the NCOs had had their revenge by sending a large squad of those responsible, including Vassia, to dig anti-tank trenches, and it was only a bit of flour after all. No one died from it. But the commissar wants to set an example: in his eyes we are a lost cause, irresponsible wasters, not the stout soldiers the country needs. He is going to make sure that we smarten ourselves up properly, all of us 'without exception'. We are in the armed forces, not in a brothel; we are to concern ourselves with aeroplanes, not with girls. His allusions appear to me to be more and more personal. Heavens! Had the Mietchotka gang denounced me to the commissar after our falling-out? Through hatred of Nievka? I feel myself grow pale to the point that I am nervous of implicating myself in the *galouchki* caper. The idea that Kola and his friends might have betrayed me is a terrible blow. What an informer-riddled country! I think to myself, without listening any further to the commissar. Since it is so I must run off with Nievka. Isn't that how they behave in all the best literature?

Bielokonienko, however, is a kind of Russian version of the drunken millionaire in Charlie Chaplin's *City Lights*. In his case it isn't vodka which changes his mood, but other factors. In my opinion he is reproaching himself with being too familiar, too tolerant towards us, and in order to re-establish his authority he utters terrible threats that he regrets almost as soon as they are made. The threats fade by the next day; Kola is innocent, flight useless, and for the New Year celebrations the commissar orders me to find a good performing artist at the town theatre to recite for us the highly acclaimed poem of the year, 'Kirov with us', by Nikolai Tikhonov, who, like Nievka, is from Leningrad.

Now, however, I have to spend the afternoon with the commissar. He has to dictate to me the speech that he is going to deliver in front of the full assembly. Its theme is: 'What are the qualities needed to become a good long-range fighter pilot?' He dictates while walking to and fro, either because it helps him think or because he likes to guide himself by the reactions of his auditor. Some say – maliciously – that as he has so many confidential reports to write to the political leadership of the airforce he uses me as secretary for other matters in order to give his hand a rest. All that I can say on the subject is that he claims that whereas my writing is very legible, he can't even read his own.

With gusto, he starts off with the specific character of Soviet man, who is animated by a great communist ideal and is conscious of the historical importance of his struggle. A digression on Pietchorine, Mikhail Lermontov's unfortunate hero who lacked any ideal, will help in elucidating the difference. Then he introduces long-range aircraft, recalling that a bomber is often obliged to fly alone, without a fighter escort to accompany it all the way. A solitary crew, in particular, wouldn't get very far, nor know how to carry out its tasks without a good communist consciousness. At this point he leans towards me, tears off the page from beneath my pen without saying a word and throws it into the wastepaper basket. Terrible. Rest.

The second version begins with a eulogy to peace. Yes indeed, we are at war but only because we have been forced into it. But our planes fly in order to guarantee *vietchnyi mir*, eternal peace, for which all the progressive elements of humanity have been striving for so long. We are the builders of a fraternal society; our five-year plans are the proof of it. Here we pause again. This sheet suffers the same fate as the one before.

A new opening is declaimed this time with a certain weariness, and gives the impression that the effort is wasted. He tries to keep himself to the mundane: fatherland, honour, victory, we Slavs, the dawn of history. In short, the *Pravda* staple. It comes so easily that I have to slow myself down: if my writing is so legible it is because I know what is going to be said. His inspiration dries up. Two more sheets are crumpled and thrust into the bin. With his nose to the wall he meditates silently. (I have a pile of other things to do myself. I am not going to stay here for hours contemplating his mute back.)

Finally he turns round and, returning to his armchair, he sees hanging above his desk the portrait of Stalin with his handsome moustache. A vague smile lights up my commissar's face: by heaven, why didn't I think of it sooner? That's the answer and it's staring me in the face. Stalin is the surest value, on this point there is no risk of being mistaken. It is in his august person that the old doctrine based on the *History of the CPSU (Bolsheviks)* and the new one based on the Slavic nations, most readily meet. The commissar sits down and starts to dictate: now there is no need to pace up and down. He is carried away. His sentences connect up like an ode to our supreme chief, our guide in all domains, our flag, our, our . . . Four sheets later he concludes: 'To be a good long-range pilot you must love Stalin ardently!' (That's it, then, I am going to be able to leave and perhaps call at Nievka's on my way to the theatre.) No; a new idea! With a grave face he has me reread the last sentence: 'To be a good long-range pilot, you must love Stalin ardently.' 'Add,' he orders, 'that you must love aviation ardently also.' (Of course, that goes without saying. Is that all?) 'No. Strike out *ardently* after aviation, and leave it simply that you must love it.' He then goes over it all again, smiles his thanks at me, and as I am on my way to the door, adds: 'On 1 January you are authorized to slip away after the assembly; go and join your nurse, but do it discreetly, without drawing attention to yourself.'

A real Charlie Chaplin character this Bielokonienko. Does he also know who my nurse is? And if so, from whom? I am terribly suspicious; this separation from my friends from Mietchotka never ceases to bother me.

'Tell me some *dietskie skazki* (fairytales).'

'Oh Nievka, we are too old for that and besides I don't even remember any now.'

'Search your memory and you will surely find at least one Polish fairytale.'

I found more than one, but for this I had to go to the Karl Marx Library of Kislovodsk, where Grimm, Andersen and Afanassiev replaced my studious reading of Korneitchouk and Ehrenbourg, to the great amazement of the librarians. Then I dazzle Nievka with my fairytales, pretending that they are coming back to me spontaneously. If she suspects the deceit she doesn't show it, maybe so as not to break the spell. At difficult times escapist fiction is as necessary for adults as for children. I shall discover the truth of this less than one year later, when Grimm, Andersen and Afanassiev, along with Alexander Dumas *père* will allow me to establish a *modus vivendi* (it was either that or *ars moriendi*) in Yerevan prison.

Why though had Nievka, who was so proud in her uniform, so much need of fairytales? To see her, tall and thin, with her determined step and satisfied smile you would think she was the most stable of people, always clear about what she wants. I sense that she is fragile, however, and unable to explain it to myself, I decide that she is too much of a 'Mama's girl', never having had the experience of living alone. I am convinced that adulthood begins with separation from the family, and Nievka, who has only just gone through the experience, is two years behind me in this. On the other hand, she is very much the 'liberated woman', very sure of her right to an emotional life of her choice. Unlike me she doesn't care in the least about what wagging tongues might have to say about us. If her superiors dared to pass comment to her she had resolved simply to tear out their eyes. Immediately after the night we went to see *La Dame aux Camélias*, she succeeded in obtaining a double bed and a second armchair. She went about the business of refurnishing the room quite openly, as if the better to inform the whole building, which was occupied by party functionaries, of the real reasons for my visits. The sexual mores not only of Nievka and Olga but also of the girlfriends of Kola's gang, are living proof, in my view, of the enduring effects of the ideas on free love preached by Alexandra Kollontai after the Revolution, and proof too of the resistance to the wave of puritanism encouraged by Stalin. In these years, Soviet women are in advance of their sisters in the West who are still imprisoned in bourgeois family morality and the religious concept of sin. Even my own sister Alicja, although an atheist, had decided to remain a virgin until she was married.

Emancipated, materially independent, often highly cultivated – as is the case with Nievka – Soviet women are still haunted by the fear of being without a man, as if they felt the irresistible need of a masculine arm in order to feel stronger, or to realize their potential. I cannot say if this is a matter of Russian tradition or whether it is a consequence of the separation of the sexes owing to the war, but I am struck by the unaffected way in which Nievka often says to me: 'You're the man. It is for you to take the decisions.' Similarly she finds it normal to take responsibility for all the domestic chores and to get up at dawn to make tea for me, so that I arrive at seven o'clock exactly at the parade where Orlov is going to order me not to sing.

My schedule depends on the imponderables of cheating and, over and above the leave to which I am entitled once a week, my time spent with Nievka is stolen from the 'eleventh school' of the VVS, and is therefore difficult to plan in advance, but she always waits at home for me and goes out as little as possible during her time off, in order to be at home if I turn up. Her devotion delights me but it also puzzles me because in American films the roles are reversed, especially during the honeymoon period, and it is for the man to woo the woman by showering her with jewels and other presents.

Except when I drink too much, Nievka says openly she 'doesn't want to lose me', as if she believes she couldn't find another man, which is clearly absurd. Her mother teaches German literature at the Lifli, one of the best institutes of philosophy, literature and history in the USSR, and thanks to her, Nievka knows by heart a good part of the work of Heinrich Heine. Her father was himself a history teacher before becoming a party functionary, so that her culture by far exceeds mine and that of my friends. She prefers though to underplay it and sometimes she spends hours writing down verses from memory in order for me to shine among my friends on reciting them. 'Here, this one will certainly delight them,' she says, and hands me the transcript of a poem in which Heine dreams of being the Lord God only to conclude: 'If I were God I would go to the Devil.' On the other hand, she doesn't talk very much about her feelings, thinking that we have already said enough on this subject to each other and that, of itself, the fact that we are lovers proves our love. I would like, however, to talk of love and to pursue to infinity the stream of tender words that began on the Persian carpet.

What surprises me most is Nievka's behaviour in the intimacy of our time together. She is terribly shy and asks me not to look at her while she undresses, as if she were ashamed of her body. Once we are in bed, I see her naked in any case, and she has a splendid body, a soft skin, very soft, softer than the silk of all the dresses of Alexander Blok's *Nieznakomka*. In my view, Nievka ought to be filled with pride by it. Only later shall I discover clues to her reticence in this respect. Nievka has a holy terror of becoming pregnant, although abortion is freely available in the USSR. In fact I have the impression that this anxiety undermines her sensuality and obliges her to control her desires to the point of blunting them. She makes love only during her 'safe' days, the safest being those during her period, with the result that I begin to entertain completely false ideas about the sexual behaviour of women. Nievka's ideal – though she obviously doesn't admit it in so many words – is to wrap herself around me under the sheets, and talk passionately, softly, about the distress of her native Leningrad, about literature, listening next to some fairytales for consolation, and then going to sleep, without running any of the risks of carnal love. In a few words rather than many, Nievka loves me after her fashion – 'I have only you in this world,' she often says – but I don't 'hold her by the senses', as Vassia claims to do with his very sensual Raia.

I have no regrets: I am happy as a king with Nievka and I think of no one else from morning to night, during military exercises or while carrying out my politico-cultural tasks. When, therefore, my commissar hints about the forthcoming formation of a Polish army in the USSR – following the Stalin–Sikorski agreement in December 1941 – I am seized with panic and declare to him: 'I am staying in the Red Army.' Pleased as punch, he concludes from this: '*ty nach*' ('you are one of us') and he congratulates me on my irremediably Russian 'consciousness and culture'.

In fact my 'consciousness and culture' have nothing to do with it. I am simply crazy about this woman from Leningrad who speaks with such a bewitching Russian accent, makes almost horizontal plaits with her short hair before going to sleep, and stares at me with her astonished, big green eyes when I tell her fairytales. Trying to explain this, however, to altogether more vigilant investigators than Commissar Bielokonienko , at the time of my 'affair' in Yerevan, will feel like a gamble.

I made up with Kola and Kostia first of all, with Vassia and Volodia soon after. It is just as well for I need Kola's help to fight against the campaign of denigration directed at me in the first squadron, on the theme: 'A Polish *pan*, a king into the bargain, found for his *karoleva* (queen) a mute, flatchested duchess from Leningrad.' Nievka is called a mute because when she is accosted in the street she refuses to answer or even to utter a word. In our detractors' little songs there are other couplets of such vulgarity that, even 40 years later, they are not fit to be written down.

The folklore with which I am landed is not in the best of taste, but it doesn't bother me too much. I am called '*polski pan*', even though I have explained a thousand times that in Poland, anybody is a *pan*, that it doesn't constitute a title, but a term equivalent to 'Mr' or 'Monsieur'. My colleagues in the 'eleventh' of the VVS don't want to believe me. They are victims of a stupid propaganda campaign against the '*panska Polcha*' (the Poland of the *pans*) which has persuaded them that in Poland it is only the rich and the oppressors who are called *pan*. They persist in singing an anti-Polish refrain behind my back: '*Perepil vseh polskii pan, v bardakié on jest ulan*' ('the Polish *pan* has drunk more than everyone else, he plays the hussar in the whorehouse'). Now this is not without a certain humour, for in order to outdrink these inveterate Russian drinkers you really would have to start early in the morning, and if someone

125

could open a bordello in the USSR they would become rich overnight, because these Russian males think of nothing else. I keep cool, even when they toss at me: '*Pan, gliadi v oba*' ('look with your two eyes'), a subtle allusion to the fact that I am blind in one eye. On the other hand I find I can't swallow this couplet on the king and his mute, flatchested queen; it sends me foolishly into a rage. And Kola is probably the only one who, thanks to his authority, is able to ensure that the first squadron stops singing it.

We talk about it one evening as we are returning to barracks after a meeting. Nievka is at the hospital and Maroussia is at her school. Suddenly, in the darkness, a shadow cries out: '*Stoi*', 'halt'. There is no mistaking it: it is clearly a military voice. A silly reflex, born from habit, sends us running off at full speed. The shadow gives chase and, good runners though we are, manages to catch up. We stop. After all, for once we are not in breach of the regulations! We turn around. Oh, no! Facing us is Colonel Gerch Yakovlevitch Zlotnikov, chief instructor and pilot emeritus, the commander most feared for his intransigence and severity. Our explanations are in vain, as is a discreet allusion to my membership of the political vertical: 'Hardest fatigue for both of you,' he says. 'I shall arrange it with the commissar personally.'

The very next day Kola and I set out for Min. Vody, to dig anti-tank trenches. It is an unending building site on a snow-covered plain where mainly women, muffled from head to foot, are assigned to work. The supervisor who stamps our papers and gives us our picks is also a woman, used to 'welcoming' offenders from the 'eleventh' of the VVS. She tells us straight off that we are going to have to 'shift our arses' and warns us against 'acting the lads'. We pick away conscientiously at the frozen earth, chiefly to warm ourselves up. January 1942 will remain in the Russian folk memory for its record cold temperatures. Kola is so incensed by the injustice of which we are victims that he pours forth an endless litany on the vile, irredeemable stupidity of the Russians. 'And for starters, what use can these idiotic trenches serve?' he asks, observing with good sense that the Germans hadn't come to the USSR to practise mountain climbing in the Caucasus mountains or to plant the swastika at the summit of the Elbrus. If they were to get as far as here it would signify that the war was lost and that the trenches had been dug in the wrong place. He is terribly persuasive, the 'Herring'; and I think that he is 100 per cent right. This mini-Maginot line makes no sense. They are constructing it only in order to torment us and these unfortunate women. Events are going to prove us partly wrong: the Germans will occupy all of this region some months later. But our derisory trenches will not slow down in the slightest their advance towards the great chain of the Caucasus, so we were right to grumble.

In the last *electritchka* – a self-powered carriage on a narrow gauge track – which brings us back to Kislovodsk after this harsh day out, we are in the mood for confidences. Kola begins with some general considerations on the aptitude of the Russians and Cossacks for suffering and for imposing suffering. 'What were my parents' first words to me? Guess if you can.' Without waiting for a reply he answers: 'Suffer, Cossack, and you will become ataman. Today though, ataman no longer means anything. And in the past, how many of these lousy atamans were there anyway? – hardly one per generation. But those who suffered were numbered in their thousands. They all suffered, my father, my grandfather, our *stanitsa* and the others. A great competition in suffering, there you have the historic contribution of the Cossacks. Let them piss off without me from now on for I have done my share of suffering. More than once my feet have been swollen with hunger and I haven't become ataman. And so much the better. On this side the chapter is closed.' He looks at me as if to check whether he can start on a second, more delicate chapter. I am all ears. He continues:

'Unfortunately the Russians, and Bolsheviks too, are great specialists in suffering. This time it is in the name of collective progress and productive forces, while with the Cossacks the competition is strictly individual, but it is of just as little use to me. I am a member of the Komsomol, sure, but of the Ostap Bender tendency.* Not that

---

* Hero of *Twelve Chairs* by Ilf and Petrov.

I want, like him, to become a millionaire in the land of the Soviets. We've gone beyond that sort of thing; but I'm sick of sacrificing myself for the happiness of my grandchildren. Productive forces? Fine. By all means. Let us develop them, but in such a way that we get the benefit from them right now and without discrimination. For if we don't, I have my own five-year plan for the progressive elimination of suffering from my life!'

'But Kola, we're at war. What plan are you talking about? Tomorrow we could be killed,' I say.

'If you place yourself in an apocalyptic perspective, clearly there isn't any plan which will stand up. Until we have proof to the contrary however, we're still alive, and we need to think about the future during and after the war. For the present I am obeying the rules in everything that touches upon my immediate duty, but for the future, I am an intransigent partisan of a policy of non-suffering. It is my personal socialism and has nothing to do with these nationalist stupidities, any more than with the theory of productive forces. I am barely 20 years old, and as far as sacrifices are concerned, I have already exceeded a reasonably calculated norm for a long lifetime.'

I can no longer hold back. I talk about all of my misfortunes. I tell everything to Kola, even about Western Siberia, although some days earlier I had taken him for an informer and, until then, had carefully concealed my Siberian adventures. 'You are 20 years old too, because your last two years count as double,' he says approvingly, like a good accountant of dangers, but he doesn't go as far as admitting that my credits surpass his. 'You were able to react, to defend yourself, while we could only suffer without being able to do much about it. I have been separated from my parents for a very long time; I don't even know where they are, perhaps even in Western Siberia. And your fine *mastier* in Zavodooukovsk could have been my father . . . After the war, all of that will have to change, is going to change, and I am not the only one to think so . . .'

We feel as though we are long lost brothers who have found each other as if by a miracle. As luck would have it we are able to celebrate the event immediately. It is Wednesday, the day the Mietchotkians regularly meet at Tania's house. When we get there the clan and their girlfriends have eaten almost everything, as they did not expect us to return, but there is plenty left to drink. Kola, who normally holds his drink very well, gets awfully drunk in the maudlin style. His story of suffering is told once more. He mutters strange things that we can't hear properly. 'What are you saying, Kola, my love?' Maroussia finally asks.

'I am saying that they are all fascists, Hitler and Stalin, Churchill and Roosevelt, and that I have had it up to here with them; and that everything here will have to change.' At a stroke it is clear; but Maroussia prudently leads him off into the next room so as to be the only one to hear what comes next.

For me, however, the evening passes off with a cheerful drunken abandon. I sing – in tune, for once – and give myself up to a number of pranks. Or so I was told afterwards, because beyond a certain threshold of drunkenness I am without memory.

We recovered quickly, with only mild hangovers: at seven o'clock the next morning all five of us are in our places in the column to sing: 'Stand up enormous country/Stand up for a fight to the death!' Sergeant-major Orlov is providentially absent and I sing along with the others all the way to Green Alley; no one is put off by it, and I experience an intense satisfaction. Then in the afternoon, I call at Nievka's place to announce to her that we will once again be taking part in the Mietchotkians' social evenings. She declares herself delighted by the news, but it is perhaps only from a spirit of submission, because 'the man has to decide'.

In the spring of 1942 the first storms break between Nievka and I. It's because we have inherited from our respective parents – she from her mother, me from my father – an inclination to jealousy. We don't contemplate putting an end to our turbulent love affair; on the contrary it is precisely because of this jealousy we ask permission to be allowed to live together. The only definite result of this foolhardy

129

initiative – in the light of my unforeseeable experience in Yerevan – is to reopen hostilities between the NKVD and me. Our blunder is perhaps explained though by the bizarre politico-military climate of this period.

Our watches are set at 1812, as Stalin has suggested in giving to us our glorious nineteenth-century ancestors as a model. At that time though, Napoleon's campaign lasted for a single summer since his army had proved unable to survive the Russian winter. Hitler on the other hand fell back some 200 kilometres during the periods of deepest cold and his troops are still here. What is going to happen in the spring? The past indicates clearly that the freezing conditions work to our army's advantage and the good weather to that of the enemy's, as Tolstoy explained in *War and Peace*. One can't deduce from that, however, that a new Battle of Moscow is inevitable and that we are going to lose it: history always has surprises in store. We approach this springtime, which is early in arriving, in expectation of grave hours ahead.

Above us, the sun rises higher each day, the months pass: March, April, May, and the front doesn't move at all. Certainly bitter fighting had taken place (there was never any 'phoney war' to the east) and the two armies manoeuvre a lot, but neither side seems to be committed to a decisive breakthrough. Our press sees in this proof of the fact that the Germans were not stopped at the gates of Moscow merely by 'General Winter', as they alleged, but that it is really the Red Army which has beaten them. Then, raising the stakes in the propaganda war, the Sovinformbureau affirms that the Wehrmacht has exhausted its capacities for offensive action because of the enormous losses it has suffered: 10 million dead, wounded and taken prisoner, 30,500 tanks and 20,000 aircraft destroyed. Presented with such figures who could resist the temptations of a measure of insouciance and avoid concluding that the German danger no longer existed? In Kislovodsk we eagerly accept this turning-point and no longer worry ourselves about the Wehrmacht, any more than we did one year earlier, in Rostov, just before the famous 22 June 1941.

This psychological turning-point hasn't the same effect, however, on Nievka and I as it has on Kola and his friends. For them the future lies on the 'fifth ocean'; they will soon be airborne, while we shall remain grounded in Kislovodsk. Nievka is already an anaesthetist's assistant and is going to resume her medical studies by correspondence; I shall probably be promoted, even though the post of junior (*mladchyi*) *politrouk* doesn't really appeal to me. But, after all, here we are in the 'pearl of the Caucasus' and we might as well arrange our future as best we can. Not that all this renders the absurd step we are going to take – that of setting up home together – indispensable. Nievka's character has a lot to do with it. She is one of the very few people in Kislovodsk not to believe at all in the exhaustion of the Wehrmacht's capacity for offensive action. This is not because of any systematic scepticism: Nievka is a 'believer', one of the Party faithful, a candidate-member of the CPSU, and not a simple Komsomol like we are. However, in her hospital she is faced each day with the harsh realities of the wounded. The latter have a lot to say and they contradict our official communiqués. You might say that they were trying to undermine this girl who had not been accustomed in Leningrad to hearing the authorities criticized. Nievka relays everything to me; but under oath of secrecy, insisting each time that I swear on my 'Komsomol's word' not to tell any of it to anyone, especially not to Commissar Bielokonienko or to Kola.

Even without these promises I would never have dreamt of repeating to my superior these remarks about the poor functioning of the Red Army medical services, or the disturbing news that Nievka had gleaned from the wounded who had come from Crimea and from the southern front. Bielokonienko in any case is going through a period of euphoria, so convinced is he that our army's general offensive is imminent and that it is going to coincide with the opening of a second front to the west, in Normandy or elsewhere. He doesn't say from what source he has this news, but I know that he receives confidential reports from the leadership of the political services, as well as the Tass Agency special bulletin which includes dispatches from Western news agencies not published in our press. He must have an overall idea of how the war is going, whereas Nievka bases what she says merely on partial testimony. The problem is that whereas the commissar limits himself to generalities – 'the Nazis' goose is cooked; they will be caught in a pincer grip between East and West' – Nievka cites individual but irrefutable cases. Wouldn't it be a good idea to bring them both together and to discuss it at length in order to throw some light on it?

Chance arranges it well. One hot day in May, Nievka and I are stretched out in a discreet and sheltered spot on the edge of a small river which crosses Kislovodsk; the water is too cold for bathing, but you can dip your feet in for a few moments at a time. It is in this position – with our feet in the water – that Bielokonienko surprises us. I shouldn't be here at this time of day (nor should he for that matter), and, without my shoes on and with my trousers rolled up I must present a fairly ridiculous sight. I am unsure about how to deal with the situation and so I introduce him very ceremoniously to Natalia Trofimovna G., who is sitting half-paralysed and doesn't even dare remove her legs from the stream. My *tchoudak* of a commissar is delighted: 'You aren't by any chance the daughter of Trofime Stepanovitch G., of Leningrad?' Why, yes, indeed, the very same. It's a small world: Bielokonienko and Nievka's father met 10 years before, at the time of God knows what national meeting on productivity in transport (of all things!), and have often seen each other since then. They are more than good acquaintances; they are 'companions-in-arms'. 'What an old slyboots, though, this Trofime is,' he continues. 'He never told me that he had such a pretty daughter. There is no hurry; let's sit down and chat for a while. It's cooler here than in town.'

After this promising beginning we have the opportunity of confronting the two visions of Russian reality. Nothing of the sort happens: I might as well have gone home, for Bielokonienko and Nievka babble on without allowing me a word in edgeways. He does his usual number on Zaporojié, his beloved town, connecting it up with the forthcoming encirclement of Germany and Hitler's ineluctable capitulation. She declares herself in agreement with everything he says, whereas half an hour before she had been tormenting me with the bad news she had heard from Crimea. She also takes advantage of what I have told her about Molotov's forthcoming visit to London, in order to ask intelligent questions on Soviet–British relations. What strikes me especially is the ease with which she paces the conversation, an ease quite at variance with the reserve that she maintains in the course of our Mietchotkian social evenings. Bielokonienko, for his part, doesn't spare the compliments, and it doesn't escape my notice that he is examining my Nievka in detail with a randy eye.

When we get back, I tell her that the commissar fancies her. By way of a reassuring reply Nievka explains to me, citing physiological reasons, that it is impossible for a woman of her age to make love to a man who is old enough to be her father. A fine joke! How could I have come into the world if women of 23 couldn't sleep with men who were 20 years older? I am not about to commit myself on this subject, however, and I go straight to the point: 'You could have taken advantage of his friendly disposition towards you to say a few words about the complaints of your wounded. This was the ideal occasion to tell him that ambulance trains are lacking and that the Red Cross convoys are not even given priority on the railways.' She taps her forehead with a contemptuous finger. 'OK, OK, but at least some references to the latest stories of the wounded from the south, with their verdict on the calibre of our command, would have interested him, especially as they come from "companions-in-arms" belonging to the army of the North Caucasus.' At this she bursts into tears, gets up from the carpet and throws herself on the bed, cursing the fate which has thrust her into the arms of such an intolerable person. To crown everything, she accuses me, in between sobs, of defeatism. That is the limit! I have been consoling her for months, struggling against the avalanche of nightmarish confidences, and it is me who is deafeatist!

It is time though for me to get back to Green Alley, where duty calls me and, so as not to leave her sad I make a little speech of reconciliation – not without a touch of irony. 'You said that in bad faith, Nievka, but it's not your fault, you didn't do it on purpose. For me alone you will remain Cassandra. The two of us, in spite of everything, will know how things are really evolving.' She acquiesces, the irony having escaped her, and recovers her smile. I am to come back this evening, after my last meeting. I am almost at the door when she cries: 'Don't eat any of their junk, I shall get dinner ready here.' Here again is this Russian mania for saying 'them', even when in this case it applies to the Red Army which she holds in such high esteem! I let it pass: the food that Nievka prepares is much better than that prepared by the canteen chef.

Ever since this episode the commissar seems to have hoisted me to the ranks of 'companion-in-arms'. He completely exempts me from Sergeant-major Orlov's exercises. So that I won't become altogether idle, he often lends me to the *zavkhoze*, Pietia Danilov, to escort the supplies lorry. At every opportunity, sometimes twice a day, he asks for news of 'the ravishing daughter of his friend Trofime of Leningrad'. He even reproaches me with having hidden her from him. I remind him that we could have met at the Kislovodsk theatre, which Nievka and I often went to. Despite this familiarity, he is very careful not to invite us to his home to introduce us to his wife, Jara. It is obvious what's going on: Bielokonienko has secret designs on Nievka. He already appears to me as a rival.

Having witnessed the scenes my father used to create with my mother, I swore resolutely to myself that I would never give way to jealousy. In present circumstances though I would have needed an exceptional self-control that was out of character; I would also have had to love a woman who didn't work at the hospital where the relations between the wounded and nurses leave a lot to be desired. It is not simply my imagination: Nievka herself measures the progress of the cure by the yardstick of the patient's sexual appetite. When they arrive in the surgery department where Nievka works, they are usually delirious or screaming against our incapacity to prosecute the war; but hardly have they recovered their spirits when they begin to chat up the nurses. The latter are relatively plentiful and some of them, who are young and incompetent, seem to have enrolled in the medical services only because the food is better than in civvy street. At this stage, Nievka pretends that she no longer has much contact with the patients because she remains attached to the operating ward and to the seriously wounded. Nevertheless she spends a lot of time at the hospital, crosses the communal halls and is often shouted at in passing, sometimes very crudely. 'Hey, you, the stuck-up one, give us at least a sniff of your big arse – and it is Nievka herself who relates it to me.'

OK, soldiers everywhere are slobs, in Russia more than elsewhere; there is nothing in that to get excited over. Nievka is indulgent towards her wounded. 'They have spilled their blood for the fatherland and are only asking for a bit of human warmth.' With us, that is to say Kola, my friends and I, when we get nicely drunk from time to time, Nievka is severe; but with the wounded, she appears ready to overlook any behaviour, no matter how far out of order it might be. I ask: 'And suppose one of them, in search of human warmth, should try to sleep with you?' 'Where? How? You can't be serious,' she replies. Now in fact she spends two or three nights per week at the surgery department; I beg her to let me know if she should sleep with someone in the hospital. Unperturbed, she tells me that it goes without saying, because she would never dream of living polyandrously.

In the month of April, because of an inspection by General Golovanov, the future air marshal, I find it impossible to leave barracks for a period of 10 days. When finally, relieved and delighted, I head for Nievka's, she greets me with a fearful scene: 'Admit it, you filthy drunkard, you took advantage of it to sleep with girls with big tits!' Had it been said in a bantering tone this might have been rather flattering, but she isn't joking at all. She is livid with anger. She knows all about it; she has proof; someone has seen me; they have told her everything; we have to tell each other the truth, etc. Anger has the effect of making her lose her fine Leningrad accent and she hits out at the '*tsytsatyie baby*', these women with big tits. Her performance is worthy of the last of the Cossacks. It takes hours for her to calm down, and to resume a normal dialogue. Then I learn in sequence: first that Nievka's father was cruelly unfaithful to her mother, allegedly because of the mother's small breasts; next, that in Russia the men go mad for big breasts and that, although I am Polish, I ogle Raia's chest in a very suspect manner. Finally that during these last 10 days she had become convinced that I would never come back to her.

I surmise that Nievka suffers from an inferiority complex because of the size of her breasts. A good analyst would free her from it in no time. At Kislovodsk, however, there are no analysts and besides, Nievka would never agree to submit herself to a bourgeois science. There is nothing to be done therefore: Nievka is not content to limit strictly my tipple of vodka during our communal evenings – increasingly rare anyway since the onset of the good weather. She also regularly accuses me of shamelessly rubbing up against the breasts of Raia, her main rival, and against those of Maroussia, Vera and even Tania. It is a sort of ritual, but painful all the same. Sometimes I suspect that Nievka throws these scenes just to keep the initiative and to prevent me from questioning her about possibly far more serious infidelities at the hospital.

The most serious incident erupts at the beginning of June. At the 'eleventh school' of the VVS the ceremony to commemorate the first anniversary of the outbreak of war is already in preparation. This time it is Colonel Zlotnikov and not the commissar who is to make the main speech. Counting on being sent into town on an errand, I had promised Nievka to take her in the afternoon to a spot on the outskirts of the town from which you can see Mount Elbrus. Now, in the morning I am sent to fetch coal from a surface mine 100 kilometres away, as a favour to the *zavkhoze*, the commissar's friend. I ask the driver, a civilian with a small moustache invalided out of the service for some illness or other I've forgotten, to make a detour through the southern quarter. I need to call and warn Nievka, so that she doesn't run off with the idea that I have decamped with a *tsytsataia baba*. Curiously, Rosa, her friend from Leningrad, is at home with her, whereas they usually arrange things so as to alternate their time at the hospital. On top of that, in the middle of the room there stands, like in an exhibition, an enamel bucket of fresh cream – 10 kilos at least. 'It belongs to Captain Pojarski,' Nievka says. 'He will be here to pick it up at any time.' It is out of the question to discuss it in front of her friend, and the lorry is waiting for me outside. I leave in a whirl, as I had arrived.

Once we are on our way, this mysterious fresh cream begins seriously to prey on my mind. Why did this damned Captain Pojarski need to leave his things at Nievka's? How do they know each other in any case? He is not from Leningrad, as far as I know. Suddenly I seem to remember that Nievka had said to me that Pojarski was one of the most presentable of the commanders of the 'eleventh'; a handsome man, in short. What's more, he is not exactly 'old', like Bielokonienko; he is barely 30 years old. The road is poor, the driver with the small moustache is obsequious and taciturn, and the landscape doesn't interest me. I don't manage either to talk or to concentrate. 'This coal is so bad that the mine was abandoned a long time ago; we are endangering the lorry's suspension along this road,' says the driver. I notice that his moustache, though much smaller, resembles my father's a little, and my father's image comes to mind. I see him saying to Chourka, my communist brother, that in Russia there is no more fresh cream. Why did I always take my mother's side against him? Perhaps she really was unfaithful to him. She could have taken advantage of her professional and political activities to meet lovers.

I ask the driver about his wife but he replies only in monosyllables. Yes, she works; yes, they have four children. Then Nievka's image reappears to me; what an air of defiance I had sensed in her smile when she announced to me that Captain Pojarski would be calling at any time. That's right! She thinks that she can do whatever she likes because she thinks I am a weakling. And what exactly did she mean by 'at any time'? It can't mean the morning, since this damned Pojarski, a pilot instructor, is busy at that time of day. At the beginning of the afternoon then? And suppose that I

137

were to turn up for the rendezvous too?

'Turn around,' I say to the driver. 'The road is too badly damaged. We aren't going to sacrifice the lorry for this bloody coal.' 'But what will Captain . . .?' the other begins. I cut him short; this morning I am in charge. With a sudden pang of conscience, I go off to announce my decision to the four fellows in the back; all of them are from the second squadron and I hardly know them. They all have their coats off and collars undone, and are lying back enjoying the midday sun as if they were at the beach. 'What sort of farce is this?' I scream, like any old sergeant-major. They rush to button themselves up; they stop short only at standing to attention. It's crazy how the army ingrains conditioned reflexes. I have no right to give them orders; they could tell me to go to hell. But no, I am travelling in the cabin, and that is sufficient to ensure that they obey. Hell, this driver is driving slowly. Is he deliberately trying to make me late?

On arrival, I burst into Nievka's place without knocking, expecting to surprise her *in flagrante delicto*. There is no Captain Pojarski, however, and the enamel bucket has diappeared. Nievka, in her underwear – it is hot – is reading Zoshchenko. She is so absorbed by her reading that she doesn't even want to listen to me until she has completed the page. When she is quite ready to hear my story it makes her laugh without any restraint. What's so funny? Here I am in danger of being hauled in front of a war tribunal for failure to obey an order, and she laughs, covering her mouth with her hands and trying not to choke. Then she switches to tenderness – it must be a safe day – and wraps herself around me before leading me onto the bed. I am powerless; it isn't even worth the bother of asking her about Pojarski.

It is she who finally talks about him. He is Rosa's lover, and has found a farm from which they get fresh cream that Rosa has to sell on the kolkhozian market. They need some money to be able to set up home together. Rosa is going to move anyway; she has already found a tiny room in the same house in which Pojarski lives. 'You will have to move in here with me. Then we shall stop tormenting each other with our jealousies,' Nievka concludes abruptly. The advantages of this arrangement are obvious, but only commanders have the right to live in town; I have no official rank, and my mission as a Komsomol special envoy is precisely to live alongside the ranks.

'No excuses, please – you have only to speak about it with the commissar,' she retorts with assurance. 'You are not asking permission to live just anywhere in town, but at the home of Natalia Trofimovna G. And if you won't do it, I'll speak to him about it myself.' Nievka doesn't take herself for a commoner but for a great lady of Leningrad society. We agree then, that as soon as the storm about my failed mission blows over, I shall take the necessary steps; it is more logical for me to do it. Moreover I don't want to give Bielokonienko the opportunity of a face-to-face meeting with Nievka.

I couldn't have chosen a better day to raise the matter with my commissar. The night before, an exhilarating storm has freshened the atmosphere and purified the air; it is so clear that from the upper part of the town you can clearly see the great chain of the Caucasus and the majestic Elbrus. My aborted expedition has created no great ripples and I am congratulated for having taken such care of the rolling stock. If Bielokonienko's mood is set fair, however, it is because we are in the process of signing, after the Pact of London, an agreement in Washington on US deliveries. Large quantities of engines supplied on credit terms are already on their way, or soon will be; with this aid, even if there is a short delay in the opening of the second front, we'll soon show the Germans what's what. Although he doesn't clearly say so, in his Ukrainian head the patterns of 1812 repeat themselves. For him the only really important front is that of Moscow: it is here, with the aid of the formidable cold, that Hitler will be beaten.

He leads me off once more towards the large waterfall to explain to me his ideas for the anniversary ceremony on 22 June. We could have an open-air evening of films, 'non-stop' as he says (reflecting the linguistic influence of the Tass Agency bulletin), and show the Maxim trilogy* at one sitting. And without waiting for my objections he begins to sing: '*Kroutitsa viertitsa char golouboi*' ('It turns, it swerves, the blue balloon'). With this song we are transported to Leningrad – on the Vyborg side rather than that of the Nievka – but a rather good sign I think anyway for the outcome of my request. The more I explain our plan the more Bielokonienko's good humour gives way to embarrassment. There are regulations in the armed forces: each one to their place. Someone of my rank cannot enjoy the same privileges accorded a commander. And anyway, who would do my work within the ranks on behalf of the Komsomol? I would have to be given promotion and a replacement would have to be found for me, and all of that takes time. My promises to carry on doing everything as before, in spite of changing my living arrangements, don't carry much weight. He continues, however, thinking out loud: he cannot, on reflection, upset Natalia Trofimovna, the daughter of a 'companion-in-arms'. I slip in the fact that she is called Nievka, and for good measure the fact that Andrei Zhdanov himself used to bounce her on his knees when she was a little girl. 'Natalia isn't a bad name either,' he says laconically, but the information has been duly noted.

A lengthy, silent meditation follows amid the splendours of the park. Near the waterfall, I think back to my first rendezvous with Nievka. At last, the commissar proposes a compromise; I can move in with Natalia Trofimovna – 'Nievka' is decidedly too familiar – but only on condition that I return to barracks two or three nights per week, to show my face and make my presence felt, and to share the life of my comrades. Bielokonienko also promises to see to my Kislovodsk residence permit. All those who live in town are obliged to have one; it is the law. He will have to withdraw my passport from my Red Army dossier, have it stamped by the NKVD and then

* Three famous films by Trauberg and Kozintsev – *The Youth of Maxim*, *Maxim's Return*, and *The Vyborg Quarters*, – about a worker in St Petersburg before and during the October Revolution.

return it. 'It is a mere formality,' he says, before getting back to the Maxim trilogy and to our current business. 'You can bring Natalia Trofimovna to the film show on 22 June,' he adds.

Three or four days later, at around bedtime, someone comes to look for me at the barracks: I am to go immediately to Bielo-konienko's home. He lives at the far end of Kislovodsk, off an alley. In daytime I can find it easily enough but at night it is another matter. I hear the chimes of midnight when I finally enter his small apartment, after having passed Captain Danilov on the stairway, a little the worse for a drink or two. Bielokonienko is in a foul humour. Jara is sleeping in the other room and he asks me to lower my voice, but he can hardly control his own when he cries out: 'Wretched creature, what terrible wrong have you done in your life?' as if he didn't recognize me. I fear the worst, the discovery of my Siberian past or something of the kind. I wasn't born yesterday, however, and I wait for him to show his hand. He repeats the question; I repeat my silence. 'Do you know, wretch,' he continues finally, 'what sort of passport you have?' I continue to say nothing because I don't know how to answer; he repeats his question several times. It is astonishing how he can drivel on when he is drunk. This will take all night if he keeps on at this rate. He gets hold of himself however: 'You hold a passport that is issued only to persons who are not allowed to change their place of residence, who are thereby declared undesirable everywhere else. It is notably the case for prostitutes, *prostitutki*. Do you understand what I'm saying?' And he insists on repeating this provocative word 10, 20 or 30 times.

What is there to say? I am not going to explain that a certain Ivanov in the NKVD in Rostov has clearly played a dirty trick on me, and that this hypocritical bureaucracy disgusts me. I confess only to my surprise: this passport has been inspected a hundred times in the Komsomol and in the Red Army – which keeps it in its own files – and no one, including myself, noticed the fact that I was marked out in it as an undesirable. 'It's because the Chekists are the only ones to recognize certain coded paragraphs; it's their way of communicating,' my commissar replies, with an ease that persuades me he is recovering the use of his faculties. I call upon him to witness the injustice done to me: I came to Rostov through love of this town, and to defend the USSR. By what right do they dare to add paragraphs to my passport that mark me off as undesirable?

The score is equalled. Bielokonienko has me sit down and brings out the vodka; the atmosphere is one of détente. 'It's true, you don't deserve it. Our Chekists are awful characters, and you're not the first to find this out. On the other hand, there is nothing to be done about it; we cannot do without them, for there are too many authentic enemies to fight against. Later, after the war, when we approach the phase of communism, we will no longer need the NKVD; everything will be socialized. Do you understand what I'm saying?' No, I am interested in the here and now and want to know if I can move in with Nievka. 'At present it's impossible. You would have to shift heaven and earth to get your passport changed, because they also hold against you the fact of your Polish nationality, which is suspect by definition. You ought to have declared yourself a Soviet since your parents come from Rostov, but now it's too late. Do you understand what I'm saying?' Of course, I understand and I shall remember. 'Don't pull a face, take a drink. Relax!' Now completely drunk, the stout Ukrainian promises to do whatever he can to aid my relationship with Natalia Trofimovna, 'a wonderful girl', an 'oumintsa' (very brainy too). At this stage of drunkenness his speech, punctuated by hiccups, becomes almost unintelligible. He doesn't even hear me as I withdraw, leaving him to mutter to himself.

On my way home I pass close to the 'fortress' hospital where Nievka is working that night; but it isn't worth looking for her. Nurses who work in the surgery department are not allowed to go outside while on duty, and they wouldn't call her away even if I had been killed in a duel by Captain Pojarski. I can't go to sleep just like that however; this discovery that the Cheka have been communicating with secret signs weighs too heavily. I wake Kola up in order to talk about it. He is thunderstruck; I had told him nothing about my plan to move out so as not to admit my intention of betraying the clan for Nievka. I spin a long yarn for him about the sacrifice I had been ready to make for Nievka's sake, to console her for her troubles at the hospital, and I spill out everything that I was not supposed to say on the Red Army medical services and the situation on the southern front. It takes Kola some time to see a way through this confusing mess; then he decrees, with the good sense of a man of the south: 'You sleep at Nievka's place three nights a week anyway. After moving house it would amount to the same thing since on the other three nights she is at the hospital!' The truth of what he says is clear and the absurdity of our undertaking becomes apparent. We have stirred up the shit with the NKVD to no purpose. As for the passport, it is of no importance since it is kept in the Red Army's files, and no one will bother with it until the end of the war. Afterwards, things will have changed, and we'll see.

Then we change the subject to Nievka. Kola is touched to learn that she takes the misfortunes of the wounded so much to heart, certainly more so than do his other nurse friends. 'I would never have believed it of her,' he says. 'She is rather haughty sometimes, you'll admit, and comes from a world that is very different from ours. Well, you will have to explain to her that people like us are used to *tieplouchki*; it is our Russian way of travelling. On top of that we are not really great travellers and our railways are almost non-existent; as for our roads, all it takes is for a cow to piss on them for the traffic to be brought to a halt. It is terrible for the transport of the wounded, but the Germans have the same problems with the evacuation of theirs; in this way our handicaps become trump cards. She ought to understand that. But don't do anything to harden her heart or to make her indifferent; we have to keep her on the side of the enemies of suffering.'

The next day I relate to Nievka the incident with the passport, without any reproaches for this scheme of hers which earned me a humiliating refusal. I watch the blood rise to her cheeks. 'They will pay for this,' she says, stressing each word. 'Just wait until the blockade of Leningrad is broken, then we shall see who is strongest. I shall go to see Zhdanov and I shall have their heads. Who do these Chekist shitheads think they are?'

The sensational Raia jumps on to my knees singing, 'Mama, *ia polit-liotchika khotchou*' ('I want a political pilot'). The Russian language is very supple and allows you to make up neologisms. In the original song a girl sings to her mother to say that she wants a pilot who flies very high and who earns a lot of money – a high flier. Raia has added the prefix 'polit' to designate me, and the trick is complete. She 'wants me' because there is a coolness between her and Vassia the 'Elephant', and maybe also to torment Nievka, whom she doesn't really like. 'You are the prettiest girl I have seen in your country,' I say, pressing her closely against me. 'You're the only one who knows how to talk to a woman,' Raia replies, under the impassive gaze of Vassia who is chatting with Kola at the other end of the table. Nievka, her elbows on the table, her head on her hands, stares silently at us.

Without releasing Raia, I catch hold of a bottle of vodka with my left hand and help myself to a large swig. 'I want some too,' she says, opening her mouth wide. Laughter breaks out around us and except, obviously, Nievka's, glasses are refilled. 'Mama, *ia polit-liotchika khotchou*' Raia begins again, and the other girls, Maroussia, Tania and Vera, take up the refrain. Volodia the 'Singer' accompanies them on a guitar, and Vassia himself joins in the chorus. I decide to have another drink and already have the bottle in my mouth when Nievka gets up: 'You've had enough to drink. Let's go home.'

The vodka has lent me courage and loosened my tongue: 'No. I have the right to drink. Sevastopol fell yesterday and my friend Motia was there. I am drinking to his survival. He is the only one who ever helped me in your country.' And I repeat 'in your country', because having already drunk a fair amount, I too feel that I have the right to go on a bit. Kola rushes over to shut the window in case things get overheated. 'So it isn't your country then?' Nievka asks, her green eyes lit up like headlamps. 'No it isn't mine, we are fighting a war together, that's all. I am not from here, I am not really Soviet.' *In vodka veritas.* Since the scene late at night at the commissar's, something inside me has snapped; it is like a game of snakes and ladders, when an unlucky throw of the dice brings you back to the bottom line. Raia is delighted. 'Great. In that case you can stay with me tonight, and after the war you can take me with you to your country; it will be terrific, my *polit liotchik*.' She is drunk. I am too, but I empty the rest of another bottle to defy Nievka. She will not impose her 200-gramme limit (vodka is sold by weight in Russia) on me any more. After it I begin to see the others' faces spin and to see double. . . . It is Nievka who wakens me some hours later: 'Quickly, quickly, it's 10 o'clock already. You are going to have problems *maltchik moi* (my lad).'

Nothing is really pressing. In this July of 1942 all our schedules are upset: the runways planned for the TB3 heavy bombers at Min. Vody are not yet ready; even some of the little single-engine training planes, the *koukourouzniki* ('maize planes' – so called because on reconnaissance missions they hug closely to the fields) have been taken away from us. At Nievka's hospital the flood of the wounded has dried up and the operating block is working below capacity; she is even able to cut short her night shifts and return home almost every night. You might almost say that on the eve of the disaster, which we still did not foresee, a kind of semi-holiday is granted us in order to live out our love affair. Yet we spend this strange month of July having rows about vodka.

At the front everything is going badly. There is no need to listen to Nievka's wounded to learn about it, it is enough to listen carefully to the Sovinformbureau's communiqués on Radio Moscow. The Red Army is falling back from all its lines of defence in the south and south west, from the Black Sea coast to Voronezh. Our propaganda takes account of this with the usual time lag. On 22 June, on the occasion of the anniversary of the war, Colonel Zlotnikov still affirmed: 'The enemy is trying to hurl itself forward, but the intensity of its attacks diminishes day by day.' So much for the line about the Wehrmacht's incapacity for offensive action. In July the tone changes: *Pravda* exalts the heroism of the defenders of Sevastopol and alleges that, despite the fall of the city, we have carried off a moral victory; but it also seems to acknowledge and adopt as its own the revelations that Nievka has been making to me

145

in the preceding months. Certainly there is no question of criticizing the medical services, but the incompetence of certain commanders is noted and so too is the lack of discipline among the troops. Still more revealing are the denunciations in *Pravda* of those promoting 'panic' and 'capitulation'. The best pens in the country, those of Ilya Ehrenbourg, Alexis Tolstoy and Mikhail Sholokhov, are now mobilized to develop hatred for the *German*. This seems to contradict the speech in which Stalin himself the previous year exonerated the German people from the crimes of the Nazis. Our troops, however, are probably not sufficiently motivated and so in addition they are warned that 'captivity in Germany is worse than death'.

On the commissar's orders, the *politrouks* abandon the *History of the CPSU (Bolsheviks)* in favour of this new literature. We have to learn by heart the poem by Konstantin Simonov, entitled *Kill Him*: 'If your brother or your neighbour has killed him it is they who are taking revenge. You have no excuses, you don't hide behind the other person's back. You don't take revenge with a bent rifle . . .' For love of our Russian mothers each of us must kill at least one German. At Kislovodsk we don't feel at all that we are hiding, we ask only for the chance to fight. And for that matter, why should we avenge only Russian mothers? Why not Ukrainians, Cossacks, Jews or Poles?

It is not so much the bad news or the annoyance provoked by the pan-Russian propaganda, however, which drive me to drink. The scene at Bielokonienko's has triggered within me a rejection of this Soviet world and its deceitful practices. It had happened to me already in Western Siberia; but this time it is stronger, almost irrational, because at bottom Kola is right: I am not the victim of any injustice, I have simply been denied a privilege that I had arrogated to myself. The commissar, what's more, is as good as his word: he facilitates my relationship with Nievka and turns a blind eye when I report late to work. The thing is stronger than me though: I need to drown it in vodka. I no longer even look for company to drink with: I often hide myself behind a tree in the park, like a thief. Lying there alone, I close my eyes, hoping to forget everything, but straightaway I hear again the drunken voice of the commissar, and the word *prostitutki* resounds in my ears.

Some odd associations of ideas are set off by it. In what ways is the desirable Raia any different from those young bourgeoise women who chase after a rich fiancé in the films from America? And doesn't Rosa take advantage of the black market even though she is, like Nievka, a candidate-member of the CPSU? For that matter, what do I know about Nievka's income? She wants for nothing and never asks me for any money although she is paid a pittance. And then in a more general way, they take us for idiots with these tedious stories about the German Army's loss of impetus, when in fact it is bearing down on us at full speed.

Nievka is convinced that I have lapsed into alcoholism. She preaches at me endlessly, even on the days when I am sober. She is as repetitive as Bielokonienko, when drunk. At least she has given up her attempts at blackmail: 'It is either me or the vodka. If you drink more than 200 grammes you can go to hell.' Now she no longer threatens to throw me out, and when I turn up at her home, well gone, she undresses me with the skill of Russian women used to drunkards. She applies cold water compresses to my forehead and wraps herself around me as if to calm me down. Early the next morning though, while serving the tea, once again it's: 'Vodka will be the death of you, wretch. I even feel pity for you. If you don't stop drinking you will be ruined,' and so on. 'Nievka,' I say to her, 'on 4 August I shall be 21 years old, and I am old enough to know myself what I have to do.' In fact I shall only be 18 but I have always lied to her about my age.

One morning towards the end of July, she asks me mysteriously: 'So your mother doesn't like socialism, is that right?' It takes me a little while to grasp what she is leading up to. I have never spoken to her about my mother, who is socialist but strongly anti-communist. I react vigorously: I don't care if I am late in reporting to my commissar: the matter might be serious. Nievka doesn't get upset however; my questions even put her in a good mood. 'You toss about a lot in your sleep but it doesn't matter that much: I know how to sleep with you. But I am not deaf, my lad, and you talk a lot in your sleep.' And what exactly did I talk about in connection with my mother? Nievka becomes more evasive, using the fact that she herself was too deeply asleep to make the effort to understand everything. She is certain of one thing only: 'It is the vodka which makes you talk in your sleep.' 'Don't the war and the setbacks suffered by our army have something to do with it?' I say to cut her sermon short. 'That isn't what you talk about,' she counters. I tell her what I have read about the unconscious, but she shrugs her shoulders: 'It is vodka and nothing else. Stop drinking or this damnable drink will be the end of you.' There is a menacing ring to what she says but in fact she is partly right. I can afford less than anyone carelessly to narrate episodes of my life wherein are found Siberian mosquitoes and a host of other things that I have no intention of divulging.

On 1 August, listening to Radio Moscow, we learn that the Germans have taken Novotcherkask, the historic capital of the Cossacks, and have even taken Rostov. *Pravda* publishes a solemn appeal from Stalin: 'Not a step backwards.' Consternation prevails in the first squadron. We are wasting our time in Kislovodsk. We no longer even know how to fill our time, while the Germans take possession of the region dearest to us. Kola does what he can to put things in perspective. 'It's not a war between Hitler and the Cossacks,' he says. 'He has the whole of the USSR against him, and on the Moscow front he is hardly advancing at all.' That boosts our morale a little. Kola is right: the Germans have taken Rostov before, in 1918, and once again the year before, and on neither occasion did the USSR collapse because of it. It is Moscow that counts; and there their advance is blocked.

Our Komsomol meetings are much longer from this time onwards, so intense is the interest generated by the reading of *Pravda* and the *Red Star* (the newspaper of the armed forces). Late in the evening I arrive at Nievka's sober as a judge, and another surprise awaits me:

Rosa's bed has been replaced by a long table with eight old chairs. 'It's for your birthday. I have already arranged everything, don't worry about a thing,' she says, and goes on to explain that she has invited all the regulars from our evenings together except for that 'cheap tart' Raia. Rosa will be here and can keep Vassia company. 'Your commissar is also coming,' Nievka adds, after a brief hesitation. 'What? Have you seen him then?' No, she has invited him in writing and hands me his acceptance. He is delighted to see her again – not a word of course about my birthday – and he explains that his wife unfortunately is busy on that evening. He will come alone therefore. Nievka, Nievka, this will never do. First, because I sense that Bielokonienko and the Mietchotkians don't necessarily have compatible styles of getting drunk, and then, because I am once again jealous.

'Nievka, you are as naive as a child; the commissar is making eyes at you because he wants to screw you. That's why he's coming!'

'I don't mind being stared at,' she says, laughing. 'I'll dress to the nines. But your Bielokonienko will not *screw* me either here or anywhere else. I have already told you that I am incapable of sleeping with an older man.'

'OK, but Bielokonienko isn't aware of your tastes. He is going to try his luck, and I shall be forced to box his ears and finish my military career in prison.'

In this Lermontovian spot, I have always had the presentiment that everything would finish in a duel. The place requires it.

This birthday will be the most memorable of my life. It is barely 11 o'clock when someone comes to fetch the commissar. He sets off staggering, but perfectly capable of understanding that something urgent is afoot. One hour later, it is Nievka and Rosa's turn; they have to get to the hospital immediately. Something is clearly wrong, but what? The Germans? According to our communiqués, they have hardly reached Rostov. Whatever the intensity of their attack, they can't have been able to cover 600 kilometres in two days. It must be something else.

It is our propaganda, however, which is lacking in logic. Very early in the morning the general alert is given and we have to pack in an atmosphere of catastrophe. The enemy has already occupied the railway centre at Min. Vody and has cut off our retreat towards the Caspian Sea and Transcaucasia. We have to save ourselves by going through Pyatigorsk, and then follow the mountain routes towards Nalchik and Vladicaucasia. Before leaving, however, we have to destroy all industrial installations including the vodka factory. And thus it is that, this 4 August 1942, the day of my eighteenth birthday, the 'damnable drink' flows in floods in the gutters of Kislovodsk, and the citizens, flat on their bellies, drink it as if it were water from a mountain spring.

The commissar orders me to escort the usual lorry, driven by the chauffeur with the small moustache, but authorizes me to take only three men: Kola, Vassia and Volodia. Kostia will take the *electritchka* with the others. We'll meet up again in Pyatigorsk. As soon as we are on the road I ask the driver to make a detour via Nievka's hospital. 'You're going to bring her with you?' Kola asks approvingly. 'You won't be doing her any favours,' Vassia objects. 'The commissar will force her off in Pyatigorsk.' 'You're kidding, sunshine! It's more likely that he'll force you off! She's coming with us!' I say categorically.

Chaos reigns in front of the hospital: the wounded are trying to escape in their pyjamas, some with their heads bandaged, their limbs in plaster, leaping about on crutches. They clutch at our lorry, begging us to let them get on. 'Brothers, show us some Russian sympathy, or the Huns will certainly finish us off.' It is awful, but we can do nothing for them. We have no right to take anyone at all. Already, if we take Nievka, we are sticking our necks out. Vassia brutally thrusts back those who are trying to climb on. Kola and Volodia do their best to help him. Insults fly on all sides.

Finally Nievka appears on the main porch steps to say: 'I am not leaving.' Fury takes hold of me and I tell her that she is ungrateful. Then I recover just enough cool to reason with her. 'Everyone knows that you are a candidate-member of the party, and that Zhdanov held you on his knees when you were a child. You are exactly the type of communist the Germans are dearly looking for; your own wounded have told you so a thousand times. Nievka, come with us, come quickly, we are already dangerously late.' She doesn't answer; silence is her weapon on those days when she is most annoyed or upset. I beg her forgiveness for all my faults: for caressing her friend Rosa once or twice, for having drunk like a fish. 'I'll be kind to you, I'll never make you unhappy again, but let us leave now, let's leave quickly. Look at what's going on around you.' She remains adamant, erect as a statue, pale as her nurse's blouse; she doesn't even seem to be listening to me. The lorry's horn sounds, my friends are calling me; they are at risk of being overwhelmed by the patients. I have to go, I can't stay around arguing.

I am already climbing into the cabin when Nievka catches up with me. She holds me tightly, very tightly in her arms. Her voice, choking with sobs, is so feeble that I can hardly hear her: 'I don't want to abandon the wounded, I cannot, it just isn't done. But don't worry, I can look after myself. I shall get out of it. But you, *maltchik moi*, take care, be prudent, and promise me not to drink any more.' We cover each other with kisses, on the forehead, the eyes, the nose, just as at the time of our first rendezvous. We can't quite manage to detach ourselves from one another. Our friends in the lorry leave us alone for a moment and stop protesting; even the wounded move away silently. Then, she is but a white speck on the steps of the 'fortress', her hospital No. 1224 (or is it 2142?). Adieu Nievka, Natalia, daughter of Leningrad, stubborn, anti-alcohol *sanitarka*. You have been good to me, and I shall not forget you.

I never saw her again; I have never had any news of her. In the beginning I often spoke of her with Kola and Vassia. They argued that we ought to have taken her off by force. After the war Kola exchanged several letters with Raia to dissuade her from taking Vassia to court about the child she alleged she had had by him. Thanks to this correspondence, we found out that Kislovodsk was savagely bombed and half-destroyed during the winter of 1942–3. The kind teacher, Maroussia, and joyful Tania, our vodka supplier, were killed. Vera had survived and rejoined the Red Army medical services. Not a word about Nievka though. That didn't prove anything, however; Raia and Nievka had always detested each other, and they could very simply have totally lost interest in each other's fate. Personally I believe that Nievka is still alive.

On just one occasion, in 1945, the whole Mietchotka clan was able to come together in Rostov to celebrate victory. Vassia the 'Elephant', a captain by now, proposed a toast (with a slight touch of malice) to the good health of 'our friend Nievka'. Our women companions, almost all of them Cossacks, were astonished. In the region of the Don they had never heard such a name. So I spoke at length of the nurse who had come from the north and, in order not to spoil the mood, I told them that in the end she had managed to return to Leningrad where she was now living happily and prosperously, just as they do in these fairytales that she liked so much.

3. Kola and the others

Few people realize nowadays that in 1942 the loss of the Caucasus would have been a catastrophe for the Allies. Even in the USSR the history books dismiss the affair in a few lines and seem to rate this battle as a negligible matter. At the time it was otherwise: the Wehrmacht blitzkrieg in the region that yields the greatest oil wealth in Europe and commands access to Turkey – and beyond to Iran – was the subject of great concern among the general staffs of the anti-Nazi coalition. Churchill hurried to Moscow to discuss it with Stalin. It was the first and most difficult of their meetings: neither had the slightest good news to communicate. Some weeks earlier the British had abandoned Tobruk and were now fighting in Egypt, their backs to the Pyramids. For the Russians things went from bad to worse after the fall of Sevastopol. They hadn't managed to hold the front either in the Kuban – their 'granary' near the Black Sea – or along the Don. As it penetrated the Caucasus, the Wehrmacht seemed to be swooping down to meet its troops operating in Africa under the command of General Rommel, the 'desert-fox'. Such a junction of forces would have had disastrous consequences for the Allies. Conscious of the danger Churchill bluntly asked Stalin, in August 1942, if his army were still capable of preventing the Wehrmacht from crossing the mountain passes of the Caucasus. (He is even thought to have offered the aid of the RAF though he doesn't mention it in his memoir *The Second World War*.) Stalin then unfolded onto the table a detailed map of the region – a Georgian in origin himself, he was familiar with the area – studied it, and decreed: 'They shall not cross the passes of the Caucasus;

we will stop them in the mountains.'

Churchill only half-believed him, and he reported to Roosevelt that his chief of staff, General Alan Brooke, placed even less confidence in these declarations. Reading this passage in Churchill's memoirs used to fill me with a secret joy as if, in 1942, I had personally played a fine stroke against both the Germans, and also against these sceptical Anglo-Saxons. Today, so many years later, my ex-combatant's pride is less keen, and I think that the success we eventually enjoyed 'in the mountains' was only obtained thanks to the extraordinary over-confidence of the Wehrmacht.

I don't propose to offer here a lengthy exposition on military strategy. A brief summary of the facts of the situation after our rushed departure from Kislovodsk will allow the reader to form a better picture. What is striking to begin with is that during the Churchill–Stalin discussions in Moscow, the name Stalingrad was never mentioned. The two leaders of the Great Alliance reasonably inferred that the Wehrmacht would hurl the bulk of its forces on the Caucasian front – where it stood to gain everything – and not on the unrewarding steppes of the Don and the Volga. Now the Germans in fact do the opposite, and drive deeper into an endless space well known for the severity of its winters. It appears that they wanted to encircle Moscow. How, though? Imagine an army at Lille, in the far north of France, hoping to encircle Paris by making a detour through Aix-en-Provence, almost on the Mediterranean coast. On the Russian scale the distances are even greater. Perhaps, these aristocratic strategists – the von Mansteins, the von Kleists (perhaps the descendant of the poet of despair?) and the von Pauluses pressed forwards on to the steppes of the Volga for no other reason than that they met, for the time being, with very little resistance.

Their second mistake becomes clear as soon as one considers the geography of the Caucasus. Until the discovery of the oilfields in Kuybyshev, and later in Western Siberia, 90 per cent of Soviet oil came from Baku and Groznyy. These two cities ought therefore to have been the prize targets of the battle of 1942, such was the belligerents' dependence on fuel for their 'war of engines'. Now

Baku is situated on the coast of the Caspian Sea and Groznyy on the northern foothills of the Caucasus, not far from the coast. To reach them the Germans were certainly not obliged to secure control of all the highest mountains. It would have been sufficient for them to have followed the path of the Moscow–Tiflis–Yerevan Transcaucasian railway, which, after the railway junction of Min. Vody winds its way through some of the lower passes and then skirts the Caspian Sea. If the Wehrmacht had concentrated its best divisions along this axis it would certainly have taken Groznyy and Baku. General Tiouleniev, who was responsible for the defence of this sector, acknowledged this in his memoirs published in 1960.

The Prussian generals, however, tried to do everything at once. They wanted the Caucasus but wanted Stalingrad also; they wanted oil, but also Mount Elbrus; and all this while encircling the adversary in order to capture large numbers of prisoners to send back to Germany. It was too much. Their appetite exceeded their means, even if, to begin with, they possessed mastery of the air and a clear advantage in armaments. After their failure at Stalingrad they were routed from the Caucasus, narrowly avoiding becoming encircled themselves. Their campaign didn't yield them a single barrel of oil; only the consolation of having reached the summit of the Elbrus.

This aspect particularly interests me – although I have a marked aversion for climbing in general, for we in the 'eleventh' of the VVS came very close to losing our lives because of it. When we abandoned Kislovodsk, our commanders had reasoned sensibly enough that the Germans were going to follow the route of the Transcaucasian towards the oilfields, thus leaving the road towards Nalchik and Vladicaucasia more or less free. These mountain towns have a strategic value only for the conquest of Georgia, and, even today, 40 years later, they are still not connected up to the railway network. This assessment neglected the Wehrmacht's taste for mountain-climbing. The main chain of the Caucasus extends to the west, close to and almost parallel with the Black Sea, and is dominated by Mount Elbrus with its peak of 5,600 metres. The Germans wanted to plant the swastika on it at any cost. As early as mid-August their press had published a photomontage showing their *Alpenjagers* on the summit of the mountain, and it had immediately provoked mocking denials from the Sovinformbureau. Wounded in their self-esteem, they no doubt decided to do whatever was necessary in order to be able to take some authentic snaps.

The Red Army command, when it saw the Wehrmacht slow down its advance on the oilfields, and head suddenly towards Nalchik, couldn't understand the object of the manoeuvre. Were they trying to cut through towards Tbilisi and, from there, towards Turkey? The enemy's numbers were insufficient for such an ambitious expedition. Far from imagining a German objective as absurd and limited as the scaling of the Elbrus, our high command decided to defend Nalchik whatever the cost and mobilized all available forces, including Marshal Golovanov's future pilots. The irrationality on the German side thus prompted an irrational reaction, and the 'eleventh' of the VVS was going to spend the second half of August 1942 defending a town of no military importance. Thanks to Churchill's *The Second World War*, I know today that we took up our battle positions on the very day that Stalin declared to him: 'We will stop them in the mountains.'

One further remark in conclusion before returning to the lorry in which we are taking leave of Kislovodsk. In the West, since the end of the war, it has become fashionable to eulogize the strategists of the Wehrmacht, to portray them as lucid men who were contemptuous of the former corporal, Hitler, and to imply that they were wholly unaware of the atrocities committed by their troops. This is demonstrated by the ready market for their memoirs, which sell like hotcakes. It is understandable: even in football the winning team always sings the praises of its beaten opponents, the better to emphasize its own merits. Nevertheless, I would like the Western victors one day to clarify the Mount Elbrus episode. For until we are better informed, I shall abide by the incontestably severe verdict of my friend Kola in 1945: only imbeciles could have consented to expend so much effort in order to climb the highest peak of the Caucasus.

*

Kola is in the back of the overloaded lorry with Vassia and Volodia, discreetly inspecting the cargo. In the cabin, the driver with the small moustache, is even more taciturn than usual. What worries me is that the zigzagging mountain road is completely deserted: there isn't a vehicle in sight. We must have been the last to leave Kislovodsk, a long time after the others. Suddenly, in a little rise between two bends which form a large hairpin, the driver parks our lorry at the edge of the ravine. We approve. It is time for a break. No sooner has the driver got down, however, than he disappears in the direction of some rocks that we have just passed by, and cries out to us: '*Gospoda russkié officery*!' ('Gentlemen, Russian officers!')

This is an extraordinary form of address: ever since the Revolution there have been no 'gentlemen' or 'officers' in the USSR. We are all comrades; our superiors are commanders.* My three companions, in spite of their astonishment, don't seem all that indignant at being so addressed. It may only be an impression on my part, however, since they say nothing. The driver only begins his speech after having taken up a strategic position which will allow him to take cover behind the rocks with a single leap.

'Gentlemen, Russian officers,' he shouts. 'Come back to Kislovodsk with me! The Reds have lost the war. You mustn't sacrifice your young lives for them. Another, different Russia is soon going to be reborn, and it will need you. Come with me; I'll hide you. I shall obtain civilian clothes for you. You will want for nothing. Trust me.' Our silence obliges him to raise his voice: 'Why do you want to get yourselves killed for the Bolsheviks and the Jews who have been sucking our Christian blood since their damned revolution? Don't be crazy. Come back to Kislovodsk!' Then he disappears behind the rock. He is off as fast as his legs will carry him.

None of us moves. His speech has us riveted to the spot. Today has provided us with more than our fair share of excitement: the panic departure, the tragic scene at the hospital, and now this flesh-and-blood counter-revolutionary straight out of the films on

* The titles of officers will only be re-established in October 1942.

the White Guards, who tells us to our faces that we have lost the war! What is there to say?

'You ought to have shot him,' Volodia, who is the first to pull himself together, says to me.

'Why me? You're a better shot. In fact it's your speciality.'

''Yes,' he admits. 'But you're the politico, and the fight against defeatists is your special responsibility.'

'You mean this creep's speech had no effect on you? That it's none of your business?'

'Leave it out,' Kola intervenes energetically. 'This isn't the Wehrmacht here. We don't fire on unarmed civilians. In any case he is now far away. Let's be on our way as well. We have already wasted enough time.'

Easier said than done. Which of us four knows how to drive a lorry? Here the discussion sours. They reproach me for not having learned to drive despite having ridden in this damned lorry so many times. How can they pretend to pilot a four-engined plane when they don't even know how to drive a wretched lorry. We outdo each other in futile recriminations – a pointless screaming match. In my view we ought to wait for a vehicle to arrive and ask the driver how to start the engine. 'A fine solution, very intelligent I must say!' Vassia mocks. 'Our driving instructor will come from this direction' (he indicates Pyatigorsk) 'and will be wearing the uniform of the Wehrmacht.' They plead with me to try and start it up; or else we are going to have to set off on foot. I agree to try. I pull the starter, depress the accelerator and release the handbrake, and – the vehicle slowly sets off! 'Bastard! You were having us on. You knew all along how to drive. You just wanted to be begged.' Heavens above! How had I ever been able to befriend these Cossack brutes? They don't seem to realize that if they carry on irritating me like this, we are all going to finish up in the ravine.

In fact I keep the situation under control only because the lorry won't go more quickly. It makes the decisions, and when I press my foot on the accelerator it simply responds with threatening noises. The traitor-driver had left it in first gear – at least this is what I think today – which allowed me to start off. As I don't know how to change into second or third however, I can't get it to run normally. Never mind. Let's go slowly. It is safer on this tortuous route, and it still beats going on foot. The others don't even seem to notice that anything is amiss. Vassia, the 'Elephant', is actually snoring in the cabin beside me. Kola is also sleeping, in the back, while Volidia, sitting behind me, is singing one of his ballads from the region of the Don in which a Cosatchka offers a ring to her Cossack and promises that, in a year's time, she will marry him. A thousand calamities follow – wars, floods, fogs – but the chorus comes back, always the same: the Cosatchka promises that, in a year's time, she will give herself to him. This melancholy song grates on my nerves. It seems to lack a conclusion. Did they sleep together? Were they happy? Did they row? Did they die?

'That's enough, Volodia! Wake Kola up and let's get down. I need advice.'

'Tut, tut. Are you thinking of running off as well?' he replies without laughing.

And to think that Volodia's best quality, in Nievka's opinion, apart from his singing voice, was his total lack of any malice. Perhaps though, in all innocence, he thinks that I am a potential deserter? I insist on apologies first of all, and then explain that our situation is getting worse by the hour. I sense that I am in the process of destroying the lorry and that it is certain that the rest of the 'eleventh' is no longer waiting for us at Pyatigorsk.

'Perhaps they will wait,' replies Kola. 'We are carrying the grub after all . . .'

'But going at this speed we won't get there until late tonight. And maybe later still!'

'What's the alternative?' Kola asks, and he cites the old Russian (or Cossack) saying that 'it is idle to complain about losing your hair when they are cutting your head off.' Right. If this is more or less the situation, my grumbles about the state of the lorry are foolish indeed. Let's set off again in first gear and not talk about it any more. Volodia is no longer singing. He is dozing like the others. You

159

would think that they were intent upon arriving on the Wehrmacht executioner's scaffold well rested.

In the distance, a sky filled with smoke announces Pyatigorsk. I have pulled off a real exploit: I know how to drive a lorry. I am a star player. It is incredible that such a trivial thing can make someone so happy. 'Hey! you bunch of timorous defeatists. Are your heads still firmly in place? I have brought you safely to port.' Instead of congratulating me, these rogues ask to stop once more. To do what? Aren't we late already? Of course. But they are Cossacks, and they must conduct the war with cunning and discernment. They do not intend to enter a burning town without first assuring themselves that it is in friendly hands. Volodia will go first to see what is happening. With such a shrewd head on his shoulders the mission belongs to him as of right. While waiting for him to return we shall examine more closely the contents of the boxes that we are transporting. For once there is no argument: we are all agreed.

The news that Volodia brings back, while not entirely disastrous, is very bad. The Germans haven't yet arrived in Pyatigorsk but our forces have already abandoned it; not merely the 'eleventh' of the VVS but also the military command, the civil administration and even the fire brigade. Part of the town is on fire, either as a result of aerial bombardment or because our own army has blown up industrial targets without observing due precautions. Crowds of disbanded soldiers of the 37th Army, which dispersed following the fall of Rostov on 23 July (and not on 1 August as we had been led to believe), have been left behind. They are starving and are prowling around in search of food. Meanwhile the Germans are at Min. Vody, in the form of a motorized column which will have to await the arrival of the bulk of their troops before advancing on Pyatigorsk. On the other hand, since the town is now defenceless, they might just as easily be planning a raid at any moment, to pick up the disbanded remnants of the 37th Army. We can't afford to delay: we shall have to cross Pyatigorsk quickly and press on towards

160

Nalchik. Everyone else is heading in the same direction.

I don't feel capable of driving our clapped out lorry through the crowd. We need a skilled driver to catch up with our unit and to avoid crushing these unfortunates who have been walking all the way from Rostov. There must be any number among them who would be happy to drive a lorry loaded with food. 'That's it! We'll place the lorry under their noses and give them a whiff of Kislovodsk sausage, then we'll question them one at a time on their driving abilities. The slight drawback here though is that they are armed and hungry.' Volodia, unquestionably, is looking for a fight. How would we be any better off by trying to drive at a snail's place through these hungry crowds? Vassia and Kola come down on my side: we shall look for a driver. First, though, we'll stash the lorry out of sight in a quiet street.

'Just a minute!' Kola says. He refuses, even in exceptional circumstances. to neglect his personal five-year plan for the elimination of suffering. He has discovered at the back of the lorry, right at the bottom, a case containing a roll of light woollen cloth intended for commanders' summer uniforms. We'll cut off a good length, and put the remainder back in place. The spoils of war, our strategic reserve, are for five: Kola is not forgetting Kostia, the 'Khan', even if he isn't here with us. We greatly regret his absence: it would take us less time to unload this ton and a half of goods from the lorry. The case that we want is right at the bottom. How had Kola discovered it? If he wasn't aware of it at the time of our departure from Kislovodsk then he must have an uncanny knack for ferreting these things out. Never mind. What's important is that he isn't mistaken. Now we can set off into Pyatigorsk in search of a quiet street and a good driver-mechanic.

It is the lorry, however, that once again decides for us. At the first square it stops dead, like a horse that refuses to approach a fire. All around us there is not a soul in sight. It's crazy: this town is twice the size of Kislovodsk, and its inhabitants must be hiding somewhere instead of fighting the fires. There can be no question of leaving the lorry unguarded however: Kola and Volodia stay in the back, rifles in hand. Vassia and I head towards the Nalchik road to try and find a driver.

We follow Volodia's directions. To get to the area where the soldiers are passing through we have to cross the city. It is a strange excursion around a town which, even more than Kislovodsk, has been celebrated by Mikhail Lermontov. Could he have imagined that it would one day burn down in this way, almost in silence, sadly, abandoned to looters? And what would Nievka have said about this humiliating spectacle? Perhaps it's just as well that she didn't come. 'Tell me, vagabond. Where are you from? What is your native land? . . .' sings Vassia, just as we are approaching the first vagabonds of the 37th Army.

Our undertaking is ridiculous. Volodia was right: it isn't all that easy to ask passers-by, one by one, if they know how to drive. Normally we would have had to present ourselves at the administrative section of the 37th Army, at least to a divisional or regimental command, but they have all evaporated. Perhaps they have already reached Nalchik and they are waiting for their troops there. The soldiers seem surprised by our questions and still more by the state of our uniforms. An abyss now separates those who, only the day before, were still sleeping in a bed, and these men who have been marching since 23 July. We soften the shock by offering them chocolate and cigarettes that we found in the lorry.

For a retreating army, night is the most favourable time for marching: the sky isn't full of enemy planes. A town abandoned by the authorities, however, automatically attracts errant troops, some of whom use the respite, the vacuum of authority thus created, to rest up. Vassia dismisses my objections to the risk we are taking of getting lost in these identical streets. His sense of direction is infallible, or so he alleges. The Cossack identity, would you believe it, exists after all. You have only to look at Vassia, if you need convincing; a novice who behaves as if he had been a soldier all his life. This ghost-town doesn't bother him at all. The older members of his tribe have described similar situations to him from childhood, in order to prepare him for such shocks. He doesn't even react when I point out to him a slogan chalked on the wall: '*Russe Kaput.*' 'You don't win wars by writing on walls,' he concludes serenely. True. It is demoralizing none the less. Even before the Germans arrive someone is already scribbling their slogans on the walls. I don't remember ever having seen the like of it in Poland in September 1939. And to think that only the day before we were celebrating my birthday with Nievka without suspecting for a moment that someone was writing '*Russe Kaput*' behind our backs!

We meet a group of *tchernomortzy*, Black Sea sailors. Had their fleet been dispersed along with the 37th Army? It is clear they have been doing some serious drinking. They don't seem in any hurry and are singing – out of tune – that 'a Russian sailor never surrenders to the enemy'. Vassia exchanges a few words with them but is careful not to ask them if they know how to drive. He wouldn't take any *tchernomortzy* with us for anything in the world, even if they were sober. They are notorious brawlers, and have a very exclusive esprit de corps. He has seen the *tchernomortzy* in action in Taganrog, the port closest to Rostov, and has no wish to repeat the experience. Prudence above everything: this is the first principle of the art of warfare.

'Hey, you bum! Hold on a minute!' Vassia calls after a figure in uniform about 20 metres in front of us. The man turns round and obeys. It's a colonel! From the back Vassia couldn't identify him because the insignia of rank are worn on the collar of the tunic. How is he going to react to this salute? A colonel without troops is only a man like any other, and in a dark street, he tends to take account of the number and size of his interlocutors. Faced with an outsize Vassia he prefers not to be too touchy. So much the better. Yet it is also demoralizing: is it still an army if you can get away with hailing colonels like that?

We're in luck: the colonel does indeed drive and it would suit him perfectly to travel in a lorry with us. Mission accomplished. We return to the vehicle. I had been proven right against Volodia's pessimism and I recover my good humour. En route we tell a lengthy story to the colonel and pretend that we have killed the traitor-driver much as you would put down a mad dog. The colonel has his own worries, however. He is preoccupied by the lack of fighting spirit among certain detachments which are dispersing with the conviction that the sheer size of the country will be enough to defeat the enemy.

The colonel is called N.N. Tretiakov, as in the famous art gallery in Moscow. It's a name that is easy to remember and it inspires confidence. He doesn't manage, however, to start the engine. He reverts to his habits of command and orders us to push the lorry near to a burning house so as to be able to see what's up. To find the toolbox he has us unload, once more, most of the cargo, and he gives me a thorough dressing-down because I should have 'given the lorry some water' – as if it were a horse. Finally, having decreed that the damage is irreparable – something having leaked from the engine and caused it to seize up – he raises his voice: 'Burn everything. We mustn't leave anything to Jerry. That's an order.'

A short while ago he was wandering around in the streets of Pyatigorsk – and in the wrong direction as well, with his back to the Nalchik road – and now he has the cheek to fire orders at us. Since we have no spare colonel, however, we are obliged to deal with N.N. Tretiakov. Kola respectfully explains that we will have to have a written order. Our hierarchy is in general very exacting, and will be even more so over a question of food intended for 500 pilots. The word 'food' seems to sway the colonel. He changes tack and suggests an arrangement. He is not altogether alone; his men are sleeping in a courtyard in Pyatigorsk, near some horses which are resting. We could travel on the *telega* (a large wooden cart), and carry at least some of the provisions from the lorry. At this he goes off in search of his men, leaving us to hold another council of war.

Vassia is not at all impressed by N.N. Tretiakov. He's not a real soldier, he says, he's an engineer who has been given his stripes on that account. His argument is double-edged: it is not clear that a career soldier is better qualified than a technician to repair a lorry. Volodia has another idea: we could lighten the lorry's load and tow it to Nalchik. Kola is sceptical. He suggests that I draft the written

164

order, since I have the most readable handwriting, and have it ready for the colonel to sign. The rest is merely idle chatter. 'One day we'll get back from Jerry a far better lorry than this old heap,' he says, proving that even if he has given up his Cossack identity, he has shed none of its fantasy. For you would need a fair amount of it on this night in Pyatigorsk, against this backdrop of *'Russe Kaput'*, the writing on the wall, to be able to talk about the trophies that we shall be taking from the Wehrmacht. I lack his imagination and my defeatist presentiments are only aggravated when the colonel's *telega* arrives. It is three-quarters full of the five occupants' baggage and is drawn by a single horse, the most skeleton-like specimen in all of Russia.

Not to worry, the Mietchotkians say, we shall all go on foot and load the *telega* with sugar, *soukhari* (biscuits) and tobacco only. In respect of the lorry we are covered: N.N. Tretiakov has signed everything, in duplicate to boot. Let's carry on then, to Nalchik. Time is pressing, that's for sure. We have emerged rather well from our first test as soldiers. 'Cheer up, *polit-liotchik*,' Vassia says, giving me a friendly pat on the back. The others also encouraged me: having noticed that I am somewhat down in the mouth they assume that it's because of the loss of the lorry.

It isn't that at all. It is this Nalchik Road, packed with a retreating army, which reminds me of Poland in September 1939. I am overcome with a sudden wave of awful gloom, and I think of my family, especially my mother, who had had this presentiment that we would never see each other again. Oughtn't I to have stayed with her instead of chasing defeat in Russia? Then I cast a last glance on Pyatigorsk, all in grey as day breaks, remembering Nievka, sadly. How many times had she asked me to take her to visit this town! I always promised her I would 'next week', 'later on' . . . I behaved like a filthy egoist towards Nievka, and now fate is punishing me. 'Cheer up, *polit-liotchik*! You mustn't regret our swopping a useless lorry for a good *telega*.' This time however I get angry: 'Stop calling me *polit-liotchik*. You aren't Raia, and we aren't drunk either.' Vassia is not wanting in tact: he will never call me that name again.

Nevertheless, the three centuries of battles that he carries in his veins prompt him to offer me some sound advice: 'You must give up all thought of women during the war. They'll be there after the war is over.'

Where can all these servicemen come from, wearing the colours of the different armed forces, mounted on improvised vehicles, perched on *telegi*, or on foot, and advancing as slowly as a funeral procession? I imagine that these dispersed elements of the 37th Army – and of several other army divisions – flowed back towards the south, over the vast plain between Rostov and the foothills of the Caucasus, across the fields, like thousands of uncontrollable streams, before joining up in Min. Vody. Here, between Pyatigorsk and Nalchik, there is only one route, a simple country road twisting in and out of the gentle slopes which lead to the mountains. The distance to be covered is not enormous: 100 or 150 kilometres – no one seems to know exactly – but it is obvious that at this pace, with the enemy in control of the air, this march is becoming a dangerous folly.

My experience in Poland in 1939 has served me well and my three companions are agreed. They are airmen as well as Cossacks and they know the implacable laws of the 'war of engines'. Kola alone is reticent when we discuss taking one of the small paths that link up the mountain villages. He is lazy by inclination and thinks, or hopes, that our planes will give us air cover and allow us to arrive in two or three days, without too great an effort. Our baggage and food supplies appear to him to be lighter on Colonel Tretiakov's *telega* than on our backs. In any case we will at least need to get hold of a map of the area if we are not to be setting out blindly into the unknown. But we search for a map in vain: nobody has one. They are all in Nalchik in the hands of authorized personnel. For want of anything better, Vassia manages to get hold of a small compass in exchange for half a packet of *Kazbek*.

We have the feeling that there is no hurry. The hours pass by; the sun climbs higher. It is warm and the sky remains empty. Our spirits pick up. On the whole, the outcome of the business with the lorry is not without its advantages, and to travel with Colonel Tretiakov is almost a pleasure. He pays no attention whatever to our dishevelled appearance, and Kola suggests that he wouldn't intervene even if we chose to march in our underwear. He has hardly finished with these wry reflections when we are under attack from the sky. Pilots of the Luftwaffe may not get up early but once they start, they work with determination.

The first raid is worthy of an airshow: everything is done for dazzling effect. One after the other 12 aeroplanes dive straight at us, making as if to land on the road, climb up again at full throttle, turn and descend once again to pass low over our heads. The din of their engines would waken the dead, and among the living it creates a fair panic. Above us these Luftwaffe aces must be chuckling at the sight of horses rearing up, carts turned over, the mad scramble of soldiers searching for cover among the bushes on the highly exposed slopes. Curiously, they don't bomb the road, as if they want to keep it intact for their own motorized columns. There isn't even any machine-gun fire, perhaps because they have run out of ammunition or, more simply, do not want to damage potential prisoners. I end up thinking that by some sort of telepathy, and out of a sense of solidarity among pilots, they have only made this showpiece raid to encourage us to get off this road before they return with more murderous intent.

After such a harrowing experience order returns slowly to our ranks. I take the advantage of the pause to talk to a civilian refugee whom I have met near a *telega* full of women dressed in black, carrying children in their arms. I know from experience that a retreating army doesn't like to be restricted in its movements and I decide to alert these people to the dangers they might be facing. The Soviet equivalent of Sergeant-major Bartczak would be perfectly capable of ordering one of these women to strangle her child, lest a simple cry should bring the squadrons of the Luftwaffe down on him. The man to whom I give the friendly advice not to continue along this dangerous road has a strangely young face, with an abundant white head of hair. He gives me a kindly smile which doesn't detract from the sadness of his expression, and explains to me that they are all Jews and therefore haven't any choice. 'The Germans are killing all of us without distinction, men and women, young and old alike. In every town and city large or small, they round up the Jews, take them to the fields and force them to dig communal graves, in which they are buried after being shot. It's happening everywhere in the same way: in the Ukraine, in Byelorussia, in the Don region. Everywhere the Wehrmacht passes through they leave behind them communal graves of massacred Jews.'

I feel myself go pale as if my Jewish identity, for so long hidden in my unconscious, has suddenly revealed itself. My blood runs even colder than it did during the Luftwaffe raid. The man with the strange face doesn't seem to notice. He introduces himself and carries on with his macabre story. He is the leader of a small Jewish community in Sablinsk, a small market town near Stavropol. I am unsure whether he was a rabbi or lay-president because, in the meantime, the first shock over, I am trying to find ways to doubt what he has just revealed to me. It is nothing less than the genocide of the Jews, even if he hasn't used the word, that he has just announced to me on this 5 August 1942. Without proof, you can't accept so horrific a statement from the mouth of a stranger. To strengthen my internal resistance, and also to give courage to the man from Sablinsk, I undertake, with as much tact as possible, to explain the danger of forming a general rule on the basis of a few isolated instances. I concede that in December 1941, at the time of its offensive in eastern Crimea, the Red Army actually did discover a communal grave of the Jews of Kerch. The Soviet government revealed it immediately to the entire world and denounced the ferocity of the Nazis. And at around the same time, in Byelorussia, the Germans raped and hung in a public square, in front of their jubilant troops, a young girl of 18 years, Zoia Kosmodemianskaia, and another, younger still, whose name escapes me. We can clearly

168

infer from this that these men are barbarians, but we cannot deduce from it that they hang all 18-year-old girls. 'The young girls, no. But they are killing all the Jews,' the man from Sablinsk replies.

Where does his certainty come from? He can't be better informed than the entire world. Bielokonienko, for example, received the Tass special bulletin with the dispatches of foreign news agencies. He doesn't. I question him politely, not wanting to give offence, and especially not to give the impression that I am trying to send him back where he came from. I help him to rearrange his *telega* while listening to him speak about the witnesses to these massacres of Jews, survivors from such and such a place who have reported to him this awful news which he now considers irrefutable.

The women remain apart. They listen to the conversation without becoming involved in it. They have marked oriental features but their clothes, especially their way of covering their head and hiding almost all the face, make them resemble Caucasian Muslims rather than Jews. The children, who tug at their mothers' long black skirts, seem very quiet for their age, as if they are afraid of crying or running about. They are on their way to Georgia where a large Jewish community awaits them and will be able to help. Already, however, their *telegi*, about 20 in all, have got separated from each other; some have got lost among the crowd of soldiers. Have they at least something to eat? The man from Sablinsk thanks me. They get by; they have few needs. Their only problem is the slow pace along this congested road, and, obviously, fear of machine-gun fire. 'Here at least we have a chance of escaping, whereas the Wehrmacht means certain death for us.'

He has no questions of his own to ask. He addresses me formally, thinking perhaps that he is speaking to a commander because of my well-cut, dark blue uniform. Had we continued together along this road I would certainly have told him about myself. But I already see in the distance that the Mietchotkians have taken their rifles and packs from Tretiakov's *telega*. We are going to try our luck on the mountain footpath. When I explain it to the man from Sablinsk, his face brightens up, and suddenly, in a voice that has become firm and decisive, he says to me: 'You are defending a just cause, my riend, *moi droug*, and God will reward you for it. You'll get out of this war unharmed.'

My face reddens. Such a prediction sounds extremely encouraging. But immediately the atheist in me starts to laugh: these believers are extraordinary; their God is incapable of protecting them and yet he confides the future of others to them! Later though, in each difficult situation, the message of the man from Sablinsk comes back to me and brings me comfort.

All four of us climb the gentle slope between the Nalchik road and the mountains. En route I describe my conversation to the Mietchotkians; it has badly upset me. 'If things go badly for us,' I say to them, 'you will end up doing forced labour in Germany; for me it will be the communal grave straightaway.' Kola loses his patience and snaps at my credulity, saying that the story is farfetched and cannot be verified. Since the Germans certainly are savage, they may have massacred the Jews of Kerch for a thousand reasons that elude civilized people, but there can be no question of their having established a system aimed at exterminating all the Jews, or any other people for that matter. In modern times, by virtue of its labour power, humanity provides the surplus value necessary to capital: to kill people systematically would be like killing the goose that lays the golden eggs.

Vassia and Volodia, who were formed in the same school, support Kola. Their history teacher at Mietchotka had demonstrated, with arithmetical rigour, the laws which brought wars of extermination to a halt. At a certain epoch, in the terribly remote past, humanity managed to produce only the basic minimum necessary to its subsistence. Thus the winners in a tribal war had no incentive to take prisoners, and they exterminated the vanquished tribe. Later, however, with the development of the productive forces, wars had as their objective the taking of prisoners and their transformation into slaves. The latter were squeezed like lemons, and from their suffering sprang up the Pyramids and other monuments of antiquity. Whence the inexorable if somewhat peremptory conclusion: the

Nazis' plan of once more reducing conquered peoples to slavery is monstrous enough, without crediting them with the intention of turning back the clock of history even further.

'You will be our Ursus, if we become slaves,' I say to Vassia, who walks in front and is blocking my view of the horizon, such is the height and especially the breadth of the man – he is a good 10 or 15 centimetres taller than the rest of us. He declines the role of the hero of Sienkiewicz's *Quo Vadis* however, and declares instead that he will be Spartacus, a fighter and not a martyr. His quip cheers us up. Yes, we shall sell our lives clearly. We shall fight and fight, and none of us will end up in a communal grave.

In the meantime we have only one worry: we are overloaded. Our guns are as heavy as they are out of date, and we are also carrying all of our winter gear – at least 20 kilos worth – poorly packed into rucksacks which press painfully against the shoulders. As we had transport, we left almost nothing behind us in Kislovodsk. I have even brought with me the outsize underwear that Moussia gave to me and, obviously, all the presents from Nievka. To throw these objects out on to the roadside would be unthinkable. It would bring us bad luck and would be unworthy of the traditions of the region of the Don. Now to this burden is added the weight of our food supplies. We haven't taken very much, counting on the proverbial hospitality of the inhabitants of the Caucasus, but even this is too much to carry. We pause every half hour, twice as often as during a normal march. Here, rising up on the horizon above us, is the outline of an *aoul*, a Caucasian village. It is well situated and seems to have a pleasant aspect; perhaps we shall find some good strong string there, or sacks that are better suited to our backs.

The time we spent studying for the baccalauréat is not so long ago – a year in my case, two years for the others – but a world already separates us from it. Tolstoy's stories no longer whirl about in our heads. All that was needed to efface them were the cold shivers that the traitor-driver produced in us, or the inscription '*Russe Kaput*', and especially the story told by the man from Sablinsk. The horrors of war now cut close to the bone. The signs are there and accumulate from day to day. Nievka had often spoken to me about other people's sufferings but I had paid little attention. They appeared abstract, because my unit was to go into action in the second phase of the war. The latter has now begun, sooner than we expected and in a place that we would never have imagined. We don't fully grasp it, however, and we don't want to think too much about it. Since the Nalchik road appears dangerous to us, we plunge further into the heart of the Caucasus without even asking ourselves why the other 'runaways' don't do likewise. We are happy not to have any superiors, to be able to decide everything for ourselves and to embark on an adventure that we can later boast about to our friends.

Wouldn't it be wonderful to meet one of those Cherkess horsemen in black capes and silver-plated arms, at a turning on the path, above a rocky peak? Perhaps a Cherkessian lady of staggering beauty would be sitting astride behind him. . . . We would give a warm reception to this free-spirited and audacious woman, and we wouldn't call her 'shameless' as, in former times, Count Tolstoy did.

In fact we aren't really hoping for anything of the sort, having learned already to mistrust our dreams as much as our fears. In the space of a few days we are going to cross a very poor, inward-looking region. Much later I shall find out that some months after we passed through it, a tragedy would overtake this part of the Caucasus. We had no intuition of it, nor did those who were to be its victims. Ever since I learned of it, our war has also appeared to me in the light of a cruel deceit. And yet at the time it was very real for us. Men, lives, paths to follow; it was all true.

In the village, which we reached after a march of four hours, there are no men in black capes nor even responsible officials dressed in a more recent Soviet style. The women are covered from head to toe, and on seeing us they rush with precipitate haste to lock themselves indoors with their children. Some of them take their goats indoors to be on the safe side. Kola is the most widely read in the literary classics and decrees that we must find the *metchet*, the mosque, the centre of Caucasian village social life. But he doesn't remember how to distinguish the *metchet* from the other dwellings. In Tolstoy, there are Muslims but also *staro-viery* (old believers) who broke with the Orthodox Church because of its compromises. Vassia bursts out laughing: he is ignorant where literature is concerned and has no arguments with which to counter Kola on Tolstoy. He is certain of one thing however: 'These people are not *staro-viery*, nor Christians of any other persuasion.'

A small group of barefoot youngsters follows us with curiosity but doesn't dare approach. As soon as we take a step in their direction they scatter. The only interlocutors left to us are some old people who have neither the strength to run nor a great desire to talk. Who is the village chief? What is your nationality? It is impossible to get the slightest response. They don't understand – or no longer understand – a single word of Russian, even pronounced slowly, and accompanied by a mime worthy of the Moscow Art Theatre.

The poverty of the place is striking. You breathe from the very air a sense of what is later to be called the Third World. It doesn't even occur to us to ask for food and hospitality from people who are so poor. Nevertheless we are at war and need information. Did the authorities leave because of the enemy's approach? Is the enemy coming from the west or from some other direction? Are there any men hiding in the forest waiting to organize a guerilla force? Unable to communicate with the old men we set an ambush for a youngster about 10 or 12 years old, who in theory ought to speak Russian, since both school attendance and the teaching of Russian are compulsory. A waste of time: the boy screams like someone possessed and the women of the village reappear to give him courage. Although they keep their faces hidden they don't disguise their anger. OK. We understand. We're going. We'll have better luck at the next village.

The only track leads, unfortunately, towards the west while Nalchik is to the south. At the first fork we take a still narrower path that we have to follow in single file and which, some kilometres further on, disappears in the middle of a meadow. Perfidious

Caucasians! You would swear that they deliberately planned these paths leading nowhere in order to waste our time and to increase our sense of insecurity. Our plan seems a good one, however, since we can no longer hear the drone of enemy aircraft. But we are too far away from the road, cut off from any news about developments in the battle, and plunged into a strangely calm, sleepy countryside. How could we have known that the villages here are built so far away from the main axis of communication and at such a great distance from each other?

We reach the next village, five hours' march later, at nightfall, and find two old men who reply without hesitation that they are Balkars and Muslims. After this promising beginning, their Russian dries up. Where are the leaders of their kolkhoz? '*Da da kolkhoz.*' What news is there of the war? '*Voina plokho, plokho.*' It is anyone's guess whether this *plokho* (bad) applies to the war (*voina*) in general or to the day's events. In telling us their nationality, however, they at least confirm that we are on the right road, and enable us to situate ourselves within the RSFSR (Russian Soviet Federative Socialist Republic) which includes the whole of the northern and central Caucasus even though the Russian population is conspicuous by its absence. Because of their national identity, the indigenous peoples were given a degree of autonomy on the regional administrative level as ASSRs (Autonomous Soviet Socialist Republics), but are always twinned: the Karachay and the Cherkess, the Kabardinos and the Balkars, the Chechens and the Ingush, and so on. No doubt this is to prevent further administrative fragmentation and to discourage any nationalist temptation. In practice, however, this twinning doesn't facilitate the task of intruders, like us, who have a very poor idea of where they are and with whom they have to deal.

Thanks to the old men in the second village we are now certain that we have left the Autonomous Region of the Karachay (and the Cherkess) and that we are indeed headed towards Nalchik, the capital of the Kabardino–Balkar ASSR. We even receive some advice on which road to take to avoid both forests and some of the more

174

abrupt mountain slopes. They do not invite us to spend the night in their village however. To tell the truth we wouldn't have accepted anyway. Vassia, always supported in this by Volodia, mistrusts these Muslims. This is because his grandfather – or perhaps his father – was a veteran of the Russo–Turkish wars, and apparently told him a thing or two about the Persians. For us, the Caucasian Muslims are all Persians. We say this without pejorative connotations, since their civilization is prestigious, but at the same time make childish puns: the diminutive of *Perse* (Persian) gives *persiki* (peaches).

Vassia takes his mistrust to the point of wanting to post a guard over our camp. Kola fortunately opposes him. 'These Persians are not our enemies,' he says firmly. 'The Revolution happened here too.' We press close to each other in our greatcoats and all four of us fall asleep at once. Not for long, alas. The Caucasian mountains are a paradise for nocturnal insects. They have less bite than Siberian mosquitoes, but they are specialists at imitating the menacing noises of hostile men. They poison all the nights of our long march, which are disturbed by nightmares and startled awakenings. We spend only one night under cover in an abandoned hut between two villages. Even here I dream that I see the Germans in front of the doorway. 'Let's get away through the window,' I cry out in my sleep, and the other three respond by sliding like snakes through a miniscule skylight. They are so pleased to find no one outside that they don't even complain about my talking in my sleep.

Our most serious problem is lack of food. Our provisions have lasted for only 48 hours. From the third morning Vassia resorts to strong-arm tactics in the villages, and manages to get us some tea, goat's milk and a small quantity of an odd sort of crumbly cheese. Try as he might, however, for something more substantial, by waving his gun about and shouting 'boom-boom', the Persians have nothing else to offer. Kola's attempt to exchange some winter clothes for food is a failure. The two of us enter unarmed into the Balkars' houses and we come back out without even proposing a barter: the stench of mutton fat proves too much for us. Their homes rest on bare earth and seem to us to be horrendously dirty. 'Russian, if you cherish the house where your mother has raised you . . .' Kola, with a taste for irony, recites this opening line of a poem by Simonov as he leaves one of them. He explains that in Russia you find all sorts, and that those of us who have been brought up under a wooden roof couldn't possibly eat the food of people who don't even have a floor.

Our situation begins to improve when we discover fields of melons and water-melons. They are hardly larger than grapefruit, and we are afraid that they might not even be edible, but they turn out to be delicious. We eat loads of them, devastating each field like locusts. There is no question of taking any with us. We are overloaded, and there is no guarantee that we shall find any more further ahead. The nutritive value of meals eaten in the locust style is doubtful to say the least.

It is the dead calm of the countryside which is driving us mad. According to our calculations we ought to be in Nalchik, or at least close enough to hear the sound of enemy aircraft. How is it that not the slightest sign of war reaches us? And suppose that my bad dream had been a premonition, and that the Germans, now masters of the region, are going to catch up with us at the next village or even before then? The silence of these unguarded fields and these almost deserted mountains presages nothing favourable for we four vegetarian sleepwalkers, who have left the war rather as you might leave the auditorium of a theatre during the interval. We have surely taken the wrong turning. But where? Could our Russian-speaking Balkars have intentionally pointed wrong paths out to us in order to keep us from our objective?

We also lack a leader. In wartime, even when there are only four of you, someone has to give orders. Now Kola, a natural and undisputed leader, no longer exercises his leadership. He sulks, and recalls at every opportunity that he had from the outset been against this detour across unknown countryside. His answers henceforth are all in the negative. Should we get rid of some of our baggage? No: it would be a waste. Ought we then to retrace our route or march east to rejoin the main road? No: it would be sheer folly. . . . In fact a situation without alternatives doesn't suit Kola's genius. He is great when it is a matter of choosing the best solution from a whole range of possibilities, when he is surrounded by a lot of people. There are some to attract, others to win to one side or another, yet others to neutralize. . . . In these situations his cunning never lets him down. He has flair. He knows how to think of a 'cushy' way out for himself and his followers. Kola, in short, needs a field of action and not a field of water melons, where he limits himself to reciting his macabre expression about heads being cut off, and even manages to discourage me, his faithful follower.

Our chief warrior is indisputably Vassia, a serene elephant, sure of his strength and of his mastery of the military arts. Fatigue never catches up with him. He could march for 18 hours a day without even feeling the weight of his awkward rucksack, his rifle, or anything else. We wouldn't of course be able to keep up with him at this pace. We belong to another category of men. Volodia, the one most attached to Vassia, his shadow and his best counsellor, permits himself occasionally to shout at him and invites him to stop setting the pace a kilometre ahead of us. Vassia, however, is a slow-witted sort who is lacking in spirited repartee and who often provokes useless rows.

On the morning of the fifth day – or was it the sixth? – a miracle happens. In a meadow, far from any village, a white horse awaits us. It isn't grazing. It is standing upright and its gaze is an invitation. From time to time, it shakes its tail to chase the insects away but no doubt also to show, in the manner of a dog, that it is contented. In a trice Vassia is beside it. He caresses it and checks it over. Could the animal perhaps be lame? Otherwise why would it have been left alone, untied? No, it isn't lame, but it isn't abandoned either. A small Persian with wrinkled features, his head enveloped in a kind of turban, emerges from the other end of the field and cries out in Russian, '*Kogn moi*!' ('the horse is mine'). This doesn't deter Vassia, who replies to him with affected politeness that the animal is not a *kogn*, but a *lochad*, a style of horse suited to work in the fields rather than the kind bred for the cavalry or for racing. The other persists for want of vocabulary: '*Kogn moi, kogn moi!*' Vassia claims that he had led this *lochad* all the way from his *stanitsa* Mietchotka, and protests that he is not about to leave it in this insect-infested field. The Persian is obstinate: '*Kogn moi, kogn moi!*' The poor man. He resembles so little the horsemen of Tolstoy's tales!

Very well then, let's fight fair. Vassia suggests a test of loyalty. They will place themselves at equal distances from the horse, each at different sides of the meadow, and they will call the animal. The horse will designate its legitimate owner by going towards him. The Persian understands the challenge and, having nothing to lose, accepts it. Each of them takes up the agreed positions and calls in his own language, modulating his voice the better to attract the horse. The *kogn*, alias *lochad*, doesn't move straight away. It hesitates, listens, turns its head towards first one and then the other; then slowly, it heads toward Vassia. It is ours, and of its own free will too! We have defended, in a Caucasian meadow, the right of animals to self-determination. The man who had shouted '*kogn moi*' disappears as silently as he had come.

Vassia, transported with joy, does a victory lap to thank his supporters. After it he packs our arms and baggage expertly on to the horse, and, like a commander-in-chief, orders us: 'Forward march! Day and night without a halt as far as Nalchik!' We set off without demur, having no wish to spoil the good atmosphere. In addition, as soon as we are relieved of the weight of our rucksacks, we discover that this corner of the Caucasus is very beautiful, most appropriate to a pleasant march.

'You ought to have entered the cavalry,' I say to Vassia to congratulate him.

'It's what my parents had planned for me. I was barely three years old when they put me on a horse without a saddle and had me grip it by the mane; then they set it off.'

'Oh, come on now, you're exaggerating. I've seen professional cowboys in American westerns who have real problems in controlling their horses in a rodeo. A three-year-old youngster would be thrown to the ground like a sack of potatoes!'

My scepticism drives him into a fury. He doesn't want to hear about either westerns or rodeos, and he calls upon Kola and Volodia to confirm his story. At the time they were of the same age as Vassia – three years old – and I doubt if they can remember his exploit. But, for the sake of peace, they agree with him.

I have a word with Kola about more serious matters. Shouldn't we have compensated this poor sod, left him a few roubles, some tobacco or a warm piece of clothing? Kola hesitates for a while but argues that the circumstances hardly lent themselves to such a gesture, and that it wouldn't have changed anything. After the war, we shall come back here and repay our debt. In the meantime are we simply thieves? 'You mustn't exaggerate,' he replies serenely. 'We are also fighting for this Caucasian, which gives us certain rights. And until the coming of the communist society no one can be totally honest.'

A precious companion and a sturdy carrier, the handsome Balkar horse will not remain ours for long. It will leave us near Nalchik without even saying goodbye, but its bid for self-determination will for years to come enjoy a place of pride in the repertoire of our Caucasian yarns, winning widespread appreciation. We enriched it with elements of suspense, including storms and German patrols following hot on our heels, in order to enhance the intelligence of an animal which had known how to make the right choice. The role of the man who cried '*kogn moi*' was impossible to ameliorate and therefore remained comic – the lot of losers. A Russian would not have fared any better than the Persian had done, in a contest with Vassia backed up by the three of us, all armed. Our laughter, therefore, was not anti-Balkar; in fact, by repeating this popular story we became attached to its protagonist and, by extension, to his compatriots. Even Vassia, who had previously been the most mistrustful, ended up declaring that the Balkars had nothing in common with the Turks – his grandfather's enemies – and that on the contrary they had come to take shelter in the Caucasus – God knows when – in order to flee from the Turks. Given this, nothing prevented us from adopting them as 'our Persians' and raising our glasses to their good health at the time of the victory celebrations.

But at that time, in 1945, the Balkars were no longer in Balkaria. Stalin had deported them one year after the battle for the Caucasus, along with the Kalmyks, the Karachay, the Chechen and the Ingush, all of them Muslims. The operation was conducted in the greatest secrecy between September 1943 and April 1944, and involved some 800,000 people of both sexes and all ages. Events taking place on such a scale could not pass unnoticed, and they were in fact marked by an amendment to the name of the administrative territory. The Kabardino–Balkar ASSR became simply the Kabardino ASSR. We were already far away by then, however, and knew nothing about it. We spoke of 'our Balkars' only to amuse our audience with this story of the horse that had been stolen with its own consent.

I learned of the tragedy of the Balkars in 1956. Nikita Krushchev, in his secret report to the Twentieth Congress of the Communist Party of the USSR, revealed that Stalin had held the people of the northern Caucasus collectively responsible for 'acts committed by certain individuals or groups', and had submitted all of them to a harsh regime of 'poverty and suffering'. Krushchev condemned this repression, which he described as 'inadmissible not only for a Marxist–Leninist but also for anyone of good sense'. The secret report stops there. Some pertinent lines on the principles of the deportation follow, but they are too short to explain what really happened in the northern Caucasus in 1943–4. Ever since 1956 silence has once again cloaked the subject: not a single book or study, not a single victim's testimony has been published in the USSR. 'Our Balkars' had the right to Moscow's official commiseration only for the space of an afternoon, and behind closed doors, given that Krushchev's report was never made public.

Another deported people, the Crimean Tatars, were even more badly treated. Krushchev 'forgot' to speak about them to the Twentieth Party Congress and didn't authorize them – as he did the Caucasians – to return to their homes or what remained of them.

These 'reject people' (aided by dissidents such as Alexander Nekrich or Pyotr Grigorenko), have, since that time, been the only ones to break through the official silence. Their testimony is frightening: half of their people perished during deportation. Everything leads one to fear that the story was the same for the Caucasians, and that they were all victims of a policy of genocide.

What had they done to attract Stalin's thunderbolts? We crossed Kabardino–Balkar for a period of eight days, shortly before the arrival of the Germans. Their patrols weren't hot on our heels as we were later to pretend in order to give ourselves airs, but the Wehrmacht wasn't far away. For 'certain individuals' or 'certain groups' among the Balkars now was the moment to commit 'hostile acts'. Had they been so inclined we would not have left their villages and mountains alive. Aware in advance of the routes we were taking and often knowing where we were going to camp for the night, they would have had no difficulty in either annihilating us in a surprise attack or in taking us prisoners and capturing our arms. They did nothing of the kind. And the coolness that was evident, a certain degree of mistrust the people showed towards us, is easily explained by the fact – we are witnesses to this as well – that, at the moment of danger, all the authorities in the region had disappeared, leaving 'our Balkars' to their fate.

I can't say whether they received the Germans with flowers. They certainly hadn't many reasons for liking the USSR: the great Russian Soviet Republic had incorporated them in order to swallow them up and prolong their former colonization. It is perhaps even because these 'Mohammedans' constituted the flagrant and unacceptable proof of this fact that Stalin had resolved to deport them at the first opportunity. The Christian minorities of the Caucasus were allowed to stay put. The Orthodox Church, restored to a place of honour in the name of patriotic unity, and infiltrated with NKVD agents, watched over them.

In the spring of 1981, in Ordzhonikidze, in Ossetia, which had in theory been spared the round-up of 1943, violent incidents broke out in which former Muslim deportees fought Christians who had occupied their homes. The battle is thought to have lasted several days; troops had to intervene, and the news eventually filtered abroad. It is clear from this that the problem of the returning Muslims is still not resolved a quarter of a century after Krushchev's secret report, and that the victims nurse a grievance against those who benefited by their misfortune. It is possible that Stalin's attempt to 'de-islamicize' the Caucasian ASSRs of the great Russian Republic, will, in the end, lead to a war of religion in the area. And yet 'anyone of good sense' (Krushchev's words) ought to understand that such great injustices scar those who have suffered them, and that they do not assess them simply as regrettable historical aberrations to be forgotten in silence.

'Our' Balkars were able to return to their homes. They are once again, alongside the Kabardinos, jointly recognized as the citizen residents of their ASSR. On the official map of the USSR nothing has changed, and I have no difficulty in retracing our itinerary of the month of August 1942. I still have two regrets: that I didn't note the names of the villages, and that I played a part in stealing a handsome white horse from one of their people.

We can tell from the thickness of the smoke rising towards the sky that we are approaching Nalchik, the capital of the Kabardino–Balkars. We can see it from the mountain slopes at a distance of 15 to 20 kilometres. In August 1942 all of the Caucasus is on fire. Crossing Pyatigorsk had given us some idea of the possibilities for foraging in abandoned towns ravaged by fire. In Nalchik we shall head directly for the *Miasso-Combinat*, the great municipal meat factory. Our stomachs, which have had enough of a vegetarian diet, dictate this plan and we quicken our pace as at the sight of a mirage. Once we reach the town we shall separate; the first to scent the smell of sausage meat will alert the others by firing three shots into the air. And after Nalchik? We'll see. . . . Someone will give us proper directions. The Caucasus is a big place and we have enough time to think about it. Meanwhile we are fully resolved upon looting, having forgotten the contemptuous fashion in which we treated the retreating soldiers in Pyatigorsk.

Suddenly, two Luftwaffe planes dive at us. Vassia runs to take cover behind a tree, first taking our baggage from the horse's back with quick, skilful movements. Frightened by the noise, the animal gallops off. It passes in front of the rest of us, as we lie huddled in a ditch. Go on, then, handsome Balkar horse, you served us well, but watch out because these Luftwaffe swine fire on everything that moves; whether you are a *kogn* or a *lochad* makes no difference to them! Vassia thinks that instinct will guide the animal back to its meadow and to its rightful owner. Let's hope he's right!

When we resume our march at nightfall our baggage seems to be heavier than ever. I suggest storing it with an inhabitant of Nalchik. The others scoff at the idea and don't even deign to reply. What's so funny? Many of our things have only a sentimental value. And it isn't all that unthinkable to find an honest citizen in this country. Volodia gently interrupts me: 'Don't waste your breath in talking about such things!' He doesn't spare his own breath, however, for he breaks into one of these pilot's songs exalting their magnificent aeroplanes and praising the sky, their 'fatherland'. This of course is very apt when you have a 20 kilo rucksack on your back and the prospect of a race on foot across the Great Caucasus!

As we approach Nalchik, we meet other marchers. We shall not be the only ones who are looking for the meat factory. I am afraid of getting lost. I don't have the Cossacks' sense of direction, and the idea of finding myself alone in this country scares me. All my fears are unfounded however: Nalchik is not Pyatigorsk. Vagabondage is forbidden; helmeted patrols stop and question each group of soldiers; orders rain down anew; the army becomes the army once more. Let's button our uniform collars, quickly, the farce is over.

These patrols treat us with consideration because of our dark blue uniforms. Without even asking us the number of our unit they point out to us the spot where the VVS is quartered. Who would have believed that our lads were still here? Quickly, then, back into the fold. The war is a collective business after all. Fine, but my situation is not the same as that of my three companions: I am not a trainee pilot in whom the Red Army has invested a lot of money. It is from me that explanations will be demanded for the loss of the lorry, since it was personally assigned to me by Commissar Andrei Bielokonienko. It would be better if we put our heads together and agreed on a version of the incident.

It proves impossible to have one last council of war. Volodia seems as excited as the hero of his ballad at the moment when he meets up again with his pretty Cosatchka. Vassia, as usual, is already far in front. Kola alone comforts me: 'Don't worry. First we'll check with Kostia the hierarchy's attitude towards us, and then we'll tailor an explanation to suit.' His inventiveness is reawakening. It is the real Kola who is going to handle the problem and not the half-hearted one we have become familiar with during the crossing of Balkaria. But an uneasy foreboding haunts me, and today, 40 years later, I know that it was not unfounded. It is in Nalchik that the intrigue against me which will come to light in Yerevan takes shape.

The 'eleventh' of the VVS is sleeping in the vast courtyard of a building that is three-quarters burned down. Our superiors are resting in rooms that were spared by the fire. The sentries don't even consider disturbing them to report our arrival. There is no hurry therefore, and Vassia and Volodia go off to look for food. Kola and I consult with Kostia, the 'Khan'. The embraces between these two friends gives an opportunity for my jealousy to manifest itself, especially as they exchange some friendly but rather paternalistic remarks about me. They don't think of me as their peer, but as a protégé whom they take along out of the goodness of their hearts, and they express surprise at the fact that I have managed to stay the course so well. I find it difficult to take, but this isn't the moment to get touchy.

Kostia gives a humorous account of the regiment's arrival in Nalchik. They too marched on the mountain footpaths, but on the other side of the main road. Zlotnikov asserted himself as the only competent leader, earning the respect of the men and at the same time generating some very pro-semitic feelings. Knowing that their fate depended on him, the comrades hadn't hesitated, during halts in the march, to sacrifice their own sleep in order to watch over his. They took turns, discreetly, to stand watch by his bedside in order to chase away any insects that threatened his sleep. Among the volunteers on this unofficial guard duty there was even one who had always bad-mouthed this 'dirty Yid', Zlotnikov. Kola isn't surprised: for a long time he has argued that if the army of the Don had been commanded by Jews instead of these idiot atamans, there would have been less suffering all round in the region. He laughs all the same: Kostia is a storyteller who knows how to add spice to his narrative.

What did the Jewish colonel's merits amount to? Zlotnikov knew how to organize a system of intelligence and supplies, and to maintain his little army in a state of combat alert. An airman himself, his greatest fear was that the Germans would take advantage of their mastery of the air to drop (by parachute) some small decoy detachments. He wanted to be in a position to destroy them. Convinced also that the enemy was not advancing towards Nalchik, he preferred to sacrifice speed to an orderly march; – unquestionably the right decision. Thus the regiment arrived in Nalchik in top condition. The military authorities took advantage of this by putting it immediately to work, assigning it to the building of fortifications around the town. Zlotnikov had nothing to do with the decision, nor had our nominal commander, Colonel Ganachek. They would have preferred to withdraw us as quickly as possible.

As for the hierarchy's attitude towards us four, in Kostia's view, the news is not so good. Believing first of all that we had perished along with the lorry during an air raid, our commanders had planned a small ceremony in our honour, as soon as circumstances would allow it. When they learned from their intelligence service that we had been seen, without the lorry, in Pyatigorsk, they had decided to reserve a very different kind of reception for us: to teach us how to protect military material and supplies. On the other hand, since everyone was now compelled to work on fortifications, it was hard to see what more unpleasant fatigue they would be able to find for us. 'There are no more dungeons in Nalchik,' Kostia notes, laughing, 'since the town has been destroyed by fire.' He advises us to declare that, threatened by the traitor-driver, we had been forced to kill him. If we don't, we shall be reproached with not having forced him to drive. Kola disagrees: he thinks ahead, and he doesn't want our careers to be compromised when, after the Red Army has retaken Kislovodsk, our presumed victim is found safe and sound. We decide therefore to be rather vague about the outcome of the incident. The driver launched a surprise attack on us; we fought back without being sure of having killed him. It is more prudent this way. Nevertheless, anxiety – or perhaps the excessive fatigue and the joy of reunion with friends – prevents us from sleeping. The next morning, when we present ourselves in front of Colonel Ganachek, we are in a piteous condition.

I would like to think that it is this which accounts for the almost insulting indifference that he shows towards us. 'Ah. There you are! Make out a report on the lorry,' he says, without even raising his voice or asking any questions about how we had acquitted ourselves. He doesn't even want to read the written order from Colonel Tretiakov, and pretends to be already acquainted with all the relevant circumstances. Since the military world is small however, perhaps he has met Colonel N.N. Tretiakov. Fine. If he doesn't want to hear the tall story about our battle with the traitor-driver, so much the better. We'll make out a report in 10 lines, attaching Tretiakov's written order to it, and that will be the end of it. Meantime Ganachek gives us the morning off duty. Here is a happy ending which, in a film, you would judge to be unrealistic and very artificial. For me, however, the matter is not quite closed: Ganachek is not my only superior; I am also answerable to my commissar, Andrei Tarassovitch Bielokonienko.

Bielokonienko wakes me towards midday and invites me to sit with him. He has aged a great deal since our departure from Kislovodsk.

His hair seems greyer and his shoulders sag badly, making him lose whatever martial bearing he had possessed. I know from Kostia that he has been seriously worried about his wife, Jara, who is still in Kislovodsk, having refused, like Nievka, to be evacuated. Also, it is said that the commissar can't forgive himself for having submitted us to over-optimistic propaganda which didn't correspond to the real development of the war. I don't find such an argument convincing: Bielokonienko only carried out the orders of his superiors. At worst he might be angry with them for leading us on, although it is not his style, but he has nothing to reproach himself with personally.

The man has changed: he is no longer the *tchoudak* of Kislovodsk days, and, for one thing, he no longer suggests talking to me while walking. We remain seated in a deserted, sinister courtyard. He listens to me while I deliver our version of the incident with the driver and the story of our Balkarian escapade. He shows no interest even when, while describing our detour to the hospital, I evoke the seductive image of Natalia Trofimovna G. In Nalchik, Nievka's charm has no hold over him. Perhaps I made an error of judgement in bringing her into the story and thereby aggravated my offence. I don't know for certain; I shall never know what happened inside his Ukrainian head while I was making my report to him.

'I am pleased that you are all safe and sound,' he says finally, without much warmth. I begin to feel a certain sense of relief, despite everything. But he continues, 'On the other hand you have rather disappointed me.' Why? Did he take me on in his service to drive heavy lorries? What, honestly, can he reproach me with? He explains in a single sentence: 'You have let yourself be led by the nose by Kola P., a comrade who is *nienadiojnyi* (untrustworthy), not to say a mischief maker.' Here he is barking up the same old tree. I don't reply. In the army you don't argue with superiors; and even if we had been in civvies, a discussion on this subject would take us nowhere. I simply ask what my duties are in Nalchik, emphasizing the urgency of calling Komsomol meetings in order to raise the comrades' morale. Only then does he give the ghost of a smile. After a pause, he drily delivers a painful blow: 'You are going to work on the fortifications like everyone else.' The conversation is over. He gets up and leaves the courtyard.

I am the only one to be punished: deprived of my special functions and thus of any possibility of distinguishing myself in my particular field. I have to melt into the mass of trainee pilots, who have a wholly different future in front of them. However, I can't make a fuss about it; to do so would be to create the impression that I consider myself as a privileged person, and am refusing to participate in the priority collective effort: the construction of fortifications. Not even Kola sympathizes. He explains everything away by the exceptional circumstances which are likely to be short-lived. Tomorrow, the 'eleventh' will be installed in Transcaucasia or on the other side of the Caspian Sea; the pilots will start to fly again, the politicos to organize meetings. It is only much later, when he analyses Bielokonienko's attitude towards me more seriously, that he will admit that the unexpected and undeserved punishment I received in Nalchik represented the first link in a chain.

For the past two days the muffled sound of cannonfire has reached the hill that we are fortifying. They are our *zenitki* (anti-aircraft batteries) which at long last are being used to stop the Luftwaffe. Others think that the Germans have parachuted in their decoy detachments, just as Colonel Zlotnikov had foreseen, and that our 37th Army is attacking them. No one though is expert in artillery matters. In a school of aviation you don't learn anything about cannons, and official information is non-existent. In Kislovodsk, while it was still far from the theatre of war, the special programme intended for the front line was broadcast every evening on loudspeakers. 'Listen Front. This is Moscow.' In Nalchik, where the cannons are booming, there are no loudspeakers.

In the evenings, we walk for a while in the town and talk with comrades from other units. They claim that new armaments supplies are beginning to arrive from Transcaucasia. But this proves only that the 37th Army is going to be reorganized and re-equipped, not that the German attack is imminent. Nalchik is a large market town, consisting entirely of white clay houses which seem to be fire-resistant. The inhabitants either ran off after the first bombs or else have been evacuated. There isn't one to be seen. In theory, we can go where we want; in practice it is not so simple. There are numerous patrols and they are the first to have been issued with *pépéchas*, automatic rifles that are the forerunners of the Kalashnikov, which make a big impression in Nalchik.

Their chief rival among the wonders of modern armaments is the very peaceful American Studebaker lorry. The soldiers gather round each one like village youngsters, discussing its 4-wheel drive, its tyres, and its elegant design. There are even some who allege that it has been designed especially for the Russian *bezdorojie*, as they call the country's backward road network. It constitutes the first tangible proof that the United States, the world leader in engine manufacture, is on our side, and this boosts our morale. In other times, Bielokonienko would not have missed this opportunity to cite Stalin's prophecy on the inevitable victory of our camp in the 'war of engines'. Unfortunately, in Nalchik, our superiors keep very much to themselves, and seldom appear either on the hill or in town. They are probably discussing the best route to take us away from here with the commanders of Marshal Golovanov's Eighteenth Airforce. Perhaps – does one ever know? – we shall be leaving on these very same Studebakers.

On the third morning: the Germans are at the gates. We are going back up on the hill – to fight not to work. It's crazy: my comrades belong to the airforce, jewel of the armed forces; they aren't common infantrymen. What's more, the colours of our uniforms don't correspond to the requirements of camouflage: we are striking blue. And what about helmets? All that we have are light peak caps, stylish it is true, but quite useless for protecting our heads against flying shrapnel. As to the *pépéchas*, we are given only one between two men, and we have no experience in using them.

'Quickly! Move yourselves! Take with you only what is necessary.

There are no whores to please where we're going,' our sergeant-majors bawl out in their customary male language. I sort through my belongings and leave all my souvenirs in the camp: those that I have brought with me from Poland and those that Nievka gave me in Kislovodsk. I shall never recover them. With greater foresight, Vassia takes our war booty – the piece of cloth salvaged from the lorry before it was destroyed – in his lightened sack. 'In war,' he will explain to me one day, 'you need to have everything that is dear to you within easy reach.'

The three squadrons form a semi-circle and Colonel Ganachek advances to the centre to speak to us. He explains only our defensive positioning on the hill and says nothing to us about how long we will remain on the battle line. To avoid concentrated fire from the enemy artillery we are to stay in groups of two, seven metres apart from each other. We are familiar with the hill since we have fortified it ourselves. We know where to find the two bunkers of our communication network and how best to reach them across broken or shelled terrain. The remainder of what he says is devoted to reminding us of the different signs by which, day and night, orders will be given. We know them off by heart; we have been on a thousand simulation exercises in Kislovodsk.

Ganachek disappears without even wishing us good luck, and Commissar Bielokonienko takes his place. Silence falls: the cannonades close by stop momentarily. Stirred by the occasion, he mechanically removes his airman's peak cap, perhaps feeling more at ease with his head bare. Bielokonienko has never excelled in his role as orator. He has always needed notes and, on important occasions, speeches prepared in advance. This morning in Nalchik he improvises. He says few things about us, and little about either the importance of the battle for the Caucasus in general or about the battle for our hill in particular. He argues only for the historic role of the USSR, the beacon lighting up the path of our class brothers in their struggle to shake off the yoke of capitalism.

Until the great proletarian revolution of October 1917 everyone had said that a society without capitalists, without the lure of gain, without the profit motive, was only a utopia that was incompatible with human nature. The USSR, by its very existence, by its successes in the fields of production and social welfare, is proof to the contrary. Since then, bit by bit, workers everywhere have drawn strength from our example, and have been trying to free themselves from capitalists, landed proprietors and other profiteers. That's why international capitalism created fascism and Nazism before unleashing its barbarian hordes on us in order to halt the march of history. This plan, Bielokonienko vigorously emphasizes, has no chance of succeeding, especially as now, we are not alone. The workers, in all four corners of the world, are ready to take up the torch of our combat.

Although optimistic with regard to the final destiny of humanity, this speech is less reassuring in respect of the immediate situation. We are left with the feeling that a defeat in such an isolated sector as the Caucasus would not weigh heavily in the balance of history.

It isn't a 'class brother' who follows Bielokonienko, but my enemy, Sergeant-major Orlov. Our squadron is the first to leave and, when we are already en route, he decides that I shall be paired with Boris T., known simply as Lovelace, and not with one of my friends from Mietchotka. I get on well with Boris T.; and in any case can no longer invoke my status as a politico in order to question orders. I suspect that the commissar has had a hand in the decision to separate me from Kola, Vassia and the others. And then I am too afraid to reason with or to become indignant over the pettiness of a sergeant-major or of my *tchoudak* commissar. I am lucid enough to realize that we have little chance of escaping from this Caucasian hornets' nest. Otherwise the far-sighted airforce wouldn't sacrifice its own men in an absurd land battle.

I am being evacuated to a hospital – where, I don't know – aboard a Studebaker which shakes me about just as much as an old Russian lorry would, despite its elegant design and its 4-wheel drive. It is all too stupid for words. Nothing was happening on our hill that day.

191

My story is straight out of *All Quiet on the Western Front*. If I manage to get out of this, I shall be ashamed to tell the tale. During a period of prolonged calm, I went off to fetch some soup. Suddenly a stupefying blast hurled me several metres into the air. There had been no whistling sounds which indicate artillery shells. I heard the explosion only after I had been sent flying.

Fortunately Boris T. saw me land and took care of everything. He alerted Sergeant-major Orlov, who contacted the medical services and signed the necessary papers for my admission to hospital. (You need these, even on the front line.) Both of them accompanied me to the ambulance-lorry and Boris kept on repeating with compassion in his voice: '*Oh, kak tiebia zaiobnoulo*', a Russian way of saying: 'Oh! What has happened to you?' but also: 'You've had it, old son!' I don't feel as though I'm dying however. The taste of earth in my mouth badly upsets me; I imagine that I shall never be able to spit it out completely. I am bleeding here and there, having received scratches all over my body. But I don't feel a lot of pain and I haven't lost consciousness. True, you can't trust appearances. In Poland, in 1939, I also felt no pain and had ended up losing an eye.

For 15 days we had been defending our hill near Nalchik, and the battle hadn't been without its agreeable moments. At night the front is sometimes very beautiful. When the artillery gunners in both camps fire at the same time, the entire sky lights up as if a gigantic firework were exploding. It takes your breath away. I also have an extraordinary memory of the introduction into the battle of our *katyushas*, these deafening rocket-propelled mortar bombs. That same night, a week or so after our arrival on the hill, I understood that thanks to the *katyushas* we were going to win the war. It is hard to call this to mind when you have a taste of earth in your mouth and you are being shaken this way and that in a lorry. One day though, when I am cured, I shall devote a special narrative to the *katyushas*, to their sound and light effects. They are incredible. When we first saw their trace in the sky, we thought that these ultra-modern machines were German, and that the Wehrmacht had surrounded us. And what can one say of the terrifying and yet melodious sound of these weapons which the enemy nicknamed 'Stalin's organs'?

The next day, at dawn, advancing by several kilometres, we were able to witness the devastation they had wrought, literally sweeping away the enemy's defensive positions. Unfortunately our adversaries were not Germans. The poor devils were Romanian; their helmets were decorated with the letter C in honour of their king, Carol, who had however been exiled well before the war. This was a great disappointment to us. We had learned endless poems exalting the necessity to kill Germans, but none of them mentioned Romanians. Later, when other ex-combatants boast of having killed lots of Wehrmacht soldiers, we shall be thoroughly embarrassed to admit that we have only ever fired on soldiers from the Balkans. Not one among us thought for a moment of picking up a helmet decorated with the letter C in order one day to show it to his grandchildren.

Along our front, which extended a good 20 kilometres in length and as many again in depth, there was a constant movement forwards and backwards. The Germans were sometimes forced to fall back as far as Beksan, a small river along the Pyatigorsk road. But these details are of interest only to specialists. I prefer to dwell on our everyday concerns, food for example, or the sometimes dangerous obstacle race we tackled to consult some front-line comrades who had a reputation either for palm-reading or fortune-telling. The Second World War was notable in the USSR for bringing about a tacit truce, which, since time immemorial, has placed materialists and idealists in opposition, and which, in the final analysis, sums up the history of all human thought. Since the October Revolution we have formed the vanguard of anti-religious materialists who are destined to emerge the victors in this struggle and to extirpate all super-stitions. In Rostov it would have been suicidal to admit that during my childhood in Lodz I had attempted to communicate with the supernatural. In Nalchik, however, since the proclamation of a truce with the idealists in the name of patriotic unity, it was possible to take advantage of certain of their side's assets. It was thanks to this

193

that several of our lads, all good Komsomols, revealed that they had learned the occult sciences from their families, and knew very well how to read palms or see into the future through playing-cards. When shells are raining down on all sides, it behoves everyone to maximize their chances of survival by observing the rules of war. But they also stand to gain by knowing as much as possible about destiny, about what is 'predetermined'.

Take the case of Boris T., alias Lovelace. He is not a Cossack but a Russian, originally from Koursk, who had settled in Rostov. I believe he was the son of a university professor, and therefore an atheist of unimpeachable pedigree. Boris, what's more, is a very reassuring optimist, for he is convinced that he has a bright future as a pilot. By the time we arrived on the hill he had explained to me that we wouldn't be staying there for long, and that he would be a flight lieutenant by the end of the year. He claimed that by the end of 1943 he would be a captain and, in 1945, a squadron leader at least or a lieutenant-colonel. All of this is accompanied by exact calculations on the salary he will earn and the medals he will have been awarded. Now even this self-confident Boris T. didn't balk at crawling along the ground like a snake for several kilometres, in search of a certain Vassiltchenko, a comrade of Ukrainian origin who was widely reputed for his gifts at palm-reading.

In my own case, after a very reassuring examination of the lines on my palm by Vassiltchenko, I went the next day to see Volochtchenko, another highly-regarded Ukrainian, to have him repeat the examination and confirm these favourable predictions. Next I had the cards read for me by two comrades recommended by Kola. According to them I was a *boubnovyi karol*, the king of diamonds, and I had nothing to fear from Jerry. I was threatened only by great disappointments with the queen of diamonds, a blonde or red-headed woman. If I hadn't had all these assurances, including the prophecy by the man from Sablinsk – 'You will get out of this war unharmed' – no doubt I would have been altogether more alarmed, in this ambulance-lorry which violently tosses me about.

*

Our sector was attached to the 'Don' bunker. It was here that the field kitchen turned up twice a day, though at irregular hours. Fedka, the cook, who was always in a hurry to leave, didn't serve out individual portions. He filled up a mess tin for four, either with *kacha* (in the mornings), or with haricot soup, with a little meat. This gave rise to two problems: first of all, getting the overflowing mess tin back across a shelled terrain without spilling any. Next, there was the problem of making sure that the fastest eater didn't eat any more than the others. We gave up on sorting out the second problem, because our foursome was made up of eaters who were all confident in their ability to eat as quickly as the others, and who accepted open competition. It was through going off to fetch the evening soup that I fell victim to this imbecile incident.

It had been a memorable day for another reason, thanks to Boris T. This tall, handsome man is a Soviet version of Gary Cooper. He is not at all aware of it; he has seen only three American films and remembers only one of them, Charlie Chaplin's *Modern Times*. The name Gary Cooper doesn't mean anything to him. His resemblance to the romantic Hollywood hero first struck me in Kislovodsk, and I had no difficulty believing him when he told me about his astonishing successes with the nurses. This had earned me his friendship: a young Don Juan always needs an appreciative audience. In the Nalchik trench, Boris also seemed to me sometimes like the male equivalent of Moussia. Despite his tender years he already had very definite ideas about amorous skirmishes. He insisted on always appearing presentable, even here on this pile of stones as if it was not the enemy but some charming princess who was going to emerge from the other side of the hill. In Kislovodsk I had noticed that he kept a piece of chamois leather in his revolver pocket so as to be able to clean his boots at a moment's notice. In Nalchik this would have been excessive, so he contented himself with shaving every day and, during each period of calm, washing himself in the 'Don'.

Despite the short length of his stay in town, he claimed that he had managed to get off with one Sergeant Galia, who was attached to artillery headquarters. 'She is the PPG (an abbreviation of 'field wife') to a colonel, but I bet you that she'll come to see me here.' And he suggested some green-pea paste or a ration of sugar as a wager. I accepted the bet, thoroughly convinced that the sergeant, even if she did exist, couldn't have the vaguest idea where Boris T. was to be found. Now that very afternoon, taking advantage of a lull, a jeep of artillery soldiers arrived to take the bearings of some target. And Galia was among them. I tried to move away discreetly but Boris kept me by him so that I should see that this colonel's PPG really was keen on him. I didn't spare my compliments, and Boris, sensitive to this homage, not only refused my green-pea concentrate and my sugar ration, but even promised to teach me a thing or two about how to charm a woman.

We were talking about it when notified of the arrival of the field kitchen. I set off, and now here I am in this ambulance-lorry. Boris had only had time to explain to me that boldness is indispensable in relations with women. Nothing very sensational; nothing which could be considered as a crucial clue to the secrets of love. I was due to hear the rest after dinner. I am decidedly a king of diamonds. The cards had not been lying.

The hospital is in Beslan, halfway between Nalchik and Vladicaucasia. It is an improvised building that doesn't bear comparison to the hospital in which Nievka worked in Kislovodsk. In fact it is only a first aid post, rather large, but on the night I arrived plunged into darkness by an electricity breakdown. We are accommodated on mattresses placed on the floor in a long ward. The mattresses are close together, to save space. There are wounded lying on a sheet in their underwear; others have their uniform on and are covered with their greatcoats, for want of blankets. I am among the better-off: I have been washed and undressed. But I am positioned close to the entry door which is continually being opened. It is the month of August, so it can't be this draught that gives me the shivers. I must be feverish. Suddenly, I have the feeling that I am a 'goner'.

A man and a woman in white overalls approach, with an oil lamp, and listen to the report from the medical officer who has transported and taken care of me since collecting me in Nalchik. I can't hear very well. I believe, however, that I hear him say he has given me an anti-tetanus jab, even though he hadn't noted any wounds caused either by bullets or by shrapnel. The man leans over me and asks me to squeeze his hand with all my strength, first with the right hand, then with the left. He presses my head a little and then my legs, without hurting me.

It is now the woman's turn, and she gets right down on her knees to examine me by touch all over, before applying her stethoscope. On getting up again, she declares in a loud voice: 'An attack of malaria.' The other doesn't agree at all, and argues that I have lost strength in my left side as a result of concussion to the right side of my brain. My opinion is not solicited. They discuss the matter without looking at me any further, their voices more or less drowned out by the groans of my neighbours. The two of them then leave arguing the bit out, without informing me of their verdict.

Could there be a sedative in anti-tetanus injections? Why are my eyelids closing when I would like to find out first what the diagnosis is? I could have found out by asking either the medical officer or the nurses but I am not familiar with the conventions. And in truth, not having much strength in my limbs, left or right, I prefer to remain in bed and wait. I mustn't miss the next doctors' visit. Once I have sunk into the darkness I am in danger of never again being able to open my eyes. It is a very common fear, it seems, among the freshly wounded. Other casualties, according to their own accounts, draw up a balance sheet in respect of their relations and their dear ones, wondering who will suffer from their disappearance and who will rejoice over it. I simply meditate on malaria which, in my mind, has always been associated with the disquieting jungles of Africa and Asia, with Tarzan and the tales of Joseph Conrad. All things considered, I prefer the concussion diagnosed by the male doctor.

The strange antics of my neighbour interrupt my thoughts once again. I find it hard to make out the features of the wounded man who is lying close by, for his head is three-quarters covered with dressings, as is one of his legs. The poor man seems to be suffering atrociously but he finds the strength to call the nurse at regular intervals and to beg her politely: 'Macha, can I detain you a moment to ask about a personal matter?' He follows this up with a stream of compliments in the same vein, spoken in a low voice: 'You are the most beautiful creature,' 'I'm crazy about you.' The woman replies each time, with great patience, that being the only nurse on the ward she is necessarily the most beautiful, that she is very pleased to hear it, and that he ought to go to sleep. Their dialogue begins again as if they were performing a play. The poor pathetic creature. This ward is the last place in the world to touch upon 'personal matters'. Somewhere in the middle of these reflections I sink into a deep sleep.

When I open my eyes, late in the day, my neighbour's mattress is empty. In an evacuation hospital this doesn't necessarily mean that he is dead. Perhaps he has been transported elsewhere. As to Macha, she looks very tired. It is ludicrous to impose 24-hour shifts on nurses, I tell myself suddenly, recalling that Nievka too sometimes got back from the hospital with her face drawn and tired. If only she were here. I would recover quickly. My spirits lift after this sleep, and I am certain once again of getting better. I think about the man from Sablinsk and of his prophecy: 'You will get out of this war unharmed.' He didn't say 'alive'; he said 'unharmed', and this word seems to indicate that in Beslan, as opposed to my hospital experience in Radom, I shall not be butchered. What do these shivers matter then, this alternation of hot and cold, these repeated plunges into sleep? I let myself go. And after relaxing in this manner, I sleep for three days and nights continuously, without thinking of anything, without hearing anything, and without recalling anything.

The queen of diamonds of the Nalchik fortune-tellers is called Liuba. Her hair is of a deep red hue, the reddest I have ever seen. She wears it in a flamboyant style, and her face, her hands, perhaps her whole body are covered with freckles. With her large green eyes, her ample figure and her original hairstyle – a bun worn behind and a fringe falling down to her eyes – Liuba would be very desirable if she weren't so fierce, aggressive even, as though she felt obliged to remind me at all times: 'Watch out. I am *boubnovai adama* (the queen of diamonds), and I shall hurt you!'

However, each time that I have tried since then to imagine my life differently, I think that those who read the cards in Nalchik were mistaken. Not only did Liuba not represent a danger to me: she was perhaps even the messenger of destiny, charged with trying to prevent me from transferring to Yerevan, 25 kilometres from the Turkish frontier, where, three months later, my 'affair' was going to surface. We spoke to one another only four or five times but always in circumstances that were too unusual to be natural. Now although I had been used to reading signs in Poland, I didn't grasp at the time that in my meetings with Liuba fate certainly played a part.

It is the middle of the night when I finally stir from my long sleep. I don't know what time it is for my watch has gone (forever, alas), but I note that all my symptoms – fever, shivering, itching – have disappeared. I still feel rather weak but as though I am convalescing, and I am able to get to my feet. Wrapped up in my blanket, I go outside and sit down in the courtyard on an old tree-trunk. Beslan sleeps in the darkness, in silence. Even the noises of the large ward no longer reach me. All around me I make out the Great Caucasus, this lacework of hill tops close at hand covered with eternal snow. We are high up and the air is sharp and invigorating, just the thing to dissipate the remaining traces of cloudiness in the head of someone who has slept for three days. Suddenly I notice a nurse approaching, wearing a greatcoat over her white overall. I hadn't seen her in the hospital before.

In the large courtyard there is no shortage of tree-trunks, but Liuba sits on mine, right beside me. She introduces herself and offers me a pouch of *makhorka*, a rough shag tobacco. The colour of her hair clearly reveals her to me as the queen of diamonds, and so I am on my guard. Hardly have I begun to complain about my confused medical situation and about having lost my watch, a precious gift from my parents, when Liuba accuses me of 'setting traps'. Every wounded soldier tries to arouse her pity, and all of them have the same calculating motives. It is too much for me to take, so I invite her to consult my medical file to persuade herself of the truth of what I'm saying. She would also be doing me a favour if she could tell me the final diagnosis. 'There can be no question of such a thing. I am not even on your ward, and nurses are never supposed to communicate such matters to the wounded,' she replies aggressively. Whereupon, just as I was thinking of getting up and going elsewhere, Liuba lays her head on my shoulder. 'You mustn't get cross with me,' she says. 'I have so many things on my mind that I no longer get a moment's peace. Day and night, whether I work or sleep, they never stop tormenting me. Perhaps you are not like the other men, pigs, the whole lot of them. I can talk to you.' And with this she begins to tell me the story of her life.

A Siberian, she fell in love at the nursing school in Tioumen with an auxiliary doctor who had been made a lieutenant upon mobilization and whom she later married. From the beginning of the war they had both belonged to an ambulance unit responsible for transporting the wounded between the first aid posts at the front and the evacuation hospitals 50 or so kilometres behind the lines. In the month of May however, in the generalized scramble of the retreat from Kharkov, their ambulance-lorry was machine-gunned by a German plane which had returned in a surprise attack to finish off the survivors. Only Liuba and one medical officer survived. Her husband, the lieutenant, was killed before her eyes, riddled with bullets along with the wounded in the ambulance. They had had to bury them with their bare hands – she shows me hers as if they still bore the traces – in a communal grave. 'I am not even sure that I shall ever be able to find it again. I was so happy with him.'

I don't know how to reply. In my regiment there had been relatively few losses because we were assigned to a peripheral sector of the front, set up to prevent any German attempt to encircle Nalchik. During an advance patrol, it is true, I had to bring back Chourik L., one of the foursome with whom I shared a mess tin,

200

who had been shot in the leg and was covered in blood. I still have a horrible memory of it, but it appears to me to be indecent to speak about it with Liuba. Having to help a wounded comrade is not the same thing as having to bury a dearly beloved husband.

But why does she believe that the men don't understand her? She straightens up immediately, in a fury, and the anger rises in her harsh voice as she tells me how the men have 'understood' her. Three days after the death of her husband, her new superior tells her straight that since they're bound to sleep together sooner or later, he would prefer to do it right away. There follows a long list of medical officers and wounded, all of whom tried to take advantage of her. 'I no longer want any man, at least until the end of the war,' she shouts. She also rages against the Red Army which won't allow her to return to Tioumen and is transferring her to a hospital in Krasnovodsk, on the other side of the Caspian Sea.

Tioumen, Tioumen. To everyone their own dream, but, even so, there are a multitude of towns in Russia that are less infested with mosquitoes. And then, Siberia is the land of deportees: to want so much to go there voluntarily is something altogether beyond me. 'There aren't a lot of mosquitoes in the town itself,' Liuba objects. 'It is in the forest that they devour you.' No, it's not true: let's be honest, Liuba. In Tioumen in summer the insects reign supreme. Astonished by the extent of my knowledge with the local conditions she only half-believes me when I tell her that I got it from a friend. But she isn't unhappy to talk about Tioumen and she puts her head on my shoulder. 'You can caress my hair provided that you do it gently and don't harbour any afterthoughts.' I do so, convinced that she is not only the most red-haired woman I have ever seen but also one of the most bizarre. And thus we continue to while away the time talking about Siberian mosquitoes, while my hand makes prudent stroking movements along her thick red hair. The day breaks and before our very eyes emerge the harmonious outlines of the majestic Elbrus, and its rival in altitude, the Kazbek. It is an astonishing landscape, and, at this hour of the day, beneath the mist, it is strangely soft and calming, uplifting.

The charm doesn't last, Liuba admits that the landscape 'isn't bad', but, she must leave. Work awaits her. She goes off with a firm step.

Some hours later an unusual noise in the ward tells me that Liuba has come back. On her way, she receives even more requests to give advice on 'personal matters' than little Macha. After scrutinizing the faces and examining the hands of my two neighbours, Liuba kneels down by my mattress and says in my ear: 'You're lucky. I consulted your medical file. I wanted to know who you were. Your report is so good that I decided to let you know about it. You are to be sent as soon as possible to the hospital in Krasnovodsk for observation, because it is feared you may have suffered brain damage.' She is surprised that I don't understand and need further explanation. The Red Army doesn't trust this category of patient and demobilizes them much more readily than, for example, a nurse who has seen her husband killed before her very eyes. 'Who is going to fight the Germans then, Liuba, if everyone gets themselves demobilized? Where would you have me go? To Tioumen?' She looks at me as I were not so much 'brain-damaged' as a madman to be tied up. Her diatribe on men's stupidity is shorter this time: we are not alone, and she hasn't the time. She leaves me without saying goodbye. Should I run after her? She would certainly accuse me of having ulterior motives. Ah, but what anguish to be alone among these groaning strangers with the sole prospect of relocation to the other side of the Caspian Sea. Krasnovodsk? That night was the very first time I had even heard the name. They teach geography badly in Soviet schools.

Framed in the doorway, a large silhouette appears, which could well be that of Vassia. With his back to the light I can't clearly see the colour of his uniform, but I know that it can't be him, since he is up on the hill near Nalchik, in the Volga sector. However, just in case, I cry loudly – you have to, to make yourself heard here – 'Hey, *Slon* (Elephant)!' The man turns his head: it is indeed Vassia, our horseman of Balkaria, the strong man of our clan. Having received my distress signal, he had hastened to my side so that I shouldn't feel alone.

Here we are then, all five of us, the Balkarian quartet and Kostia the Khan, on a tree-trunk, at the bottom of my hospital courtyard. The VVS, withdrawn from the front following the arrival of reinforcements from Georgia, are taking advantage of a halt to clean themselves up in Beslan. It is *bania* day, this great Russian institution which takes the place of bathrooms, and which also allows you to disinfect clothes, blankets and personal belongings. But it takes time. The *bania* in Beslan was not built to scrub down a whole army. We have time to tell each other everything at leisure.

They can't get over having found me in such good health. Boris T. had told them that I was stuffed full of shrapnel, as fit to burst as a turkey on Christmas Eve. Certainly, to judge from my pallor, I seem a little ill; but Napoleon himself in underpants would not have made a better impression. 'Let's drink to it,' Volodia suggests, and he discreetly hands me a little bottle of vodka. I hesitate. '*Za Stalina*' ('To Stalin'), he encourages me. This is something new: in Kislovodsk we never once drank to the health of our supreme commander-in-chief. A toast to Stalin would have seemed incongruous. It was at the front that the cult of Stalin developed. At each advance, I saw comrades cry out '*Za Stalina*.' Why did they? Because this name alone expresses our hope of living and of conquering? In Beslan, on our tree-trunk, Kola and Vassia take in turn a little vodka and pronounce religiously: '*Za Stalina*,' and the others drink to the toast.

Kostia has an exceptional item of news: the commissar, eaten by remorse after my injury, suggested to Kola that he propose him, Kola, for membership of the CPSU. Membership formalities are greatly simplified at the front, and a commissar could enrol half of his troops in the party. (It was even written about in the press at times.) It amounts to such an unexpected gesture and one so rich in implications that we find it hard to assess. But the other news is very, very sad: the palm-reader Vassiltchenko had been killed on the day of departure from Nalchik. He was a good comrade and doubtless would have made a fine fighter pilot.

I don't bother mentioning Liuba – what would I have been able to tell them about her? – but I explain that my next destination is Krasnovodsk. All of them then agree that 'observation' is good for crazies but not for me, and that they are taking me with them. Vassia wants to do it on the spot, without formalities. The hospital is unguarded and they will find a uniform for me at camp. 'To cover 500 metres in your underpants isn't such an impossible task. The *bania* is close by.' But Kola, confident in the knowledge of the commissar's offer, is for respecting the rules. Why cheat when you can do it all legally? He knows his geography: the Great Caucasus is fine to look at but difficult to cross; a hospital will not hold on to a wounded man who, covered by his unit, prefers to leave of his own accord thus relieving the medical services of the obligation of transporting him. Kola's efficacy is astounding: one hour after our decision my papers are already in order and I am free to return to the 'eleventh'. The hospital refuses to accept my formal complaint concerning the theft of my watch. I am given a sealed letter addressed to my superiors. Although tempted to open it, I decide finally to remit it to Bielokonienko unopened. It is our day for observing the rules.

I have already donned my dark blue uniform when Liuba makes a noisy appearance. As she is not attached to my ward she is not supposed to be aware of my departure, but she knows about everything and suggests a private conversation. She takes me amiably by the arm but holds it so tightly that it hurts. I don't protest; I let myself be led to the quiet spot that she has chosen to avoid the other patients. Here she relaxes her hold on my arm and drops the pretence of a smile. You only have to see her flushed face to tell that she is angry and that it is not a simple matter of a farewell. 'You stupid man,' she bursts out. 'Who do you think you're impressing by leaving here with concussion that still hasn't been properly diagnosed or treated, and an attack of malaria on top of it all?' She tells me off as though she had a right to do so. Who has given her the job of looking after me? She repeats herself endlessly in a voice which gets louder and louder, becoming more and more harsh. I reply feebly, murmuring some empty phrases about the comradeship between men, and the 'eleventh school' of the airforce which is my only family. But I daren't remind her that I am an adult and that my affairs do not concern her. There is something which both touches and troubles me in this woman. Liuba wears herself out, then turns brusquely on her heel and tosses at me over her shoulder a parting 'See you, combatant,' which is equivalent to: 'Go ahead, idiot, get yourself killed!' Too bad; our paths have no chance of ever crossing again.

At the exit to the *bania* in Beslan, Adrei Tarassovitch Bielokonienko, closely shaven and clean as a new pin, has recovered his former self. He greets me in the way he used to in the best days in Kislovodsk, when I was almost a 'companion-in-arms'. And although he doesn't suggest facilitating my entry into the CP of the USSR, as he did for Kola, he gives me several items of good news. I shall be on a lorry with a military driver, without any risk of bother. The 'eleventh' of the VVS will take care of my health. Upon recovering properly, I shall have much more important tasks than in Kislovodsk. 'The socialist fatherland,' he adds, 'will never forget its debt towards those who have spilled their blood for it. You, what's more . . .' But his sentence stops midway. He probably can't decide whether I deserve supplementary thanks in my capacity as a 'class brother', or whether I deserve them because I am 'consciously and culturally' Russian.

It hardly matters. What counts is that I feel myself to be a creditor of the entire USSR, and also feel that I am promised a brilliant career in the armed forces. I bear no grudge at all against Bielokonienko for having sent me up on to the hill in Nalchik instead of keeping me busy in his command bunker with political scribbling. All's well that ends well, the episode having turned out to my advantage. I have no worries at all, not even about the situation of our army, which is deteriorating on practically all fronts. It is only later that I realize that in this month of September 1942, the USSR found itself even closer to defeat than during the Battle of Moscow. With the Germans in the Stalingrad suburbs and in the very heart of the Caucasus, the Red Army didn't seem to have much hope of reversing the course of events.

It is hardly surprising then that just now the role of the long-range action aircraft was not in the forefront of the plans formulated by *Stavka* (the high command, which many called the 'politbureau' of the Red Army). The 'eleventh' of the VVS will receive contradictory orders on its destination; our departure from the Great Caucasus, which is difficult enough to cross in normal times, will be marked by several demoralizing episodes. But my memories of this journey are very confused. Sometimes they even contradict the official facts of geography.

I know that we stopped in Vladicaucasia ('the one which dominates the Caucasus'). Before 1941 it was called Ordzhonikidze in honour of Stalin's companion of that name who died in suspicious circumstances in the 1930s, and it has borne his name once again since 1945. In the interval, however, it was well and truly Vladicaucasia. This capital of Ossetia is linked to Tbilisi and to the Georgian coast of the Black Sea by two famous passes: *Voienno-grouzinkskaia daroga* (Georgian warpath) and *Voienna-ossetinskaia daroga* (Ossetian warpath). I am almost certain that we took the first of these roads, and that our driver found it even bumpier than it had been in the days of the czars. What is surprising is that we ended up in Makhatch-Kala, on the Caspian seaboard, and not in Tbilisi. To complicate matters I can't find either a pass or a road between Vladicaucasia and Makhatch-Kala in the Soviet atlas. How did we manage to get there? It's a mystery to me. I had, I suppose, suffered concussion in Nalchik after all, and no doubt my brain only gradually began to function normally.

In Makhatch-Kala, my brain was functioning and my memories of the place are of great clarity. This is chiefly because of a further meeting with Liuba, but also because at Makhatch-Kala I saw the sea for the first time in my life. Such strong impressions are unforgettable.

Our arrival in Makhatch-Kala on 6 or 7 September, is pervaded by uncertainty for us. Here, we are at a crossroads, from here one can go by sea to Asia or by rail to Transcaucasia. All of us would prefer Georgia or Armenia. We fear however that the farsighted airforce will send us to safe but distant destinations on the other side of the Caspian Sea. Finally, we hear the good news: we are ordered to assemble at 5.30 pm in front of the railway station. We can now give free rein to our taste for tourism and barter: we are going to pay a quick visit to Makhatch-Kala and exchange whatever we have in excess for some good Caucasian grapes.

The town, for people who come from the plains, is astonishing: it is made up of terraces hewn out of the mountainside, which go down in stages to the sea. Its white clay houses, in the same style as those in Nalchik, are surrounded by flowers and an abundant vegetation. It is a town of great beauty. The inhabitants are clearly Muslims. (They too will be deported by Stalin in 1943, accused of being collaborators, although their town had never even been occupied by the Germans.)

I am among the first to go down to the station, for I lack the strength to climb the street-paths, and I discover that the port is close to the station, only about 50 metres away, but one terrace lower. From the quayside, I notice almost immediately Liuba's head of red hair on the bridge of a boat beneath me. Standing alone, she is shading her eyes with her right hand against the sunlight. She seems to be looking for someone among the airmen. I hurry down, almost knocking over as I do so, the ticket inspectors, who are still not letting passengers go aboard. For once, a contented smile lights up Liuba's face. She says to me quietly, almost tenderly: 'I was waiting for you. I am pleased.' How had she been able to predict that on this day and at this time I would be at Makhatch-Kala? The airforce command itself didn't know when we would arrive. Was Liuba trying to make me understand that destiny was one last time holding out a hand to me? It was too subtle for me.

'Come with me,' she says. And she explains that having committed an offence in Beslan by communicating the contents of my medical report, she feels that she is to blame for my precipitate departure and for its consequences. Everything can still be made good if I go with her to Krasnovodsk, where she herself will see to my admission to hospital and take care of my health. Liuba's suggestion seems absurd to me, almost insulting. The Soviet Union is indebted to me and I have great expectations of reward. How can someone suggest to me that I should enter hospital for observation and get myself demobilized?

The queen of diamonds has a trump card however. She has chosen her setting perfectly. The light of Makhatch-Kala and its reflection in the calm Caspian Sea underline her singular, red-headed Siberian beauty. 'You are beautiful, Liuba,' I say to her foolishly. 'Cut it out. I am anybody. In this light you simply don't see my freckles.' She insists that you have to mistrust wounds or uncured illnesses. They are like enemy aircraft: you think they have flown past and then they swoop down on you once more, brutally and, 'Bang, your goose is cooked.' It was exactly like this that her husband was killed: he had prematurely relaxed his guard, believing that he was out of danger. Anything that happens to me will weigh on her conscience; I ought to go to Krasnovodsk for my own good as much as for her peace of mind.

Is it merely a question of her peace of mind? She is no longer ferocious in the least and says nothing more about her decision to remain chaste until after the war. But I lack boldness. Instead of reflecting on the inner meaning of Liuba's message, I can think only of the immediate circumstances, of the temptation to kiss her, and of my fear of being snubbed.

'Run to the station and ask permission from your commissar,' she continues. 'Tell him that your health is at stake, and we shall leave together.' But our convoy of *tieplouchki* is already alongside the station platform, and my comrades are making themselves comfortable on the carriage roofs (their favourite way of travelling).

'No, Liuba. I can't go to Krasnovodsk. I'm sorry. You are a very beautiful *boubnovaia dama.*'

'So they tell me,' she replies, giving to me, on a scrap of paper, all her civilian and military addresses, in Krasnovodsk and in Tioumen. 'Write to me if you meet with any problems.' She makes no reference to those problems that do not allow any correspondence. Even the messengers of destiny are required to observe some discretion.

4. 'Pojarnik'

The colonel with the Boudiennyi-style moustache, the commandant of the Volgalag,* a camp situated in the region formerly belonging to the Volga Germans, has me summoned to his office on Friday 13 January 1944, at 14.00 hours exactly. He reads out a short communication issued by the public prosecutor of the Soviet Union. It is so short that it fits into a single sentence: 'Sanction for the arrest of Citizen (my family name, and first name are inserted) is refused because of the absence of material evidence to support any accusation.' The colonel, still standing, solemnly explains: 'No one can be placed under arrest in the USSR without this *sankcja procurora*; the law is explicit on the matter and tolerates no exception to it.' Then, revealing two rows of long, white teeth, he smiles at me: 'Therefore comrade, your arrest in Yerevan, on 10 December 1942, never took place. We have to arrive at a clear agreement on this point.'

His style, which is worthy of the great tradition of Russian surrealism, will delight my friends in Rostov some months later. So too will the rebounds of the conversation that follows. Kola will persist in searching in it, beyond its comic aspect, for the key to the future of the USSR. He will ask to hear my story a hundred times over – adding to it details of his own invention – and introduce on to the stage the shadow of Commissar Bielokonienko pulling the colonel along by his Boudiennyi-style moustache, in order to

* Gulag is the abbreviated form of 'General Administration of Camps', but each *lager* (camp) has its own name, generally deriving from the place where it is situated.

demonstrate that injustices were beginning to disappear from our society. He will advise me after each retelling always to begin with the end of the story of my voyage of 13 months and 3 days across the Gulag Archipelago, from the prison in Yerevan to the camp on the Volga.

The Armenian convoy's journey towards the Volga camp during the summer of 1943 defies imagination. It travelled at an extremely slow pace, taking two or three weeks for a journey that a slow train could do in two days. Beneath the summer sun this snail's pace alone would have been enough to have sorely tried the inmates, who were closed up in poorly ventilated *tieplouchki*, but there is more. Fearing that someone might take advantage of the interminable halts to escape, the guards come along every three hours, day and night, and use wooden mallets to tap the carriage doors and check that no one has tried to tamper with them. 'Everyone with their things to the left,' they shout; then 'Everyone to the right.' Now this type of movement, which is very inconvenient during daylight, is catastrophic in darkness. The occupants of the carriage bang blindly against each other, lose their bundles and the niche they had made for themselves to sleep in. They need two to three hours to recover, which is the length of time that separates one inspection from the next. In other words we hardly sleep at all, we eat very little and we drink sparingly. The only plentiful commodity is the heat. Not even Solzhenitsyn, who has described the Gulag transport system at length, seems to have undergone such a journey.

Once we arrive at our destination the surprise is rather agreeable. The NKVD had not planned ahead for the deportation to Siberia of those who had settled on the banks of the Volga two centuries earlier. They were packed off in a hurry without distinctions being made between the communists and the rest. Refugees from western territories, city dwellers especially, who had fled from the Wehrmacht came here to settle. The authorities were unable to train a population unaccustomed to agricultural work in time for the harvest and so they called in the help of Gulag labour. The deployment of this great labour army raised a lot of problems though: there was no question of accommodating it in the comfortable villages that had belonged to the Volga Germans, nor of allowing it to circulate freely. The authorities therefore opted for the creation of provisional camps located near the principal harvesting centres.

In the Soviet Union the 'provisional' can last a long time, so long in fact that our convoy from Armenia, on arriving (in the late summer of 1943) in the Volgalag, finds total chaos. Communication between camps is virtually non-existent; the brigades get to the fields only after long delays and often have to wait for the arrival of armed NKVD guards who are lodged in the villages. This massive escort is explained by the peculiarity of agricultural work: on my previous site of work, in Armenia, where we were building a bridge, our superiors were not afraid of us eating the concrete, whereas here they know that *zeks* just love raw vegetables and consider corn-on-the-cob a great delicacy.

My camp has 10 brigades, each of 30 men, grouped according to their physical strength; we are housed in barracks with three-tiered bunks. The best places are taken by those who have been there longest, the 'veterans'. My neighbour is a veteran, a professor of organic chemistry – one of the most cultivated among the *zeks* that I knew. He observes that I seem to have been exhausted by the Armenian convoy and suggests to me that I get myself cared for. Better still, get myself hospitalized. I come out of my state of torpor to plunge myself into an obstacle race in which the prize is this dream-like place where you sleep between sheets, eat your fill, receive vitamins and do nothing. But, in our camp, there is no hospital.

My problem is getting myself accepted for a medical visit in another camp, 30 kilometres from this bizarre agricultural penitentiary. Neither complaints presented to superiors nor simulation of illness is of any use whatever. What you have to do is pull strings. The problem is that I have no money to distribute 'tips'.

Nevertheless I have got some connections among those whom my neighbour calls the 'permanent delinquency'. His expression strikes me as apt, because it doesn't just designate recidivists, but also conveys the cohesion of the criminal fraternity. These people are well organized, whether in prison or outside it; they have their hierarchy, their code of honour and their system of communication. It is more difficult to be admitted into their midst than into the Communist Party, because they don't hold either with words or with oaths of loyalty, and they know how to recognize their own. They don't proselytise nor try to corrupt the *frayer* ('free man'), by which term they contemptuously designate the others.

The big wheels of the 'permanent delinquency' neither work nor move around: their code of honour forbids them to do so. And the penitentiary administration generally bows before this case of *force majeure*. Those one rank down do work and even take on responsibilities in order to protect and control the small fry who are in danger of losing their strength and sapping discipline. The 'full-timers' (those who didn't work at all) gave me the nickname of 'student-raconteur', in remembrance of my performance as a narrator in a prison cell in Yerevan, where, suffering from boredom, they had greatly appreciated the story of the *Count of Monte Cristo*, which I had adapted to Russian conditions and improved upon as I went along.

In acknowledgement of Yerevan, the 'full-timers' secure a medical visit for me. In three months they manage to get me three visits, which proves both my determination and their benevolence towards me. The fact remains, however, that at the hospital there are 10 candidates for every available bed, at least in my category, classified as suffering from *pelagra* or *distrophia*: 'weaklings' in lay terms. To avoid favouritism and to expose malingerers, the administration introduced a 'scientific' test: the only ones admitted to hospital are those whose red blood corpuscles, as measured by a blood count, do not exceed a certain threshold. Above this limit access to the hospital, with its sheets and its vitamins, is impossible.

Even though my results 'improve' from one visit to the next; –

meaning that my red blood corpuscles count goes down, I am still above the threshold. I am given only consolation prizes: after the first visit, I am transferred from a normal brigade to one for 'weaklings of the first degree' (*Slabcommanda* No. 1), after the second, to the brigade for 'weaklings of the second degree' (*Slabcommanda* No. 2), and after the third, to the post of *pojarnik* (fire-fighter) in an almost uninhabited area of the camp. At this third failure I give in: the competition is too great and I shall always have too many blood corpuscles.

What's more, if changing brigade in the same camp is no big deal (it even represents a small advantage sometimes), changing camp is a leap into the unknown and can end up badly. It is a labour of Sisyphus just to resettle when faced with brutes who take advantage of your difficulties in order to vent their aggressiveness. But you can't appeal against the verdict pronounced by the camp doctors: they alone determine what level of blood corpuscles correspond to what job. So off I go on a cart driven by a *zek* who consoles me: 'You won't have a lot of work to do, *pojarnik*. While it is under snow the steppe never catches fire.' Why then do they need a firefighter? 'There was one in the days of the Germans,' he replies, as if the explanation suffices.

That's no explanation. Aren't the Germans cruel and stupid, and aren't we at war with them? 'Yes, but they know how to build; your hut is better built and better equipped than our dormitories.' And, to help overcome my remaining doubts, he adds: 'You are lucky. You will have 54 women for neighbours, blondes and brunettes, young and old, beautiful and less beautiful.'

An Eskimo would not feel out of place in the *pojarnik*'s hut. Everything around is white; there is endless snow. The nearest village, two kilometres away, squats behind a small rise in the road; there is another village beyond the horizon. The illusion of being free is perfect but cruel; there are no warders, not even a lock on the door, but where is there to go to? Near the hut in a strange windowless, red-brick barracks, the female brigade is housed; they work in a canning factory in the village. The rest of the landscape is empty, without a tree, without birds; a desert where the wind shifts the hills of snow. The winter of 1943–4 is less severe than those which preceded it and the cold is manageable. From time to time, ignoring the ban placed on wandering off, the *pojarnik* goes along the road to look at the village from afar. It is exhausting but he feels himself less excluded in knowing that there is still life elsewhere.

His relations with the women are better than he had feared. To all appearances their world is less harsh, less unpitying than that of the male *zeks*. Officially the *pojarnik* has to keep an eye on their stoves and help them to operate a water-heater twice a week, but in reality they have no need of him at all. In the days of the Volga Germans the red-brick barracks was used as a depot for inflammable materials – no one is too sure what these were – this explains the water-pipe fittings and the firefighter's hut.

Because they aren't so crowded, the *pojarnik*'s neighbours hardly notice his presence. Their barracks is never empty since, in addition to the *dejournaia* (day warden), there are always a few sick or absentees who haven't gone to work for the day.

The brigade leader, predictably, is a foul-mouthed permanent delinquent. Her four deputies, the *nariadtchitzé* (distributors of work), are no novices either and could have shown Sergeant-major Orlov a thing or two in the matter of profane oaths. Towards the *pojarnik* however they have no reason to be aggressive; they have practically no dealings with him. Of course they insinuate in jest that he is a cunning firefighter, who has managed to get off working and 'feasts his eyes' on 54 women. In fact so little do they believe it that when a place becomes free in the barracks for a night or two they are the first to invite him to take advantage of it: 'You'll be a lot warmer here than in your hut.'

What surprises him most is the kindness of some of his neighbours. Such kindness is very out of keeping with his experience of the Gulag. Lioussia 'the Peasantwoman' (or 'the Christian-woman'; in Russian these two words are almost identical) cleans his hut and brings him wood for his stove; Nadia does his washing, mends his clothes and even cuts his hair for him. And their friends approve of their doing it.

Why do they do it? How can they allow themselves such selfless behaviour in this world which never gives them something for nothing? In respect of supplies their brigade is not particularly well favoured; if anything, their food rations are rather inferior to the norm. Most of the women, as soon as they return from work, collapse from fatigue on to their bunks. They are frighteningly thin and the *pojarnik* sometimes says to himself: 'These women will not be of this world for much longer.' In the mornings, when the brigade goes out, some of them shout openly in the face of the *nariadtchitzé*: 'I can't take any more of it. I'm going to end up in the morgue.' The latter threaten them: 'Don't play the fool or they will come to get you. They'll take you away under escort and you will finish up in the dungeon.' These noisy scenes are the most distressing moments of the *pojarnik*'s day.

Whether he sleeps in his hut or in the barracks, Lioussia comes each morning to check that he is still alive. She obviously doesn't admit this; she is merely bringing him a little boiling water for his breakfast. But her manner of always calling him *biednyi pojarnik* (poor firefighter), combined with her worried expression, gives him to understand that he is in danger. He will have to start the obstacle race to the hospital all over again. How, though, can he set about it? With whom can he negotiate or simply talk? Nadia is more intelligent by far than Lioussia. She rarely speaks of herself and doesn't meddle in the lives of others. The camp, like the Foreign Legion, effaces the past; it is not forbidden to talk about it but you can just as easily be silent about it.

The best moment in the firefighter's day is when the work brigade returns and his neighbours bring him his rations from the village. He quickly eats the mess tin of *kacha* intended for two meals, the 300 grammes of bread and the half of herring. Sometimes Lioussia and Nadia make him reheat the food; his nerves are set on edge at the delay. He knows that his manner of eating is not rational but he can

216

do nothing about it; he is incapable of storing food. In the prison in Yerevan, when there had been a wait of only an hour or two between the bread, the herring and the tea, he never managed to eat the whole lot together. He certainly can't wait now when the food comes at the same time.

In his dreams, Nievka, Liouba, Clarissa – along with Kola and his friends – have been eclipsed by herrings. It is distressing and degrading; where will it end? In Yerevan he still dreamed about cooked dishes or Polish croissants; now he no longer sees anything but herrings.

There are two versions of what happened on the morning of Friday 13 January 1944. In the first version, the *pojarnik* has gone back to sleep in his hut after the daily uproar which precedes the departure of the women for work. Suddenly, a man in uniform wearing a fur cap shakes him: 'Hey, firefighter, you are a real fire risk. Quickly! Put out this smoking stove.' He doesn't remember the man's face, but the remark, which is deeply wounding to his self-esteem, engraved itself for ever on his memory.

However, that same morning – and this is the second version – Nadia came to look for his spare set of clothes because she is day warden today and is taking advantage of it to do some washing. She has promised him that afterwards she will heat some vegetable soup that she has pinched from the canning factory.

When you have no food to look forward to until the evening you don't easily forget such a savoury promise. The *pojarnik* settles down close to Nadia after having helped her to place her washing on a stove. Suddenly, contrary to all her habits of discretion and reserve, she asks him if he really believes Lioussia's story. The 'Peasant-woman' is rather prolix by nature and tells to whoever is willing to listen that she was sentenced to 10 years for having sheltered a deserter, an unfortunate stranger, who had hidden for a year in the forests near Tambov. Why shouldn't he believe her? She is a Christian and probably capable of such a charitable gesture; the *pojarnik* sees nothing suspicious in her story. Nadia keeps an eye on her washing and, as though she were talking to the saucepan, observes: 'The only suspicious thing is that Lioussia lived with this man; he wasn't a stranger therefore. A woman ought never to be ashamed of having loved, even when it concerns a deserter.' Then she turns to him and says: 'Did you know that I was beautiful once?'

At this he feels ill at ease. Courtesy requires that he reply: 'You are still beautiful,' but he doesn't wish to take any risks in this mine-field. But, without awaiting his reply, she continues: 'Men have killed one another over me. I was beautiful, *pojarnik*, I am not boasting; I shall tell you the story by and by.' It is at this exact moment that the barracks door opens and the man in uniform with the fur cap makes his entry.

In both versions of the story, he begins by addressing to the *pojarnik* the classic question asked by the Cheka: 'What letter does your name begin with?' They never pronounce the name of a 'wanted suspect' first themselves, so as to avoid any mistake. As it happens, everything is as expected, and the *pojarnik* has to leave with him for the commandant's office where he has been summoned for 14.00 hours.

Of course, the officer reveals nothing of the interrogation to come; it is contrary to camp conventions. In the first version, he expresses surprise that the *pojarnik* was sleeping so deeply at 9.30 in the morning and hadn't heard the arrival of his jeep – an arrogant and disagreeable reflection on his part. Later, after an hour's journey, he relaxes a little and expresses surprise also at the absence of a radio in this forgotten corner of the steppes, which is thus deprived of good news from the front. In each camp, there are loudspeakers everywhere which broadcast special programmes intended for the front – 'Listen, Front, this is Moscow speaking' – whereas in the red-brick barracks there is only silence. The officer and the *pojarnik* concur in regretting this anomaly and their conversation becomes more relaxed, too relaxed even, if you consder the enormous differences of rank and condition (especially physical condition) which separate them. The normally taciturn *pojarnik* talks to his escort about his preference for the meridional climate and extols the beauty of Yerevan and especially of Tiflis (Tbilisi) where the noisy River Koura flows, and from which a fine view extends over the nearby Caucasus. Emboldened, he even breaks into a little Georgian song: 'If you fall from the summits of these mountains to the bottom of the Koura without fastening on to something en route, the odds are that you can kiss goodbye to life.' It is a childish sort of song and the *pojarnik* can't stop himself from laughing at it, while adding: 'I am also in the process of somersaulting to the bottom of the Koura.' The officer takes his laugh for a sob and retorts: 'What's all this about somersaults? A man shouldn't whimper like this; it isn't seemly at all.' His tone, however, isn't threatening and that is enough to reassure the *pojarnik*.

In the second version everything passes off much better. The departure is preceded by two curious scenes. While looking for his things in the hut, the *pojarnik* racks his brains for the significance of this new transfer. He would like to have had Nadia's opinion at least, but she has remained in the barracks with the officer and 10 or so absentees. The *pojarnik* thinks hard about the best way to carry off the maximum of things from his hut: in the camp everything is sold and exchanged, even a firefighter's bucket and spade. Where can he hide them though? His bundle is too small to disguise objects of this size in it, or even the very thin blanket. He tries to put it on beneath his trousers, but doesn't manage to come to a decision about it, for fear of being searched and thrown into solitary confinement. In this version, he really does cry before leaving the hut, such is his confusion at this new transfer mingled with regret at the thought of leaving his neighbours.

When finally he returns to the red-brick barracks, Nadia and the officer are drinking tea. In his frightened rush, the fire-fighter forgets to ask Nadia to give him back his spare clothes, which are still boiling in the saucepan.

He only mentions this to the officer when it is too late to turn back, but the latter reassures him: 'You will be given other clothes, much better ones too.' This triggers an immediate thought: 'I am going to be admitted to hospital; they must have recognized the mistake they made in their last analysis. That's it, and it is in hospital too that you get given good clothes and sometimes even new ones.' It is the officer who asks questions however, and he asks him: 'Do you remember the circumstances in which you were incarcerated?'

By heavens, does he remember them! It was like a scene from a horror film. On 10 December 1942, at dawn, four Chekists with their dog burst into his room at the student residence in Yerevan, instilling in him a fear greater than anything he had experienced at the front. To make matters worse he was suffering from a terrible hangover, having celebrated the previous evening with Kola and the gang. But the *pojarnik* no longer knows how to describe such a scene, and he doesn't even know how to refer to the Chekists. As comrades? No. This is forbidden to *zeks* and he was warned against it from the first day of his arrest. Well then, four citizens with a dog? But that sounds more like a sequestration. He gives the date and otherwise talks only about Yerevan, of its three large avenues, Lenin, Stalin and Akopian, the last named of which – though he doesn't say so – is the most beautiful. His escort listens to this as if it were a rather boring geography lesson.

The jeep arrives in the wooded courtyard of the camp's central administration building well in advance of the appointed time. The officer offers a bath to the *pojarnik* who feels perfectly clean and prefers to wait alone in the antechamber of the commandant's office. There is a handsome earthenware stove in this room, like the one in his apartment in Lodz. He warms his back against the clean, lukewarm tiles and slides to the floor where he sleeps a deep sleep.

The *pojarnik* is offered the chance of becoming a free man in a world without enclosures, without barbed wire. All that he has to do is sign some forms duly prepared by Colonel Boudiennyi on the instructions of a good public prosecutor anxious about socialist

220

legality. With a signature, a nightmare of 13 months and 3 days would come to an end as suddenly as it started. Personally, I would have signed without even reading this official document. The *pojarnik*, however, sees things in a different light: he wants to recover his freedom, but he also needs a minimum of security such as he enjoyed in the firefighter's hut. Conscious of the fragility of his strength, he doesn't feel himself capable of leaving for just anywhere in any old fashion. What's more, conditioned by this harsh school of mistrust that characterizes the Gulag, he has learned to scent a trap behind every offer from a superior or a co-detainee. Even when it is a trifling matter – as, for example, when Lioussia offered to clean his hut for him – he hesitates, takes his time, and only accepts with a certain reluctance. But this explanation still seems too vague: it is difficult for me today to retrace the particular logic of thought processes shaped by a limited number of red blood corpuscles. In the 'heroic' version of the events, I shall credit the *pojarnik* with a stirring speech against an administrative forgery which attempted to cancel after the fact his arrest and all the sufferings that followed from it. I shall even introduce a note of irony: just because the *pojarnik* had dreamed of becoming a firefighter while he was still a youngster doesn't mean to say that he had appreciated this training course in the forsaken hut of the Volgalag.

In reality, in front of the colonel, the *pojarnik* is not in any state to construct such a complex speech, nor to display the slightest trace of insolence. A *zek*, even when miraculously cleared by a mysterious public prosecutor, doesn't imprudently throw disagreeable truths in the face of his gaolers. The *pojarnik* simply says 'no', and regrets that he is unable to sign anything whatsoever.

Although they are taken aback, the colonel and his assistant are extremely patient. (They have probably received a very elaborate communication from the public prosecutor, recommending that they handle this delicate case with tact.) They explain to the *pojarnik* the advantages that he can expect to obtain from the cancellation of his arrest and the destruction of his dossier. Their reasoning proceeds on the basis of the peculiarly Soviet attitude of complete confidence in the sacred authority of the written word regarding history as well as the destiny of individuals. We know that in the USSR by virtue of this principle, an event which is erased from the textbooks is considered never to have taken place. According to the colonel, a former prisoner who no longer has a dossier would no longer ever be so classified, even by the relevant state organs.

All of this eloquence, decked out with articles of the Code of Criminal Procedure of the RSFSR, is in vain. It is not even clear that the *pojarnik* has attentively followed the arguments of his interlocutors. In the 'heroic' version, he squares up to them in the name of justice – of vengeance even – but in reality he is more concerned with the immediate material advantages to be gained from the apparent goodwill of the colonel. So when the colonel, by now somewhat exasperated, asks him: 'But what do you want exactly?' he replies immediately: 'I want food. I haven't eaten since yesterday and hunger is preventing me from thinking properly.'

A bustle ensues at the other side of the table. The colonel, now indignant, reproaches his deputy with having left the *pojarnik* without food and orders him to bring him some sandwiches. The scene livens up: the deputy runs off to look for a secretary, who declares herself incompetent in the matter of sandwiches and who rushes off to find a cook, who in his turn arrives breathless, and asks the *pojarnik* a question from another epoch, another world: 'What would you like in your sandwiches, comrade?' 'Herrings,' the *pojarnik* replies like lightning, letting himself be guided by his unconscious which has discovered in this fish the sole source of protein in the *zek*'s diet. A new difficulty arises: inexplicably, in the canteen of the administrative centre of the Volgalag, there are no herrings. Someone can be sent to fetch them from the nearest camp but it will take time. The commandant's cheeks are flushed with anger, but it is aimed at his subordinates and not at the *pojarnik*. Towards the latter he becomes on the contrary more benevolent, as if he had suddenly been saddened by learning of the prevalence of hunger in his camp. He has a whole tin of corned beef brought to the starving *pojarnik*, and takes advantage of the refreshment break to ask about his life as a firefighter. Later, Kola and Vassia, basing their theory on the shape of his moustache, will say that he was surely from the Don region, and sensitive to human suffering for this very reason.

His attitude contrasts starkly with that of the arresting officer who, furious at having been lectured by his superior, now lays the blame on the *pojarnik*: 'Why didn't you ask to see the public prosecutor's "sanction" at the time of your arrest? Ignorance is no defence; no one should be ignorant of the law,' he says spitefully, without noticing the preposterous nature of his remarks. The commandant's cheeks turn a deeper red: he does not appreciate the intervention of his 'legal advisor'. 'Let's drop the mistakes of the past,' he says, in an almost paternal tone, 'and look instead towards the future. Where will you go after leaving here?' Silence. A very hard question. The *pojarnik* sees no answer to it. 'Have you any parents or family?' 'In Poland.' The commandant raises his hands in the air. This case seems insoluble.

A bright idea comes to him all of a sudden: 'According to your dossier you belong to the political service of the airforce and you were granted for health reasons six months' leave which expired on 1 April 1943. Go back to your post and I shall see what I can do to get the public prosecutor to authorize me to enter in your military papers that you have never left it. That will extricate us from an embarrassing situation. What do you say?'

'No,' the *pojarnik* persists. The deputy immediately advises him to 'stop being impertinent'. He accuses him in addition of being a lecher: the women with whom he had spoken that morning had told horrors about the firefighter and he is in a position to have him condemned to 15 years of camp for attempted rape. 'We aren't in Poland here you know, where the lord is the one who has the biggest prick. Here, the public prosecutor will immediately approve of the arrest of a hooligan who harasses defenceless women.' The commandant gets up to make his assistant be quiet, and the *pojarnik* takes advantage of the contradictions in the adversary's camp to refine his reply.

223

He isn't going to say that he no longer has the heart to organize Komsomol meetings and propagate the just socialist cause. He gets up and shows his emaciated arms, his swollen legs, and declares that he can't present himself in this state in front of the fighter pilots of the airforce, an élite unit. This argument sways the discussion: the commandant orders the *pojarnik* to be placed in the camp infirmary for officers, while he consults the public prosecutor on how to deal with this perplexing case.

Less than one hour later, the *pojarnik* is sleeping in clean sheets and pyjamas. He has a handsome room all to himself, in the well-heated house of a Volga German, deported in 1941. It is much better than in Moussia's home in Rostov. In fact, it is the most comfortable room that he has ever slept in since coming to the USSR. What's more he is soon to enjoy a deep sense of moral satisfaction: the nurse, after taking a blood sample, reveals to him that he ought to have been hospitalized a long time before, because of the very low red blood corpuscles count. The tests inside the camp, were as he had thought from the beginning, a con. Science has finally vindicated him.

The officers' infirmary in the Volgalag almost seems to have been designed for sleeping. Some ten fairly quiet patients are in the six rooms. The double windows insulate them from outside noise, while indoors, even the nurses seem to walk on tiptoe. Minor noises occur only at mealtimes and are rather agreeable to the ear. The food is brought in but reaches the patients still hot and is in a different class from that in the prisoners' canteens. The infrequency of medical visits doesn't worry the *pojarnik*: he is only here to rest before the next discussion with Colonel Boudiennyi.

It would be best in these conditions, following an old Russian saying, to unplug the brain and let the time flow by. In practice, however, he would have to be possessed of an unassailable serenity. Now the *pojarnik* has one point in common with me: a very strong propensity to hold himself culpable for things that he thinks he has done the wrong way, or hasn't done at all. Thus, he is tormented by the memory of a particular day in the prison in Yerevan, the day on which someone mentioned for the first time the public prosecutor to him. His scruples don't go as far as forcing him to agree with the arresting officer ('Ignorance is no defence; no one should be ignorant of the law'), nor to the point of making him regret his inability to articulate his demands to his gaolers. They torment him more subtly, by forcing him to remember once more everything which happened before and during that day that was so unlike the others.

Everything begins one evening in January 1943, one month after his arrest, when Captain Streltzov – let's say Strel – puts an end to his interrogation by the NKVD and accompanies him on foot to the prison in Yerevan. The town is already asleep and they walk through the empty streets like old acquaintances who are taking advantage of the fine weather to go for a nocturnal stroll. This last walk in semi-liberty made a deep impression on the *pojarnik*: never before had he known a town in which the air was so warm, so mild, right in the middle of January. Captain Strel is not very loquacious but, in contrast to his Armenian colleague, Captain Abak, he had never appeared violent in the course of the interrogation sessions. Tall, thin, with a long bespectacled face which gives him a vaguely professorial air, he is convinced that he is right about everything and maintains to the end that the accused – the future firefighter – has terrible crimes on his conscience that sooner or later he will admit to. He tells him that in the meantime other state services are going to take his case in hand and that they will inform him of charges brought within their jurisdiction. It would be in the accused's own interest to make a full confession, because these other services are capable of keeping him in prison or in a camp for eternity. On this note, Strel departs. His very special service doesn't distribute visiting cards but the prison management know how to contact him.

The prison in Yerevan is an historic monument. A former fortress, built in the time of the Turks, it appears rather splendid from the exterior, with its imposing, unscaleable walls. Inside, it is made up of very sombre vast rooms or halls. The one to which the *pojarnik* is assigned is crammed full with a whole battalion of detainees. Since the ceiling is very high, five metres at least, it should have been possible, like in other Soviet prisons, to instal tiered bunks, giving prisoners, if not exactly comfort, at least the possibility of sleeping without disturbing their neighbours. The explanation for this absence of furniture is immediately obvious: the real rulers in this place have always been the bugs, and any wooden fittings would only be for their benefit. During the daylight hours the detainees try to drive the bugs up the walls but under cover of darkness they come down again.

Only one of the detainees deigns to raise himself in order to greet the future *pojarnik*: the cell leader.

'What are you in for?' he asks authoritatively but without raising his voice, so as not to waken his companions. Having neither confessed nor been confronted with any formal charges, the newcomer can only protest his innocence. His interlocutor points out that all of the occupants of the cell are in the same situation: 'We are all innocent.' To explain the specific character of his innocence the future firefighter, avoiding any mention of Captain Strel's accusations, introduces himself as a student who has problems with his papers. The cell leader immediately draws a peremptory conclusion: 'So, you're a Trotskyist, eh? a Trotskyist student.' It is the word 'papers' which sets off in him this irrational reaction, and he laments aloud, as if a calamity had just befallen his hitherto peaceful cell. It is impossible to clear up the misunderstanding or to persuade the cell leader to go back on his decision to allocate to the 'Trotskyist student' a place to sleep, in between the toilet tank and another tank of almost the same height which contains the supply of drinking water.

A drama erupts on the very first night. The future *pojarnik* – we know that he is a restless sleeper – kicks the water barrel towards the wall near which are sleeping, in relative comfort, the leading figures of the 'permanent delinquency'. An unbelievable scrimmage immediately follows, leading to a generalized clamour of protest against this latest cold-blooded Trotskyist sabotage. Blows rain down on the future *pojarnik* and, if the cell leader had been armed, the culprit would have been executed on the spot, to the unanimous applause of the inmates.

Ostracized, he barely dares to try his luck when the big wheels of the 'permanent delinquency' announce a story-telling competition. The first three candidates fail abysmally, beneath boos and thumps, and so, the *pojarnik* opens his act in a state bordering on panic. He risks a lot; where he's concerned they won't forgive anything. But thanks to Nievka's taste for fairytales, he knows some of the stories by the brothers Grimm, which are ferocious enough to lend themselves, with some adjustments, to the taste of this public. The first story is listened to in silence; a good sign. The second, in which a frail orphan becomes superpowerful and ends up punishing a wicked prince – changed for the occasion into a chief of police – by plucking out his eyes, his tongue and tearing off his testicles, raises grunts of approval close to enthusiasm. He is asked for more, and from the next day, the future *pojarnik* has the good sense to go on to Alexander Dumas and *The Count of Monte Cristo*. This serial, to be spread over 15 or so evenings, will mark the first great turning point – and the only happy one – in his prison career.

The story of Edmond Dantès, a young sailor who falls victim to a public prosecutor consumed by political ambition, but who will succeed in escaping from his dungeon, find a fabulous treasure and usurp the title of Monte Cristo in order to seek justice for himself, seems to have been written expressly for the detainees in the prison in Yerevan. To begin with, the idea that a prisoner could escape and become immensely rich excites their imagination and their dreams; then, none of them would hesitate to take ferocious reprisals against the public prosecutors, the magistrates of the NKVD or the criminal militia. Thus far, credit for the spectacular success of the future *pojarnik* belongs entirely to Alexander Dumas.

But that is true only of the first part of the tale – the detention of Edmond Dantès, his friendship with the Abbé Faria, another forgotten inmate of the dungeons, and his escape. The second part,

227

devoted to his revenge, drags on 'for want of bum and tit'. Therefore Monte Cristo appears as a rather forlorn figure who doesn't know how to reconcile his legitimate thirst for vengeance with a love life more in keeping with his great wealth. With this in mind, the *pojarnik* feels justified in claiming that his adaptation of the work for the Yerevan audience not only improved the original but added to it a certain piquancy which his public appreciates. The method followed by this adaptation derives from two perfectly fair premises: firstly, that a well-matched Zorro couple is more efficacious than a single man, and secondly, that Monte Cristo could very well have met a Russian countess in Italy, for the St Petersburg nobility had a predilection for this country. All that is required is to place the treasure island in the Adriatic instead of the Tyrrhenian Sea, and to imagine that the former Edmond Dantès falls in love in Venice with his Russian accomplice-to-be, who is superbly beautiful and as Machiavellian as himself. As it is, their first rendezvous in St Mark's Square brings into the prison gloom in Yerevan a much needed poetic light, and brings out the taste for romance buried in the souls of the bosses of the 'permanent delinquency'.

The heroine invented by the future *pojarnik* borrows first from Alexander Blok the appearance of the mystery woman dressed in rustling silk, who is elusive and yet perfectly capable of inflicting a thousand torments on your careerist attorney. But as the tale gradually progresses, the accomplice of Monte Cristo begins increasingly to assume the traits of Natasha Rostova, the heroine of *War and Peace*, who has always been adored by Tolstoy's male readers, all of whom would like to have her for their wife. This is an audacious stroke, for the beautiful Tolstoyan heroine in no way seems inclined to cruel reprisals. In the company of Monte Cristo, however, her apparent innocence lulls the vigilance of those who are to be chastised. Also, she is an authentic aristocrat whereas they are newly ennobled. This enables me to emphasize the prestige that 'our' compatriots enjoyed and to improvise some comic episodes ridiculing the pretensions of the French nouveau-riche establishment.

The reader will appreciate of course that it would have been impossible to invent the vengeful ruses of Edmond and Natasha during the actual recitation itself; everything must be prepared in advance. However, it doesn't displease the future firefighter to turn over these episodes in his mind, to recite them to himself; even though the place which has been allocated to him, between the malodorous toilet and the leaky water tank, is not really propitious to inspiration. Fortunately, cell opinion is moving in his favour. One of the big shots, a recidivist who specializes in train hold-ups, understands immediately the enormous injustice that has been done to the 'student-raconteur', and promptly slaps on the cheek the cell leader who had been stupid enough to call the future *pojarnik* 'Trotskyist-student'. In the collective memory of Soviet prisons, Trotskyists are not people who are renowned for their skill at reciting the uplifting adventures of the Count of Monte Cristo. The big shot's orders are irrevocable: there is to be no more mention of 'Trotskyist' in relation to the student-raconteur; he is to be given a comfortable place on a mattress and he is to be properly fed, with the cream of the soup and not with the pale juice.

It is already a remarkable improvement, comparable to the transition from a third-rate hotel to a suite at the Ritz, but there will be more advantages to come. The godfathers of the 'permanent delinquency' will allow all the prisoners to listen to the serial on Edmond and Natasha, but, as it is a suspense story, they forbid anyone to approach the student-raconteur with a view to learning the rest of the story. Now if it is true that these godfathers are not very hot on grammar – Solzhenitsyn in *The Gulag Archipelago* will even claim that they can't conjugate verbs – they are very strict about everything that pertains to their code of honour. If they have proclaimed a law they themselves are the first to respect it scrupulously. Even the big shot who did train jobs doesn't try to take advantage, during the daily exercise period, of the influence he has with the story-teller. On the other hand he does show a certain interest in his prison dossier. Unable to make either head or tail of it he summons the cell leader once again and orders him to arrange a meeting of the story teller with a godfather versed in matters of jurisprudence who is detained in another block. Since moving around between cells is strictly forbidden, the cell leader will have to use great ingenuity to carry out this order. But with his own position at stake, he manages to pull it off. One fine morning after the toilet break, a warder takes the story teller to the legal expert's cell.

This cell appears suitably imposing, as befits the prestige of a detainee of distinction: it is a former hall of arms, as vast as a railway station hall. It is also relatively uncrowded. The man who is expecting the future *pojarnik* seems astonishingly young – no more than 30 years old – but the mysteries of the hierarchy in the 'permanent delinquency' are as difficult to penetrate as those of the Central Committee of the CPSU. A self-assured Armenian with a harsh unsmiling face, and lively eyes, he has a whole corner of the cell to himself. To obtain yet more privacy, he enjoins his 'bodyguards' to move off the *frayer* and his subordinates. He indicates a stool near his bed, places a bowl full of grapes and oranges on a little table and relaxes himself, stretched out on his double mattress. 'Tell me everything, keep nothing back,' he says. 'I can only be of help to you if you tell me the whole story with all the details.' He closes his eyes, not to sleep but to concentrate. In the course of the narration he will react indignantly from time to time, either at the behaviour of Captains Strel and Abak or at the stupidity of the future *pojarnik*.

The same evening, at the officers' infirmary in the Volgalag, here then is how the *pojarnik* recollects his report to the legal expert.

'At the time of my arrest on 10 December 1942, I was very frightened, more so than I ever was at the front. It happened at dawn, at the student residence. There was something that was both brutal and paralysing about this intrusion of four Chekists and their huge police dog. To crown it all I had a terrible hangover. The night before with my trainee-pilot friends, from the village of Mietchotka, Kola, Vassia, Volodia and Kostia, I had celebrated our army's success at the Stalingrad front, and the anniversary of my arrival in the USSR, three years earlier. We had drunk a good deal at the Intourist Restaurant . . .'

'Where? You must be crazy! It is the most expensive and most closely watched place in all of the southern Soviet republics, if not indeed in the whole of the USSR . . .' The legal expert blows his top.

'We knew that, but for one thing we had a fair amount of money, having acquired a fine length of pure woollen cloth during the retreat from the Caucasus and this had earned us a small fortune at the fleamarket in Tiflis; for another we didn't know where to go, our attempts at picking up girls having failed. Obviously we would have preferred to spend our evenings at the homes of some girls. We were fed up and we discovered that you can find everything at the Intourist, so we became regular customers of this restaurant and the waiters, whom we tipped generously, seemed to appreciate and looked after us. I didn't see why I should be arrested for that.

'My conscience wasn't entirely easy though. The mild climate had gone to my head and, because I had been wounded in Nalchik, I behaved as though I were a creditor of the Soviet Union, authorized to do whatever I liked, or rather to no longer do anything at all. I had obtained six months' leave from the airforce to convalesce and to resume my studies but, in fact, I had no need of any further medical care and never went to hospital. Similarly, my desire to study Russian language and literature was less than wholehearted, and yet it was the only faculty that I could attend at Yerevan University since all the other courses were in Armenian.'

'There is no crime in that; a serviceman on leave has the right to do nothing. What were your official resources?' my listener asks, his eyes still closed.

'Everything was above board in this respect. I continued to receive my salary and a student grant. I was housed for almost nothing in a shared room at the student residence. I had access to the university canteen and I also went sometimes to the airforce mess where I was well known and liked. Recalling the difficulties I had had in obtaining a residence permit in Kislovodsk, because of my Polish origins, in Yerevan I declared that I had been born in Rostov, of Russian nationality.'

'Not so quickly!' the expert interrupts, asking me to tell him about the episode in Kislovodsk. The digression will be a long one, for he wants to know the details about Nievka and Commissar Bielokonienko, as well as those concerning the papers issued to me in Rostov in 1940. Even though I am convinced of my listener's goodwill, I avoid all mention of Western Siberia and of my Muscovite cousin, Stepan Vladimirovitch. One is never 100 per cent sincere, even in a confessional.

'It seemed to me that Commissar Bielokonienko, also recalling the distressing incident in Kislovodosk, deliberately emphasized, in the character reference he gave me for the local authorities and the university, the extent of my "Russian consciousness and culture". I still hesitated before making my false declaration of identity, even though I knew full well that, for the moment, the authorities would have to take my word for it. Since our papers of origin had been burned in Kislovodsk, and since Rostov remained under German occupation, they had absolutely no way of verifying what I told them. But I was also afraid of remaining stuck in Russia forever. In the future, how could I obtain permission to return to Poland after having declared myself Russian, and having said that I was born in Rostov? My friends in the Mietchotka clan quickly dispelled my apprehensions on this score, saying that it was simply a subterfuge without any consequences for the future. "On 1 April 1943," Kola said, "you will come back into the 'eleventh' of the VVS, where even the kitchen mule knows that you are a *Polskii pan*." My friends wanted to see me transferred to the student residence for the safety of our war treasure; in barracks there are often searches and also thefts.'

'Your code of honour can't be worth much,' the expert remarks. 'Otherwise you wouldn't steal from each other. But let's get to the heart of the matter: what did the NKVD say about your papers?'

'One further detail, if you will bear with me. As ill luck would have it, all my acquaintances at Yerevan University were from Rostov, and most of them were the homesick type who talked about

232

their town, morning, noon and night. I used to go out quite a lot with Svetlana, the daughter of a history professor, and she soon guessed that I wasn't really from Rostov. It wasn't important in her case because she liked me and we trusted each other. With Oleg, my room mate, the situation was more complicated. From the first Kola found him unsympathetic and we never invited him to our social evenings. I wouldn't have minded inviting him; I felt sorry for him because he had lost a leg at the front, but Kola, guided in this by his sixth sense, declared that he was an informer. Whether true or not, each time that I came back a little the worse for liquor, Oleg would wear me out with questions about Rostov, about girls there whom I might have known over the years. Generally I coped well with it, but on the night of 9–10 December, after an evening of celebrations, I told Oleg to go to hell: "I don't remember either your blonde-haired Nadia or your brunette Vera because I am Polish, and not a *kacap* (a pejorative for Russians) like you!" This was the drink talking: such remarks are futile and could only prove insulting to an injured war veteran. His revenge though was swift; some hours later the four Chekists were already searching our room.'

'Your friend Kola was right. You can't be too careful with informers. But tell me now about your interrogation by the NKVD,' the expert concludes, handing me a fine bunch of Armenian grapes.

'For the first two or three days Captain Strel confined himself to checking details, in such a way as to make me feel that the NKVD had been keeping a close watch on me since my arrival in Yerevan. His dossier seemed more detailed than my own diary would have been, particularly in respect of finances and relations with Svetlana. All my expenses were meticulously noted – I am notoriously incapable of keeping such accounts myself – as were all my outings with the professor's daughter. Svetlana was more excited by the opportunity to explore southern Armenia than by the study of her native language. Since our relationship was platonic (through no fault of mine) Strel's corroboration of events in no way embarrassed me. The two of us often went to the picturesque market in Yerevan to enjoy the strong-tasting Kurdish cheese. Yes, we had sometimes held hands so as not to lose each other in a crowd, but it could hardly have been construed as an outrage against public decency. I freely admitted that we had skipped lots of our classes at the university – especially those on Old Slavonic, which were particularly uninspiring – and Komsomol meetings too, but this "misconduct" surely wasn't a breach of the law.'

'Are you sure that this girl isn't their informer?'

'No. She has other failings, but not that one. Svetlana is an old-fashioned 22-year-old virgin, who loves her father and is resolved upon becoming a history teacher like him. Tall and well-built, attractive in a very Russian way, she would have been an ideal prey for the young blades of the "eleventh", but I always kept her out of circulation in the hope that, sooner or later, she would give herself to me.'

'That is neither here nor there,' the legal expert comments. 'It doesn't prove that she wasn't reporting on you to the NKVD. But carry on, and stick to the point.'

'With the appearance of Captain Abak, my position worsened. This little man, who spoke an execrable Russian, was out for blood. "You have left your honesty on Mount Ararat on the bulls' horns," he said to me. I replied that Ararat was in Turkey and that I had never set foot there. Then he asked me: "How would you like to taste some Iranian sausage?" – and he produced a rubber truncheon from his drawer.

'OK, throughout each interrogation there is a good guy and a bad guy; it's part of the game. It has nothing to do with the fact that Abak is Armenian. If he were Russian he would have told you that you had left your integrity in the Caucasus, on the Elbrus or on the Kazbek. Don't confuse the national question with your personal troubles.'

(An Armenian himself, the expert clearly doesn't appreciate my criticisms of his Chekist compatriot.)

'But it was Abak himself who started it by accusing me of being anti-Armenian. He possessed a whole dossier proving that on such and such a day, at a given time, I had called the Armenians "Persians"; that on another occasion, also duly recorded, I had made fun out of the small drinking-water fountains at the street corners in the centre of Yerevan, and that I had time and time again insulted Armenia. He even forced me to repeat 10 times, under threat of his Iranian sausage, that water in Yerevan is a lot better than the vodka of the Russians.'

'Let's not waste time with this childishness; an Armenian interrogated in Russia would meet with more problems than you have encountered in our republic.'

'That's a poor consolation. You don't seem to realize that even here, in prison, half of the staff don't speak a word of Russian. When the disinfected clothing is handed out how am I supposed to understand orders that are given only in Armenian? They call out: "*Es oumné?*" In Russian, *oumno* means wise, intelligent, so their question would seem to mean: "The one who is intelligent, take one step forward." Here it means: "Whose is this?" And whoever doesn't reply in time is punished and receives his disinfected clothes last.'

'You can enter that in the prison complaints book,' the expert says, laughing for the first time, clearly amused at the discovery that Russian speakers felt ill at ease in this country.

'To support his accusations, Captain Abak wanted to give a particular – and xenophobic – significance to an episode of no importance. Right at the start of our stay in Yerevan, we had diverted a tram. It happened like this. Our gang had missed the last tram home one evening, and we managed to persuade a tram driver who delivered bread to the bakery shops during the night, to take us back to the barracks, which were situated quite far away, near the synthetic rubber factory. We paid him more roubles than he earns in a week's work, and we also tipped his assistants, who were well pleased by this excursion across a sleeping Yerevan. No charge was brought against us at the time. Now, suddenly, Captain Abak unloads the entire responsibility for the incident on me, alleging that

235

because of me, the workers in Yerevan were deprived of bread. In his opinion this crime alone is going to earn me a few years in prison.'

'Tall tales. A red herring to get you muddled,' the expert declares. 'Come to the point more quickly.'

'The "point" was a very long time in coming, at least two weeks. Each evening I thought that they were going to release me since Strel and Abak beat about the bush without anything definite emerging. At the time of my arrest I had only about one thousand roubles of our war treasure left – hardly something over which to create a major fuss. I pretended that this sum had come from the sale of my watch, which was a mistake. They knew about everything, including the fact that my watch had been stolen in the hospital in Beslan. I had to confess therefore, and claim sole responsibility for salvaging the woollen cloth, which had been sold in Tiflis. They seemed indifferent, and Strel even remarked with a hint of irony that I had applied the scorched-earth tactic after a fashion by leaving nothing to the enemy.

'After this, I spoke to them, unprompted, about the question of my Polish nationality, and this outburst of sincerity also made them laugh. Well informed from their dossier, they obviously knew that I had lied in order to get my residence permit in Yerevan. An unnecessary lie in their view, for residence would have been granted to me in any case. Here too, though, from their point of view, there was nothing to make a fuss about – "to skin a cat over" in Captain Strel's own words. Why then did they keep me locked up in this seedy little basement cell?

'Finally, when I began to get impatient and started to mention at every opportunity my claims to consideration in virtue of military service, Strel got up and threw in my face, syllable by syllable: "*Ty Ger-man-skaia pros-ti-tut-ka* (You are a German prostitute)." This vulgar invective, unworthy of a Chekist intellectual, overwhelmed me. At the time of my concussion, I had tried in vain to get up again, whereas this time the chill caused by the uncontrollable terror prevented me from speaking at all. I ought to have protested, for even a captain in the Cheka hasn't the right to insult people in this

236

way, but my tongue would not obey me. By a violent effort of will I managed eventually to articulate, in a trembling voice, that I had damned near lost my life fighting the Germans at the front. "Damned near lost my life," he mimics sarcastically. "Yet here you are, well and truly alive. Spies are always above suspicion, otherwise they would easily be caught." His spine-chilling irony was even more disturbing than his initial abusive taunts, and yet, little by little, I lost my fear and even fell prey to an immense indifference.

'Master of the situation, Strel resumed his verbal assault: "The Krauts are holding your family hostage. They placed you clandestinely in Rostov. You then found cover as a Komsomol and infiltrated our airforce. They have never stopped paying you and controlling you, even in the Caucasus where you feigned concussion. In Yerevan however, when they put pressure on you to obtain information about our aviation, they made the mistake of exposing you and at that very moment we were waiting for you!"

'If it were only a nightmare! Am I not still in hospital in Beslan, stretched out on my mattress? But Strel lowers his bespectacled head closer to me: "Don't be afraid; I am not bloodthirsty. Tell us the names of your accomplices in Armenia and Turkey, and you will get off with a light sentence." '

'Heavens above, this is no laughing matter!' the expert interjects, his eyes wide open, flabbergasted by the gravity of my case. His astonishment doesn't last though; a minute later he is already reproaching himself for having taken me so seriously: 'If you were a spy, even of the smallest calibre, you would already be in the morgue, and not in this cell with common mortals. Carry on. Your case is an interesting one, and it amuses me.' He seems to have a pronounced taste for espionage stories.

'It was just like at the front. After the heavy artillery fire they explore the terrain, slowly, systematically. To destroy my lines of defence, Strel put aside my presumed accomplices in order to first lay bare my entire history. Why had my parents left Rostov after the great proletarian revolution of October 1917? The answer I offered, that my mother wanted to complete her studies at the University of Warsaw, didn't hold up to Strel's assaults for very long. In a household, he declares, it is always the man who decides on the place of residence. Right then. They were property owners, and not office workers as I had declared earlier on the forms. Next? Hold on, sunshine. Are there, or have there ever been, any property owners who were not anxious to recover their goods and who are not militant counter-revolutionaries? But my father, who was Jewish, surely couldn't be suspected of backing Hitler, who had set himself the objective of exterminating the Jews; it would have been suicidal on his part . . . What a blunder! Strel couldn't get over my ignorance: according to him rich Jews prospered in Hitler's entourage, because the links of class take precedence over all others; this is one of the first principles of our knowledge about the history of humanity, from primitive communist societies up to socialism, at which point class differences are finally suppressed.

'Laying cards on the table but changing the game each day, he claimed at one moment that my parents were hostages, at the next, that they were accomplices of the Third Reich. He claimed that I was an infiltrator in the Komsomol, then that I was a real Komsomol whose duty it was to help him in the name of our 'common cause'. Over and above this refined dialectic he possessed an advantage which assured him of victory in this war of attrition: during the day he sat behind an imposing desk while I was on a stool a good distance away; but more importantly he went back every evening to his home in town, as free as a bird, whereas I returned to my basement cell. I was exhausted and yet, in his own words, we were only at the stage of the *hors d'oeuvre*. To get to the main dish more speedily, I submitted to a self-criticism. I admitted to the nefarious influence of my parents, to having always remained a narrow-minded petit-bourgeois, and to plenty of other similar blots. My soul was so black that I could have become the agent of practically any power, even the Japanese or the Italians. Strel interpreted everything the wrong way: "Good. Now tell us about the undertakings you gave them." "What undertakings?" "That is for you to reveal to us," he would reply with his patient air, as if he were ready to spend his life in this room to pluck my soul from the claws of the devil.

'In fact his dossier on my past in Rostov and in the airforce was so empty of any incriminating material that the only real weapon he possessed was his patience. To be sure he had harvested some bits of gossip from the army barracks, which proved only that in the lives of every one of us there are a lot of small facts that take some explaining. Someone had told him, for example, that at the beginning of 1942 I had decided to join up with Anders' army – I probably mentioned it in order to put an end to the tedious anti-Polish jokes and Strel had deduced from it that my mythical German "bosses" had forbidden me to enlist in it. These same chiefs had allegedly ordered me to leave Beslan and to refuse to have myself treated in Krasnovodsk. All of these fabrications proved only one thing to me; that Strel had a network of spies within the 'eleventh', which in other circumstances would have surprised or even shocked me. In the frame of mind I had reached, it all appeared to me absurd and interminable – inconsequential also, because when I asked him who the witnesses of my supposed crimes had been, he replied coldly: "We still don't know who your controllers are, but you will certainly finish by identifying them for us."

'Abak intervened periodically in this dramatic atmosphere, as though to destroy whatever small complicity his colleague had created in the name of our "common cause". In Captain Abak's version my parents personally had put Hitler in power and as for me, I had been active since early childhood in the most fanatical Nazi movements. He said whatever came into his head. He made Nievka a nymphomaniac, and made it clear she had nothing to do with my not joining the Polish army. Coming as they did from a crazy, violent character, these insults simply filled me with disgust. "Just wait and see, you Chekist shithead," I'd say to myself, remembering Nievka's oath. "If she survives the German occupation of Kislovodsk, she will make you pay dearly for that insult. Andrei Zhdanov in

239

person will twist your balls off to avenge her." '

'Don't create too many illusions for yourself,' the expert says, his eyes closed once more. 'It is odd that they didn't try to implicate your reveller friends from the airforce. Are you sure that they weren't aiming, through you, at bigger game? Didn't they ever talk about a third party, another suspect, or about a compromising acquaintance?'

'Yes, but he was an Armenian whom I had met and spoken to without having a common language. It is another of these inexplicable things which happen in life.'

'Try me and see,' the benevolent expert challenges, 'we have plenty of time.'

'The gang may well be revellers, as you say, but we're prudent. Because we feared our superiors as much as the NKVD, we used to take a very discreet table at the Intourist Restaurant, hidden from the rest of the room by a large column. In the corner, there were two other small tables, one of them always empty, the other regularly occupied by the same customer: a solitary, thoughtful young man, who ate very little and supped a lot of wine, as if hoping to drown his sorrows. Who could he be? A waiter reassured us that he wasn't trying to eavesdrop on us since he didn't understand Russian. He had been repatriated from France with some thousands of Armenians in 1938, and had simply kept up the habit of drinking in public, like they do in France.

'When I heard this I immediately felt a keen empathy with this loner who had come from the West, whose fate resembled my own in some ways. In addition, since my brother Boris had been a student in France, I was sure that we would have lots of things to tell each other. In what language though, since he didn't speak Russian, nor I French? One evening, having still not found any solution, I approached his table, saying simply: "*La Grande Illusion*," the title of the last French film that I had seen in Poland. The Armenian hesitated a little, fixed his melancholy gaze on me, then he guessed my intention. "Jean Renoir," he replied. He knew this film then. I continued: "Pierre Fresnay, Erich von Stroheim," picturing once again in my mind's eye these actors during their last dialogue in the fortress. The Armenian visualized them at the same time as I did. "Jean Gabin, Jean Carette," he said, thus indicating the following scene to me, and I concluded with "Dita Parlo," the German woman who helped the two fugitives to escape. It was a marvellous discovery; we had found a means of communicating and, at the same time, of mentally projecting works which were dear to us both.

'He invited me to his table, ordered some wine and passed on to other films, *Quai des Brumes*, then *Pépe le Moko*. The rule of our dialogue was simple: we had to cite the names of the protagonists in the order of their appearance on the screen and follow them from one scene to the next. All commentary would have been superfluous, or worse, an interference, in the game of re-viewing the films in our memories. His choice was rather morose, so I tried to lead him towards René Clair and to make him laugh a little with *Le million, Sous les toits de Paris*, or *A nous la liberté*. He appreciated this and, for the first time, mimed some gestures, probably meaning: "I would give anything to be able to see these films once more." His eyes appeared less sad to me and even began to sparkle when, in sign language, he tried to explain something to me about Annabella and Michèle Morgan. Intrigued by all of this, Kola drew close to listen but I begged him not to disturb us; in any case these titles, these names and faces belonged only to our world.

'Since he had been brought up in France it was inevitable that my new companion would know the repertoire of French cinema better than I did, and, at the end of our first bottle of wine, I was already having problems in following him. Some of his titles meant nothing to me. They probably hadn't been released in Poland, or else I just hadn't seen them. In order not to let the conversation flag, a change of subject was necessary. Since politics was to be avoided, I tried my luck with a foray into sport. Racing Club de Paris? Arsenal of London? Rapid of Vienna? Juventus, Sparta, Ferencvaros? Yes, he nodded his head for each of these clubs, but didn't say anything. Who was the best goalkeeper then, Planicka the Czech or the

Spaniard Zamorra? And the Austrian Wunderteam? And the English football ace Alex James? No, he didn't follow. This young Armenian was not a football fan. Nor a boxing fan either, and it was to no avail that I mimed for him the two "fights of the century", between the Jewish American Max Baer and the German Max Schmelling. Even Marcel Thil, the great French middleweight champion, didn't raise the slightest tipsy smile from him.

'We had no desire to leave each other. It would have been a great pity to return to the tedium of our daily lives after having awakened the splendours of another time. And so, suddenly, by tacit agreement, we moved on to Hollywood. There, we could go on ransacking the archives for ever, and sigh, thinking of stars whose like will never be seen again. I said "Al Jolson," and the Armenian mimed his response; he also knew this singer who had starred in one of the first talkies. He kicked off with *The Champ* because, inexplicably, while being totally uninterested in boxing, he rated this film, starring Wallace Beery and James Cagney, very highly. "Bang, bang," what do you say to the westerns? Fine. "Ralph Scott," he replied, while making clear from a torrent of names that he preferred the great romantics, Clark Gable, "the King", and, obviously, Gary Cooper. He even remembered Rudolf Valentino; bravo! I was too young myself to have seen his films.

'Behind the column, a group of drunken officers were singing and stamping their boots on the floor. "Fred Astaire and Ginger Rogers" – the Armenian cited their names with a wink of complicity. There is indeed a difference between the stylish tapping of feet at our table and the brutish din coming from behind the column. Then, with a single voice, we pronounced the same words: "Paul Muni" and "I am a Fugitive from a Chain Gang." What a coincidence! Perhaps because both of us in our different ways feel that we are "fugitives". But our language was too limited to express concepts.

'After the second bottle of strong Armenian wine, we called up the international superstars, these women who succeeded in making all of the men in the West dream about them, Marlene Dietrich or Greta Garbo, the Blue Angel or Queen Christine. "I refuse to choose between them," my Armenian gestured with all the ardour and dexterity of a Southerner. "I want them both." And the blonde vamp Carole Lombard? At the mention of this name, forgetting our conventions, he switched over into rapid and serious speech, in French. Was he in love with Carole Lombard? Did he find it disagreeable to talk about her in this prosaic restaurant, the Intourist?

'I had to go; they were calling for me at my table. Not wishing to leave on a note of misunderstanding, or at least on a question mark, I went back to the first film which had allowed us to communicate. I began with "Dita Parlo", and he said by way of farewell: "Ah! La Grande Illusion!"'

'And that's the long and the short of it. I never saw my Armenian again and I don't know his name, his age, or his address, yet he is a friend.'

'I understand, but of what use was it to you to search in your memories for people and things that you will never see again?'

'We couldn't help it; it was in our heads, and anyway how is one to know what is useful and what isn't?'

'What about our own Liuba Orlova; isn't she as beautiful?' he asks with chauvinist curiosity.

'Certainly, I find her extraordinary, particularly in *The Circus*. What's more I am a great admirer of Trauberg and Kozintsev, and of Eisenstein, a little less so of Pudovkin. But my friendship with the Armenian from France doesn't depend upon the cinema. I warned you that I was incapable of explaining it.'

'All right, all right, let's get back to Strel and Abak's investigation, and not linger over each isolated episode.'

'But it was isolated episodes that they were so interested in uncovering! For want of witnesses they tried to use against me gaps in my timetable: "In Makhatch-Kala, you disappeared for two hours." "I was with the red-haired nurse, Liuba, whose address I have here on me." "Your alibi is worthless. Anyone can have a nurse's address." Continuing along this track they explored all the opportunities I had had for secret meetings in Yerevan. Do you know Maxim's song in the trilogy by Trauberg and Kozintsev: "Where is this street, where is this house, where is this girl with whom I'm in love? . . ." '

'Everyone knows it; you aren't the only one who goes to the cinema.'

'Well then, replace "girl" with "spy", and "love" by "complicity", and you will have the chorus of the last phase of their investigation. In the film, Maxim wasn't long in finding his fiancée, whereas in Yerevan I couldn't manage to help them find anyone. For some peace I would have admitted perhaps to meetings with suspects of their choice, but to invent "this street and this house", and the "first name and family name" of someone I had neither seen nor known, was beyond me. For sure my conversation with the repatriated Armenian gave them a pretext to harass me. According to their informer, we had spoken in German and the Armenian had called me by my first name ('Carole Lombard'). But if he had really been the one they had been talking about, my controller, they had only to arrest him at the Intourist Restaurant!'

'You bet your life they could have! As if they didn't already know all the regulars of this restaurant. Why, they even know the colour of their parents' eyes!'

'We were stuck – Strel and Abak in their armchairs and me on my stool. The trainee pilots having been cleared of any suspicion – "Don't touch our airforce" – I was in no position to give them anyone other than Svetlana, whom they knew already and who didn't quite fit as the Mata Hari of Yerevan. Her historian father, a relative of a friend of Lenin, the (formerly) famous Professor Pokrovski, was also excluded. As for my accomplices in Turkey, this part of the accusation was not helped by my ignorance of geography. I know nothing about this country or its inhabitants. When I arrived in Yerevan I was even surprised to see Mount Ararat on the other side of the frontier; I had always thought that this mountain, on which Noah's Ark ran aground, was somewhere in the Middle East, between Egypt and Babylon.'

'Don't make a virtue of ignorance. Mount Ararat occupies an important place in Armenian culture, and it isn't merely a matter of ancient history.'

'All right. If I get out of here I promise you that I'll plunge myself into Armenian culture, and anyway I was delighted by the view over Mount Ararat. At the time, however, I didn't know what to believe. During the final interrogation sessions, I felt that Strel no longer believed in his initial accusation. He simply claimed that he no longer had time to devote to my case, and regretted my obstinacy in keeping to myself a secret which was going to poison my entire life.'

'Right. Well done. Tell me once more what he said to you while taking you to the prison.'

'He assured me that since he really wasn't bloodthirsty, he genuinely wanted to help me, but that I needed above all to free my conscience of the weight which was crushing it. In his view, once my dossier was taken up by state agencies less well-disposed towards me, it could well earn me long years in prison.'

'Let's walk a few paces to stretch our legs,' says the expert. His minders immediately clear a path for us, moving people to one side and warning them to be quiet. 'My friends in your cell have asked me to give you some advice, because I know by heart the criminal codes of the former Republic of Transcaucasia, the Republic of Armenia, founded in 1936, and of the USSR,' my host explains, as though to let me understand that he could have been a Minister of Justice and enjoyed altogether more significant perks than that of being the only prisoner to have the use of a double bed. 'Unfortunately your case leaves me perplexed. It's hard to know which way to approach it, because it is one which has no due form. In our codes of criminal law, there are no articles relating to people found in possession of a thousand roubles who have made a partially erroneous declaration of identity. Perhaps in administrative law there is something on the subject of these trifles, but I'm not sure. To put it another way, legally speaking you don't exist, you have no juridical profile. Is that clear?'

'Perfectly so. But what must I do then to acquire one?' Even while replying to him I start feeling my face.

'Just a moment. Because of these minor matters you aroused the curiosity of the most important wartime service, the formidable "Death to spies", known by its acronym *Smerch*. The latter have certainly established that there was no link between your one thousand roubles and any espionage, otherwise you would already be dead and buried. In the course of their enquiry you admitted various inanities about your parents or about yourself, which may serve as a pretext to expel you from the Komsomol, but are insufficient to charge you with anti-Soviet activities under Article 58. Ah, my dear story teller, had your objective, in planting yourself in Yerevan, been to rob the Gosbank branch, I could have given you some advice. But you are merely a *frayer* who has succeeded in attracting the attention, for no good reason, of the most important security services of our republic. I have never, myself, met a *frayer* like you; you are here but your head is elsewhere, in a world about which we Soviets know nothing.'

'My head is here, and the rest of me also, in this bug haven, and I would very much like not to have to rot here much longer!'

He sympathizes but sees no way out. Back in his corner and stretched out once again, he searches in his archival head for some clues from the legal codes of the USSR.

'They are going to deport you or send you to a military labour battalion. You wanted to hoodwink them to get your residence permit in Yerevan and now they will make it a matter of honour to expel you from this town. It has nothing to do with the law, the criminal codes provide no justification for it. I am going by precedents, by their current administrative practice. Just now though, there is frightful chaos in their prison system, because they recently transferred a large number of prisoners from the prisons and camps of the Caucasus to Yerevan, and many of them have no dossier; they are not in due form, like yourself. What should you do? If you were Armenian and a little more on the ball, I would have advised you to complain to the public prosecutor about wrongful detention. Since however you are neither from here nor from there, you would perhaps do better not to protest. Sooner or later they will have to put your case in due form.'

Towards the end of the day, before the roll call of detainees, he had me accompanied back to my cell, recommending that I return to see him for a further consultation as soon as I should come into the possession of a presentable juridical profile.

Some days later, a typical prison uproar put the future *pojarnik* in a state of alert. Some of the prisoners are being led off, but which ones and where to? He is one of them! He's going – orders: quickly, shower, disinfection – is it a good sign? Do they want him to be clean for his release? Perhaps. Besides, he finds the bathing ritual almost agreeable, but there are about 30 detainees with him and he is doubtful at the idea that they might carry out a collective release of prisoners, as happens after an amnesty. On the other hand the legal expert has explained to him that they had brought to the prison many prisoners without dossiers who were therefore potentially scheduled for release. Under the shower the future *pojarnik* questions his neighbour, an Armenian who is neither happy nor sad, a young detainee with a dreary expression. 'We are going to work,' he replies in an approximate Russian. So, it is still not freedom. But if they place the *pojarnik* into a military labour battalion he will know how to get by; once on the outside he will find a way of returning to the airforce.

The lorry journey lasts less than an hour. The 30 prisoners, the future *pojarnik* among them, are taken to the nearest labour camp and not to a military labour battalion. With or without dossiers, the *pojarnik* and his companions were to be used to replace exhausted *zeks* at the construction site of the bridge across the River Zanga.

In his infirmary bed, it comes to the firefighter: 'That's the moment when I should have protested with the utmost energy to the public prosecutor, if I hadn't been such a dunce!' Angry at the arbitrariness of it and his own passivity, he says aloud: 'It's a scandal, to be brought out of your cell one morning, asked with what letter your name begins and told to go and build a bridge for four months! Even the expert, who knows all the codes of the Armenian Republic and of the USSR hadn't foreseen such an eventuality. Someone had definitely overstepped their authority here. Is it Captain Abak who continues to work unceasingly against me out of sheer xenophobia?'

A nurse pushes the door open, thinking that the *pojarnik* is calling for her or kicking up a fuss about something, but he calms down. In any case, as the old Russian proverb has it, there is no point in waving your fist after the brawl is over. The *pojarnik* notes that, at the time of the facts recalled here, not only could he not have found a public prosecutor – there wasn't one around – but he wasn't even interested in finding one. For on the day of his transfer to the construction site, he was really rather pleased about it, almost happy.

To leave behind him the bug-infected prison, for springtime sunshine, on the banks of a sparkling river, was not a change of luck to be disdained. The site delighted him, and he also enjoyed the sensation of inhaling, in deep breaths, the famous Armenian spring air. In the cell those who were from the region had often spoken to him about this time of year when the sun doesn't yet beat down too strongly, but already makes all the colours of the exotic, southern vegetation vibrate in a warm haze. They had exaggerated somewhat, to be sure. On our construction site, to begin with, there isn't a single flower. But in the middle of a war who could claim to have been transported to a perfumed garden?

Viewed from the outside, our living quarters, situated in a gully near the river, were not those of a penal work camp. There was only one watchtower and little barbed wire. The citizens of Yerevan strolling along the cliffs wouldn't have suspected the presence of a labour camp. In the USSR at the time there were plenty of construction sites, both military and civilian, that were protected for security reasons, and ours aroused neither curiosity nor suspicion. From the cliff-tops, it would have seemed as if the men working here belonged to an Armenian construction company. Its concrete mixers poured out a concrete-mix which we had to spread rapidly on the piers of the bridge under construction. Such speed was essential, in my opinion, because of the poor quality of the cement, which immediately hardened.

There was very little concrete during the first few days because the mixers broke down. Overseers swapped insults in Armenian while we, with our wheelbarrows, took advantage of the springtime warmth. Who, in such circumstances, would have had the idea of going off in search of a public prosecutor – who in any case was nowhere to be found? Afterwards, it would be too late. To cap it all, these damned concrete mixers didn't have a single breakdown for an entire month: a record in the history of civil engineering in Armenia, probably even in the Soviet Union.

What month was it? April, or maybe May; it is of no importance anyway. It was an awful month, less because of the heat than because of the infernal rhythm of work: '*Choute, choute, choutareque*,' faster, faster, faster still. The concrete mix flowed while we pushed our wheelbarrows: an endless marathon. Even to go for a piss, permission was necessary. All the supervisory personnel on the site spoke only Armenian and discriminated against those who didn't speak their language.

In the evenings, after the marathon along the planks, the *pojarnik* collapsed with fatigue. He wasn't yet as skeleton-like as some of the prisoners he was to meet in the red-brick barracks, but he was already behaving like them, scarcely able to take advantage of his free time to walk in the evening air or to talk to his companions in misfortune. He dreamt not of herrings, but only of concrete mixers breaking down.

At the beginning the overseer had favoured him when it came to food servings, probably in tribute to his skills as a narrator. Each morning before work the overseer gave him an extra mess tin of soup without explanation. One day though, one of the small fry came and told him an improbable story about his forthcoming escape: he claimed that he needed the *pojarnik*'s shoes to organize it properly.

249

Why? Because they are better, more solid than his. In Yerevan prison another would-be escaper had taken a sweater from the *pojarnik* under the same pretext (he had later been obliged to return it on orders from the 'permanent delinquency'); you don't catch a fish twice with the same bait. After this refusal, however, the overseer stopped dispensing favours to him and remained deaf to his entreaties and explanations. As it happened, this reduction in his food supply coincided with an acceleration in the concrete mixers' output. And so it came about that the *pojarnik* lost his red blood corpuscles.

A last recollection of the construction site brings him back to the enigmatic public prosecutor. He remembers an event which gladdened his heart one evening, when he was on night shift: he had seen, on the cliffs, behind the floodlights, the silhouettes of four airmen alongside a young woman dressed in white. Blinded by the light, he hadn't been able to recognize their faces, but their silhouettes corresponded exactly to those of Kola, Vassia, Volovia and Kostia. As for Svetlana, she always wore white.

It must have been them: his friends, the last friends he had made. The *pojarnik* had been moved to tears, and was comforted by the fact that he had caught a glimpse of them and at the thought that they were talking about him. Throughout their interrogation, Strel and Abak had never questioned him about his friends as if unaware of their existence. It was obviously very strange, for their informers must have told them all about the links between the Mietchotka clan and their friend from Poland. But this silence didn't prove that the clan had been left in peace: the reasoning of the NKVD is too complex to allow such a simple deduction.

For Svetlana the problem was different. Strel and Abak slyly used her as a kind of indirect witness, but without ever quoting her: 'Instead of attending the hospital at such and such a time, you went with the student S. to the museum,' and so on. Had they questioned her? Had she suffered because of his 'unsavoury company'? And yet, it seemed that Svetlana was free. Kola and his clan too were safe and sound, and looked on from afar as the future firefighter shifted

250

concrete mix on to the bridge foundations.

'But what, in fact, did they see from up there? Nothing!' the *pojarnik* shouts, forgetting his decision to 'reflect calmly' and not alarm the nurses. He realises for the first time just how ambiguous the memorable scene of the bridge must have seemed from the cliff-top. From the height of the cliffs his friends no doubt knew that they were watching a man obliged to do an exacting job, but they surely didn't guess the slavery to which he had been reduced. Faced with the ferocious beasts who bullied him incessantly, he was already no longer the same man; he was merely clinging to life as a drowning person clings to the first plank that comes along.

'My good, dear Kola, on the roads of Balkaria you explained to me all the stages of the evolution of humanity, from the remote epoch when tribes killed their prisoners who were of no use to them, to the stage of slavery when, on the contrary, prisoners were squeezed like lemons to make pyramids for their captors. Isn't the bridge on the Zanga, which will one day be the pride of Armenia, a modern pyramid? Except that neither you nor other free citizens suspect anything. And in the USSR, how many other bridges, factories and towns have been built in the same manner, by men and women who were sacrificed, squeezed like lemons?

'No, I wasn't asking for anything,' the *pojarnik* replies to the nurse who has put her head around the half-open door. 'I have got into the habit of speaking aloud to myself; I'm sorry.' She suggests some drops of valerian which would help him sleep, but doesn't insist and is content with the *pojarnik*'s promise to speak a little less loudly, so as not to disturb his neighbours.

In fact the poor *pojarnik* has plenty of things to ask about. Things that no one will be able to help him with. He would like to know what the mechanism of his own transformation had been. How could the man who had dazzled his cell-mates in Yerevan by recounting from memory a 1,000-page book, and composing, on the basis of it, another which was even more action-packed, be the same person as this wreck from the Volgalag who is capable only of fantasizing about hospitalization and food? He will never know how to describe this transformation because it occurred without his being aware of it, in stages that he didn't understand in time. Since he hadn't completely lost his memory he recollects that this degradation resulted as much from physical exhaustion as from the humiliation endured. It had been impossible to remain himself, to resist, to cling to a hope or to a friendly hand. At the end of the day, a camp is a pack of wolves which are obliged to work for even fiercer animals. The Pyramids themselves are a mystery: who in this far off epoch could have built them, and how? One day the same question will be asked about those who built the bridge across the Zanga and similar works, but it will be too late once again. There will no longer exist any witnesses and the future will hear only the official version of those who had the whip hand. These tigers will mention in passing some regrettable errors, inflicted on the victims. They will pretend at the same time that these victims ought to have used the due process of law, that of the Socialist Code of Criminal Procedure, the most advanced in the world just as the Constitution of the USSR is the most democratic.

'That's the way they'll tell it in the books of the future. They'll say that there were people who could have lived happily, free as the air, if only they had presented themselves to the good public prosecutor, who of course never wished to sanction their arrest!' And the pojarnik laughs aloud, in his nice warm infirmary bed, intended for NKVD officers, the very authors of future books on the harmony of socialist legality. And this scum, well stocked with red blood corpuscles in the middle of wartime, will also escape unharmed as did during slavery their precursors, whose version of history is the only one that survived. Spartacus didn't know how to read or write, and after the massacre of his followers, his corpse was not even found. In our days the *zeks* are better educated, but in the camps they quickly forget their learning; they even forget their itinerary through the Gulag. The *pojarnik* laughs, remembering that an accused person must get hold of a defence lawyer and not a prosecutor, and that a 'legal advisor' in the Volgalag should have known such elementary facts. Clearly this whole story about appealing to the public prosecutor had been invented in order to put pressure on him, in the hope that he would sign whatever was put in front of him.

Now, the arresting officer is in the *pojarnik*'s room, his arms full of clothes. 'Get up, you are to get properly dressed for the road.' 'But why? What road? Nothing has been decided yet.' 'Yes it has. You have been resting for four days, and now the commandant will explain things to you.' The *pojarnik* would prefer his own trousers and his padded jacket, which are certainly inelegant but very warm and well suited to the Russian winter. 'No,' the officer retorts. 'You are to dress like a free man and not in rags like a *zek*.' He has, however, brought for him his spare set of old clothes and a note from Nadia: 'Dear *pojarnik*, I am very happy for you. In 10 years' time, if I am still alive, call in at my former address in Moscow which is as follows.'

Colonel Boudiennyi approves of the *pojarnik*'s new outfit – inherited from a deceased *zek* – and informs him of the results of his consultation with the public prosecutor. As the *pojarnik* ought never to have been 'taken away' from the Red Army, his dossier will show uninterrupted military service, and, so as not to complicate matters, even the six months' leave granted him in Yerevan will be erased. On the other hand, to spare him long journeys and distressing reunions with his former friends, he will go first of all to Saratov where he will be given his new assignment at the Commissariat of Military Affairs. He will have to go there on foot, but it is only a matter of a few dozen kilometres, a fine walk on the Volga: a pleasure rather than a vexation.

'I have assigned you dry rations for three days,' the moustachioed colonel continues amiably, 'and I arranged to have added to them several of the herrings that you like so much. But I am certain that you will not take three days to get to Saratov. There are quite a few lorries which use the road and you will surely find one to take you to your destination. Finally, given the solution suggested by the public prosecutor, it isn't necessary for you to sign a discharge form for the penitentiary administration. You have been in the armed forces without a break since September 1941; you know nothing whatever about the camps. If, through carelessness, you do speak about them, you run the risk of being charged with anti-Soviet propaganda, under article 58 of the Code of Criminal Procedure, paragraphs 5 and 6. But you are a reasonable man, cultured as well. You have made an excellent impression on me, and I am sure that you have already forgotten this whole embarrassing affair. I wish you a safe journey.'

Free now, and already half-transformed back into a soldier thanks to a long, rough sheepskin jacket, worn inside out, the *pojarnik* begins by sitting down upon a tree trunk on the edge of the Volga and eating one kilo, 200 grammes of bread and his three herrings. This is his three days' rations: instead of *kacha* he had been given extra bread and a double portion of herrings. The commandant had been generous in word only, but it is too late to protest. Besides, had there been one herring more, the *pojarnik* would have swallowed it like the three others. Unless a lorry picks him up, he has the prospect of a long walk along the Volga on a soon-to-be empty stomach.

He is not in a hurry to get going. He is haunted by a strange memory, a little distressing and yet rather funny; he pictures his neighbour in Lvov once again, the one who had asked the Chekists: 'Why are you insisting on throwing this youngster overboard from society?' At the time this sentence had imprinted itself on his memory because it had been so bizarre, for society is not a boat and nor is Lvov situated in the middle of the sea. Today on the other hand, he understands everything and he says to himself: 'Here I am then, thrown overboard on the Volga, but fortunately it is frozen over, and I am in no danger of drowning.' And then he bursts out laughing, because to go for a walk on the Volga is not an experience which happens every day. He will not be able to describe the Volgalag nor his time spent on the construction site on the Zanga, but with his walk along the Volga he will be able to astound all his listeners once he returns to Poland. 'That's for sure. I'll dazzle them with a fine display,' the *pojarnik* says to himself, very pleased altogether to find himself 'thrown overboard' in this marvellous place.

In all truthfulness, it is a unique river. In comparison to the Volga, the Vistula is only a stream while the Bug is, well, so insignificant that it hardly seems worth mentioning. The Volga is so wide that you can barely make out the white trees on the other bank. It exudes a taste and a feel of Russia more pronounced than elsewhere, much more, certainly, than on the banks of the Don, the river of the Cossacks, which is far narrower than the Volga.

'It's a funny sort of country all the same, Russia, for in Poland you would never go for walks on the rivers. Here and there you can see people ice-skating, but we have never thought of using them as roads in winter,' the *pojarnik* reflects. If his imagination embellishes the Volga in this manner, it is so that he might delay the start of his march and savour the first moments of his newly recovered freedom. It is already a good sign that he daydreams of telling the story of his march to Saratov on a frozen river and that he is no longer obsessed by the red blood corpuscles he has lost, or by food. 'Go on, don't be lazy; look carefully at what surrounds you, then go back in the society which has thrown you overboard.' Thus he encourages himself and eventually sets out on the most unusual walk of his whole life – a long walk on the Volga, '*mat rodnaia, Volga rousskaia rieka*' ('our beloved mother, our Russian river') . . .

Frozen and covered over with snow, this national river really is beautiful, but it bears no resemblance at all to a busy main road. The beauty of the Volga in winter consists rather in its cheering calm, which no traffic disturbs. No doubt lorries pass over it from time to time – the tracks of the wheels in the snow are there to see – but whoever was stubborn enough to wait for one would be in danger of freezing. The *pojarnik* doesn't walk for long on the Volga. His practical sense prevails: he climbs the bank and takes to the paths that link up the villages, hoping to be fed by the local inhabitants.

This unavoidable choice is risky. Russian peasants, reputed for their hospitality, are also very mistrustful; reticent in normal times to open their doors to strangers, they are always ready to lay the

255

blame for thefts or accidents in their village on them. During these years of war and hunger, women predominate in the region: widows, mothers, wives or sisters of soldiers – and often too, of *zeks*. Because of his clothing, these women have no difficulty in seeing a resemblance between their dear ones and the *pojarnik*: half-soldier, half-*zek*. They are able to read the misery of the camps in his eyes, but also that of the labour battalions, and of the poorly-fed soldiers at the front. The welcome is not the same everywhere: in certain izbas the stranger is not allowed to enter, in others he is given only a piece of bread, like a beggar. Sometimes he is offered some hot soup, a little meat, some dried fish, and is allowed to rest in the warmth.

The women are moved to tears watching him eat, but they avoid asking him questions about the reasons for his winter outing. They ask instead about when the war is going to end and when their loved ones are going to return. On this subject the *pojarnik* acquits himself rather well; recalling the optimistic speeches of Kola, he knows how to reassure the most anxious and to promise a better future after victory.

Although it has been spared the ravages of bombs the region around Saratov is not exactly opulent. In the villages, which are often very near to one another, social distinctions are easily spotted. After three or four experiences, the *pojarnik* concludes that it is the middle peasant who represents his best hope: those who are too poor have nothing to offer him, while the rich ones are quite capable of setting their dogs on him, so concerned are they to protect their property. Unfortunately, the middle peasants, who are the most generous with their food, don't have the space to shelter a stranger, despite the departure of conscripted men. During the summer, he could have slept in a stable or a barn but in January it is much too cold.

At the end of the first day, the *pojarnik* comes upon a kindly family who offer him hospitality. While he is eating an excellent cabbage soup the grandfather produces a photograph of one of his sons, saying: 'We have had no news of him. He looks a bit like you;

he is surely there where you have come from.' A queer kind of resemblance indeed; son is old enough to be the *pojarnik*'s father, and is also much fatter. The grandmother realizes her husband's mistake and pours a large spoonful of fresh cream into the *pojarnik*'s soup, which she hopes will instantly cure him of his thinness. Then she gives him some good advice: 'Go and sleep in the kolkhoz administrative centre. The building is heated and, as far as I know, it isn't closed at night.' Is it allowed? 'Leave early, before the office workers arrive.'

The next morning in another village ten kilometres further on, the kolkhozians question the *pojarnik* about a vagabond dressed in rags whom they are looking for in connection with a theft that was committed the night before in the same building in which he had spent the night. There had been no one else in this room. Had the old woman attempted to pin on him a crime committed by a member of her own family? True, she had given a false description of his clothes. Had this been in case he had been seen in her home? The *pojarnik*, who had become mistrustful in the camp, understands then that he has to be even more so in the 'free' world outside. He quickly learns that peasant hospitality has another side to it, and that to travel in the Volga region involves unforeseeable dangers.

He decides to return to the river. None of the very rare lorries stop, and Saratov is still far off. He knows not what distance he has still to cover and, on top of this, a strong southerly wind blows him off the road. It's obvious that freedom is dearly paid for. The *pojarnik* walks on, taking advantage of the villagers' hospitality while trying to avoid the consequences of their hypocrisy.

Immediate problems, among which is the wind from the Lower Volga (as it is called in the villages), preoccupy him so much that his sense of time begins to desert him. He is expected in Saratov, at the Commissariat of Military Affairs, on Friday 20 January, but this date has already gone by and the city is not in sight. 'This is going to end badly. The colonel and the arresting officer have concocted this odyssey on the Volga in order to be able to stick me once more in their Volgalag, this time with the sanction of the public prosecutor,' the *pojarnik* laments silently. And then, a miracle, an old lorry stops for him; takes him to the *voienkomat*, the Commissariat of Military Affairs in Saratov.

This will be one of the *pojarnik*'s strangest evenings, the one in the course of which his *zek*'s obsessions and complexes almost destroy him. He presents himself at the Commissariat on a Sunday. There is only a sergeant on desk duty, who grants him leave to spend the night in the waiting room. Tomorrow those qualified to do so will deal with him.

Some hours later, however, the *pojarnik* smells the appetizing smell of cabbage soup – a great regional speciality, not to be confused with bortsch – and, noting that the sergeant is sleeping behind his desk, he advances into the corridor, letting himself be guided by his sense of smell. A light behind the door indicates the route to the kitchen, and he enters without knocking. A colonel as bald as Taras Bulba or Yul Brynner, knits his eyebrows in anger or surprise. The *pojarnik* apologizes profusely for his intrusion, his late arrival in Saratov, for his very existence. The colonel says nothing, but his expression still seems threatening. In a desperate effort to appease him, the *pojarnik* mumbles something about being hungry, but immediately proposes to clear off and return to the waiting room. 'No,' the bald colonel orders severely. 'Sit down and don't move,' and hurries off without even closing the files on his work table.

For the *pojarnik*, this hasty departure indicates punitive intentions; superiors who go off in this fashion are the most dangerous. 'Why should I wait here for the worst to happen rather than try my luck outside?' the *pojarnik* asks himself. To be sure he no longer has his papers, the desk sergeant held on to them, but he has just been on the road for five days, without having had to show them. An inner voice within continues: 'Go on, take courage, run. Don't let yourself be sent down for another 13 months by these bastards. It will be a fine consolation when they announce to you a second time that you have done nothing and that the public prosecutor doesn't accuse you of anything.' The *pojarnik* glances down the corridor: everything is still, an escape is possible.

It would be futile to look for an unguarded official building in the city. Suppose I went to the station? But there frequent checks are made on passengers' papers. Had it been daylight, in the country-side, the *pojarnik* would have fled, tempted by this subterranean, unpoliced world which exists throughout the USSR. Every *zek* has heard tell of those who have lived for a time without any fixed domicile, of those who belong to the 'permanent delinquency'. By listening to the latter's folklore, you learn that they have their regular pubs, their hideouts, and complex system of communication. The *pojarnik*'s neighbour in the Volgalag, the chemistry teacher, had scientifically demonstrated to him that any society which is incapable of putting an end to criminality for social and economic reasons, ends up by making a pact with it in the hope of controlling it and minimizing the damage it causes. Why not try to enter into this other world? But it is too late: in the corridor he can hear a large number of energetic footsteps approaching; he closes his eyes convinced that he is, once again, about to meet up with four Chekists accompanied by a large dog.

In fact it is a group of male nurses with a stretcher and a woman doctor. The bald colonel shows them the *pojarnik* while explaining certain matters in medical jargon. Then he summons the duty sergeant and asks him some questions so he can sign the papers for the *pojarnik*'s admission to hospital. What an extraordinary country! The moustachioed Colonel 'Boudiennyi' had judged him fit to march 100 kilometres on the Volga, while the bald-headed colonel doesn't believe him capable of getting to the hospital without help.

The *pojarnik* has been lucky: the Saratov hospital (No. 1683) is one of the three best in the Soviet Union, and has just been awarded the Order of the Red Flag for notable results in the struggle for socialism. Thus the bald-headed colonel has put him in the hands of genuinely competent doctors, who inspire the greatest confidence in their patients.

259

During this transition period, our memories – the *pojarnik*'s and my own – intermingle, and they are doubly confused. Something had persuaded both the bald-headed colonel and the doctors of hospital No 1683 that the *pojarnik*'s life hung only by a thread and that he needed urgent care. Had he been overtaken by a bout of fever as a result of exposure to the cold on the Volga, or had he grazed his face in a fall, or was he lame after a march that had been beyond his strength? Frankly, I don't remember. His case must have been serious though; the nurse in the communal ward, a believer, blessed herself each time that she approached his bed.

The seriousness of his condition is indicated by the intensity of the treatment administered: endless transfusions and injections, intravenous ones which generate an agreeable warmth, and also intramuscular ones, which give him a sore backside. The dietary regime is unexceptional in either its quality or quantity, and the *pojarnik* has to appeal more than once to the Christian feelings of his nurse to get a second helping. By chance, his neighbour in the first few days is an officer who has had an operation for appendicitis and who, having no appetite himself, discreetly passes his food to the *pojarnik*. Apart from these fragmentary recollections, neither the *pojarnik* nor myself can say very much about this obscure post-Gulag illness which was combatted so efficaciously by the doctors of hospital No. 1683. Once I had been cured, I convalesced for a month in a sanatorium for officers, in Khvalynsk, on the Volga. This sojourn, which was prescribed for health reasons, will be useful for catching up with news from the front.

In the Gulag the war is followed with a detached, distant curiosity: the story of the victory at Stalingrad, in February 1943, would not have met with as much success as the story of the Count of Monte Cristo. On the whole, whether by prudence or conviction, the 'permanent delinquency' were clearly on the side of the Red Army; but their interest in the war's goings-on went no further than this.

Fortunately, convalescing Soviet officers are not only living encyclopaedias of military strategy, they also love to argue over the comparative merits of the famous protagonists of the Great Patriotic War. Stalin's wisdom is never questioned: his star shines more strongly than ever and he is already celebrated as the greatest military genius of Russian, even world, history. All that can be speculated on is how early he had prepared his plan for the encirclement of 3–400,000 Germans in the steppes of the Volga and the Don. Had he purposely allowed the Wehrmacht to penetrate during the preceding summer in order, six months later, to inflict on it a most spectacular defeat? The officers in Khvalynsk are convinced that, at the time of his famous speech on the occasion of the twenty-fifth anniversary of the October Revolution, on 7 November 1942, Stalin had hinted at glad tidings to come because he knew full well that on 19 November von Paulus's army would be caught like a rat in the Stalingrad trap.

After this feat, everything still remained to be done. The Germans who were caught in the trap were in fact as numerous and well armed as the Soviet troops which encircled them. At the beginning of the war there were only three marshals in the USSR: Voroshilov, Boudiennyi and Timoshenko. By the time of my stay in Khvalynsk there were about a dozen, each with his fans who are convinced that theirs is the best of all. Zhukov, certainly, is ranked above the other contenders; he is the only one to figure immediately after Stalin in a new war hymn: 'S nami Staline rodnoi, S nami Joukov gueroi' ('We have with us our beloved Stalin and the hero Zhukov'). But the partisans of Rokossovski, Vatoutine, Koniev, Cherniakhovsky, Chouikov and Malinovski claim with a vehement passion the second place for their favourite in this competition.

The convalescents of Khvalynsk are not of a sufficiently senior rank to know these heroes personally, but that doesn't prevent them from holding very decided opinions. I am excused from expressing mine because of my belonging to the airforce which is considered separate. Nevertheless my account of the battle of Nalchik is often appreciated and even gives rise to some flattering comments. According to one of the convalescent officers, by immobilizing the Germans in the Caucasus and by inflicting severe blows on the

Romanians, the 37th Army in Nalchik greatly contributed to the triumph of Stalingrad. This extremely dialectical reasoning will delight Kola when he hears about it and he will enrich it with additions of his own. On the whole, however, the 37th Army is held in low esteem in Khvalynsk (it is a *slabaia armia*, a sickly army).

This month in Khvalynsk reminds me of my stay in Moscow in 1940. In both instances I learned or relearned to behave like a normal Soviet citizen, by trying in Moscow to forget my Polish habits, here the experiences of the Gulag. Of course during this convalescence, I don't know that I shall be returning to Rostov. At the beginning of April, after a medical examination, I am to receive a military assignment and to rejoin either my original unit or another unit of the Red Army. But the doctors in Khvalynsk don't seem to think that I am entirely cured, and they demobilize me for one year until April 1945.

Two surprises await me. For want of an airforce uniform I am given an infantry officer's uniform and greatcoat – remarkably elegant even without the epaulettes (a demobilized officer hasn't the right to wear them). Secondly, I am paid all of my salary dating back to 10 December 1942, amounting to some hundreds of roubles, a fortune almost as fabulous as the unfortunate war booty that the Cheka had confiscated from me in Yerevan.

Miraculous meetings sometimes happen in real life just as they do in the movies. In Rostov Station, upon getting off the train from Saratov, I catch sight of a tall, slim airman with a snub nose: it's Kola! He has been demobilized and is no longer wearing epaulettes. What is he doing here? He is asking himself the same question about me. Our voices are choking with emotion and we both just about manage to say 'You haven't changed at all.' It isn't customary for men in uniform to show their emotions in public. So we behave with cool, as if, one and a half years earlier, we had arranged to meet in the time between the arrival of the train from Saratov and the departure of the train for Mietchotka. A look, a smile, suffice to express our happiness; for the first time in a very long while I feel that I am no longer alone, even if I still don't know what I am to do next.

Kola knows: we shall go to Mietchotka, after I have invested some of my roubles in buying a load of herrings, which are relatively cheap in Rostov. His Aunt Valia will be delighted to have the two of us for a day or two, and we certainly need this time in order to tell each other everything. 'Great, but tell me, why were you demobilized?' 'Stomach ulcer,' he replies laconically. What on earth is that? A minor matter; you don't die from it. The airforce nevertheless decided to demobilize this valuable 'ulcerous' pilot. Their reasoning seemed absurd to me, but I rejoice in their decision. Haven't I recovered my best friend thanks to their medical stupidity? Kola is not complaining about it either: he misses flying, but now, since the war is almost over, all his thoughts turn to jockeying for position in the 'post-victory' race. 'We shall become public works engineers. Everything has to be rebuilt from scratch in this country, starting with our own Rostov. This task will guarantee us a future without suffering.'

We return to the station just in time to catch the next train for Mietchotka. Kola remarks: 'You are a little bit thinner than you were but it suits you.' He wants to travel on the roof to avoid the crowded carriages and indiscreet ears. 'It's not allowed, Kola.' 'Don't worry,' he assures me. 'All you need do is give the ticket collector a small tip, one herring will do, and not a very big one at that.' It works, and he is delighted. 'In Russia, the roof is the best place on the train,' he says sententiously, recalling our magnificent journey between Tiflis and Yerevan. I agree with him, although the wind is definitely too strong for my taste: it is only the beginning of April and the climate of the Don is not as mild as that of Transcaucasia.

'Well then, begin!' Kola tugs his ear in anticipation and puts his arm on my shoulders. But I don't feel at ease on this curved roof – those of the *tieplouchki* are flat and therefore more comfortable – and anyway, the Gulag is not a fairytale by the brothers Grimm. So it is Kola who will talk most, but this time without embroidering his narrative.

'Our first reaction – I mean of Vassia, Volodia, Kostia and I – after your arrest was quite banal: it was one of fear, the conditioned reflex of our age. We were petrified at the thought of being interrogated, taken from the airforce and thrown into a hole somewhere. It appeared inevitable, first of all because of the principle of collective responsibility that operates in our country, which applies as much to a family or to a group of friends, and next because we were jointly guilty with you of the offences with which we thought you would be charged. Of course, you represented the "weakest link" in our chain, as Lenin would have put it, but we really didn't feel much more secure. Aren't we the sons of *lichentzy*, people who were deprived of civic rights up until 1936? The airforce hadn't taken this into account and had believed in us, but the NKVD is not so indulgent towards those who are guilty of "original social sin". Logically, therefore, we ought to have been arrested and we feared it would happen from one day to the next. Perhaps it would be for having, along with you, made off with a small war treasure, or for having come out with stupid remarks in the Intourist Restaurant, within earshot of Armenian informers.

'At the end of a week, however, since nothing had come of our darkest forebodings, we took courage and went to talk to the only witness of your arrest, one-legged Oleg. Because he is such a suspicious character we were obliged to put the fear of the devil in him. Vassia took him squarely by the collar and threatened to throw him out of the window. Suicides are commonplace among disabled ex-servicemen, Vassia explained, to convince him that we would have no hesitation whatever about arranging his 'suicide'. He ended up by agreeing to talk and, while swearing that he had had nothing to do with it, he told us that you had been lifted because of your false declaration of nationality. He claimed that this was what he heard during the search of your room by the Cheka. For us, this changed everything: we were in the clear. As soon as we understood this we decided to act, first by asking Commissar Bielokonienko's advice.

'At his office, the commissar claimed to know nothing of what had happened. He wasn't play-acting either, he was really thunder-struck at the news. How could someone have been arrested for an offence with political implications, without his former superior having even been informed of it? "Right then," he answers without further ado, "it is obviously possible since it has already been done, but it won't be left at that." We tried to fan the flame of his indignation, assuring him that you had been planning to return to the regiment on 1 January 1943, without waiting for your leave to expire. "Enough's enough. I've had as much as I can take from them," he shouted like a madman. "I've told them a thousand times that he is *nach* (one of us)." It was clear then that "they" had spoken to him about you, but had kept from him the news of your arrest, and this had put his commissar's authority and honour in question. Quite forgetting our presence, he telephoned Colonel Ganachek to express his indignation and to arrange an urgent meeting to discuss the matter. Perhaps he did it on purpose, to let us know that he was going to intervene on your behalf in the name of the regiment. Remembering for my own part the way in which he used to go on at you in Kislovodsk about being culturally Russian, I told myself: "Maybe he is going to declare to the Cheka that it was he himself who advised you to falsify your declaration of nationality, and in this way you might be freed." Another week went by, however, without us receiving the slightest confirmation of my hypothesis.

'Then, in a further dramatic gesture, Bielokonienko had the four of us come to his office and drily instructed us not to reply to any summons which might arrive from the NKVD, "Tear them up or bring them to me, but ignore them. That's an order." Vassia, who was somewhat baffled by this, came very close to asking him to confirm this order in writing, but the *tchoudak* didn't even give him time to open his mouth: "Your only concern is aviation and nothing else. Is that understood?" Perfectly.

'After that he used to summon me alone, under the most diverse pretexts, but obviously we always ended up talking about you. In the course of these conversations I gradually gained the impression that he knew a great deal about us, our Caucasian past included. In my view this proved that he was in touch with the NKVD, and also, unfortunately, that the Cheka had forced you to talk. Frankly I didn't hold it against you: they are capable of making the dumb speak. No one resists them for long. Nevertheless our legal situation became precarious, for to salvage a roll of cloth amounts to looting, and in the forces they take a dim view of that. Vassia and Volodia became very pessimistic, while Kostia and I searched hopelessly for a means of getting in touch with you to find out what you had told them. In Rostov, we would have found a way but in Yerevan, without the right connections, there was nothing to be done.

'When Bielokonienko summoned us all a third time, at the beginning of 1943, I expected the worst and hadn't prepared a defence. "I know all about it and I don't care," he says, "but I would like you to help me find the Georgian who bought this stolen cloth from you in Tiflis." He said that he needed to find him for personal reasons, because he had made a bet with a friend, or something of the sort. Now that I know that these Chekist assholes had accused you of receiving money from the Germans, I realize that he simply wanted to find a witness who could confirm your story. At the time though, to be honest, all four of us thought that he had gone mad. How else could such a foolish wager be explained? However, Volodia described to him the *tolkoutchka* of Tiflis: the greatest fleamarket in all of Transcaucasia, or maybe even in the whole of the USSR. It is a place where you can buy or sell anything, even a Hero of the Soviet Union gold star medal, but where it is impossible, four months on, to track down an anonymous individual. "Couldn't you at least try? I shall find a pretext for sending you to Tiflis." It was tempting. As you know, we regard Tiflis as the most marvellous of cities; but we refused because this search had no chance of succeeding and to accept would have been an abuse of trust. He was so disappointed that he showed us the door without saying goodbye.

'Some days later, he invited me to accompany him on a walk from the barracks to Yerevan city centre to talk again to me about the fleamarket in Tiflis. Volodia's suggestion that you could acquire the title of Hero of the Soviet Union in exchange for banknotes bearing Lenin's effigy, had visibly shaken him. But, bit by bit, he delivered a lengthy speech against indiscriminate repression, and in fact against the NKVD, with precise charges directed against its Yerevan branch.

'I offered him my help and this made him smile. "In this matter I would need the help of four air-marshals, not four trainee pilots," he said. In his view the only thing that we could do for him was to become the best pilots in our squadron, and not furnish the slightest pretext for any criticism of our conduct. That, then, had been the object of our walk, to alert us to the fact that we were being watched. Vassia and Volodia, who are always inclined to pessimism, then pointed out to me that there are only two air-marshals in the entire Red Army, and that if Bielokonienko needed four of them to extricate you from this fix, you really were in trouble. Vassia has never been very quick to understand figures of speech. Kostia, on the other hand, was the first to grasp, well before I did, that on the basis of your false declaration of nationality, the Cheka in this frontier zone could be trying to fit you up for contacts with the enemy.

'At the beginning of February 1943, at the time of the victory of Stalingrad, there really was a "festival in the streets" both literally and figuratively. After all the speeches possible and imaginable, we were given two days' leave to get as drunk as we liked, with the proviso that we neither offend the native "Persians", nor divert their bread delivery trams. Returning home on foot after a party, Vassia met the *zavkhoze* Captain Pietia Danilov, staggering but still capable of speech. Vassia willingly helped him home as he wanted to find out more about the captain's buddy, the commissar. Thanks to Vassia's strength, we learned the following.

'Before the war in Zaporojié, Bielokonienko had already had a run-in with the NKVD over a fellow whom he knew to be innocent but who had been condemned to endless years of labour camp. He had never ceased to reproach himself with not having saved this man, as he thought he could have done. As soon as he learned of your arrest he therefore raised a hue and cry. This time not only the "eleventh" of the VVS, but also the command of the Eighteenth

Airforce, exasperated by the Cheka's interference, had given him a free hand to do so. However, the NKVD were not easily frightened and they claimed they could prove that you were a German spy, and that after such an accusation the airforce should close the case. The commissar, who had already been "had" in Zaporojié, replied that they were bluffing and insisted on seeing the proof. This was very risky on his part, for if they had proof, he himself would have been in danger, accused of complicity with a German agent. On the other hand, according to Danilov, even if they were bluffing they would still send you far away to hell's gates if need be, rather than admit a mistake. Luck nevertheless came to Bielokonienko's aid for several of his friends from Zaporojié secured senior positions in the leadership of the political services of the armed forces, as well as in the Party. He immediately enlisted their support in his local war against the Yerevan NKVD, and also their help in obtaining his transfer to the army which was about to advance to the Ukraine.

'Danilov knew nothing further. Vassia tried to revive him, but in vain. He simply repeated himself and added nothing new. The next day, however, we went to see him to ask for authorization to send you a parcel. I had thought of this as a way to establish at least indirect contact with you, taking advantage of the friendly attitude of the captain. At first he refused, claiming that it was too dangerous, but as he isn't such a bad sort, he eventually agreed, on condition that we didn't indicate the address of the sender. All of us put together a handsome parcel of five kilos and sent it off addressed to you care of the NKVD in Yerevan. At the end of February, the parcel returned to Danilov's shop – he didn't sleep properly for nights afterwards – with the handwritten inscription: "addressee unknown". How strange! They were not supposed to know the sender – whom they found nonetheless – while they couldn't not know the addressee. It was the world turned upside down, and it would have been funny had it not been so sad. We arranged to see Bielokonienko for we hadn't even notified him of the parcel. But he was very calm: "Forward the package to Yerevan prison and don't complicate life for *them* by concealing the names of the senders."

So, all four of us signed but I confess to you that I understood nothing any longer, really nothing at all of the tactics of the *tchoudak*, nor of your situation as the accused.

'The package was returned one month later, at the end of March, accompanied by a standard note saying that only close relatives may visit and help detainees. Svetlana, who had come to ask for news of you, had the idea of taking it to the prison in person, and declaring that she was your fiancée and therefore a close relation. It didn't work, but as she is a stubborn Rostovian and a born fighter she gave them something to chew over, threatening to lodge complaints with heaven only knows who. Thanks to her laborious negotiations, the prison administration – it was April by this time – informed her, and us along with her, that you had been transferred to the construction site on the Zanga bridge. Bielokonienko knew nothing about it himself but he made no comment.

'We saw you there one evening, hard at work, and it was awful. Svetlana couldn't stop crying. She really is a terrific girl. She was already engaged and now she is married, but she liked you a lot and was ashamed of her country for having reduced you to the condition of a convict, a *catorgenik*. She was quite fearless and showed her claws everywhere in Yerevan, like a tigress defending her young. Her father too, told us not to hesitate to call upon him if we needed either money or influence.

'In practice though, no one knew what to do. To all appearances there were only condemned men on this semi-camouflaged construction site, whereas you hadn't even been tried. When I questioned him privately, Bielokonienko limited himself to saying: "He hasn't been, nor will he be, tried or condemned." Well, then? Nothing. He shrugged his shoulders. "In Nalchik," he asks, "did you believe that four months later the Germans would be encircled in the steppes of the Don?" "Not with this precision, but I knew that we were going to win," I say, failing to see the points of comparison. "This time, it's the same," he replies, with his mysterious *tchoudak* air about him. Take it or leave it; he didn't ask for our help in this particular war, simply for our patience. To be honest, though I don't want to offend you, I didn't believe you were capable of standing this regime of forced labour for very long, and I lapsed into the blackest pessimism, worse than when we were put to rout in the Caucasus.

'In the autumn of 1943 they started to send us to operational bases in Georgia, not all at once but in little groups. We took part, in turns, in bombing raids against Romania, on the far side of the Black Sea. It was a real war between Cossacks and Romanians: they had come to take our petrol and now we were bombarding theirs. In the month of November – or was it December by that time? – when I saw the commissar for the last time, he gave me a wink then whispered: "It's all fixed. You'll see him again soon." Who? "You know very well. Come and see me, both of you, in Zaporojié, after victory, or as soon as it's possible." Now you can understand why I wasn't altogether surprised at meeting you in Rostov station this morning, although your smart uniform took my breath away. And now, "look and admire," as Mayakovsky would have said, we are coming into the *stanitsa* of Mietchotka, of the region of Mietchotka, in the department of Rostov-on-the-Don!'

In other times I would have found this journey extraordinarily moving. For better or worse, the four musketeers of Mietchotka had become my best friends in the USSR and had promoted me to the rank of honorary citizen of their *stanitsa*. I feel that I know almost every house in it, having had it described to me in the smallest details. This large village, almost a small town, is altogether worthy of the stories I have been told about it, especially at this time of year when its streets are clean and verdant, after the mud from the thaw has disappeared and before the summer dust from the steppe has invaded.

But I arrive as an ex-*zek* who, three months earlier, was forced to wander from one village to the next along the Volga. Despite myself, this all too vivid memory eclipses older ones and dulls my enthusiasm. While visiting my friends' school, and then the municipal buildings, I think neither of Vassia nor Volodia but of my nights spent exposed to risk on the road to Saratov. Here everyone is friendly towards me, but I wonder if they would have been as kind towards the vagabond *pojarnik*. My personalized criteria are biased, and they falsify everything. The Chinese saying, 'Better to see something once than to hear about it a thousand times,' doesn't take the visitor's frame of mind into account.

Remarking upon my sullen mood Kola imagines that it is because I am disappointed by the absence of visible signs of Cossack folklore, or disgruntled at the fact that the quiet Don doesn't flow through the middle of the village. Instead of joking and trying to relax, I reply abruptly that I am well versed in geography and especially in Soviet methods of handling whole populations. All that surprises me in Mietchotka is that the entire Cossack people haven't been deported, as had happened for example with the Volga Germans, and the fact that no prison has been installed there. And anyway how can Kola be sure that, a few kilometres away from here, there isn't hidden behind high palisades a camp of forced labour employed in agricultural work. 'You can't hide anything here because the steppe is so flat.' Kola talks his way out of a difficult situation.

It is clear that the news of our arrival has spread through the village. We are surrounded by young women, dressed in their Sunday best, smiling like the springtime sun and eager for masculine company. They take us by the arm and invite us along the same evening to their dance, the *tanzplochtchadka*, making bold allusions to the pleasures which await us. This reversal of roles altogether vindicates Moussia's aphorisms right at the start of the war: it is absurd to separate men and women for years on end; it is against nature.

We shan't be going dancing. Kola, unruffled and watchful, outlines to me his austere plans for our studies, our political careers and our whole future. Before the start of the academic year we ought to take advantage of the travel facilities granted to demobilized ex-servicemen to accumulate some money by buying and selling between Tiflis and Rostov. Given the huge disparity of black market prices in these two metropolitan centres, we could make vast sums of

271

money out of each return journey. Then, once assured of a solid material foundation, we can apply ourselves to becoming public works engineers. We shall begin by earning the title of *otlichniki*, first in the class, which will automatically open the doors of the Party to us. As regards women – in Rostov he thinks there must be 20 or 30 for every man –, we shall avoid flirtatious dissipation by each choosing a proper, serious girl, preferably one with accommodation in the centre of town, not too far from the Institute of Public Works. On the basis of his preliminary soundings he thinks that we shall easily find candidates with the requisite attributes.

'Haven't you understood anything of my 13 months and 3 days in the camps?' I break the spell abruptly.

'Quite the reverse. It is because I know you have suffered so badly that I am seeking to eliminate suffering from your future and from mine,' he replies imperturbably. How can I be angry with him? He is at his best, cleverly resourceful and loyal to his friends, sceptical, yet convinced that everything will work out for the best. But it is no longer 'my' society. I am too frightened even to consider these plans for lucrative journeys between Rostov and Tiflis. 'Just as with Bielokonienko and his native Ukraine, Kola, I have to concern myself with only one thing: my departure for Poland. In a few months, maybe even before then, I shall be able to leave, and I want it to be by the first available train.'

My desire to go home seems natural to him, but he is saddened that I am so bitter, almost vindictive. How could I so easily forget our good times together in Kislovodsk, in Tiflis and even in Yerevan. He reminds me of the vow we made in the *bania* in Tiflis to go back there for our respective weddings. 'Don't you remember the all-marble, luxury compartment in that *bania* which astounded you so much? And the wine cellars, and Chota Roustaveli Boulevard? Why not take advantage of our situation as demobilized servicemen to go back there?' 'I am not the same as before, Kola, I have more recent memories than those of the *bania* in Tiflis.' He becomes very gloomy. Let's go home. We'll have it out over dinner.

272

The *pojarnik* would certainly have classed Aunt Valia among the rich peasants. Her house looks well-kept: it is surrounded by a rather large vegetable garden, and all the windows are fitted with clean, lace curtains. But I haven't the vaguest idea of the source of this wealth. Aunt Valia is in her forties, and has been living alone since her husband and son left for the front. If it weren't for the absence of men in Mietchotka you would infer that Aunt Valia had seduced some regional leader, or a kolkhoz president at least, who has lavished presents and gifts of food on her. Perhaps she isn't rich at all and is simply making a ruinous effort to give a fitting welcome to her favourite nephew, Nicolai – as she ceremoniously calls Kola – and I, whom she decreed straightaway to be an 'artillery man', praising this branch of the army. 'Artillery is the god of war!' she says. One thing is certain: on the black market in Rostov the dinner we enjoy would have cost a fortune.

The menu is both classic and original: bortsch with meat, mutton stew with potatoes, then as many blinys as we can eat; they are Aunt Valia's speciality. Honey and fresh cream are set out in magical quantities. The grandfather plays the part of wine waiter, then leaves vodka on the table and withdraws to a corner of the room. His daughter is too busy making blinys in the kitchen to join in our conversation. Here are Kola and I served like princes, as happy as reunited brothers, but still, somewhat tense and anxious. The vodka has something to do with it: I am no longer used to drinking and he is no longer allowed to because of his ulcer. He is drinking only in honour of the exceptional occasion.

Like all *zeks*, I am convinced that Kola cannot imagine what a camp is like; those who haven't been there themselves are not capable of grasping the unspeakable atrocity of this singular world. But I try, tactfully, to explain to him, recalling that his deported parents have never returned whereas I had managed to leave it, in part thanks to him. As I listened to his story I realized just how much he had encouraged Commissar Bielokonienko.

'Look at this charming cat. See how nice and quiet it is, how it lets us eat, without miaowing, without bothering us. I saw an almost identical cat enter the Volgalag by mistake. A pack of starving men immediately threw themselves upon it; the first three crushed its head with a stone, tore off its skin and put the rest into a saucepan. All the others watching, myself included, envied their good luck and admired their cunning.'

'In our villages, in time of famine, they have always eaten cats,' Kola answers.

'In a camp you wish for the death of your neighbour, who has done nothing against you, simply in order to receive an extra ration for helping to dig his grave – half a herring, or a bowl of repulsive soup. I buried a man on the Zanga bridge construction site, and another after my arrival in the Volgalag. Others were eagerly awaiting my death, and didn't even try to hide their desire to collect the reward for my burial.'

'That also could have happened in a free community struck by extreme famine. People hang on to anything to survive; in such circumstances instinct gets the better of dignity. It has been the case since the dawn of time,' he says in a less assured voice, helping himself to a large measure of vodka.

'In the camps the famine is organized, Kola, not produced by any natural calamity. In the same way, work serves only to destroy the *zeks*; it is a simple instrument of death and not of production. You would have to have seen a brigade of men, no longer able to hold themselves upright, harried all day long, prodded with bayonets by guards of the NKVD who could have performed the same work in an hour. No free community, nor even any penal system, however irrational, organizes production in this way.'

'Russian indolence, aggravated by the stupidity of a bureaucracy with a police mentality. You only have to read Lermontov and Mayakovsky to understand the aberrations that you're describing,' Kola persists, but his eyes reveal a gloomy turn to his thoughts. 'Is it like that everywhere, or are there some camps which are a little more human?' he asks in a suffocated voice.

Aunt Valia's entrance with a new mountain of blinys saves me from having to answer. She senses however that something is wrong.

274

Anxious, she begins to blame the poor quality of the flour, but I assure her that after I have left the Soviet Union I shall keep a fond memory of these blinys all my life. The dish almost drops from her hands. Is Kola's friend drunk or is he teasing her? How could the young artillery officer possibly leave Russia? Kola avoids her baffled, incredulous stare; he tells her gently to go back to the kitchen and to continue making blinys. He goes off to fetch another bottle. To hell with the ulcer!

'To Vassia's health!' he proposes, but his toast has a precise objective. He wants to know if the 'Elephant' would have been capable of carrying out the work on the bridge under the work regime that I have described.

'As a labourer, no. Not even the most solid and robust of men could long withstand the rhythm of *choute, choute, choutareque*, or being driven across fields under threat of the cudgel. In order to survive you need to obtain a job in the supervisory hierarchy, or else you have to become a specialist at something, nurse, shopkeeper, locksmith. In the Volgalag Vassia might perhaps have been lucky and found a job as a groom, looking after the officers' horses; otherwise he would have been broken even more quickly than I and the others were, because the rations are the same for everyone and his "Elephant" needs are much greater than ours.'

I try to change the subject, considering that after this explanation Kola has understood, if not exactly what it is to live in a camp, then at least the reasons for my haste to leave the USSR: 'Tell me about these wonderful TU-2 bombers, the Soviet equivalent of the American Flying Fortress, which you mentioned earlier.' For him, the discussion of the Gulag is not yet over, and he remarks that according to a rumour that is widespread in the Eighteenth Airforce, Tupolev conceived of his four-engine bomber while in a camp. He had doubtless enjoyed working conditions that destroyed neither his red blood corpuscles nor his brain, but, even so, the airforce could have launched its famous aeroplane at least two years earlier had he been left to work in freedom. And during a war, two years sometimes count for more than two decades in peacetime.

'That's enough of these sombre topics. Let's go to the local dance,' I suggest. Kola disagrees. We must continue our discussion, while eating blinys, for they have a calming effect on agitated spirits. In any case we ought to avoid the girls of Mietchotka because they can be as dangerous as the NKVD. 'Tomorrow, in Rostov, we'll go to the dance, but for this evening, let's unburden ourselves on this subject.' I am happy enough to go on with the blinys. But what more is there to say? My 'burden' is the memory of the Gulag which weighs on me as heavily as the mountains of the Caucasus, and I know no way of making it lighter.

'That's not what I'm asking of you,' Kola replies. 'I know from experience that bitterness makes a poor counsellor. Now it seems to me that it would be a pity to forget, out of spite, the scientific truths concerning the march of history. Certain people have tried hard to sabotage our war effort but, despite them, we are on the way to winning the war. That goes too for the construction of our socialism and for the transition to communism. Victory will bring dividends: the material foundations of our society will be enlarged and people will be motivated, active, different from how they were before. I still consider changes inevitable whether it pleases you or not.'

'Who are these saboteurs of our war effort, Kola? Doesn't my case prove that a general improvement on one front doesn't exclude individual unfortunate "errors"? Don't you know in your heart of hearts that after victory it is likely to be the same?'

'No, no and no again. By refusing to place your trust in the future, you simply become the pawn of these bastards who are trying to delay our victory. You know them well, you have suffered because of them. Don't ask me in this pointless way who they are. They are the all-powerful who abuse their power, jackals of all kinds, who don't even realize the harm that they are doing. But tomorrow they will no longer have the opportunity of wreaking such havoc, and later still, under communism, they will disappear; our children won't even be able to believe that such people ever existed. Look at my grandfather: under Czar Nicholas he was a soldier for life, and he struggled in this world like a fly which keeps on thumping against a windowpane without seeing it, without understanding anything about it. We are lucky to have studied the science of how societies develop; we have learned Marxism–Leninism and can predict the course of events. What good would it do you, as a result of bitterness, to become like grandfather!'

The old man in his corner, as if he understands that we are talking about him, raises his head, which had been resting on the handle of his walking stick. Maybe he isn't as deaf as Kola thinks. Aunt Valia too comes rushing in; she wants to make a nice omelette to break the tyranny of the blinys. 'You are an authentic woman of the future, of communist society, Aunt Valia, both fraternal and disinterested,' I say to her. This earns me a still more incredulous stare than when I declared I wanted to leave the USSR. But she laughs – she is good humoured – and she assures me too that it is a family trait, that Nicolai is like herself.

By nature Kola is lighthearted – but this evening so long as I disagree with him on his theory of the future he continues to sulk. We talk a little about my mother, who has a different idea of socialism, but he assures me that she too, after the changes in the USSR, will want to return to Rostov and that yesterday's debates will no longer have any importance. Since these are mere generalities, I give in and finally adhere to his thesis, rejoicing in anticipation of the withering away of suffering and injustice. But after we have drunk to our renewed concord, I declare my total disagreement with some of his future plans: 'I shall not be taking the shuttle back and forth between Rostov and Tiflis, for fear of finding myself again in these unspeakable places. And I have no intention of becoming a public works engineer, since I have no vocation for such a profession were it ever so well paid. Finally, I have no wish to become a member of the CPSU.'

But Kola is now too elated to worry about all this. If I don't want to become an engineer, we shall examine possible alternatives in Rostov. I might become a poet – they are very well paid – or a teacher. The range of possibilities is almost infinite in his view. He understands too my reticence about joining the party, but advises me to re-apply for my Komsomol 'ticket'. Otherwise he declares for prudence, and decides it would be better if he undertook alone to feed our common coffers. After all, he is a flight lieutenant and a CP candidate-member.

The honey, spread plentifully over the blinys, contributes to our rediscovered harmony. Kola has been advised to eat a lot of it because it is thought to be good for ulcers, while according to Aunt Valia it is a source of eternal youth, especially for women – it improves the skin. In my opinion, judging by the experience of this dinner, honey has the virtue of increasing one's appetite while at the same time mitigating the effects of the vodka. On a bliny diet, we could easily have spent the whole night eating and drinking without getting drunk. But it seems unfair to leave Aunt Valia in the kitchen and exclude her from our reunion celebrations. We invite her therefore to come and join us, but only after she has presented her crowning glory: a magnificent cheesecake.

With an audience now, the two ex-combatants relate their stories with brio. To dazzle Aunt Valia I repeat the Khvalynsk officer's argument on the importance of our front in the Caucasus. Its effect had been to immobilize 400 Wehrmacht tanks and inflict a decisive blow to the morale of the Romanian troops. During the decisive phase of the Battle of Stalingrad it was precisely these 400 tanks – not one more, not one less – that had made all the difference. If the Germans had had them they could have broken out of their encirclement. On the other hand, to cut off the encircled Wehrmacht from the rest of the German lines, our men had struck the Romanian sector, which collapsed easily because it had already been so severely tested. 'Imagine that now!' Aunt Valia is lost for words, but even Kola is pleasantly surprised. 'There you are now, we are heroes of Stalingrad too,' he says, cutting another slice of cheesecake with hands that are becoming a little clumsy.

The old man at the far end of the room suddenly interrupts our strategic considerations: 'I have seen four generations of Cossacks eat at this table,' he says in the loud voice of the deaf, 'but I have never seen so much eaten as this evening.' Is this a reproach or a compliment? Kola staggers over to the old man, and shouts to make himself heard: 'Your four generations of Cossacks, *Dzied*, never did any good; they were just so many flies beating against windowpanes. We are different and have thoroughly deserved our meal, for we have won the greatest war in history!' Aunt Valia thinks he is drunk and sends us all off to bed; she is not far off the mark.

Before nodding off, the haunting memory of the camps takes hold of me once again and, in a moment of lucidity I call out to Kola: 'I am leaving for Poland.' When? 'On the first train.' Too befuddled to discuss the matter, he replies tangentially: 'I forgot to tell you that one of your schoolfriends, the *Cosatchka* Klava, often asks for news of you.' 'What difference do you think that makes? She is a youngster, a nice kid.' 'You have become very demanding; this "youngster" is more beautiful than Nievka, Liuba and Svetlana together.' At this, we fall asleep, half undressed, half unconscious.

I would leave for Poland in April 1946, two years to the day of this dinner in Mietchotka. Not on one of the first trains for the repatriated, but on one of the last. Klava had a great deal to do with this delay.

5. Klava

It was destiny that made me fall in love with Klava; Kola's eulogy to her beauty had nothing to do with it. He even tried to put me off her, with horror stories about Cossack women and their families. I remained indifferent to them, for I already knew by then whom to trust on the subject of my beautiful friend from school No. 44. Klava had blossomed into a young woman with an irresistible smile but had retained her round cheeks and schoolgirlish ways, which reminded me of our carefree adolescence. Extremely diligent, Klava had the gift of being at once serious and playful, very stubborn – 'it's in my character' – and very gentle. She admitted to being one of the most accomplished liars in Rostov; she had cultivated this art so as to pull the wool over the eyes of her very traditional Cossack parents, thereby imposing her will on them while feigning the whole time to be a dutiful daughter.

In August 1944, we 'registered our marriage', as they used to say there. She was 21 and I was 20, we were in love and everything was going our way. Klava had just passed her entrance examinations for the Rostov Institute of Public Works Engineers while I had obtained, with ease, a job with a fancy title in a factory in the heavy industry sector. The war front was increasingly distant from Rostov and we greeted the approach of victory with more and more frequent parties which brought together our best friends: Kola, Chourik and Jorik, known as Zeus, three fellow veterans of Kislovodsk and Nalchik, and their wives, Fira, Galia and Cathinka. What more could we have hoped for? 'It's not so much a life as a raspberry,' as they say in Russia when someone is lucky, and we sang lightheartedly:

'Onwards, joyous band of Komsomols!'

Under socialism, however, '*hay problemas, hay contradicciones*,' as a Cuban leader asserted in 1967. Our problems and contradictions, in Rostov, were as large as the Caucasian mountains. We were used to them but this was no consolation. After the war we hoped for a world without nationalist discrimination, permanently exorcised of the old, hateful ideas which had engendered Nazism. Now, at the approach of victory, our official propaganda, while remaining resolutely anti-fascist, became more and more pan-Slavic, as though the better to fuel Russian national pride. Cut off from the world in 1943 by my 13 months in the Gulag, I had only learned rather late in the day that the Comintern, this general staff of the world revolution, Lenin's brainchild, had been dissolved. Some time later, the *Internationale*, which calls upon proletarians to 'arise', ceased to be the national anthem of the USSR. In its stead came an anthem whose first sentence celebrates the merits of *Vielikaia Rouss*, the old name for 'Greater Russia'. What's more, our 'Red Army of Workers and Peasants' was rebaptized the 'Soviet Army'. Even today, foreign commentators persist in ignoring the fact that there hasn't been a Red Army in the USSR since 1944; this name no longer appears in any official publication. And that's not all. The cinema, according to Lenin, is the most important of all the arts as far as communists are concerned, and film directors did their best to act as propagandists. After having glorified the great military chiefs, Alexander Nevsky (Eisenstein) and Souvorov (Pudovkin), they devoted themselves from this time onwards to uncritical apologia of the czars of Holy Russia: Ivan the Terrible (Eisenstein) and Peter the Great (Petrov) were the result.

I was the last person to want to see the Red Army export the Revolution and make a seventeenth Soviet republic out of Poland. All of us hoped that the Great Alliance would be maintained whatever the cost, so that the English and Americans, though capitalists, would help the USSR raise itself from its ruins. The pan-Russian propaganda therefore did not go against the grain of our proletarian leanings, but it was responsible for an eruption of

281

the most retrograde prejudices, including anti-semitism, which found open, public expression and met with the indifference of the authorities. Then, instead of dispelling these misunderstandings, Stalin added his own 'patriotic' tuppence worth: on 24 June 1945, during the victory banquet in the Kremlin, he raised his glass and thanked 'the great *Russian* people' – because they had trusted in their government even during the period of defeats. 'Another people would have taken advantage of them to overthrow their rulers,' Stalin added, as if socialism, which had been held to be irreversible, had survived only thanks to the goodness of the Russian people. Chourik, who was studying the complete works of Marx at the time, claimed that Stalin had been drunk on this occasion. Kola and I shared a regretful and respectful sigh for our Ukrainian commissar. Didn't he deserve – he and so many other non-Russians killed during the war – a little bit of gratitude from our supreme commander-in-chief?

Our worst 'problem and contradiction' was the crash of the official economy. In theory we were living in a society in which the interests of the individual merged with those of the collectivity – this was one of the cardinal points of Soviet doctrine. In practice, however, the collectivity evidently didn't care a fig about our individual interests and we repaid it fully in kind, especially where 'socialist property' was concerned. By behaving in this way we were not demonstrating an asocial state of mind so much as simply manifesting our elementary needs: the will to survive, to satisfy our hunger, to dress ourselves decently and to be able to go out to the entertainments of our choice. At the start of the war Moussia's graft had appeared shocking to me; at the war's end all of us had become her emulators with even more sophisticated rackets to help us get by.

This style of operating didn't help calm my anxieties as a former *zek*, and it tormented my friends, for they would have liked their actions to be more in keeping with their professions of Komsomol faith. We felt the situation to be humiliating, even incomprehensible, in total contradiction with the evolution of the war. Explaining our army's victories in terms of the cleverness of our generals and the heroism of the Russian nation was short-sighted. In this 'war of engines', to use Stalin's famous phrase, productive capacity was all important. Each breakthrough by our troops seemed to demonstrate that the USSR was very powerful in all the sectors of the economy – a lot more so than we would have believed or imagined possible. Hadn't we always thought that victory would only be possible thanks to concerted action on two fronts, to the west and to the east, thanks also to the deliveries of 'engines' manufactured by the West? Now, our army was marching triumphantly on Berlin, alone, with its cannons, tanks, aeroplanes and engines 'Made in the USSR'. Admittedly, in June 1944, the Allies had finally landed in Normandy, but they were progressing at a snail's pace – 'at the rate of a spool of thread per day', as we joked in Rostov, for their slowness had no longer any importance for the outcome of the war. A single unknown factor remained: who would be the first to enter Berlin to plant the Red Flag on the highest building still standing in the capital of the Third Reich. Would it be Zhukov, Rokossovski or Koniev?

All these facts clearly contradicted Soviet inferiority complexes: our society evidently harboured potentialities that we had never suspected. Even before dazzling the rest of the world, the victorious Soviet Union had astounded its own citizens. It had concealed immense productive forces and it knew how to use them to the best effect. Doubt was no longer possible: 'The possibilities of socialism are unlimited.' Stalin had been right.

It is well known, however, that certain exceptionally gifted people are incapable of simple arithmetic; our society was like them. Peerless in matters of dizzying complexity, it was unable to distribute herrings in the Don region, or water-melons in Rostov. Such trivial matters failed to interest it because of their extreme simplicity. Certainly it was hoped that one day, when the accumulation of minor matters had attained gigantic proportions, it would 'do the lot' and resolve all the problems in one master-stroke. Meanwhile the workers had to queue up to buy every basic necessity and they suffered the consequences of an inflation which reduced their official salaries to a pittance. The black market economy imposed its laws upon the victorious Soviet Union even more thoroughly than during the grimmest phase of the war.

When my marriage was registered, I was questioned about my attitude towards the National Liberation Committee of Poland, recently set up in Lublin. It was explained to me that in the event of my returning to Poland, Klava would not be allowed to follow me there. 'Your marriage will be annulled at no extra cost,' they announced to me as if it were a piece of good news: in this manner I would economize on the 50 roubles charged for a standard divorce. Admittedly I was offered the opportunity of remaining in Rostov and of opting for Soviet nationality, but, if I did, I would, like all my fellow citizens, forfeit the right to go abroad, even to Poland.

I now recall that Klava had never thought of keeping me. For one thing, she sensed that my mother was still alive. For another, she knew that I had been too badly scarred by the Gulag to remain in the Soviet Union. Once it had been accepted as inevitable, the prospect of our separation no longer seemed to frighten her. The others, especially Kola, thought that her reserve on the subject was due to her preoccupation with her studies at the Institute of Public Works. In fact Klava understood perfectly the torments I suffered as an ex-*zek*.

We detested melodramas, scenes and tears. Klava declared that she belonged to a non-migratory species of bird from the Don region: 'My wings are too small for long-distance flights and, if I clung on to yours, we would end up together in the middle of the river.' Suppose though that Kola's optimistic hypothesis proved true, and I were to return to Rostov with my mother and my dear ones? At the thought of it she gave her most bewitching smile and then answered straightaway with the cold calm of a sceptical Russian: 'Rostov will not become the ideal sanctuary for a foreign bird that has already been wounded by the ferocious poachers of the NKVD.'

We lived from day to day and didn't bother ourselves with the future. We succeeded so well in this that people said: 'It's a pleasure to see a couple who really are so much in love.' But everything was paradoxical. We arranged parties on the occasion of each advance made by our army, while knowing that final victory would hasten the separation that neither of us wanted. During these celebrations, through force of habit, our friends always proposed the old toasts of soldiers at the front: 'May it not be the last one!' Yet they no longer had to fear enemy bullets, nor measures that would prevent them from drinking together until the end of their days.

I prolonged my stay in Rostov as long as possible, then left for Poland in April 1946. In spite of the Cold War, Klava and I continued to write to each other, and this correspondence only came to an end in 1949, at the moment when I broke with 'People's' Poland and with the Eastern bloc. In my memory, our separation took place gradually, gently, in the least painful manner possible. Klava's letters – which I reread once more when this chapter was almost completed – show that in fact it wasn't quite like that. She frequently alludes to a rendezvous that we had given each other, to the hope of resuming a shared life together. She even offers me financial help, for, having completed her studies, she had found a well-paid post as an engineer in the Ukraine. So I have to accept that my memory misleads me, that we had always planned to meet up once more.

At the time of our reunion in April 1944, I experience suddenly an extremely strong attraction for Klava which doesn't seem to be reciprocated. I have fantasies about how different my life would have been without the Gulag. On seeing my former classmate, I say to myself: 'You imbecile, why didn't you show more interest in her in 1941? Why, instead of enlisting in the armed forces, didn't you go off with her to Central Asia to study, to work and to fall in love?' But Klava quickly brings me back to earth: she is happy to see me again, that's all. Love? What love? There was never any question of it between us. Is there another man in her life? Her answer is evasive. 'All girls have men who hang around.' Well then, not to worry. I shall soon outdistance these rivals; after all, at school No. 44 she hadn't thought too badly of me.

But paying court to a Cossack girl in a half-destroyed town is not only a full-time job, it is also an obstacle race and an infinite torment. Using various pretexts, Klava obtains without difficulty permission from her parents to go out, but there is no question of her inviting her suitor to her home. As for me, I live in the tiny apartment belonging to Chourik's family, the same Chourik who had been my messmate and who had had a leg amputated after his injuries in Nalchik. There is no question of entertaining Klava here.

The second obstacle is the sense of insecurity that prevails in the darkened, ruined streets. The times are propitious to criminals and to the drunkards who drown their war memories in vodka. With the exception of Gorky Park, where there is hot competition for unoccupied benches, lovers stroll around Rostov after nightfall only at their peril. I have heard far too many stories about people who get relieved of their goods, including all of their clothes, ever to expose Klava to such a misadventure. Where then can we shelter our potential love?

'In the central post office,' Klava suggests. She has fallen by chance upon a small, inter-city telephone and telegraph office which stays open all night. It is a godsend, for the people of Rostov seem to be unaware of the existence of this night-time facility and rarely intrude upon our interminable conversations. The discreet post office clerks don't bother to ask us what urgent matter keeps us in their office for nights on end.

Klava and I have lots of things to tell each other about these three years of war and separation. We sit far enough from the counter to allow us to talk without fear of being overheard; we are better off here than we used to be in school No. 44. Unfortunately, the atmosphere of the post office is hardly conducive to passion. It is hard to imagine Mikhail Lermontov composing poems about the lovers of the 24-hour post office in Rostov. In this mundane setting I hardly dare to take Klava in my arms, fearing her resistance as much as the look on the face of the counter-clerk, who is likely to wake up suddenly and put an end to the frolics of the 'postal lovers'.

The absence of a romantic setting didn't stop us from spending many a happy evening on our bench. Klava told me a great deal about her life as a young woman in Rostov, which changed hands in 1941, in 1942 and 1943. I had never thought of the war from this angle. A woman, in addition to the fear of shells and bombs shared by everyone, has to be wary of 'bad soldiers', including alas, some of our own. Immediately after the entry of victorious troops, there is a period of uncertainty during which armed soldiers make their own laws. In Rostov, except in 1942, these terrible periods had coincided with the periods of extreme cold, and Klava, hidden in a cellar, had endured fear, hunger and cold. She went out only in cases of dire necessity, disguised as an old woman, realizing anyway that her camouflage afforded her only small protection. 'Some of them even raped grandmothers,' she says.

After the terrors of the interregnum and with the stabilization of power, certain women decided to take advantage of the times, and presented a sorry spectacle of debauchery and venality. Once again, Klava had to hide in her cellar in order to avoid 'voluntary work' in Germany, but she knew that, among the women of Rostov, volunteers were not in short supply. 'The Ataman Krasnov came back to recruit a new Cossack White Army; yes, yes, I also believed he had been dead for a long time, and yet, I swear to you, there he was parading in Novotcherkask, in Rostov and in the Kuban. At that time a lot of people, thinking that Stalin had lost the war, thought they could achieve Cossack autonomy within the German Reich.' She talks without hatred for 'these foolish people', but for the women who have gone off to Germany, these 'witless whores', she has no pity.

As I listen entranced, Klava's trust in me grows. She explains her conflict with her parents, her break with their values, their way of life and their nostalgia for Cossack ways. She can no longer stand their traditions, which she defines as 'humbug', having seen under the occupation that these outdated ideas are far from innocent. 'Our reputation as warriors weighs like a curse on this region; it only deserves the epithet "special" in recognition of the suffering that it has endured.' On this point her criticism of Cossack mythologizing echoes Kola's. But Klava continues to live among a family of traditionalists, surrounded by friends who all remain attached to their specific identity as Cossacks. 'They are not counter-revolutionaries,' she adds, 'and they haven't thought of enlisting under the flag of the Ataman Krasnov's collaborators. But, they hold on to their own hierarchy of values which forbids them, among other things, to learn anything whatever from those younger than they are, or simply even to entertain any real dialogue with them.' Remembering certain passages from *And Quiet Flows the Don*, I ask her if her parents have ever beaten her. Klava bursts out laughing: 'They worship me, I am spoiled much more than my three brothers, all of whom were called up in 1941. I love them too, I have no wish to hurt them and I prefer to lie to them rather than confront them head on.' Is it wise though, to sacrifice, if not her principles, at least a part of her freedom just to keep her parents happy? 'I try to sacrifice as little as possible. And what is the alternative?'

For want of a solution I take her in my arms and offer her my kisses. Each movement, however slight, causes our bench to creak strangely. This warns the clerk of the threat that we represent to the socialist property of the post and telegraph department. 'Let's not make anyone jealous,' Klava says, indicating to me the head behind the counter. We get back on to the subject of her parents: are they practising Christians? My ignorance makes her laugh aloud once more: her father is a public servant of the Soviet state, and he would never put his position at risk for the pleasure of lighting a candle in an Orthodox church. Even her mother, through fear of compromising her husband, only ventures into one very rarely, and then only by stealth. I mention that my commissar in Kislovodsk recommended suspending anti-religious propaganda, but Klava's opinions are unshaken: the patriotic alliance with the Orthodox hierarchy doesn't imply the right for everyone to frequent the churches. Do her parents suffer because of it? Probably not. Nevertheless, nothing in the world would give them so much pleasure as seeing their daughter get married in church in a white dress with all the fuss of the old days. 'Dear, oh, dear. On this point, Klava, I hope that you won't give in to them?' 'Of course not, *golubtchik* [my dove] there is not a chance of it. Get it into your head that my papa, Emilian, is a good public servant, well disciplined, and that he truly loves Stalin.'

She asks me to describe the Gulag; she will understand. I doubt it. Not even Kola, who is the son of deportees and who has suffered since his childhood, is in a position to grasp this unspeakable world. She insists and I talk to her at length about my nightmare journey across the archipelago of *zeks*. The Zanga bridge construction site fascinates her, as if her intuition told her that it was there that I had begun my life as the *pojarnik*, this deformed shadow of myself. 'Twelve hours a day with your feet in water, my goodness! Even a stout horse from the Don would not be able to stand it,' she says, with such compassion that I feel obliged to clarify matters. We didn't work in the water, and in any case, the great problem in the camp is not merely hunger or physical exhaustion, but their consequences inside the *zek*'s head. 'Just what I thought,' she maintains, and yet she asks me new questions about each day of these four months of work on the bridge. Certain aspects – the sadism of the convict-guards, the brutality between *zeks*, or the dead buried like animals, right beside the construction site – make her shiver, and she presses against me, frightened, as she had in 1940 at the theatre, watching Anna Karenina's suicide. 'Let's change the subject, Klava. I don't want you to feel pity for me.' 'No,' she persists, 'it isn't pity.' And she wants us to talk about it even if it frightens her and even if she suffers as a result.

'Aren't you afraid of becoming a counter-revolutionary if I carry on telling you about it all?' 'The new Zanga bridge is not the Revolution,' she replies. 'The Revolution is made to change people, to give them their liberty, not to destroy it, or to fill their heads with diabolical thoughts.' Of course! She has also found the word! The chemistry teacher in the Volgalag, my only interlocutor in the Gulag, had been the first to say to me that each of us *zeks* henceforth carried within ourselves a portion of the devil. A believer, he held that precisely because of this, those from the outside, even the most impoverished, wouldn't understand us. I repeat this to Klava to warn her that I am no longer the nice boy from school No. 44. 'I am not afraid of the devil himself, and still less of a portion of devilry,' she says: 'It's not in my character.'

She swears that she will avenge me and settle accounts, starting with the traitor Oleg; since he is from Rostov he will come back here sooner or later. This must be the influence of her Cossack family, and I plead with her to forget any ideas about pursuing a vendetta: it could lead her straight to the red-brick barracks in the Volgalag. 'We shall see, who lives will see, the blind say,' she replies with a mysterious smile.

Escorting Klava home, I am allowed a few kisses: that's my lot.

It's a small world, it's well known, but this sometimes favours friendship between demobilized ex-servicemen like Jorik, known as Zeus, and I. In Kislovodsk we hardly knew each other at all, for he belonged to the third squadron, housed at the other end of the barracks. To tell the truth, I still don't know why he was nicknamed Zeus, nor who had been sufficiently learned in Greek mythology to give it to him. Having suffered concussion on the Nalchik hill, Zeus had passed through the hospital in Beslan before ending up 'under observation' in Krasnovodsk. There, a ferocious nurse had told him a lot of stories about the medical dossier of another soldier in his unit. Having ascertained that it was indeed me, Zeus continues to offer me his protection, out of a sense of solidarity between the brain-damaged. This tall, fair-haired lad, something of a dreamer, isn't lacking in resources, or at least in luck.

At the beginning our relations were distorted by our respective reputations: I didn't greatly appreciate being considered as a headcase who hadn't been adequately treated, and I was convinced that Zeus remained a little cracked in the head. For he had me read his poems commemorating our battle on the Nalchik Hill, poems with lame rhymes which described in detail the terrible damage that we had done to the Germans. It was probably intended to be metaphorical, for Zeus couldn't have forgotten that our enemies on the hill were Romanians and not Germans. Besides, after so many more important battles, why ought the Germans to remember Nalchik? We two, who had suffered concussion, and Chourik, who had lost a leg there, had good cause to remember this place, but that was hardly true of the Wehrmacht. Diplomatically avoiding an argument, I advised him against sending his poem to the Rostov daily, *Molot*, because of certain formal imperfections.

At about this time Zeus lands the job of canteen manager at the Rosa Luxembourg tobacco factory, and he invites me to come along to discuss the writing of poetry. The next day Kola joins us and, after making rapid inquiries, decrees that our friend has the right to feed us every day, without tickets or money. It is indeed perfectly legal and Zeus quickly understands the advantages of his job. Two or three times a week he calls upon Klava to replace a cashier who is often absent on account of illness, and helps her to fix her till so that she makes from it much more than her wages.

Some time later, Zeus gives us conclusive proof that he isn't at all crazy. He concludes an agreement with the factory management which allows himself, Kola and I to make some extra cash. This factory, like all the others, operates at a spasmodic rhythm and when it has to speed up the line to meet its quota, it finds itself with large stocks of cigarettes which it hasn't managed either to pack into cartons or to send off in time. For these busy periods it needs additional packers, who are neither planned for in the labour flow-chart, nor easy to find in a town where workers (especially male) are in short supply. The three of us are ready to help at Rosa Luxembourg on condition that we are not paid mere pin-money. The simplest thing would have been to pay us in cartons of cigarettes, but the law forbids it: on the one hand tobacco is rationed, and on the other all the factory workers are searched on their way out. It is at this point that Zeus intervenes. His plan proves his common sense: after work we shall leave by the canteen exit, where there is no search, with cartons in trouser pockets cunningly designed for the purpose. In short, he obtained permission for us to make off discreetly with as many cigarettes as our custom trouser pockets would hold. 'It's not theft, we are authorized to take them,' he insists, in order to dispel my fears as a timorous ex-*zek*. I fall into line with his plan and, morally pure, stuff the packets of Belomor-kanal into my trouser pockets, taking care not to crush any. The ironic touch here is that this very popular brand of cigarettes bears the name of a canal built in the far north by common-law prisoners who, if we are to believe a film made about them, had been reformed by this forced but highly re-educative labour.

The humdrum of our life as Zeus's guests doesn't satisfy Kola, who is thinking further ahead and is more ambitious than we are. He argues very firmly that we have to take advantage of these few months' respite to create for ourselves a solid material foundation, given that after the start of the academic year we shall no longer have the time to work as warehouse packers, and still less to travel. Kola and I have a shared kitty, and this gives him the right to demand my help in carrying out the plan that he had previously sketched for me in Mietchotka. Unfortunately, this plan involves numerous return journeys to Aunt Valia's home – with herrings on the outward journey and honey on the return – and I am reluctant to leave Rostov and loth to abandon Klava. Kola, more and more angry, inflicts upon me interminable lectures on the laws of the market economy: 'We need capital to invest in my expedition to Tiflis. If I set off there with the pathetic 500 roubles that we still have left between us, and if I spend the half of it on the way, the profit will be derisory.' And to whom is he explaining these elementary matters? To me, the son of a former Rostov proprietor who, among his other properties, owned the whole post office building! I don't give a toss for this lost patrimony; I simply prefer my humdrum routine as Zeus's casual worker to the roof of a train for Mietchotka. 'Right,' Kola declares threateningly, 'if you insist upon dying of hunger in a few months' time, just so you can talk all night to a Cossack girl, I shall be forced to look for another partner. But you ought to pay heed to my opinion: a Cossack woman is a curse.'

Thanks to a surprising reversal, Kola will be even more stubborn about ever leaving Rostov than I am. One evening in the middle of May 1944, he invites me to a show at the Theatre of Musical Comedy – someone has given him two tickets. Though no fan of operetta, I accept his invitation. I am enchanted; an intrigue unfolds on stage which stirs a responsive chord in me. Gentlemen of leisure, in evening suits, deplore in song the fact that they are never able to go bed early because they are so attracted by the ladies' boudoirs – do they even know what a boudoir is in Rostov? – and by these beautiful courtesans for whom life is just a large bowl of cherries. At the end of their song, irresistible temptresses come fluttering onstage, very scantily clad by Rostov standards, smiling contentedly as they shake their legs about and pirouette underneath the noses of the idle gentlemen. I would never have believed that in Rostov there could have been shows like this one. Kola wants me to pick out one of the dancers on the stage. No, not that one, the other one, the blonde, yes, that's the one, that's her, and he concludes: 'Her name is Fira. She's my girl.' 'Your girl, but what do you mean?' 'She's mine, all mine, and not just on a central post office bench either,' he says proudly.

After Fira's entry into Kola's life, there will no longer be any talk of journeys through Georgia, and a good-humoured atmosphere envelops our little circle. Fira is always ready to help, to comfort or to distract a friend in distress. Having guessed that I felt cramped in Chourik's place, she set up a bed for me in her kitchen – which doubled as a bathroom – and, with a peculiarly Cossack energy, she dispelled my fears about being a nuisance. By an irony of fate, Kola has taken up with a 'pure-blooded' Cossack, a native of Novot-cherkask, capital of the atamans, and she speaks in her region's broadest accent, full of harsh 'o' sounds. On stage she pronounces perfectly 'How do you do Mr Brown?' but she really doesn't know how to say *Maskwa* or *pajar* like a Russian – it is beyond her.

Fira is a very independent woman. Her days are filled with exercises, rehearsals and performances, and she cares little about whether it suits Kola or not. She even has her own income, which is just as well for us, and prefers to keep her savings out of our 'crackpot schemes'. Fira, as a performing artist, belongs to the privileged sector of the official economy and, in addition, receives two tickets from her theatre each evening. Entrusted to a skilful tout these two tickets earn her 60 roubles net. That represents a stable income (whereas ours is uncertain) and it is threatened only by the Muscovite composer Dunayevsky, for whose performances there is no black market in tickets. Therefore, Dunayevsky is a kind of personal enemy of Fira's, though his operettas featured very rarely in the repertoire of the Rostov musical comedy theatre.

A digression on this theatre is in order here since it brightened up our last two years of wartime. Light opera for the Soviet regime is the least important art, virtually unusable for propaganda purposes. It would indeed have been incongruous and to a certain extent indecent to take the Revolution, and even the history of Czars Ivan, Alexander and Peter as the subjects for musicals. That is why works such as *Princess Csardas*, *The Gypsy Baron*, *La Vie Parisienne*, *Mr Brown and Lady Gil* and many others remained popular. In this period of alliance with the Anglo-Saxons, the management of the 'Muscomedia' in Rostov revived a good twenty of these operettas, sometimes giving their titles a proletarian twist – *Princess Csardas* thus became the more democratic *Silva* – but without altering anything at all of the content or decor: Austro–Hungarian castles, Parisian or London luxury.

These were not lavish West End or Broadway productions but there was no need for that. The operettas were a roaring success and our group of Komsomols never missed one of them, and even went back to see some of them two or three times. While fully realizing that this decadent art should not be taken seriously, we gladly abandoned our war songs in favour of arias on the torments and pleasures of love. After all, our women, even if modestly dressed, also 'set our hearts on fire' and 'inflicted incredible sufferings in return for some sublime moments' . . .

The infatuation of the people of Rostov with light opera had inevitable economic consequences since the law of supply and demand operates as harshly in the entertainment sector as in all the other sectors of the economy. To see a new film – be it only the worst of B-movies on the war – you had to pay the touts 15 roubles a ticket, which, at the booking office, cost only five. It was perfectly normal to pay 40 or 50 for an operetta; the people in Rostov, in spite of their modest official wages of between 300 and 500 roubles a month, were clearly not short of money. Fira generally managed to obtain seats for us at official prices, but sometimes, so as not to create problems for her, we played the part of big spenders and bought our tickets from the touts. 'They have to live as well,' Kola used to say.

This phenomenon reached its peak when Alexander Wertynski came to Rostov. Wertynski was a singer of great charm, an emigrant who had decided to return to his native country with an entire wagon-load of medical supplies. The prices on the black market for his performance went through the roof: 300 or 400 roubles per seat. I couldn't possibly miss this performance because Wertynski had been the idol of my parents and since my early childhood I had known his languorous songs exalting his love for Yvette (an uncommon name in Russia), and many others. So it was with a lump in my throat that I heard this elderly man, with a sad expression, take up again his *v bannanovo limonnom Singapouri** accompanying it with gestures of his ring-covered fingers. But the others in the audience, who had never been able to buy even one record by Wertynski, how was it that they knew these great 'smash hits' by heart? I see before me once more the audience in the Theatre of Musical Comedy giving an ovation to Wertynski such as I have never seen at any performance in Russia, and calling out in chorus: 'Yvetta, Yvetta!', 'Encore!' and 'Bravo!'

---

* Russian neologism to say that Singapore is full of banana and lemon trees.

295

How are things progressing with my courtship of Klava? We are no longer limited to the post office bench, for it is now the beginning of the summer of 1944 and the longer days make it possible to go for romantic strolls along the Don. As the circle of our friends grows larger we go out together to the cinema, to the Musical Comedy, or else we play games at Chourik's place.

One of Klava's friends, Cathinka, who sings in the Don Cossacks Performance Arts Ensemble, moved in with our friend Zeus barely a week after having met him. And even Chourik found a soulmate in Galia, the assistant librarian and daughter of the deputy director of the Karl Marx Library. From her Jewish mother Galia inherited a slightly Mediterranean look which contrasts sharply with the blondness of Cathinka or Fira. She is highly cultured, as is Chourik, and together they form the most intellectual couple of our circle.

I ask Klava why, since we are both grown up, in a hurry to taste life and to make up for the lost war years, we must remain chaste. She has a good answer: 'What good would it do us to become even closer to one another since you are soon going to leave?' What she says is true, I ought to leave her in peace and let her find someone else. But, as they say in Russian: 'Love is not a potato, you can't throw it out of the window.' I don't manage to overcome my feelings. Without Klava, my life in Rostov simply wouldn't make any sense.

It is Fira who most encourages me to pursue this 'serious love'. She informs me that their bed is at our disposal when she is on stage in the evenings and Kola is off elsewhere. 'You will be much better off than on your post office bench,' she says. Next she insists upon the fleeting character of love: 'It is a magic moment that you have to grab hold of; think of nothing else, because it is possible that it will never happen to you again.' Finally she suggests to me that I explain to Klava that her own marriage to Kola has neither brought him closer to nor distanced him from her: 'It cost us five roubles, no more than a cheap theatre ticket. It won't break your bank.'

Fortified by such advice, I arrange evenings with Klava on Fira's bed, that she accepts with a challenging look that says: 'You don't scare me.' Then, one July evening, she turns up for our date dressed as though for a party: a white bodice in very fine linen, a dark made-to-measure skirt and high-heeled shoes. She casually announces: 'I've decided to get married.' So as to be clear in my mind about it before strangling her, I ask her who the lucky fellow is. 'You,' she says, and our marriage is consummated there and then.

Was it Fira who had prompted her miraculous decision? 'As early as our school days I knew that it would come to this,' she replies. 'Sooner or later I had to catch you, my dear little bird from afar.' It is flattering but it doesn't correspond to my experiences of these past four months. 'I had to put you to the test, because otherwise you would have taken advantage of me and then thrown me overboard, like Stienka Razin with his princess: "Here you are, Volga, take this pretty offering. It is a Don Cossack who makes you a present of her!"' 'You're the Cossack, I have nothing in common with Stienka Razin!' 'Yes you have! All men are Stienka Razins after a fashion. And if you think that I owe you apologies for having made you be patient, you've got another think coming.'

I haven't time to answer: a noise on the stairway persuades her that either Fira or Kola is about to come in. Dressed with speed, she has just time to tell me: 'Tomorrow, at 10 o'clock in the morning, you will meet Papa Emilian, who will give you my hand. I have already prepared the way. But whatever happens, don't neglect to tell him that you have killed 10 Germans, and I *mean* 10; eight killed and five seriously wounded won't do at all. And if you can manage it you might also slip in a kind word on the Ataman Skoropatski – it will increase the size of my dowry.'

Fira arrives first and congratulates me. 'You will see, this bed brings happiness, you will be very happy.' 'But I haven't killed 10 Germans, Fira, and I haven't the vaguest idea of who the Ataman Skoropatski could be.' 'What of that?' she expresses surprise. 'Wait for Kola, he will tell you all you need to know. Kola is capable of charming all the Cossacks on earth. He succeeded in charming me!'

A middle ranking inspector in the government department of agriculture, 'Papa Emilian' is not a very senior public servant, but nor is he a nobody. He spends most of his time sorting out different reports, but once a month he acts the part of government inspector with more efficacy than his predecessor in Gogol. You sense it as soon as you set foot in the family-owned maisonnette whose furniture exudes a comfortable ease: a large clock in perfect working order under a glass cover, an opulent settee, a magnificent rustic table for eating on and another, smaller one, for the samovar. We sit down on the settee, facing a portrait of Marshal Boudiennyi, and the conversation is very cordial because he remembers me from before the war, when I helped 'little Klava' to do her homework.

This man of about fifty, rather shortish, with white hair parted in the middle, is the very picture of the tranquil father, and I hesitate before telling him the bloody tale about the 10 Germans skewered by my bayonet. But it is he who eggs me on through this episode which is supposed to raise my prestige as a prospective son-in-law. He tells me that during the occupation of Rostov, a German officer who was billeted in the end room of the house used to go, stark naked, to the toilet. Had the officer tried to rape Papa Emilian's wife and daughter, as commonly happens in wartime, Klava's father would have defended them to the death. But, without such a pretext, he couldn't attack this shameless brute who attached no more importance to the gaze of a Russian woman than to that of a dog. Wounded by this attack upon his Cossack honour, Papa Emilian had informed his three sons in writing that unless each of them killed at least 10 Germans, they would no longer be welcome under his roof. As I narrate my Nalchik saga, Papa Emilian punctuates each mortal blow of my imaginary bayonet with nods of approval.

The Ataman Skoropatski problem is overcome even more easily: Papa Emilian brings in from the next room a photograph, taken in 1915 in Novotcherkask, showing the ataman presenting Papa Emilian with a sword on the occasion of his twenty-first birthday. 'What a coincidence,' I say. 'My parents were hosts to the Ataman Skoropatski that very same year and preserve a splendid memory of it.' The success of this revelation is stunning, but double-edged: Papa Emilian is going to introduce me to all of his acquaintances as the 'son of some of the ataman's Polish friends, who had later gone abroad'.

Before bringing out another souvenir, he delivers a very tactful speech about the Poles. What the devil is he leading up to? Papa Emilian slowly unfolds on the table, with the kind of care usually reserved for works of art, a large, old poster: a Red Cavalry soldier on horseback soars high above a town; '*Warchawa nacha*!' 'Warsaw is ours!' proclaims the caption in black letters. Klava hadn't told me that her father, after having been a White, came within an ace of conquering Warsaw with the Red Army. . . . Running short of things to say, I mutter some banal remarks on the reputed rivalry between Boudiennyi and Toukhatchevsky, which is supposed to have allowed the Poles to attack their troops separately and to win the battle. He sweeps this thesis aside: 'God didn't wish us to have the victory,' he says, as though he could see Abbot Skorupka make the sign of the cross in a corner of his own poster.

He had promised his daughter not to discuss politics with me, and so we stay silent therefore, looking at Semione Boudiennyi, whose portrait hangs on the wall facing us. In his youth, he was a legendary character, one of the founders of this Red Cavalry which played a decisive role in the victory of the Republic of Soviets during the Civil War of 1918–20. The finest songs of that period are dedicated to the heroic struggle against these 'ataman curs', in the hope that their bleached bones may be scattered by the wind of the steppes. And hadn't Isaac Babel written a classic on the epic of the Red Cavalry?

Klava is right: her father's head is full of nonsense, otherwise he wouldn't have been able simultaneously to admire Boudiennyi and Skoropatski. During the Civil War he changed sides four times before ending up 'by God's grace', on that of the victors. He congratulates himself and reminds me that the Whites, after the fall of the Crimea, were reduced to exile and became 'folk dancers who live from their tips'. Papa Emilian's sincerity prompts me to a certain indulgence: he is attached to the memory of Ataman

Skoropatski because he is the most important man he ever met, the one who, at the time, reigned over the Don region. The fact that the younger generation, beginning with Fira and Kola, doesn't even know his name, proves that he wasn't one of the worst atamans, and that he hadn't tried, like Krasnov, to capture Petersburg in order to hang Lenin and all the Bolsheviks. In Russian, Skoropatski means, 'he who falls quickly,' which made Kola express doubts about his very existence – suggesting that Klava had invented this name to make fun of her father's obsessive nostalgia. But he well and truly existed, a fine figure of a man in white uniform, and Papa Emilian's souvenir photo confirms his existence.

Unlike her father's, Klava's ideas are clear-cut, but three-quarters of the things that she has told him about our love, about my family (of Polish noble stock) and about me, are pure fabrication. I am obliged to confirm them even if, in their details, they are ludicrously improbable – for example, that we had maintained a lovers' correspondence throughout these three years of war, without ever losing contact. In my heart of hearts, I wonder if Klava hasn't pushed her taste for invention too far. Why deceive her father who, judging by my impressions, wouldn't put any obstacles in the way of our getting married? The answer will be given some weeks later.

On the matter of the dowry, there isn't a lot to discuss: the most beautiful girl in the world can only give what she has, and that goes too for a father attached to his only daughter. Since his only material wealth is his wooden maisonnette, he offers us a large share of it, proposing to extend Klava's room to include that of her three brothers. He has already arranged for some carpenters to come and take down the partition wall. 'You will have 28 square metres of space, which is not to be sneezed at,' he explains, adding that the reconstruction plan for the area around the station unfortunately provided for demolition of the maisonnette. But the implementation of this plan will take years and then, 'they' will have to rehouse us in an equivalent space. For the moment, he notes, laughing at the incongruities of bureaucracy, our house has, as its address, 'apartment Number 22' of the building next door, destroyed by German bombs.

It's amusing, I agree, but the real problem is knowing where Klava's three brothers, who still have a chance of killing 10 Germans apiece and demanding their space under the parental roof, will be housed. Papa Emilian's answer seems to me to be very evasive – 'they are all stout lads' – clearly, he can only deal with one problem at a time. Later the Soviet Army will extricate him from his embarrassment by sending his sons, after victory in the West, to go for a double in the Far East.

From the Bug to the Vistula, the Nazis destroyed half or three-quarters of the houses – in an area whose population was poorly housed even before the war. Our 28 square metres represent for Rostov the equivalent of a suite at the Hilton, a luxury that is better hidden from outsiders. With our close friends, it is different. Our parties nearly always take place in our home, around a table that is very long and narrow. Ten can sit at it comfortably but without room to place the serving dishes in between the guests' plates. Still, Rostov is not Mietchotka, our meals will not be banquets, and Klava doesn't aspire to match Aunt Valia in producing an endless supply of honey-filled blinys. At the end of the war, only the peasants are able to stuff themselves with food. Food which they sell little of at high prices – or at least so it is claimed in the cities.

Inspired by our bright sunlit room, Zeus composes a poem rhyming in the manner of Zhukovski, Pushkin's teacher, in which he wishes us the leisure to loaf about in bed until midday and to cultivate the roses (without the thorns) of love. In practice though things work out otherwise: by day, when it is bright and fine, we don't use the room. In the evenings, on the other hand, there are four of us studying around the long table: Klava and Kola at one end, Chourik and I at the other. They tussle with the sciences, we with history; in the middle, a lamp parsimoniously gives out light – in Russia they manufacture only low wattage lamp bulbs. Each couple has to speak in a low voice, which gives a vaguely conspiratorial atmosphere to our long evenings of study. Then, Fira makes a flamboyant entry. She is here to fetch Kola after the show but, asked to wait a while, she falls asleep on our bed as suddenly as a tired child.

Why do we study with so much determination? It is because the war isn't over and all sectors of education are under a military style regime. This Prussian discipline is especially pervasive at the Institute of Public Works – Kola had foreseen as much – which offers an advance salary and not merely a grant to its students. Its students are assured of rewarding careers, but it is the institute itself which finds them their jobs. So, those students who fall behind are in danger firstly of being relegated to an establishment of lesser prestige, and secondly of being sent upon completion of their studies to work in regions distant from Rostov.

Kola of course is less threatened than the others. He has fought in the war, and all the authorities must take this into account: a demobilized officer won't let himself be intimidated by some teacher who has spent most of the war hidden somewhere in Asia. Not that Kola has any need of preferential treatment: he had already studied in the air-force academy the basic sciences on the institute's syllabus. He is to become *otlitchnik*, the most brilliant of this year's intake. Nevertheless he comes to our study sessions in order to help Klava keep on top of things.

At our end of the table, Chourik and I are more relaxed. We are enrolled at the University of Rostov, which, like all old institutions, is more accommodating in matters of discipline. Chourik studies full-time and therefore receives a maintenance grant; whereas I study by correspondence and without a grant since I get a good salary as supplies foreman at the Savelit factory. I have rather over-estimated my capacities and my resources of energy in wanting to work full-time and to study. In the evenings, after leaving the factory, I am too exhausted, physically and mentally, to go to the library or to a class that is specially arranged for students on correspondence courses. Without Chourik's help I would not have entered for any examination except Latin, which I had already studied in Lodz.

Chourik is very gifted and he teaches me with great patience.

Having read Marx and other classic socialist theorists, he maintains that the teaching in our faculty is a load of rubbish and that Stalin's dialectic, in the fourth chapter of the *History of the CPSU*, is less than accurate. These things reawaken the *pojarnik* buried in me and instantly conjure up the faces of Captains Strel and Abak. Chourik though, is not afraid of anything: he has fought in the war and he thinks that everything is permitted, just as I used to think in Yerevan. What is strange is that the number of these 'invulnerable characters' has increased prodigiously and that those who are still in active service generally share their frame of mind. My friends Vassia and Volodia, on the line of the Bug, and Kostia on that of the Dnestr reveal military information to me (that I have no desire to know about) in their letters, as if censorship no longer existed in the USSR.

When I beg Chourik not to indulge in attacks on Stalin, he answers with the old adage about the mouse convinced that the cat is the most fearsome animal in the world, exactly like my cousin Stepan in Moscow in 1940, when making fun of my fear of the Wehrmacht. Be careful, I say to Chourik, remember that the German cat came close to devouring us and, in your place, I wouldn't underestimate the NKVD cat. It was a waste of time: Soviet citizens know, or think they know, how to read the secret intentions of their rulers by observing the shifting expressions of their eyebrows, which announce either a hardening of attitude or a greater tolerance. In this period, they are convinced that these barely perceptible signs presage a thaw. Let us not forget that at the same period Captain Solzhenitsyn, himself a native of Rostov, wrote to another captain at the front without troubling to conceal it, that Stalin was neither a worthy heir of Lenin, nor a good supreme commander-in-chief. That remark earns him 10 years in the Gulag.

Do I really know what I'm doing? I have enrolled at a university in which it takes four years to get a degree – a lot longer than I plan to stay in the USSR. Also, I spend a lot of effort studying subjects which will surely never be of the slightest use to me, including the tedious history of primitive communist societies. In fact what most interested me was Chourik's Marxism, but I am too badly burned by my experiences in the camps to pay it much attention. The sole thing about which I'm sure is that Klava is pleased to see me there at the other end of the long table and that she would think less of me if I didn't study. She often tells me that the value of a man is measured by his cultural progress. 'Your friend,' she says, of a former airforce trainee in Kislovodsk of whom in fact I see very little, 'is an insolent fellow, but I have to recognize that he is a decent sort. Today, in physics, he scored the highest marks.' And when I point out that he has already studied physics in the airforce she gets angry and invites me to trust her judgement. Come to think of it, it's obvious: if I weren't making an effort at my studies, Klava and I would certainly get on less well together.

From Turgenev's *Fathers and Sons* to Zoshchenko's *The Joyful Life* there is a tradition in Russian literature that describes the conflict of the generations, and the difficulty, after the Revolution, of their cohabiting in communal apartments. Our life perfectly illustrates this conflict. Klava and I haven't even a wash-hand basin of our own and cannot avoid the other generation, from first thing in the morning onwards. It is the lot of many people in Rostov, where accommodation like Fira's, which is small but self-contained, is a rarity. Sharing a wooden maisonnette between four people oughtn't to present any problems, even though Kola had warned me before my marriage: 'You won't be able to stand living with Cossacks, not even for a week.' An exaggeration: our first few weeks were, on the contrary, quite idyllic, and I only discovered the serious pitfalls of cohabitation with Papa Emilian in the course of a rainy August Sunday.

At first, the Cossack tradition of leaving the young couple in peace works in our favour. Klava's parents disappear nearly every evening to join their friends and only reappear in order to serve us in one way or another. Klava's mother, Maria, even though she goes out to work, is used to taking responsibility for most of the domestic tasks. She heaps praise on me when I help her to hang up her washing in the kitchen, as if no man had ever done it for her. Convinced that my émigré parents still have a score to settle with the Republic of Soviets, she whispers to me by way of thanks: 'The Revolution didn't bring much good to my family either. But that's between you and me, don't breathe a word of it to our Klava.' This prematurely grey-haired woman regrets not having seen her daughter dressed in white for her wedding party, but she doesn't hold me responsible in any way: the times are ugly, and have made people lose the taste for fine ceremonies and pretty dresses.

With Papa Emilian, the conversations are always more complex and usually about the war. He took at its face value the slogan postered around the centre of Rostov: 'Cossacks of the quiet Don, smash the German invaders just as your ancestors smashed Napoleon!' and deduced from it that the entire credit for the earlier victory belonged to the Cossacks. With his friends, he has made comparative studies on both the development and the duration of the two patriotic wars and succeeded in discovering facts that even the officers of Khvalynsk, who were experts in matters of strategy, didn't know about. For example the ratio between the time taken by the invaders during the attack and the time for their retreat is exactly the same during both conflicts: in 1812, Napoleon's army had taken eight weeks to get from Beresina to Moscow, and only five to retreat, pursued by the Cossacks of the Don. With the Wehrmacht it's the same story. To reach the Volga, it had needed two summers (1941 and 1942), but a single counter-offensive (spring 1944) had been sufficient to drive it back to its starting point. And a closer analysis suggests an indisputable conclusion: the rate of advance (and retreat) of the Germans and the French was of similar order.

'What lesson do you draw from that?' My jaw drops in response. This is just what he has been waiting for in order to give me a lesson on the invincibility of the Cossacks. It would be better not to speak to him about the possible influence of the social system ushered in by the October Revolution on the outcome of the struggle against the Third Reich. Anyway I have sworn to Klava not to discuss politics with Papa Emilian.

Let's talk then about his predictions for what will happen next. He prudently endorses the official line at least in respect of the first stage: our troops are marking time after the longest victorious offensive in contemporary military history. But he doesn't share its optimism for the second stage which predicts an imminent march on Berlin. 'Jerry will not resume their blitzkrieg but our army will not succeed in forcing their lines of defence,' he declares gravely, adding that he had seen these Polish rivers, the Bug and the Vistula, with his own eyes. 'You'd need to set out early in the day to cross them.' The history of the preceding patriotic war shows in any case that, having crossed the Beresina, the Cossacks no longer advanced swiftly: they had taken eight months to arrive in Paris. Although Berlin is less distant, the comparative chronology of the two wars suggests that our army will not take the German capital before the summer of 1946. At this I make a mild protest, drawing attention to the revolt against the Nazi yoke, which is smouldering everywhere in Europe, the exploits of Tito, celebrated on the walls in Rostov, the resistance of the Germans themselves. Papa Emilian doesn't answer me, either because we are getting too close to politics, or because he can detect the official wooden optimism in my remarks.

Events will prove me right: during the second half of July 1944, Rokossovski's army sweeps away the German defences on the Bug, liberating Chelm and Lublin. In Lublin the Provisional Committee for the National Liberation of Poland is quickly set up. At the beginning of August, this same army establishes a bridgehead on the western bank of the Vistula, very close to the Demblin Fortress where I had been held as a prisoner in 1939. On the other hand I don't recall any mention in our newspapers of the insurrection which begins in Warsaw on 1 August, nor of the fact that this had been the signal for the advance of our troops in the direction of the Polish capital. The imprudent Vassia writes to me at about the same date that his squadron is bombing Eastern Prussia and not Poland.

To the north-east of Lublin, our troops liberated Majdanek, the first Nazi extermination camp discovered by the Allies. It is total horror, with oven crematoria and an industrial apparatus of human destruction. The shock of Majdanek is felt very keenly, even though the Soviet people themselves had already been victims of sustained massacres and destruction during the German occupation, more so than any other people in the world. With Nazi barbarity, reality transcends anything in fiction, everything is organized so as to end in death, it is even worse than in the 'kingdom of darkness' that we denounced in our war songs.

On the same day as the revelations on Majdanek appeared in the press, two German carpenters, POWs, have come to knock down the partition separating our room from that of Klava's brothers and, while they're about it, to repair a broken joint which is warping the whole house. Skilled craftsmen working at a rate unknown to Soviet workers, they finish the job in less than a day. On my return from the factory, I find them seated on the settee, admiring with Papa Emilian their respective photos. That of 1915 with the Ataman Skoropatski impresses the carpenters – 'Schön, sehr schön!', 'Kosaken gut, sehr gut,' – but their own photos also please Papa Emilian. He calls me to his aid and asks me to tell them in German that their wives are pretty and their children so lovely that he wouldn't mind them for his grandchildren. But I don't speak German and, in any case, am in no mood to talk to Germans. 'Come and see how nicely they are dressed,' Papa Emilian insists, and he will not let me leave until I have looked at these two nice German families. 'It was Russian deportees, women like Klava, who made them these pretty clothes,' I say to break this ambience of fraternization. Before being taken prisoner these carpenters had perhaps built barracks in a camp similar to Majdanek. Later, I shall reproach myself for having so upset Papa Emilian. He would like his sons to create orphans in thirty German families, but he feels no hostility towards these German prisoners who no longer bark out orders and who are learning to speak once again like normal people. Perhaps he is right after all.

Rostov is built rather high up on a bank of the River Don. This bank climbs in a gentle slope as far as the Sadovaia, an avenue as long and as wide as Broadway. On the other bank is the plain which, in spring, is transformed into an immense lake. In summer when it is hot, you only have to cross the river and go off a little way to find spots that are ideal for picnics and bathing (although the greyish water of the Don looks rather suspect). Swimming costumes are impossible to find either in the shops or on the black market: the demand for them is so small that no one imports them from the bathing resorts of Georgia. But our underwear is perfectly suited to these summer outings: men's underpants look like the Bermuda shorts that will be in fashion a quarter of a century later in the West, while women's underwear has nothing provocative about it. Neither Klava nor I go bathing: we don't know how to swim. The fresh air and the relaxed atmosphere of the green beaches of the Don are enough of a pleasure, the more so as proper holidays, just like swimming costumes, do not exist in Rostov.

On the last Sunday of August 1944, two or three days before the start of the exhausting academic rat race, the conflict of generations in apartment No. 22 broke out. The rain was the cause of everything, including our sullen moods, and presaged an awful day from the start. Klava and I confined ourselves to our room to mark clearly our independence, and it is only in the afternoon, on hearing the agreeable, sonorous sounds of gypsy music – one of Papa Emilian's great passions – that I venture out to pay them a visit.

Things are fine. Mama Maria makes room for me on the settee and her husband puts on the gramophone the very lively 'Gypsy Caravan'. Hardly has the record stopped than he heaves a sigh of regret: 'Stupid Hitler, why does he kill the gypsies, who sing so well? He would have done better to slit the throats of a few more Yids.' He says this with conviction. As if he had merely stated the obvious, he cranks the gramophone in order to play the next record. He is not expecting any answer.

Well, he's mistaken. I'll show him what I'm made of. Enough is enough. Unfortunately, my brain reacts in a confused manner, and I let myself be dominated by contradictory impulses. The first simply was to refuse to accept the evidence of my senses (just as in Yerevan, I hadn't wanted to believe that Strel was really accusing me of espionage); the next prompts me to assault him physically, while the third suggests irony: explain to him that, according to his daughter, Outiossov, a Jew from Odessa, is a far better singer than all the gypsies put together, and that if Hitler were to slit Outiossov's throat, his daughter Klava would be inconsolable.

But I have to think of Klava, for whose sake I have sworn not to discuss politics with her father, and who wouldn't be at all happy if I were to make a scene. While I am trying to put some order back into my thoughts, the second record finishes and Papa Emilian repeats himself: 'Stupid Hitler, why is he killing all the gypsies?' I leave without waiting for the end of his monologue.

Klava is standing in the middle of our room, leaning against the long table; two tears are running down her face. Her sixth sense has enabled her to guess everything. The look in her sad, green eyes invites me to wait patiently without making a scene. However, I feel that her method is not the right one: 'You should discuss with the older generation in order to drill a bit of sense into their heads.' She shakes her head: 'No, no, no.' I insist: 'You ought to have told them the truth, because I don't want to hide my origins the way they had to do under the German occupation.' All she can do is shake her head. I mutter something about the value of giving Papa Emilian a kick in the arse, and the real reasons for his fraternization with the German carpenters.

After a long silence, Klava says: 'Along the Don they threatened a penalty of five years in camp for anyone who uttered the word yid, and that sanction still applies. Well then, your kick hasn't much better hope of succeeding. As for the German prisoners they have nothing to do with this matter which can be explained entirely by reference to the culture – or lack of culture – of the Cossacks, and their nostalgia for the lost paradise. According to it the Cossacks were a nation privileged by fate or by God, having received as their heritage lands so fertile that women could cultivate them without difficulty, which enabled the men to charge round the world on

horseback and to slit the throats, here and there, of Jews and other
infidels.'

Perhaps this is all true, but it doesn't resolve our problems. 'Let
me think it over for a day or two,' Klava replies. 'I shall find a means
of preventing him from talking about yids.' In my view to
prevaricate with Klava's parents isn't the right method. She feels
that it is the only one that can avoid creating trouble. 'You take a
condescending view of your father in claiming that he is incapable of
understanding the horror of Majdanek,' I tell her. 'No I don't, I
simply know him well, that's all. He and his friends are a lost
generation, poisoned by religion and the myths of bygone days.
Majdanek, Majdanek . . . Don't think that they only use our
newspapers as cigarette paper; they also read them.' 'Let's not talk
any more about it now, we could go to the cinema, that would take
our minds off it.' I make this conciliatory suggestion knowing that I
lose my temper easily and because, deep down, I don't care about
Papa Emilian, while Klava, torn between her attachment to her 'old
folks' and her frustration with their 'old ideas', really suffers because
of it. To my astonishment she prefers to go instead to the central
post office. It is a strange idea, but having laid on her shoulders all
the weight of the conflict between the generations, I can't refuse her
this choice.

Here we are once again on the rickety bench in the post and
telegraph office waiting room. The counter clerks seem delighted to
see us back again and imagine that we have just made up after a
lovers' quarrel.

'I ought to have spoken to you from the beginning about Cossack
anti-semitism,' Klava says. 'They drink in this poison along with
their mother's milk. In the days of the atamans "the special region of
the army of the Don" was forbidden to Jews. Why is this? The only
possible explanation, outside of their cultural primitivism, is that
they were more pious than other Russians, more faithful to the
Orthodox Holy Church.' I object that not all Christians are
automatically anti-semitic, but, in her view, the overwhelming
majority – in the region of the Don, at least – has always been

310

anti-semitic because of the accusation of deicide against the Jews. 'When I was small *they* spoke to me about it too, because they would have liked me to become a Christian even if I didn't go to church.'

Later, at school, she always had Jewish friends and it is thanks to them that she understood the inanity of the traditions of the older generation in general and of her parents in particular. 'Because if it was hard for me to verify for myself their legend about the fertile land that yielded its fruit with a minimum of labour, this wasn't at all the case where Jews were concerned, since I mixed with them every day, and they didn't correspond at all to the description given to me. Then in my adolescent head the idea took root that the Cossacks' lost paradise was as grotesque a lie as that about the yids. I was fifteen or sixteen years old at the time and I turned my rebellion against my parents, who couldn't get over it and gave way a little. As I failed to get my brothers' support however, I realized at a certain point that this frontal assault was going to poison our lives – theirs and mine. I thought I could perceive in my parents' eyes the unstated fear that I might denounce them to the NKVD – at the time this was commonplace. For another thing they accepted without protest my entry into the Komsomol, and they suggested the basis of a truce: let us eliminate politics from our discussions and love each other as is fitting a "healthy family" – an expression of our government. It was obviously more easily said than done, for you can't get away from politics, but ever since then I have made do with lies or simple omissions. My Jewish friends, Liza and Arkadi, to name but two, have always been well received by Papa and my mother, who, as luck would have it, have never pronounced the word yid in front of them. If, however, you insist that I break the truce, I shall, although such a step runs the risk of complicating our lives enormously.'

Since the ball is in my court, I consider a practical solution and ask her about the feasibility of fitting a wash-hand basin in our room to reduce our contacts with the older generation. Otherwise I tell her to act as she sees fit, without worrying on my account. 'I shall sort something out,' she says and, on the way back, having recovered her enthusiasm, she talks to me about the 'new culture' which will suppress prejudices, ignorance, hatred, and make people in every way better and happy. *Cultura, culturnyi, culturnoié culturich, nie-culturnoié* – Klava's vocabulary abounds in expressions dovoted to learning, which alone is capable of changing the mentalities of the people of today and of tomorrow. But not those of the past, her parents for example whom she loves, even preferring her eccentric father to her self-effacing mother.

Two days later, she puts on a record to please Papa Emilian. He lets himself be charmed by the gypsy music and, when the record is over, he concludes it with a sigh about stupid Hitler. Klava is ready, smiling: 'In fact, Papa Emilian, just what harm have these Jews done to you?'

'To me?' he replies, amazed. 'But I have never met a single one of them. God forbid that I ever should,' and he makes the sign of the cross.

'It is just as well that, thanks be to God, you haven't had to suffer personally at the hands of the Jews. The Germans on the other hand have brought much misery on you, your family and your country. Isn't that so?'

'Of course, my little Klavotchka.'

'Well then, since the Jews have done nothing to harm you, and since the Germans have overwhelmed you with woes, you really ought, logically, to wish for the Jews to kill the Germans and not the other way round?'

'Logically speaking, you're right, but in reality things are different because the Jews engage in commerce and not in warfare.'

'Papa Emilian! You surprise me,' (and she affects an astonished air). 'We have Jewish marshals, generals, colonels, Jewish combatants in every rank, their chests are covered with medals. Yet here you are claiming that they don't engage in warfare! You let that slip out but you don't really believe it, do you? You're a reasonable man, you wouldn't go as far as denying the evidence. You know perfectly well that not only do the Jews fight very courageously in the present war, but that they also did it in biblical times. For what is your Holy

Bible, Papa Emilian, if it is not the history of the wars waged by the Jews? When I was still a youngster, your friend Stepanovitch once said, in this very room, that the Old Testament is an epic song to the glory of the Cossacks of Jerusalem.' Seeing her father run short of arguments Klava pushes on. 'Hitler only slits the throats of defenceless Jews, those who have already been disarmed, just as he came close to slitting our own throats, in this very house. But you cannot describe someone who has committed such monstrosities against innocent people, including women and children, simply as stupid, nor encourage him to slit the throats of even more defenceless people. Papa Emilian, Hitler is a *dzikii zvier*, a ferocious animal, and we have to put him down, nothing else will do.'

At this, she leaves the room, casting over her discomfited father a glance that has more sympathy than anger in it.

'How did I do?' she asks me afterwards.

'Brilliantly, but I didn't realize that you were so well-versed in the Bible.'

'It's all part of the war of positions: you have to listen to what the adversary says in order to turn their own arguments against them. I have also looked into the possibility of acquiring a wash-hand basin: we can do it through the black market.'

She is like that, Klava. All that she needs is a day or two to think things over and then she fixes everything. From now on my contacts with the older generation will be greatly reduced.

'It is by setting out from the small things that one arrives at a better understanding of the larger matters in life,' Josip Vissarionovitch Stalin teaches us, and with good reason. Take for example the wash-hand basin. Why do we attach so much importance to having one while the idea of having a separate kitchen installed never crossed our minds? Because even in a period of penury we wash every day, whereas we cook very little, limiting ourselves now and then to boiling some water for tea. We take our main meals in canteens. The canteen at the institute, intended for the future scientific and

313

technical *nomenklatura*, is one of the best in town and even serves two meals, one at midday and one at five o'clock in the afternoon. Frankly, I don't believe Klava when she claims that 'it is more or less enough for her.' If it were true, how is it that Kola, who eats there too, goes off so often to the Rosa Luxembourg where Zeus looks after him. In my view, Klava prefers to put up with a slight hunger rather than buy food on the black market. This raises for me a genuine problem of conscience.

My canteen's food is poor, and since I have a rather flexible timetable, I am terribly attracted by the gastronomic display of the kolkhoz market, the very one in which Moussia sells her bortsch. In this marvellous place you can find, at a price, the most varied of dishes, cooked by the most welcoming of *babas*. Have I the right to spend my illicit income while ignoring the fact that we are short of so many things in the house? Is it reasonable to let the money vanish into the steam rising from a bowl of bortsch or *somm*, a fish from the Don which fries in its own fat? In this conflict my stomach more often than not gets the better of me, from which I deduce that it is particularly demanding, having thirteen months of the Gulag to make up for, or else that the others, having more character, resign themselves more readily to living a life of semi-starvation. One thing is certain: the people in Rostov think of food above everything else and, because they are unable to satisfy their needs, are often aggressive, as though a good fight could free them from their obsession about food. One of these incidents, which erupts over nothing, made a particularly strong impression upon me.

One day the four of us are out for a stroll along the Sadovaia dressed up in our uniforms. We walk there to keep Chourik company – he is too disabled to cross the Don.

At the corner of the Voroshilov Prospekt, at the most animated crossroads in the city, a disabled man on crutches, reeking of vodka, awaits our arrival in order to launch into a harangue of the sort you hear at Speakers' Corner in Hyde Park: 'You there, Russian officers, why aren't you doing something about these Jews who are leading our country to rack and ruin?' It is a typical anti-semitic speech: the

314

Jews are in command, while the Christians, reduced to the role of simple executors, carry out their orders. You don't need a diploma in political science to know what he is leading up to. While listening to him I feel myself go back in time five years, his style of speech reminds me of that of a Polish right-wing group which fought against 'Judaeo-Communism'.

To hear it all once again in Rostov, even before the anti-fascist war is over, produces a strange effect on me. Gaping onlookers, the young and the not-so-young gather round. The militiaman who is controlling the traffic doesn't intervene; he doesn't concern himself with what happens on the footpaths. The plainclothes police – there must be some of them among the small crowd – don't come forward. As for the honest citizens they listen to the anti-semite with the most benign air.

How do we react? Zeus attacks: 'Pathetic creature, who has filled your head with so much crap?' but Chourik dissuades him from further insulting and provoking a drunkard. Kola has an idea: he will whisper discreetly to him that Djougachvili means 'son of a Jew' in Georgian, then when the drunk begins to pick upon Stalin personally, the militiaman and the plainclothes police will have to intervene to put him away. But this stratagem, suggested by a rumour that was once widely current among the Cossacks, only makes us laugh, and Kola himself wasn't serious about putting it into practice. We continue on our way therefore, discussing anti-semitism. 'It's simply a phenomenon of the superstructure,' Kola says. 'It will disappear when the material base of society has been broadened.' From the height of his Marxist learning, Chourik immediately reproaches him for being so 'simplistic': 'You don't understand anything of the relations between the base and super-structure; things are a lot more complex than you suggest.'

Absorbed in our controversy, we don't pay a great deal of attention to the appearance of Klava, Galia and Cathinka, who are pretending not to recognize us. Attired in their Sunday best, in flowered dresses, they gather around us to make fun of our 'silly habit' of putting on our uniforms from time to time (which they themselves have ironed). 'My my! Would you look at that. What pretty little soldiers. And we are all so alone. Please take us with you when you go to war.' We don't rise to the bait. Cathinka takes it a bit too far: she pouts sexily at Zeus and then takes him by the arm, saying: 'Officer, I think I really like you. Show me some attention 'cos I'm terribly alone.' A passer-by of about 40 years of age, outraged by these provocative gestures, calls her a 'virgin in heat', and she bursts out laughing. 'Virgin, did you say? Come and look a little closer!' Zeus doesn't take the matter lightly and, driven on by jealousy, he lays into the prudish 40-year-old, calling him a sexual maniac and a coward – one of those who '*nie voieval*' [who hasn't fought in the war]. The other man bares his fists and Cathinka has to separate the two of them. A large crowd gathers, even more numerous than at the crossroads where the drunkard had been holding forth, and infinitely more interested.

The debate quickly spreads from the particular to the general. Some use the 'old' man as an example of all the dead-beats in the Soviet Union, who make poor patriots and are known to rape young girls. Others rail against the arrogance of demobilized soldiers who, because they have fought in the war, believe that they can get away with anything, for on this occasion (rumour has it) the airman had violently tugged the girl by the arm, seriously hurting her. Cathinka's age diminishes as these exchanges progress, and we hear in the background the raised voices of a woman passer-by outraged by the behaviour of the men – in a city like Rostov where there are so many single adult women too! – who can shamelessly attack a young girl of 15 years of age, a 'virgin' who will be scarred for the rest of her days. A brawl finally erupts and is said to have produced two knife-wound casualties, one of whom was taken off to hospital in a serious condition on the back of a *telega*.

I say 'is said' advisedly, for I heard this snippet through the agency of 'OBG' – '*odna baba govorit*,' a granny speaks – which is not 100 per cent trustworthy. Nevertheless, as far as local news is concerned, and more particularly news about topical trivia, it is the only agency which functions. Tass Agency only mentions Rostov in order to inform the country of the reopening of 'Rosselmach', our large factory for agricultural machinery (which is producing, according to the OBG, JS – Josip Stalin – tanks, the best in all of Russia, of course.) There is no question that the local newspaper *Molot* should open its columns to small ads from citizens who wish to exchange their flats or simply to find a place to live. To resolve these problems, to find out what is going on in town – why, for example, following a breakdown, the tramway doesn't work for three whole days – you have to go to the market. That suits me very well: I have a perfect alibi when I go there to stuff myself selfishly with bortsch and fried fish. Unless I am actually caught in the act, neither Klava nor anyone else can contest the information-seeking character of my visits to the *babas* of the OBG.

Largely preoccupied with the chronicle of local affairs, the OBG agency doesn't give out any international news, unless it has implications for the town market. Such was the case in 1946, two months before I left Rostov, when Winston Churchill's speech at Fulton gave rise to a very pessimistic OBG interpretation, precipitating a run on the shops the like of which I had never seen before. And I remember that on this occasion Mama Maria, forgetting all our conventions, came in to admonish us. 'My little Klavotchka, the Grand Alliance is finished. Run out quickly and buy some salt and sugar so we won't be caught without them if a new war should break out.' Obviously we explained to her that there wasn't going to be another war but this stubborn woman didn't believe us and ran from one queue to another, until the foodshops had run out of stocks.

I have never liked the Savelit factory where I work: it is dirty, noisy and situated behind the station in the poorest area of the town. In July 1944, the regional Bureau for the War-disabled, set up by Stalin's personal decree, assigned me to the post of stock manager in this factory, which belongs to the People's Commissariat of 'Black Metallurgy', a branch of heavy metallurgy. At first I was pleased, but Kola somewhat dampened my enthusiasm by citing me an old proverb: 'Those who work at churning butter never run short of it, but those who manufacture needles have only needles.' Now my factory produces heavy duty thermal-isolaters which are totally non-negotiable on the black market and which are therefore worth even less than needles. In the matter of incomes however the future will vindicate me, since Kola's folk wisdom is no longer operative in the age of a centralized, planned economy.

My first visit to the factory misfired. Ivan Petrovitch, the manager, a man of about 40 with a paunch and a square-shaped head, could think of nothing better by way of welcome than to ask me if my brain was working more or less normally after my injury. He was not embarrassed about not having fought in the war, having been kept in the 'black metallurgy' factory by the Moscow authorities, who deemed his presence indispensable to the smooth running of the economy. I try in vain to make him understand that the bureau looks after all of the demobilized, including Kola, who suffers from a mere stomach ulcer. From the moment of our first meeting, this unpleasant man's arrogant behaviour will continue to feed my aversion for his factory even when he feigns to be well-disposed towards me.

What upsets me most however is a visit to the workshops bordered by railway tracks on one side and by a piece of wasteland on the other. In Savelit, as in the whole of industry, women came to work as replacements for their husbands or brothers at the front. It was the same story at the Rosa Luxembourg factory, except that cigarette manufacture doesn't require the same physical effort as that needed in the production of thermal-isolaters. At our place, they make white sheets of metal as large as a mattress, each one weighing a good fifty kilos, by smelting yellowish ore imported from the Donbass region, in furnaces fired by coal which comes from Chakhty. Everything in the factory is covered with a film of dust which clings to the faces of the (few) men and women workers who protect their hair with peasant-style head scarves. In these noisy and overheated surroundings, one thinks at first of a forced labour camp. The comparison doesn't stand up: these women haven't the sadly resigned eyes of the *zeks*, they leave their workshops freely and decide many things on their own initiative. Some of them bring their kids to the factory; they play on the waste ground, and their mothers join them when breakdowns in the plant occur, or during breaks. Unlike women *zeks* they don't tremble in front of a man, however aggressive his manner, and often pull him up sharply, joking about it, as though in these times of role reversal he were only a timid slip of a girl. If Savelit therefore has none of the attributes of a camp, neither is it the sort of place that you go to with a carefree step.

My assistant is a woman, Vera Pavlovna, named after the heroine of Chernyshevsky's *What is to be Done?*, who dreamed of Fourierist communes. She is an accountant, little given to daydreaming and efficacious in her dual role as my assistant and also assistant to the chief accountant. She is in her thirties, fair-haired and very careful of her appearance, but rather stiff and reserved. She insists on keeping her distance from the other women workers and won't allow her 10-year-old son to play with their children. From the time he leaves school at two o'clock until his mother leaves work at six o'clock, he waits patiently in our office without making any noise, busy reading books by Chukovski, inventor of the famous 'Doctor Aibolit' who is adored by Russian children. According to Kuzmitch, the lorry driver who is often put at my disposal, Vera Pavlovna has had an affair with our antipathetic manager, whom she calls with a touch of irony 'Caesar Imperator'. I haven't noticed though that he shows her any special consideration; quite the reverse, he barks aloud at her over even the smallest mistakes that she occasionally makes in the calculation of wages.

In our factory, employees' earnings are determined according to a rigorous hierarchy, and everyone earns a different amount. Some work at piece rate and earn bonuses for exceeding fixed norms; others are paid by the hour – between 1.67 and 1.89 roubles – but the rate for the two hours of overtime (the factory operates a 10-hour day-shift) is higher and varies from one category of worker to another. I also qualify for a supplement of about 50 roubles a month, which is added to my basic salary of 400 roubles, although I never work 10 hours a day. There is a great deal of arbitrariness in Vera Pavlovna's calculations, and this is further exacerbated by the interventions of 'Caesar Imperator'. But it is the useless nature of these calculations that most astonishes me. Is there any rhyme or reason at this time of labour shortage in maintaining a whole cohort of productivity inspectors and chasing after the phantom of socialist competition at work? To the old question of Mikhail Zoshchenko: 'Why does the nightingale sing?' the Russians in wartime reply, 'to receive a larger ration of bread.' Experience has taught them that bread coupons are usually honoured and that you don't die of hunger when you get more than half a kilo per day. The women workers in my factory could have found less physically demanding work in Rostov but they have chosen to work here because it entitles them to a first or second category food ration card, that is to say, 800 or 600 grammes of bread. I do not underestimate the importance of the ration of 600 grammes of bread that comes with my job – Klava, like all other students, receives only 400 grammes.

For the other food items rationed, the situation is more complex. Their prices have remained stable since the start of the war, at a very low level, but they are considered to be interchangeable and, in the shops, you can get only what is in stock. So, instead of two kilos of meat per month, you might be given some fish, a few eggs and also some tinned food or honey, without ever being able to penetrate the mysterious rationale that governs these substitutions. At all events the lion's share of the coupons for meat, wheaten bread, dairy products and sugar, is used up by the canteen. Since the beginning of the war, salaries have increased in Russia – particularly as the working day is longer – while the opportunities of spending them have been drastically reduced. For our canteen meals and other fixed expenditure, Klava and I pay out only three hundred roubles, maximum, or the equivalent of her monthly maintenance grant as a first year student. In the Kremlin, they are so well aware of this imbalance in the private citizen's budget that we are obliged once a year to subscribe one month's salary to a State loan.

Unfortunately, on the black market, money has a derisory

purchasing power. It is almost as if, in switching from one market to another, we were changing country, and entering a world where everything has increased in price a hundredfold. Klava with her monthly 300 roubles could buy a mere three kilos of bread on the black market, and I could afford on my salary only four and a half kilos. And our two incomes combined wouldn't even be enough to purchase 750 grammes of butter (in Rostov a kilo is worth more than a thousand roubles). What is the sense in offering material incentives to encourage productivity in such circumstances? Much later, at two opposite ends of the world, Mao Zedong and Che Guevera will explain that these incentives in any case play a harmful role under socialism. But in Rostov, without having elaborated any theory, this already appears obvious to us. The promise of a bonus of 20 roubles – half the price of a bowl of bortsch from Moussia's stall – cannot encourage anyone to exert themselves.

I obviously refrain from discussing this with Vera Pavlovna and don't even dream of raising it with 'Caesar Imperator', who thinks that his managerial authority rests also on his right to hand out bonuses to the 'best' workers and to penalize the 'slackers'. The fact is that some people do work more than others and exceed the norms, but I refuse to rack my brains to discover why.

I have neither the inclination nor the time to do so, particularly as my own job brings me more headaches than I had imagined would be the case. At first sight you don't have to be much of a wizard to do it and my predecessor, before returning to his native Ukraine, initiated me into the job in less than a day. As our economy is centrally planned, I have to carry out orders contained in a very detailed document – the *raznariadka* – countersigned by I.F. Tevossian, the People's Commissar of 'Black Metallurgy'. Everything in it is minutely calculated, the quantities of raw material that will be delivered to us on such and such a date on the one hand and, on the other, the schedule of delivery dates for our isolaters. My job therefore consists in reminding our suppliers of their obligations towards us and encouraging our chief engineer to ensure that our deliveries are on time. For the smooth running of this ingenious

321

system, all that it takes is for everyone to carry out punctually the imperatives handed down by the centralized Plan: this would contribute to the greater good of all and, in particular, to the well-being of my nervous system.

In practice it operates altogether differently and, from the beginning of September 1944, only a few weeks after I have taken up my post, I receive my baptism of fire on the economic battlefront. One day, armed with duly stamped requisition papers, I arrive in a lorry at the *Neftsbyt* supply depot to take delivery of a tonne of petrol. On our way there, Kuzmitch, my driver, who is an affable and talkative man, had confessed to me his scepticism about our prospects of success, and had advised me to settle for a half-tonne or even less. But the supply manager of the depot is not at all inclined to haggle. He claims to have no petrol at all, and declares that this has been the case for so long that he has even forgotten the smell of it. 'What fuel there is goes to the front,' he informs me, and he offers me in friendly fashion 100 grammes of vodka and half a salted cucumber as consolation. Convinced he is acting in good faith, I don't insist; tomorrow, or in a week's time, the petrol will arrive and Kuzmitch and I shall come back to fetch it.

At the factory, Caesar Imperator doesn't view things in this light: '*Davai benzine*,' ('bring me that petrol') he screams, as if I had a tank of it at home. Approaches made to the powerful Industry Committee of the Rostov CPSU yield nothing, as motor-fuel is temporarily scarce throughout the city. My boss refuses to understand this and he harasses me without respite. 10 times, 20 times a day, he puts his head around the half open door of my office and hurls at me: '*Chantrapa, davai benzine.*' Now *chantrapa* is a grave insult, although it derives from an impeccably polite French expression *tu ne chanteras pas* (you will not sing). It goes back to 1812, the year of the occupation of Moscow. By this phrase the French signified to certain Russians that they didn't have the right to sing in honour of Napoleon. In Russian, the expression was eventually condensed into a single word, *chantrapa*, which designates good-for-nothings, louts, crooks even. To be called this in front of Vera Pavlovna and her son seems to me both humiliating and unfair. I return with Kuzmitch to the depot to try to appeal to the sense of solidarity of its foreman. He sympathizes and promises to phone me himself as soon as he receives any petrol.

Two days later the telephone rings. It is a *zamzav*, assistant manager of the Port of Rostov, who claims to have made my acquaintance the previous May, during the ceremony for the award of bronze medals 'for the defence of the Caucasus'. His name doesn't mean anything to me and, in any case, I have no business with the Port of Rostov. He thinks otherwise; he is going to put my way something which should turn out 'mutually profitable': 'There are five freight-cars on their way to your factory loaded with Donbass ore. Give them to me for 48 hours.' 'What? But I have to load them with isolaters in accordance with the Plan. How can I lend them to you?' 'Your isolaters are not perishable goods, whereas fish from the River Don are, especially in this heat.' And he informs me that the catch of fish this year is miraculous, because all the armies that have passed through Rostov have been throwing their food reserves into the river so as not to leave them for the enemy. 'The fish have taken advantage of it to fatten up and to multiply, but I need a means of transport to distribute them to the different towns in the Rostov region. Lend me your five freight-cars and I promise you that you won't regret it.'

Why doesn't he directly approach the management of the railways, particularly as 'my' freight-cars, which are very dirty, appear to be so unsuited to his needs? He has an answer for everything: railway workers are notoriously unco-operative and it is almost impossible to deal with them, but they wouldn't place any obstacles in the way of an agreement between us. For another thing, refrigerated freight-trucks are so rare that they have almost become collectors' items; fish is transported nowadays in ordinary *tieplouchki*, filled with lots of ice. I agree to keep my part of the bargain but I want to be sure of recovering 'my' freight-cars. 'In forty-eight hours they'll be back. You don't imagine do you that in this heat I could transport my fish any further than Salsk to the

323

south and Novotcherkask to the north?' While I am thinking this over he begins to make the oddest suggestions. In fact he is ready to deliver 100 kilos of fish to the canteen of my factory. But the canteen is not under my control. 'Don't worry about that,' says my friend on the phone. 'I can deliver your merchandise to whichever address you care to give me.' The deal is becoming clearer now and a lot more worth my while, although I begin to wonder where I could hoard 100 kilos of fish. I promise to give him an answer in an hour or two and I leave in a hurry in Kuzmitch's lorry to look for Kola. He will come up with a solution and, should it prove necessary, he will know how to get rid of this heaven-sent merchandise.

But a lorry can't leave the factory grounds without reason and I indicate as our destination the supply depot, which means that the lorry logbook will have to be stamped there. As I am obliged to call in at the place I use the occasion to ask the supply manager who has forgotten the smell of petrol if a large amount of fish would tease his sense of smell back to life and allow me to obtain my order more rapidly. 'Why didn't you tell me that you had such a treasure?' He seems almost angry, and doesn't ask any questions about the origins of this miraculous catch. Having decided against consulting Kola, I telephone the port *zamzav* straight away: 'You will deliver your fish to this address.' We set off again, Kuzmitch and I, with a tonne of petrol in our lorry. When it comes to private arrangements, the supply managers of Rostov conduct business boldly, relying on the spoken word, as in Wall Street.

In 1944, according to the official figures, the USSR allotted 27 per cent of available foodstuffs to canteens in which over 40 million meals a day were produced. Yet it never occurred to anyone to instal a self-service system, which would have made life easier for consumers while simultaneously saving labour. In 1959 on a visit to the IBM plant in San Clemente, California, Nikita Kruschev was carried away with admiration, not for the most modern laboratories in the world, but for the self-service cafeteria. Also in 1944, in order to compete with the kolkhozian market, the Soviet government created its own network of shops and restaurants designated as 'commercial', which, for exorbitant prices that bear no relation to the workers' official incomes, offer practically everything without coupons, as well as *à la carte* menus. These innovations, which were said to be temporary in principle, mark Soviet society in a lasting way by accentuating its inequalities and by encouraging a race for money.

In Rostov I didn't understand in time the deeper significance of this development. That day in September 1944, I go back home relieved at having got rid of this fish so quickly, rather as if it had been burning my fingers. But Kola arrives shortly afterwards and, in front of an impassive Klava, launches into a fierce attack on me. Just as it is better to go to bed a thousand times with one woman than to go to bed once only with a thousand different women, so too it is preferable to earn a pile of roubles at a stroke rather than repeatedly circumvent the law by many petty schemes. A kilo of fish, in Rostov, costs at least 700 roubles – and more than a thousand in Mietchotka – so my 100 kilos would have allowed us to live honestly and studiously for many months. Besides, if I had insisted, the port *zamzav* would have delivered to us not just one hundred but probably two or three hundred kilos.

I don't share his views, for I still recall the interrogation sessions which dealt with our 'war treasure'. I have no desire to become a 'millionaire in the land of Soviets', and it is perhaps the instinct of self-preservation which drove me to allow these fish from the heavens to slip through my fingers. Kola answers angrily that I had been put away in a camp not because of my ostentatious expenditures in Yerevan, but because I give myself the superior airs of a Polish gentleman who has only contempt for proletarian Russia. And what does Klava say to all this? Nothing. She leads Kola towards her end of the table to study maths.

It is only a row between friends but it badly upsets me. For the first time since falling in love with Klava I feel an overwhelming desire to flee from Rostov. I certainly don't despise the Soviet Union for its poverty, but I want nothing to do with the dilemma that Kola poses – is it better to risk everything once or to risk a little bit every day? Anyway, I am the only one among us to know what the word 'risk' really means in this context.

Kola doesn't even realize that he has hurt me and, after a short respite, he continues: 'We can still salvage something. Tomorrow I shall offer our help to the port *zamzav* for the work to be done loading your freight-cars; that will allow us to make a few thousand roubles from this lost opportunity.'

The *zamzav* gladly accepts Kola's offer: in order to accelerate the dispatch of the fish, he needs an additional crew for Saturday night and he gives Kola the go-ahead to recruit it himself. The pay is 200 roubles officially, and authorization to leave the port twice during the shift without being searched. According to the *zamzav* it will take 10 of us 10 hours to load the freight-car, but he sees no objection to a smaller crew which would be willing to work 12 hours.

But where are we to find eight or 10 likely lads? I can bring only Kuzmitch, a solid old worker. Zeus gets hold of an Armenian who manages a canteen in Nakhtchevagne, an area some distance away; according to Zeus he is as robust as Joe Louis. Lastly Kola finds two dancers who work with Fira. 'Between the seven of us we'll manage,' Kola declares, and he runs off to deposit the list of names at the port. Klava meanwhile finishes sewing immense pockets on to the insides of my greatcoat, veritable sacks with a capacity of four or five kilos of fish. A final detail of our expedition: two *babas*, wholesale fishmongers, are going to spend the night near the port exit to buy whatever merchandise we bring out to them.

The good mood in which we set out begins to evaporate from the moment we assemble at eight o'clock in the evening. Each of us has exaggerated the strength of his recruits: we discover that the dancers are rather puny, that the Armenian is as frail as a delicate southern flower and that Kuzmitch is a bit old to play the navvy. The layout of the site presents us with a second disagreeable surprise: between the fishing boat and the freight-car the slope to be scaled is by no means gradual. To cover this distance carrying large baskets loaded up with fish is no picnic. After an hour or so my legs feel like lead weights and I choose a less exacting job, transporting the ice from a container that is stationed at the same level as the freight-car. The dancers have the same idea though, so the quantity of ice in the freight-car increases a lot more quickly than that of the fish. Kola calls me to order and I return sheepishly to the steep slope where we form a chain and pass the baskets from hand to hand. Eventually we decide to take our first break, nowhere near the halfway stage as we had planned.

Our collective exit goes off smoothly; the guards pretend not to notice that our greatcoats, not needed at this time of year, literally flutter about on our backs, as the fish which are still alive try to leap out of our pockets. Then comes the third disappointment: the two wholesalers behave just like a cartel and arbitrarily fix the price of our fish at 250 roubles per kilo, a third of the market retail price. They reproach us for not having selected larger and fatter fish and, in a remarkable display of bad faith, each of them reiterates that the other *baba* knows what she is talking about. There you have a perfect illustration of the dictum that social being determines consciousness, and proof of the fact that a good Soviet citizen who gives herself to commerce behaves no differently than a bourgeois profiteer of the worst kind. We have no choice and are obliged to sell these goods for a pittance – goods that we have really earned by the sweat of our brows. Each of us comes away nevertheless with the sum of 1,000 roubles, less than we counted upon but enough, despite everything, to give fresh vigour to our efforts.

The second phase of the work is the hardest and arguments inevitably break out amongst us. The dancers, both of whom have decided never again to set foot inside a port, would like to stuff the freight-car full of ice only. Kola rebuffs such plans, and is supported by Kuzmitch, who reminds us of the principle of the job well done, and also of a well known proverb: 'Never spit on the plate that you may want to use a second time.' Zeus wants to know if our second exit has to be at the very end of the shift. Since no principle is at stake we decide to check this clause of the agreement without further ado. The guards let us pass through once again, with no questions asked. And the second thousand roubles pay-off renews our efforts. 'Right lads, let's go. Didn't we dig anti-tank trenches in the Caucasus in far worse conditions during the winter of 1941?' Kola asks cheerfully.

The port controller arrives at the appointed hour. After having examined the load aboard the freight-car and also the state of our faces, which must arouse pity, he says: 'That will do.' Below us, the hold of the boat is far from empty but, he tells us, by packing too many fish in the freight-car you run the risk of crushing them and, in any case, on Monday there will be another car to be loaded. I get the impression that he produces these reasons to allow himself to let us go – we are clearly past it. His sympathetic understanding contrasts with the ferocity I encountered on the part of the supervisory personnel in the camps. The latter delight in seeing exhausted *zeks*; it is their chief satisfaction in life. Executives or supervisors in civilian life, on the other hand, either because of their proletarian origins, or out of the goodness of their Russian hearts, often show themselves actively sympathetic to workers, like us, who are overwhelmed by the job. And the controller then gives each of us, over and above the terms agreed, a large fish for our personal consumption. He escorts us to the exit to ensure that there are no difficulties. 'You have done a great job, my children,' he declares, despite his youth: he could have been Kuzmitch's son.

Once outside, Kola, Zeus and I decide to rest our legs on the bench abandoned by the *baba* wholesalers, so as not to waken Klava, Fira and Cathinka at this hour of the morning. 'It is for them, when all is said and done, that we have made these efforts,' Zeus proclaims pompously before beginning a recitation of love poems to his darling Cathinka: 'Cossack siren sprung out of the Don, flower of the steppes, nightingale of the muses, incomparable daughter of the most splendid region in all of Russia . . .' As far as his rhymes go, Zeus is not always up to the mark, but in this misty September dawn, with the sleepy River Don before us, his poems harmonize well with the scenery and something stirs in my heart. Of our trio,

Zeus is the only one to invest everything in the love that he feels for his *blondinka*. Kola remains attached to Fira for convenience only. And me? I am happy with Klava but, from the moment of our first vexation, I dreamed of running off to Poland to punish her. I already feel some remorse over this, and I tell myself that had I not been so selfish, I wouldn't have let slip through my hands an amount of fish which could have guaranteed Klava's material security for a long time to come. In any case I myself am one of the first to be punished for it since I have been obliged to perform an exhausting job for, as it turns out, a much smaller reward.

Throughout the vast territory that separates Leningrad from Rostov there are probably no other two women as resolutely anti-alcohol as Nievka and Klava, and a strange fate willed me into the arms of first one and then the other. Like the nurse from the north, the *Cosatchka* from the south never hesitates to criticize me in public: 'You are drinking far too much.' Kola and Chourik smile, almost certainly recalling the scenes that Nievka used to make in Kislovodsk. I am not even supposed to think about Nievka, having sworn to Klava to efface all memory of her rivals. And I keep my word, I don't even attempt to contact Nievka's parents in Leningrad to find out whether she survived the German occupation of Kislovodsk. This evening, however, during our party following the 'miraculous catch', when Klava starts once again to tell me 'you are drinking far too much,' her green eyes become mixed up in my mind with Nievka's eyes, as if their two faces were suddenly superimposed on one another. What has become of her, my anti-alcohol nurse whom I left on the entrance steps to the fortress hospital in Kislovodsk? With Klava I am at least still in a position to redeem myself by showing towards her all the tenderness I can, but I also owe a great deal to Nievka and I can no longer do anything for her. Only a good tipple of vodka allows me to surmount such regrets. After this, I see Nievka parading in Bucharest and in Sofia – cities captured by our forces during this first fortnight of September 1944 – and I console myself with the thought that she no longer needs me, that she is well cared for, that Soviet officers, perhaps friends of her parents from among the *nomenklatura* of Leningrad, pay court to her.

Vodka also acts as an excellent remedy for aches and pains, and this evening, after the back-breaking work in the port, we need strong doses of it. We went off to the baths to get rid of the tenacious smell of fish and, in the meantime, Fira and her friends decided to organize a culinary competition between them to see who could prepare the fresh fish in the most delectable manner. Galia wins hands down with her stuffed carp prepared in the Jewish manner, a dish that was also widely appreciated in Poland where it used to delight even the most rabid anti-semites.

Chourik contributes to the party's success with a sumptuous present of five litres of vodka. His father, a high-ranking figure in the government supply department, receives plenty of presents, but he won this particular jackpot at cards, for he is a dab hand at 'preference', a Russian variety of bridge. The abundance of vodka allows me to drink with a good conscience and provides the opportunity to make it up with Kola. He takes back his phrase about the 'disdainful Polish gentleman' and assures me that by giving myself airs, I gain both in charm and authority. On my side I commit myself publicly, under oath, to make a better use of the next load of fish that falls into my lap. Klava shows her approval of us both but reiterates her appeals for moderation in respect of the vodka. She drinks only small quantities herself, to keep us company, but her favourite tactic consists in replacing the vodka with water on the sly. With me it is just the opposite: I swallow vodka as easily as I do water. It doesn't burn my stomach, or make my eyes water. If there is none around I can easily go without, otherwise I drink to quench my thirst, especially when as now it makes my aches and pains disappear.

In addition to its curative powers, the national Soviet drink causes a certain amount of drowsiness. Possibly as a result of the Gulag, I am more prone to sleep than the others. Seated on the bed, I slide imperceptibly onto my back as if under the pressure of an invisible force, although I want to follow the fascinating discussion taking place around the narrow table. I intervene very little, not because I have drunk too much but because I don't wish to side with Galia and Chourik, the critical intellectuals, against the optimists led by Kola and Klava. Zeus's position is as changeable as the mood of the poets, while Cathinka only raises her lovely voice to plead occasionally for a little order and to let each person speak their piece.

It is the Donbass coal miner, Aphoniev, who is the cause of a great debate. Along with the vodka, Chourik has brought with him a cutting from *Pravda* which states that this exemplary worker has earned over 10,000 roubles a month since the beginning of 1944. Nor does he owe this astronomical sum to the circumstance of being paid in coal which he then sells on the black market, as happened with our fish; not at all. He receives his 10,000 roubles at the pay counter, alongside the other workers, some of whom are content to receive as little as 250 or 300 roubles a month. Certainly, this Aphoniev is probably even more productive than Alexei Stakhanov, the record-holder of 1935, but he is unlucky with the newspaper coverage of his feats: the liberation of Bucharest and Sofia takes up more space in *Pravda* than does the chronicle of his exploits in a Donbass coal mine. For Chourik it is significant, however, that our press talks only about Aphoniev's pay slips and doesn't even indicate his rate of coal extraction. 'It's on account of the war,' Kola replies. 'You don't reveal your levels of productivity to the enemy.' This quip of Kola's sets the fuse alight.

Galia and Chourik consider that we no longer have the right to joke about such matters, for our emergent 'new society' is in the process of absorbing into its system some of the most retrograde forms of capitalism. They have prepared this indictment in the secrecy of their library, complete with quotes from Marx, Engels and even Lenin, and were awaiting an opportunity of producing it. Their adversaries, Kola and Klava, try to play the devil's advocate by arguing that the egalitarian levelling-down effect, due to the absolute pauperization of the workers, is one of the characteristics of capitalism condemned by Marx, and that our sacrosanct principle, 'to each according to their labour,' also derives from his writings. They have read it somewhere in an old speech of Stalin's on Marx's 'Critique of the Gotha Programme'. But they are no match for the 'professionals' who are familiar with the original short text in its entirety and not merely with an interpretation of it. 'Just because a society cannot become egalitarian overnight,' Chourik raises his voice, 'is no reason for it to aggravate existing inequalities between workers.' Then he adds for Klava's benefit: 'And as for these stupid references to capitalist ultra-egalitarianism they are completely untrue.'

I ought to fly to defend Klava, yet I know that Chourik is telling the truth: there is no egalitarianism under capitalism, 'ultra' or otherwise. After all I have lived in a capitalist country and I was able to observe that equality is the least of their worries. Kola takes up Klava's defence, but at the same time shifts terrain because he feels more sure of himself when talking about the priority given to the development of the productive forces. And it has to be admitted that he knows this subject well and expresses himself with great clarity, even after half a litre of vodka.

Tempers continue to rise. Galia and Chourik retort that socialism is not simply a technique for broadening society's material foundations, that it constitutes rather a phase in the transition to communism in the course of which hierarchies and inequalities will be systematically abolished. 'Right, I agree,' Klava intervenes, 'but these things will only be possible when people are better educated, *cultournyié*, fully developed, and have got rid of their egoistic individualism.'

'Well then, is Aphoniev in your view *cultournyié* and fully developed?' Galia adds sneakily but gently. 'My dear Klavotchka,' Galia continues, still more tenderly, 'we shall be truly fully developed when there is no more social division of labour and no more difference between town and countryside. Our full development will not come about simply from studying a large number of books.' 'Yet it's what you do yourself,' Klava replies swiftly. 'She studies in order to understand why things are going wrong and how new social stratifications are crystallizing in our society,' answers Chourik, who is in no mood to allow Galia to be teased.

Lying back with my eyes fixed on the ceiling, I am suddenly transported to Lodz, several years before, to the time when my mother used to debate these themes of socialism with her friends. You would have said that, this evening, a new generation was taking over from them, with similar cultural reference points but in strange conditions. For how can we forget that our discussion takes place after we have enjoyed stolen fish in a country in which you cannot even live on your wage unless you happen to be Aphoniev? No Klavotchka, I haven't drunk too much; it is our absurd paradoxical situation that renders me speechless.

The others do not remain lucid for very long and Chourik, fairly tipsy by now, attacks Kola on the differences between town and countryside. Straying away from theory he specifically lays into Aunt Valia: 'First she was squeezed like a lemon, and now she is getting her own back by holding us to ransom for a mouthful of bread.' 'Just because she gives you a good dinner you turn around and call her a profiteer! My aunt is no wealthier than your father!' 'Search around a bit beneath her mattress and you'll find enough roubles to buy a tank or an aeroplane,' Chourik retorts, alluding to a campaign for patriotic donations for our army. It took place in 1943, when I was in the Gulag, but I learned with utter astonishment that it had begun in the region of Saratov and that a certain Golovatov was able to contribute 100,000 roubles from his personal savings for the construction of a tank. His example had been followed by other kolkhozian 'small savers', and *Pravda* published Stalin's personal thanks day after day to different substantial donors. By these means a total of 13,000 million roubles was collected – almost the total annual value of our agricultural production. Just now it was not unreasonable therefore, for Chourik to wonder by what miracle such considerable sums were still in the hands of our peasants who, so it was supposed, had been squeezed like lemons throughout the phase of 'socialist primitive accumulation' in the 1930s.

The bitterness of the exchanges between Chourik and Kola obliges me to intervene. I propose a toast to friendship. By suddenly jerking the bed, I waken Fira who, invigorated by a nap, lashes out against the 'thoroughly corrupt nature of the artistic world'. It is no longer a party but a critique of Soviet society on the eve of victory. And who would have thought that Fira, our cabaret artist, was so scandalized by the 'star' system, by the privileges and corruption of the entertainment world? And that she finds it intolerable that our aeroplanes bear the names of those who designed them, just as in the West they carry the names of their owners? 'Mikoyan and Gourvitch give MIG, while a TU comes from Tupolev, and a Yak from Yakovliev. It's ridiculous!' she maintains. After Klava, Fira is my favourite. But she gets carried away quickly and when she declares that our heaviest tank shouldn't be carrying the name of Josip Stalin, I stop her from continuing: 'Right! That's enough discussion for this evening. Cathinka, give us a song instead.'

Cathinka doesn't need to be begged, she knows a new song that has been translated from the English: Put dalokii do Tipperary (It's a long way to Tipperary). I seem to know this song. Yes, of course, I remember now, the English prisoners sang it in *La Grande Illusion*. And Cathinka lowers her pretty blonde head close to mine, as though she were dedicating her song to me: 'Goodbye Piccadilly, farewell Leicester Square,' – and I feel that there is a hidden meaning in this unexpected evocation of the faraway home of my brother Genia. That's it, I shall soon be going to see him in London. It is the only possible significance of the message.

While waiting for my journey to London to come off, I have to leave on 30 November 1944 to spend a day in Moscow, where I no longer have any family. Letters addressed to Aunt Lisa are returned officially stamped 'addressee unknown', and I have never had the addresses of any of her sons. But going to Moscow is something of an event in itself, even with the prospect of spending the night in a hostel. The renown of this city grows endlessly: capital of the proletarian revolution, it has become the capital of victory to boot, because it was in the suburbs of Moscow that the Wehrmacht suffered in 1941 its first great defeat. It is also on the large squares of Moscow, beginning in August 1943, that the *saliouts* are organized – sumptuous fireworks displays and artillery salutes – to celebrate each significant advance made by our army. In Kislovodsk, admittedly, Nievka used to argue that the history of modern Russia and of the Bolshevik Revolution is in reality inseparable from that of Leningrad, the site of the Winter Palace – four stops by tramway from her home. Moscow, though, is incontestably more prestigious. As a fugitive from Western Siberia, I had arrived there in 1940 overcome with emotion at the prospect of seeing the white walls of the Kremlin, Red Square and all the other monuments. Since that time our poets have added a verse to Lermontov's *Borodino*, so that his famous poem pays homage to those who 130 years later, on the same battlefield, kept their oath to Stalin: 'We shall not abandon Moscow!'

Moscow is the best supplied city in the USSR, doubtless on account of the presence of numerous foreigners, diplomats and journalists. Though 'commercial' shops have been opened throughout the country in order to compete with the black market, there is still no doubt that you will find in those of Moscow consumer goods that are impossible to find in the provinces, items as rare as swimming costumes in Rostov. Everyone knows that even a short sojourn in the capital offers the opportunity to combine business with pleasure and, for those with nous, it can be a lucrative experience.

Obtaining a seat on the Moscow train is a notoriously difficult undertaking which requires patience. I didn't choose to leave on 30 November, but this date, decided by chance, is a good omen: it is the fifth anniversary of my arrival in Russia, and the fourth anniversary of my engagement to Klava – the two of us deem it to date from the performance of *Anna Karenina* at the theatre in Rostov. Without these two events we wouldn't have been together, that's clear, and, although neither of us is that superstitious, we think that 30

November is a lucky day for both of us.

Our entire group applies itself to organizing the trip properly. My friends know how fragile I feel, how often I am a prey to persecution obsessions which, on certain days, totally confuse me. I sometimes run off when a passer-by approaches me for information, or I make Kuzmitch take detours around the streets of Rostov to shake off a lorry which I suspect is tailing us. Thanks to Klava and her soothing reassurances, I recover my equilibrium quickly enough, but we don't know exactly what provokes my crises. The solicitude of my friends on the eve of my departure on 30 November in no way upsets me, and I too prefer that what I have to do in Moscow should be carefully arranged in advance.

This isn't possible with respect to every detail. Klava and Fira would like me to spend my Moscow evening at the Bolshoi in order to see Galina Oulanova, 'the best ballerina in the world,' but the big shots of the entertainment black market in Rostov don't have any contacts among the ticket touts in Moscow and are therefore unable to reserve me a seat. Luckily this is not the case with the food market wholesalers and the employees of the state commercial sector.

To make it to Moscow, you need only have the magic formula and the rest becomes easy. This is the *commandirovka*, a document certifying that its bearer is travelling on urgent state business. It is impossible to enter the capital without it, as identity controls have become very rigorous. The Rostov–Moscow line is closely watched. But I have a mandate from my factory: I have to go to the People's Commissariat of 'Black Metallurgy' to collect my plan schedule for the first six months of 1945. This dossier could of course have been sent by post, which in the Soviet Union, all things considered, isn't working too badly. Tradition has it though that the *zavs* and factory managers go periodically to the capital, which allows them to fatten their wallets and to contribute at the same time to the distribution of durable goods around the different cities of the USSR.

However, my mandate doesn't come under 'normal administration procedures', as they say in Russia; it has come from the office of

'Caesar Imperator' in circumstances that I shall never manage to explain.

Soviet trains do not devour the kilometres, they merely nibble at them. But the passengers in the 'soft' carriages have a few hours to spare and spend the time playing cards, chatting and picnicking as though they were on board a cruiser. In my compartment, an enormous wooden chest serves as a table on which we play 'preference'; this chest is mine and contains a large sack of sunflower seeds, that I am carrying with me to present to the workers' supplies section of a factory in Moscow that is twinned with mine. A likely story. In fact a wholesaler will come to collect it at the station and, this time, we have taken every precaution against being conned as we had been by the *baba* fishmongers. Sunflower seeds are obviously a bulky commodity but we decided upon them because they yield a very high profit margin: the contents of my chest cost us 6,500 roubles and will be resold for 26,000, which is a good deal by any standards. A comical detail: in the airforce, Colonel Ganachek tried to prevent us from munching *siemitchki* during film shows; he said loud and clear that the habit was undignified for pilots; indeed for any ordinary citizens of good breeding. We must believe, however, that Muscovites are not very well brought up since they are willing to pay very high prices for these seeds, as if a visit to the cinema without *siemitchki* is without flavour.

On the return journey, with the profits from the sunflower seeds, I shall bring back a smaller suitcase filled with underwear, rolls of cloth and clothes selected by the manager of a 'commercial' shop. He is a friend of Chourik's father, who asked him to choose items that are not available in Rostov.

My business transactions take rather longer than necessary. In the evening a curious idea comes to me: to look in upon the address that Nadia had given to me, the one at which I was to call to see her in 10 years' time 'if she were still alive'. Hardly a year had elapsed since I left the Volgalag and, barring a miracle, Nadia cannot have returned home. What's more it is not very prudent to stroll about with 25,000 roubles in the suburbs of a large city in which you don't know your

337

way around. But I must go to Nadia's home; this impulse is stronger than my fears. One thing is certain: reaching her address is no mean feat, for the road signs in the streets of Moscow are most inadequate.

A dark-haired woman of about 30 shows me into a room in which two children are getting ready for bed. She is very mistrustful and asks me to wait: we can only talk in a *pivnaia*, a bar, not far from here. It is clear that in communal apartments even the walls have ears.

The *pivnaia* is 'commercial', and therefore recently opened; it is expensive and already very dirty; and it reeks of beer and crayfish. It is as if the terrible smells are an indispensable part of Soviet gastronomic establishments. The dark-haired woman is also called Nadia, she is the cousin of the one I know and not the sister as I had thought at first. Two beers and a dozen crayfish cost 100 roubles, as much as a theatre seat, or one third of the legal minimum wage of the ordinary worker. 'That's a bit steep,' I say, and the dark-haired Nadia agrees with me. A typical conversation between people who have nothing to say to one another. Suddenly, the dark-haired Nadia becomes animated and says, as if the sentences had been on the tip of her tongue, 'The kids up there are the children of *your* Nadia, and she suffers a martyr's torment from not being able to see them. You must have known about it since you were friends with her.' What am I to say? It seems simple in Moscow but in a camp, nothing happens the way it does in normal life. Should I explain the Gulag to this mistrustful woman? I simply reply with another question: 'And do the kids miss their mother badly?' 'They were very small when she left, it's five years now.' The calculations become muddled in my head: she has been in the camp for five years and has still another nine to go? 'Seven,' she corrects me, since she was condemned to a dozen years. 'Men killed each other for her and she got 12 years?' 'She told you that?' More shadow-boxing, and I give up because a wall of mistrust separates us.

In the darkened staircase in front of her apartment, I withdraw a thousand roubles from my pocket and give them to her 'for the children'. She hesitates, uncertain as to whether she has the right to take them. Why not? 'You can write to Nadia that it is a little something from the *pojarnik*, she will understand.' 'It would be better not to write,' she replies. She takes the money and murmurs a few words of thanks. 'Are you thinking of coming back to Moscow?' 'I have no idea, but if I do, I shall come back to see you.' 'Not here. Come and look for me instead at the exit to the bread factory, where I work.' Agreed. I leave in an ambivalent frame of mind, now reproaching myself for having come, now for not having left a larger amount. In the darkness it is getting colder and colder; not knowing the route to the hostel I get lost on the way back and am in danger of freezing. Even in bed I shiver from the cold, like during an attack of malaria.

On the train back to Rostov, a good half of the passengers are old acquaintances, my mates on the outward journey. Moscow is a big city only in appearance; one of them saw me with Nadia in the *pivnaia*. He doesn't ask any questions but instead congratulates me on having 'picked her up'. The others, not to be outdone, start to tell stories of their own sexual exploits, each of them having found a Muscovite to his taste and spent the night performing incredible feats, far more interesting than those they get up to with their spouses. If boastfulness wasn't such an important part of the Russian man's character, you would have to conclude that Moscow is the capital of debauchery and not of victory.

Klava is disappointed by my trip. The fate of Nadia's children, deprived of their mother, saddens her most: 'It is inhuman, they shouldn't have done that, whatever crime she had committed.' Then so as not to add her own melancholy to mine, she changes the subject and makes fun of the erotic delirium of my travel companions, most of whom are no doubt cuckolds who tell each other these stories to forget their own inadequacies.

The trip to Moscow brings to a close my parallel earnings. According to my rough estimate, our joint expenditures (Klava's and mine) rise to 3,000 roubles a month, even without my illicit gastronomic purchases in the market. We are probably better dressed than average, thanks to the clothes brought back from Moscow, but otherwise we live very meagrely, like our friends and most other people. I find it hard to believe that anyone could have survived throughout this period on their official earnings alone. There were perhaps citizens in Rostov who made do with their official incomes. But for whom, in that case, did the state create a 'commercial' network in which two beers and a dozen crayfish cost one hundred roubles? These are questions that will remain unanswered for me in Rostov, but which, later, will help me to reflect upon the nature of the USSR and the societies that take it as a model.

6. *'Nieznakomka'* (the unknown one)

Spending half the night of VE day on a park bench, alone in the middle of a crowd gone wild with joy, will be for Solik one of the last episodes of his stay in Rostov and, to tell the truth, one of the best. Even before I was given this nickname, I dreamed secretly of a surprise attack by the USSR against Hitler, and of the collapse of the Third Reich under simultaneous blows from the British and the Soviets. (In 1940, the United States had still not entered the war.) But neither then nor later had I ever imagined that the Nazis' unconditional surrender would be announced in the middle of the night. Here was Rostov, an early-to-bed town pulled from its slumber by a party, exuberant, though without alcohol.

The next day, May 9th, Stalin, in an address to the Soviet people, explained that 'knowing full well the perfidious nature of the German leaders and having no confidence in their word,' he hadn't been able formally to acknowledge the Wehrmacht's surrender until the moment when 'the German troops had actually begun to surrender their weapons and to give themselves up en masse.' Certainly he was a man who was mistrustful to an unhealthy degree – all of his biographers concur – but not to the point of still fearing in May 1945, after the capture of Berlin, the treachery of the surviving German generals. He surely preferred to announce this great news at night-time so as to make a better impact in his own country. This time it was not a matter of just one more celebration, but of Victory with a capital V, conclusively bringing this tragic and glorious chapter in the history of the USSR and of Europe to a close.

It is common knowledge that this chapter had already come to an end on 7 May when, in Reims, the Germans signed the provisional act of surrender. For that matter, all the other victorious countries celebrate VE day 24 hours before the Soviets, but this discrepancy is probably the result of the slowness of the Soviet administrative machine in the USSR: extra time was needed in Rostov to instal along the Sadovaia, in Gorky Park and along several other city centre avenues, immense searchlights borrowed from the anti-aircraft defence forces, and to assemble the military bands and civilian orchestras essential for the occasion. At the time ordained the desired result was achieved. No daytime ceremony would have generated such emotion.

Had Klava and I been less busy at the time we might have noticed that the searchlights were being installed on the Sadovaia and we would have guessed for what purpose. However, we were taken by surprise, and immediately wanted to find our friends in order to celebrate together.

Stirred from sleep, I left the house in a hurry, without even pulling my trousers on. Halfway to Kola's place, we met, embraced, and began to weep. At the time of our reunion in 1944, we had been able to contain our emotion. Tonight, however, everything was different: we were intoxicated by this victory – no less of a miracle for having been expected and awaited. 'Now we really are going to be happy,' Kola repeated in between sobs. His voice was drowned by the cries of an agitated young girl: 'Wherever Stalin is, that's where victory is!' It was no exaggeration of the truth.

In Gorky Park, Kola is whisked off by a blonde with pigtails and I am left alone on a solitary bench. Not far away, sitting underneath a tree, a grey-haired woman, also on her own, was singing a famous aria from Eugene Onegin: 'What does tomorrow have in store for us?' as though she were inquiring into her future or obliging me to reflect upon mine. It was as obvious to me as the truth of the slogan about Stalin and victory, that my time as Solik was reaching its end; the 'tomorrow' of the people of Rostov wouldn't be mine. Soon our paths would part; it had been on the cards, like victory, for a long time, but things were now going to happen all at once. The new chapter would signify one future for my Rostov friends and another, in Poland, for me. Each of us would, after this party, return to reality.

Almost all those dancing close to my bench were women. Since my return to Rostov I had learned a great deal about the misery of the women during this final phase of the war. Some of the scenes in the Savelit factory left an enduring impression: women workers breaking down over notifications of the death of one of their dear ones, fallen somewhere in Germany or the Balkans. Yet these women continued coming to work as usual, and their mourning was keenly felt by the whole of the workshop – everyone raged against the injustice. What indeed could be more painful than to lose a loved one after an interminable wait, and just at the very time when everyone else was getting ready for victory celebrations.

'A kopek for your thoughts, my child,' a woman sang. A fair request but there was no song for my reply. No doubt the *Internationale* would have fitted the bill. On that night of victory, I thought a great deal about the worldwide swing to the left after the defeat of fascism, which rekindled my desire to renew the fight for socialism. It might seem paradoxical to leave the 'socialist father-land' the better to fight for socialism, but there too I remained faithful to Solik's early ideas. Even before crossing the Bug in November 1939, I knew, thanks to my mother, that Soviet political culture was based upon the Stalinist interpretation of the history of the workers' movement. I had discovered for myself in practice how it was applied without the slightest effort to arouse people's interest, let alone their participation, in political life. This country that is so widely reputed for its gifts of 'indoctrination' simply kept on repeating the themes of a single book, *The History of the CPSU (Bolsheviks)*. Under the colonels' regime in Lodz I knew more friends who read Marx and the classics of socialist literature than ever I did in Rostov, where my earliest protector, the mathematician Motia, had straightaway advised me to concern myself only with the natural sciences. Hadn't I been admitted to membership of the Komsomol without having been asked a single question about my opinions or my reading?

A single mystery in my behaviour remains. In 1942, when Commissar Bielokonienko had sounded me out about enlisting in General Ander's Polish Army, I had said no as if, out of love for Nievka, I was then ready, despite everything, to stay in the USSR. Had this woman exerted such a hold over me that I was ready to renounce the ideas dearest to me for her sake? Or had I secretly allowed myself to be tempted by the promise of a career among the *nomenklatura* of 'her' Leningrad, under the protective eye of 'her' Andrei Zhdanov? After the Gulag, I had never sought to find her, perhaps so as not to give her the opportunity of trying to keep me in the USSR. Something told me she was still alive and capable of punishing my persecutors. This idea had taken firm root in my head during the interrogation sessions at the NKVD headquarters in Yerevan, and had poured balm on my heart.

During victory night I would have loved to see Nievka once more. She had more than deserved her place among this rejoicing crowd. Under the bright glare of the searchlights, half-destroyed Rostov resembled an abstract painting full of discordant forms, strange shadows and luminous stains. The people of Rostov gave themselves up to a display of genuine kindness.

Although it was now almost six months since Poland had been liberated, I hadn't made the slightest effort to find out what had happened to my family. Yet I had only to write to my brother in London. Later, once I reach Poland, it is thanks to him that I am able to locate my other two brothers, but not my mother nor my sister, who had disappeared without trace, probably during the insurrection in Warsaw in August 1944. Had I received the bad news in Rostov I might not have had the heart to leave Klava, saying to her, like Stienka Razin: 'Farewell my lovely, we have been happy together, but I am setting off now for distant lands because yours no longer pleases me very much . . .'

It is difficult to hold any certainties on the future of this Soviet Russia. Suppose it were to become more bearable to live in after victory? Perhaps it would learn to govern itself differently, allowing its citizens to decide on their own affairs and to discuss matters openly. Kola hoped for the arrival of a Soviet Union without suffering, Klava for a society in which everyone was well educated, Chourik and Galia for a USSR less dependent on hierarchy, more egalitarian. . . . All of these aspirations seemed to me to be legitimate, and, in this hour of victory, had I had some vodka to hand, I would happily have drunk to their realization. But while not altogether excluding the possibility that their desires become reality – who would have dared to on victory day? – I couldn't wait to see what would happen. In Rostov, I was in danger of becoming a permanent burden on Klava. In Poland and in the West, I would be able to contribute my building-block to the construction of this freer and more just society, the dream of which we shared.

Living in the Soviet manner among Soviet people, sharing their joys and sorrows, doesn't help much in getting to know the intentions of the Kremlin, for the Soviet people are the last to know what they are. Thus it is that in Rostov neither Klava nor I, nor any of our friends, had guessed that at Yalta, three months before the end of the war, Stalin had come to an agreement with Roosevelt and Churchill on a division of Europe into zones of influence. Although we discussed politics endlessly and considered a thousand hypotheses for the future, we didn't even suspect the correct one, the one which shaped the political map of post-war Europe: an Iron Curtain at the heart of Europe, and Cold War between erstwhile allies. Was it simply for want of information, a traditional flaw of Russian life?

Forty years later, I think I am in a position to claim that our mistake resulted also from a flaw in method: we confronted Stalin's speeches with his own bible, *The History of the CPSU (Bolsheviks)*, either to criticize them (Chourik and Galia especially), or in order to draw optimistic conclusions from them (Kola and, in a lesser measure, Klava) without realizing that this doctrine restricted our vision. Everything combined to maintain us in this false perspective, from our university syllabus to our repertoire of films. In fact, our supreme commander-in-chief was above all else a pragmatist, guided by his conception of Soviet '*raison d'Etat*'; he didn't care a toss for the rest, certainly not the opinion of mere citizens.

So, we were victims of an enormous misunderstanding. In Stalin's pan-Slavic accents we thought we heard the kind of fable that Klava spun for her parents' benefit, whereas Stalin, on the contrary, was in deadly earnest and was clearing the way for the expansion of his empire in the name of his conception of the 'national interest'. On 9 May, a few hours after the victory celebrations, Papa Emilian had come into our room to propose a toast to Josip Vissarionovitch Stalin; 'May God bless him, and allow him also to capture the Dardanelles' (an old Cossack obsession)! We laughed at his anachronistic ambitions and Klava simply said that she was going to give up trying to reconcile her father with the Turks. In reality Papa Emilian had shown more flair than us in refusing to take at their face value Stalin's assurances that he would never covet any territory nor interfere in the affairs of neighbouring states. The Russian nationalists were unerringly accurate about his determination to make other peoples pay dearly for the aid of the USSR against the German invaders. We believed, on the contrary, that the Soviet Union would be satisfied with these countries' grateful acknowledgement of Soviet aid, and that it would rapidly demobilize its large army. Didn't it need as a matter of the greatest urgency the return of its men to continue with the country's work of reconstruction?

We fondly imagined that all the POWs or civilian deportees in Germany would soon return to their homes, covered with glory and honour for the sufferings they had endured. Better still, in one of Stalin's phrases of 24 May 1945 ('our government has made a rather large number of mistakes'), we thought we could detect the beginnings of self-criticism. Was he regretting his pact with the treacherous Hitler? We discussed at some length the negative consequences which the pact had had on the political consciousness and morale of the Komsomols. But neither Stalin, nor his critic Nikita Krushchev, nor any other Soviet leader, ever expressed the slightest regret at this 1939 major operation of realpolitik which, clearly, never troubled their communist conscience for a moment.

The morale of Klava and the friends of our small circle must have been very badly shaken when, shortly after my departure in 1946, the great deportation of ex-POWs towards the Gulag began and again when, two years later, Stalin decreed that all the countries liberated by the Soviet Army belonged to the 'socialist bloc' – a concept that was unknown in my time. Neither then nor later had my friends the slightest opportunity of influencing the course of events, but I am certain that they retain nostalgic memories of the few months which followed the great victory festival, during which we dreamed together of the advent of a fraternal and more just world. We were not the only naive ones in the USSR; for example, Pasternak, along with so many others, never felt so free and confident as during this brief period of hope.

In my own case, having already acquired a certain political culture in Poland, I would not have found it possible to love Klava, nor to feel so attached to my friends, had they shown any nostalgia for a Greater pan-Slavic Russia or attachment to the values that derive from it. On the contrary, they too believed in equality and freedom, in the incessant quest of men and women for the right to determine their lives, their fate. That is why we got on well with each other; that is also why the journal of Solik's last months in Rostov is devoted to the problems that flowed from this mutually accepted, though painful separation.

It is no simple matter to repatriate to Poland almost two million of its former citizens who are dispersed throughout the USSR, especially if you bear in mind that at this time, by virtue of the Yalta agreement, Poland lost its eastern provinces, inhabited chiefly by Ukrainians and Byelorussians, and recovered by way of compensation vast tracts of Silesia and Pomerania, which were historically Polish but which had been in German hands for hundreds of years. To carry out such a transfer of population successfully in a country that was ravaged by war would have needed an effective administration that

347

the Soviet Union clearly didn't possess, and a political consensus which was also lacking.

In fact, the government of the USSR, which is still set against allowing any of its citizens to go abroad, punctiliously checked all the dossiers of applicants for repatriation to Poland, a precautionary measure guaranteed to delay departure still further. There are no problems where I'm concerned: the dossier compiled on me by Captains Strel and Abak in Yerevan was destroyed, but sufficient documents remain to prove that I am not a Soviet 'in origin'. Even better, immediately after 9 May, the Rostov authorities offer in friendly fashion to allow me to leave on my own, without delay, suggesting that 'People's' Poland probably has need of the services of an ex-combatant of the Red Army. I decline this offer, on the pretext that I want first of all to complete my year at the university and my year's experience as a planner at the Savelit factory. We decide by mutual agreement that I should await the arrival in Rostov of a Polish mission which will be organizing a convoy for all those to be repatriated from south Russia.

Not knowing even the approximate date of this convoy, Klava and I live in a state of uncertainty which prevents us from fully taking advantage of these last months of our life together. We begin to worry about what will become of us after our separation; we sometimes ask ourselves what our destiny would have held in store had it not been predetermined in this way.

Since I have committed myself to completing the first year of my studies, I take six exams and pass with an ease which astonishes me. It is no mystery to anyone that, at the university, preference is shown to students who have fought in the war, and that they are given an easy ride by their examiners in acknowledgement of their services to the country. At the same time, Klava has to face a panel of hostile examiners who have probably been ordered to fail the majority of women students. In Rostov, as soon as the examinations are over full-time students like Klava are sent off to the countryside to help the kolkhozians, or else are incorporated into brigades working on urban reconstruction. Klava's brigade in Rostov isn't one of the worst, but it doesn't leave her much time to study, especially as we count upon spending the evenings together, alone or in the company of friends.

Overall, things are going rather well for me: at Savelit I enjoy an easy ride; in addition I have the agreeable surprise of seeing my airmen friends once more – they are the first servicemen to return home on leave to Rostov. Klava is happy to get to know them and goes to some trouble to ensure that they will keep fond memories of our reunion parties, but, at the same time, I sense that she is a little irritated, and is concealing a mounting bad temper, which she finds hard to control.

The uniform of flight captain fits my friend Vassia as if it had been created expressly for him. In the outfit of a trainee pilot he had already cut quite a figure, but with his silver-braided epaulettes and his three stars he looks quite magnificent. You only have to hear him to measure the enormous distance that separates his generation of officers of Cossack origin from that of the former 'army of the Don'. Vassia is a highly qualified pilot who knows how to observe and understand everything that is going on around him. He is capable of recalling the war's closing stages and of commenting upon it with a skill worthy of the Mikhail Frunzé Military Academy. I sense that we were wrong to appreciate only his elephantine strength, and to underestimate his warrior's intelligence. Besides, at the moment of danger during our crossing of Balkaria, it was he who got us out of the fix by keeping a cool head and carrying off the prize in the duel over the white horse.

To begin with everything passes off marvellously. Vassia arrives at dawn at our place. Then he is able to get us permission to go to Mietchotka. It is thanks to his air of authority, for when he goes to ask the leader of Klava's brigade for two days leave for her, the leader is obviously impressed. At the approach of so large an officer, he agrees without argument. These two days in the countryside will be the only time that Klava and I spend together outside Rostov. Mietchotka admittedly isn't Sukhumi or Sotchi, but we are just as happy there: it is circumstances and the people which determine the beauty of places and, on that day, everything worked in our favour. Vassia is busy with his family and leaves us to go for lovers' strolls through the village and its surrounding countryside. We dally a while in the cool of a picturesque wood traversed by a stream. What were we dreaming of, as we sat dangling our feet in the water on this hot July day? I believe – but this is merely a supposition formed in the light of Klava's letters – that our holiday came soon after Labour's landslide victory in the elections in Britain. I was at first surprised at the country's ingratitude towards Churchill, but I then felt a great hope, seeing in this Labour victory the proof that all of Europe was moving to the left. I didn't know much about Attlee but my mother had read some books by Harold Laski, the Party's outstanding intellectual figure; – socialism in Britain, the first industrialized country in the world, was a turning-point in history. It rendered more plausible the prospect of the progressive unification of the European continent, and thus my eventual reunion with Klava, perhaps even in London at the home of my brother Genia who had always had a weakness for the Russians.

In Mietchotka, Klava feels at home because she is a 'bird of the Don' and everyone recognizes her as such. It is a real mystery to me but the Cossacks, on this point, are infallible. As soon as she sees Klava, Aunt Valia, with whom we are spending the night, has guessed exactly the region of origin of Klava's family, and even the district. 'You are one of us.' To me she whispers, but loudly enough for Klava to hear: 'You lucky rascal, you have won a real prize. In the whole of Mietchotka there isn't a single woman who can hold a candle to her.' And the *dzied*, who has watched four generations of Cossacks at table, and who has probably seen much else besides, is also favourably impressed. Overjoyed and purring with contentment, Klava says as we are about to leave that she has been happy in Mietchotka, in particular because it was the first time for many

350

years that she hadn't had to busy herself with the house, her work, her studies. In this heartfelt cry, she summed up all of life's difficulties for a young woman overwhelmed by the many chores in a world of scarcity.

Aunt Valia does some shopping for us: agricultural products cost only a fraction of their price in Rostov. Aunt Valia doesn't forget her nephew Kola and when we leave her home, we are overloaded with bulky parcels. At the station, Vassia (who is also bringing back quite a few items) has a surprise for us; he apologizes, but the regulations forbid him to have his hands loaded. I suppose, right enough, that an officer of the victorious Soviet Army should never be seen carting around a sack of flour in one hand and a basket full of butter and honey in the other – it would be undignified. So we form a strange trio: the strongest and largest advances with nothing to carry while two feeble creatures are collapsing alongside him under the weight of baskets and bundles.

I know that Vassia isn't responsible for the regulations and that we have just spent a magnificent two days thanks to him. In the train, however, Klava grips me by the arm, and whispers in my ear: 'It's intolerable, he only invited us here so that we could run after him like porters. It's shameful! I shall tell Chourik about it.' When Vassia moves some way off from us I try to placate her with a jest: 'Among the Cossacks the men are asked to fight, and it is up to the women to look after everything else.' 'Be quiet, Stienka Razin, I have clearly noticed that you are just like them and that their nonsense amuses you, but believe me, if you stay a little while longer in Rostov, I shall soon knock it out of your head and teach you to mend your mule-headed ways!' Klava has me laughing and she laughs too, but her green eyes have a fiery look.

According to an old Soviet saying, 'from the height of the Kremlin tower you can see things that are outside the field of vision of common mortals.' From the height of a heavy bomber this field of vision becomes immeasurably wider, and Vassia was well placed logistically during the final stages of the war. In fact, Vassia says he is certain that our supreme commander-in-chief couldn't 'from the height of the Kremlin tower' see certain operational opportunities because his subordinates didn't inform him about them. Apart from me, no one wishes to believe him, and Kola, in order to reassert his shaken authority, openly makes fun of Vassia: 'Of course, I suppose if you had been our supreme commander-in-chief we would have won the war three months sooner and taken Hitler alive!'

At this point our dinner party gathering becomes agitated. Luckily we are at home and not at the Don restaurant, to which Vassia had wanted to invite us. During the trip to Mietchotka, he had disclosed certain details which greatly interested me: on 19 January 1945, his squadron came within an ace of bombing Lodz, but the order was annulled at the last minute because the town had fallen without resistance by the Germans. Having corroborated his impressions with other pilots, Vassia maintains that by the beginning of February, when our forces had arrived on the Oder, the Germans no longer had the means to defend Berlin, and that a swift attack would have allowed us to take the capital of the Third Reich with many fewer losses than in May 1945.

'Whose fault is it then?' asks Zeus. Vassia replies obliquely: he knows those who are blameless – Stalin and Marshal Golovanov, the commander of the Eighteenth Airforce – but not who is to be blamed. In his view, our generals tend to be one war behind, and in this war they underestimated the capacity of heavy aircraft to protect our troops heading towards Berlin. His arguments, coherent and illustrated with subtle examples, run up against incomprehension from Kola and Klava. This enormously irritates Vassia and drives him to increase his intake of vodka.

Roughly 20 years later, I was furnished with the formal proof that Vassia had thoroughly grasped a real problem and that we had been wrong to disbelieve him. During the period of destalinization, Marshal Vassili Tchouikov, who master-minded the defence of Stalingrad, published his contribution to the criticism of Stalin's 'errors'. Stalin assigned Tchouikov the command of one of the

352

armies engaged in the winter offensive of 1944-5, and Tchouikov found himself, at the beginning of February 1945, a lot sooner than planned, some 80 kilometres from Berlin, ready to swoop down on it without delay. He told how, in the course of a meeting with all the senior officers, he had already obtained the green light from Zhukov, when suddenly the latter received a telephone call from Stalin in person. Although Tchouikov hadn't himself heard Stalin or even taken notes, he summed up in his testimony the drift of this conversation, which resulted in the cancellation of the attack on Berlin.

Tchouikov's study provoked, however, a prompt and energetic retort from Marshal Zhukov, who flatly denied ever having taken part in the meeting in question and cited documentary proof of his claim. On the date cited by Tchouikov, 4 February 1945, he was in a totally different sector of the front, in Pomerania. But in the second part of his refutation – this is the only public controversy ever in the USSR between two such highly ranked military officers – Zhukov loses his way in unconvincing historical analogies, claiming that a premature attack on Berlin would have resulted in a failure comparable to the one that the Red Army had suffered in 1920 on the outskirts of Warsaw. And even I know that the balance of forces in 1945 was not the same as at the time of the 'miracle on the Vistula'.

As soon as he returns to East Prussia Vassia sends us an enormous chest filled with war booty. When it arrives, we round up some friends. The scene resembles one in *La Grande Illusion*, although we are in the reverse situation, that of the victors who are to enjoy the fruits of victory. Is it wholly in conformity with our principles? The Soviet Union, according to its dogma, has always been opposed to either territorial annexation or war reparations as practised by the rapacious imperialists. Nevertheless, Stalin has just annexed East Prussia, and here we are with a chest containing war plunder. Here is food for thought indeed, the discrepancy between our ideological discussions on the future of the world and the reality of this treasure chest.

When one is very poor, the here-and-now counts above everything and we think more about the contents of the trunk than about its suspect origins. With regard to the Germans, in one of his speeches, Stalin quoted an old Russian proverb: 'You don't hunt the wolf because it's grey; you hunt it because it has eaten sheep.' Vassia has simply recovered in East Prussia goods which correspond to the sheep that we and our close friends have lost in the war. To be sure, if we devour too many stray sheep belonging to the Germans sooner or later the proverb will turn against us, and everything will start all over again like in 1941. A brief anxiety on this score troubles me; probably Chourik feels it too, but we keep it to ourselves.

Hurrah! Kuzmitch has finally managed to break open the lid of the chest and a thick pile of sky-blue velvet cloth appears. What is it? A length of cloth? It seems improbable that it had been packed up like this in Germany. 'Stand back please, we have to get it all out,' Klava says. It is only when all of it is unpacked that we realize it is an immense curtain. Devil take them. Does this mean that they have such high, wide windows in East Prussia, or had Vassia found it in a theatre? 'It comes from a chateau,' decrees Kola, who could recognize a stage curtain. While the velvet is being unfolded, a rectangular casket of polished wood falls to the floor and the entire gathering exclaims: 'That's the real treasure!' The wily Vassia has used the curtains to protect it during the journey and probably also to ensure that it would escape detection. The opening of the casket makes us tremble with impatience: it contains a brand new microscope, a triple lens Zeiss Ikon, with all its accessories.

It is very handsome, a worthy example of German precision engineering. But what can it fetch on the Rostov black market? 'Really, the simplest thing to do is to sell it to our Institute of Public Works, whose laboratories are very poorly equipped,' Kola suggests, and the men among us discuss the price to ask for it. The women examine the curtain. Klava points out that there are two layers back to back and that once the two lengths are separated there is enough cloth to make several winter dresses. Klava can sew, Cathinka too, and already they are taking orders and sketching patterns for Galia, Assia and two other friends. 'And the price for the microscope?' 'Ask them for 100,000 roubles for it,' Klava replies with an expert's assurance. She also asks me to find a dyeing company that will clean the curtain without damaging it: 'You often do business with people from the chemical industry at Savelit.'

A battle on two fronts commences. Kola is unsuccessful at the Institute because the latter doesn't pay cash for its equipment: it receives it through government allocations. Chourik and I try our luck at the university, which does have the necessary funds at its disposal and would like to acquire our microscope, but only on condition that we give a series of guarantees about its origin. The negotiations illustrate in exemplary fashion the Soviet bureaucracy: it invents pointless obstacles for each situation it has to confront and then finds that it can't surmount them. Getting tired of the protracted discussions and having nothing to hide, I ask for an interview with the dean of the Faculty of Sciences, who turns out to be the worst of the lot: mistrustful, he even inspects my university record, as though he suspected me of having stolen the treasure. Then he blathers on about the difficulties and the risks of such a transaction.

Since nothing comes of this interview I leave Kola to do the rounds of different laboratories – he has more time than I have – but, in the end, he brings back this non-negotiable object and suggests that we write to Vassia, asking him to make out a report to Marshal Golovanov in person. An exasperated Klava decrees that we shall not try any further: 'We'll keep the microscope for ourselves, on the shelf, as an ornament.' It was not the intended destination, obviously, and we could have made a present of it to these muleheads at the university, but I share her anti-bureaucratic anger and agree with her decision; this Zeiss Ikon is far more handsome than Papa Emilian's old samovar.

Some time later it will be stolen from us. Sadly, in Rostov everything is stolen, and from private homes as well as state enterprises. It is a traditional calamity in Soviet Russia if I am to believe a short story by Zoshchenko which is set well before the war. In it he describes a crowd of people who give chase to a monkey, not in order to return it to the zoo but in the hope of selling it on the black market. One of Papa Emilian's guests must have noticed the microscope and made off with it. What consoles me is that they will have a lot more trouble finding a purchaser than the fellow who caught the monkey in Zoshchenko's short story.

On the second front, that of the velvet cloth, we have more success, but I wonder if it's worth the bother. To have a dress cleaned in Rostov means a wait of several months, and for a curtain probably one of several years. Thanks though, to Savelit, I found a dyeing factory in Salsk, which, in return for a backhander, agrees to clean and dye our velvet, half black, half dark blue. Cathinka spent a whole week supervising the work. It amounted to a ruinous investment, which absorbed all our savings and forced on us draconian economies. Still, after Klava and the others had made up some beautiful dresses, we recovered most of our outlay by selling the rest of the curtain. What saved us is the fact that the price of cloth had risen rapidly since the end of the war. We even manage to keep a little nest-egg of three or four thousand roubles for the 1946 New Year celebrations.

These various operations greatly preoccupy me. I abstain from talking about them with Klava for fear of upsetting her, but I have the presentiment that the mental habits, the ways and customs of Soviet society will not improve after this victory which seems to enrich it only in appearance. It is winter already, a sad season, and every morning on my way to the factory, I see the drivers of buses seized from the Germans make superhuman efforts to turn their vehicles round on ice-covered roads. There are no onlookers to cry out their advice: it is too cold. The people prefer their old trams or trolleybuses, which, at least, work in these harsh conditions even if they don't commemorate the joy of victory. The giants of the German autobahn are useless in Rostov, just like our microscope.

It won't concern me for much longer: the representatives of the

PUR (Polish Office for Repatriation) have already arrived in town and I will soon be leaving. Since I am privileged to be able to travel and to try my luck elsewhere, I experience, if not remorse, then at least a measure of anxiety thinking of those who remain behind. Most of the disadvantages of their lives result from flaws that are inherent in their society and are not the consequences of wartime. I still sincerely wish for the sake of Klava and our friends that their hopes for the future are realized but, as the euphoria of the night of victory grows distant, scepticism overtakes me.

Stretched out flat on her belly with all her concentration focused on a textbook placed on a cushion in front of her, Klava is studying for her midwinter examinations. I have no more exams to sit since I have abandoned the idea of adding one subject more to my university record. Our study group of the previous year has dissolved: Chourik no longer comes to help me, nor Kola to help Klava. She manages now on her own and I spend my time watching her while pretending to read Maupassant. I find it a moving sight to observe her obstinate struggle with science, and I know that she has chosen the correct path. As early as 1940 my protector, the mathematician Motia, had repeatedly advised me to opt for a scientific career. Yet it is only now, six years later, that I finally understand all his reasons. Professional specialization in the USSR is a way forward for those who want to do something useful without risking falling foul of the *nomenklatura*. I imagine Klava surrounded by other engineers, discussing their projects together, as Motia used to do during our night-time walks in pre-war Rostov. I shall always regret his death at Sevastopol in 1942. I want, for her sake, to see her attain her goal as a woman of science who enjoys her work and has the time to read Alexander Blok and listen to serious music, as Motia did.

She will succeed in any case though. I am sure of it, and it isn't simply something I have convinced myself so I can leave with a good conscience. Kola also tells me that after a difficult start last year, she does better and better and that she is even more diligent and conscientious than he is. Certainly she has to pay the price for it and takes less and less interest, or none at all, in the international news relayed to me by the 'hard-liners' as the PUR people are known. Of what use could it be to her anyway? I had paid only cursory attention myself, the previous year, to the changes of government in King Michel's Romania, because the names of the new ministers meant nothing to me, no more than those of the outgoing group, and because the overall picture resembled a fragmented jigsaw puzzle. The differences dividing Poles are no more comprehensible to Klava, and I have no desire to distract her from the subject that is dear to her, mathematics, in order to initiate her into the byways of Polish politics, which at this moment are the most complicated in all of Europe. But I see the 'hard-liners' only by day, for I am eager to spend the evenings at home watching Klava make her way towards her highly qualified engineer's diploma. Although I am pretending to read she knows that I am looking at her, and it probably gives her pleasure for, from time to time, when she changes the book on her cushion, she flashes at me that smile of our happiest days together. I know how to recognize it among the range of her engaging expressions, and that of this evening means: 'Gosh! but I'm so happy, and you mustn't worry on my account.' And even her favourite sally: 'I am a bird of the Don and my nest must remain on this side of the River,' is perhaps not simply a phrase of consolation after the refusal of the authorities to allow her to leave with me. She is right to want to complete her studies, to become an engineer, and only to contemplate a flight towards such far-off places (if circumstances allow) after equipping herself with this 'baggage of learning'. If the opportunity doesn't arise she will always have a very different 'nest' from that of her parents for she is in the process of laying the foundations of a fuller life which, one day, will perhaps give her all that she could wish for. The act of concentration embellishes her, and it is also one of the reasons why I am looking at her, bent over her books, sideways or face on, slowly stirring a limb to remove the creeping stiffness with the grace that only she possesses. But she doesn't like me to call her 'my pretty Cosatchka': 'Pretty is fine, it's always a pleasure to hear although it doesn't amount to anything essential, but I am not an exotic bird, I didn't choose my origins.' For the others however she is still 'Cosatchka Klava', and that doesn't upset her. No doubt from the lips of our friends the reference to her nationality has nothing of an exotic ring. Anyway, two and a half years later she will be above all 'engineer Klava'. And what will have become of my friends by that time?

Kola will graduate in the same year, but I don't think that he will be satisfied with specialization, even supplemented by music and highbrow reading. We often see each other because he presses me, justifiably, to pull off one last coup in order not to leave Klava without a strategic reserve in roubles. Now Kola has an unrivalled eye for the main chance, but it would be unfair to present him simply as a 'great schemer', the heir to Ostap Bender of Ilf and Petrov's *Twelve Chairs*. He is a leader of men, he has a political temperament and in other climes he would not have wasted his time in studying to become an engineer. In Rostov he was eventually admitted to membership of the CPSU with some difficulty, and only after an exceptionally long wait. He had already been proposed for the party by our political commissar, Bielokonienko, in 1942, in acknowledgement of his exemplary conduct during the defence of Nalchik. Kola is well aware of the reasons for this delay and of the handicap he will still have to overcome: he is the son of White Cossacks, resolutely White, who were deported to an unknown destination, perhaps even shot, in 1926 when he was four years old. A lot has happened since then, certainly, and he didn't choose his origins any more than Klava chose hers, but it is recorded in his dossier and it cannot be erased, even if he were to spend days on end explaining all the harmful consequences that he attributes to the Cossacks, and especially the Whites.

He stubbornly assures me that this page will soon be turned and that he will have to get into position in the race for posts of responsibility. With what end in mind? 'It is the only means available, in our country, to carry on the struggle against suffering,' he replies, reminding me that he remains attached to the programme that he explained to me one evening on the *electritchka* between Min. Vody and Kislovodsk, and that he hadn't become a simple careerist therefore. Kola has made a great impression by the way on the Polish 'hard-liners' and this has confirmed for me that he is astute, sensitive and quick-witted, and that I don't merely attribute these qualities to him through my liking for him or from nostalgia for the innumerable adventures that we have lived through together. I wonder though what his chances are of making his way in life while remaining faithful to his beliefs and avoiding compromises. His initial refusal to divorce Fira (now it is done), was perhaps a small foretaste of things to come. For the moment he is only a candidate-member of the CPSU, enjoying no particular privilege. He doesn't give himself any airs but doesn't for all that relinquish his efforts 'to broaden his own material base', nor to help me to do the same for Klava's benefit. In fact he is even more of a 'Don bird' than she is because, being neither obsessed by the sciences nor very interested in the outside world, he dreams of utopias only for his native region: 'If they leave me to it, we shall transform this region into a flourishing garden.' This 'we', coming after the 'me', is an apt account of his links with socialism.

Chourik, the most cultivated of our friends, has a weakness for Kola although he didn't belong to his clan in Kislovodsk. Of course that doesn't prevent him from often calling him a political ignoramus, even in public. This happened recently during a dinner for an all-male party at the Don Restaurant, in honour of our friends Volodia and Kostia who were home on leave. The next day he admitted to having got carried away because of Kola's poorly thought out peroration on the subject of Germany, but he added that he didn't think of Kola as a lost cause by any means. 'He has unquestionable merit. Moreover, since early childhood he has experienced hardships such as we have never known,' thereby implying that we two, from families of intellectuals, have benefited from the patrimony of our parents, which is not the case with Kola, nor for that matter with Klava.

In the matter of hardships, however, it is Chourik, at the end of the day, who has suffered most. I call by at his place occasionally during the day because he is often unwell and, each time that I see him hop on his single leg, holding on to the furniture for support while he opens the door for me, I understand the extent to which this mutilation is an ordeal for him. He has a very sharp mind, is very polemical, and his reading has made of him an impeccable analyst of texts, which he knows how to dissect in detail and explain, better than all the teachers in Rostov. In my view, in different circumstances, he would have made an excellent satirical essayist, but in the USSR I don't see an easy career open to him. Not that he is against the regime: on the contrary, his demands on the latter derive from the original ideals of the October Revolution, as though he were enjoining it to remain perfectly faithful to them. Conscious of the fact that during the 28 years which separate us from 1917, all too many things have occurred that were neither foreseen nor consistent with the aims of the Revolution, Chourik doesn't attempt to put the entire experience in the dock, an experience that was the fruit of exceptional circumstances which are broadly explained in the *History of the CPSU (Bolsheviks)*, but he does hope that after the war Stalin will give a new impulse to Soviet socialism and take it in another direction, more in the spirit of Lenin's *State and Revolution* or Marx's *Critique of the Gotha Programme*. I don't entirely understand him and I know that he is unrealistic because the impetus for a socialist democracy would have to proceed from the grassroots and not from the summit of power, but in particular I am afraid for him when I think of the chemistry professor I met in the Volgalag who had been condemned to fifteen years of Gulag for less subversive ideas.

A great deal will depend, however, on Galia. I knew a different Chourik when I stayed at his home in 1944, and I am well placed therefore to appreciate the effects that his librarian wife has had on him – and to imagine the problems of their daily life together. At the time he hadn't even an artificial limb and used to say to me that he would never succeed in coming to terms with his disability, nor in interesting himself in other problems. Then Galia took him in hand and gradually gave back to him the taste for reading, discussing and studying. Admittedly he already possessed his analytical gifts, but she helped him to use them more fully and to discover the joys of knowing more and understanding better than others. In our circle we are used to seeing Galia always echo Chourik, and we sometimes think of her as 'second fiddle', whereas in reality the entire weight of this couple rests upon her shoulders. Now since she is not herself one of the war-disabled (some of whom imagine that they can get away with anything), Galia has a shrewder appreciation of the point beyond which it is unsafe to go in the USSR. Her 'orthodox' mother is well-connected in academic circles and will help her to temper Chourik's exacting idealism and make of him, in time, a good history teacher who will teach the official syllabus and consign his private thoughts to his study drawers.

And Zeus? What will become of him, this god of gods who helped us so much on our arrival in Rostov? He is still dozing on his Olympus, for he only wants to study in a 'technicum' for aircraft technicians and this institute doesn't yet exist. In the meantime he remains as manager of his canteen and composes poems for our ears only, because we can't manage to persuade him to send them to *Molot*. Remaining neutral throughout our discussions, he shows a great concern for objectivity, but he always appears to be floating in the clouds somewhat. His lack of ambition is patently clear, and Kola sometimes invites him to shake himself. 'No thanks,' he replies, pointing to his head, 'I have already been shaken sufficiently.'

His case is really bizarre: Zeus is not a nutcase by any means and his behaviour cannot be explained by the concussion he suffered in Nalchik. He is the meditative type who prefers to listen and who talks very little about himself. I don't even know, for example, whether he is Cossack or whether he has any family in Rostov. Last year, when Cathinka began to doublecross him with 'Caesar Imperator', he read to me a very worrying poem which took as its inspiration Lermontov's famous exclamation: 'No, I am not Byron,

I am another exile, and with the Russian soul!' Zeus declaimed in the same tone 'No, I am not Pushkin, nor Mayakovsky either!' – only to conclude that, like them, he would die young, with a piece of lead in his head. I deduced from this that since he had been overtaken by feelings of jealousy he no longer contemplated imitating Peter the Great and decapitating his rival, but thought of committing suicide instead. Klava and Fira, the only ones to know about my fears, have assured me that in Russia all poets, even those who are most attached to life, write at least some poems on suicide and death.

Throughout the night of victory Zeus remained at home on the pretext of composing an ode to Stalin, which he never read to any of us. The visits from Vassia and others on leave don't make him particularly happy since he didn't belong to our squadron in Kislovodsk. Curiously his jealousy has diminished and he allowed Cathinka to bill and coo with Volodia 'the Singer', well beyond what would normally have been expected of a singing duo. You can always rely on Zeus: he never misses an appointment and never arrives anywhere empty-handed, but something prevents him from enjoying himself like the others. What could it be? It's a mystery to me; he never complains about anything, he eats his fill, he has a little money put aside; what's more since he is a good-looking lad and works in a factory full of women he would have been able to replace Cathinka by a whole harem. It seems likely though that Zeus just belongs to the category of people who let life pass them by, day by day, without ever undertaking anything. Perhaps despite everything he will end up deciding to study or to become a proper poet, but it is too early to predict what life has in store for him.

That leaves Cathinka, a sort of little sister to Klava, her childhood friend, who feels perfectly at home in our 28 square metres, sings, dances, changes her dress (she is the same size as Klava), but never reveals what she is really up to. In my view she is leading a double life, with Zeus and 'Caesar Imperator', and when the opportunity arises, fooling the pair of them with Volodia, 'the Singer'. Klava tells me that I have an overactive imagination and that in any event it is none of our business. She is perfectly right, except that I am soon going to leave and therefore risk never finding out the truth, which bothers me. Despite Klava's ban I eventually asked our favourite *blondinka* an indiscreet question, but she simply confused me further: 'That's it, you've guessed. I'm "Caesar Imperator's" mistress, but I also tried to go to bed with you, because I find you interesting. Unfortunately, apart from Klava, you had eyes only for Fira, and you never even noticed any of my oblique signals.' Kola though is probably right: I don't understand women well enough to guess what goes on in Cathinka's head, or to imagine what she hopes to achieve by playing around with the men in her life. Thanks to her bewitching voice, which is a great asset in Russia, Cathinka will probably spend the rest of her life in the Don Cossacks Performance Arts Ensemble: age is immaterial in the career of a singer as opposed to that of a ballerina. Provided that the men don't kill each other on her account, as they did for my poor Nadia in the red-brick barracks . . .

Meanwhile she keeps her men well under control and Klava and I are among the first to benefit from it, as on the occasion of my trip to Moscow last year. Shortly before my departure, 'Caesar Imperator' gives me a kind of courteous talking-to by way of farewell, and chides me for having replied too readily to his clients: 'Savelit? What savelit? I don't even remember what they smell of,' adding, as though he knew about our caper with the petrol and the fish through Cathinka, that the *savelit*, unlike petrol, hasn't any smell. Next, he hands me a *pridel*, a requisition voucher, for a hundred pairs of men's rubber-heeled shoes, asking me to explain this mystery if I still have the time, because we don't even have one hundred male workers and haven't any need of rubber-heeled shoes. It is a gift from providence: Kola and I go off like a shot to Kharkov and manage to sell the entire stock on the spot to a wholesaler. The latter barely examines them, so well accustomed is he to their poor quality, and throws them on top of an impressive pile of similar pairs, as though this shoe factory kept on working just for him. Even Kola, who is usually capable of finding a positive aspect to the most wretched situation, says simply on this occasion: 'What a total shambles, our industry . . .' But we bring back a respectable sum with us to Rostov, all of it for Klava, because Kola had relinquished in advance his share in this last of our joint coups.

The last phase unfolds at an accelerated pace, like a succession of snapshots. February 1946: the elections to the Supreme Soviet take place, an astonishing spectacle of self-mystification that the USSR presents as though to complete my acquaintance with Soviet life. Had I not witnessed it I wouldn't have believed that they spend fortunes in this country on an electoral campaign, as though the (only) list of 'Bolsheviks of the Party and of those without party' cannot fail to be elected. Nothing is spared in order to entice the electors: meetings, of course, but also free entertainments, buffets at competitive prices and meat rations that actually mean something.

It is Kola's baptism of fire as member of the CPSU: he has been entrusted with the role of 'agitator' in our area of the city and he obtains for us the best seats at a very good non-political concert in the Theatre of Musical Comedy. During the interval a buffet table groans under the weight of exquisite *pirojki*. Then, to spoil it all, a speech by someone called Boris Ponomarev, head of the electoral list in Rostov, who appears to me to be even more stupid than the average Russian apparatchik (he is still at it today, 38 years later, and even sits on the Politbureau of the CPSU). On the way out I warn Kola, 'I've no intention of voting for that fellow.' It doesn't bother him in the least: 'You have only to cancel his name in the polling booth.' Kola's duty is to make sure that all the voters go to the polling station, preferably early. Whoever does best in this socialist competition between 'agitators' will earn special praise in their dossier.

Chourik can't stop laughing: 'We need Japanese-style elections.' It was a favourite joke in the history faculty. A lecturer who was denouncing electoral corruption, but who couldn't criticize the democracies of our British allies had told them that in Japan, on the occasion of some election, the bosses paid cash for each vote. The students, who are always broke, privately aired their views in favour of 'Japanese-style elections' declaring their readiness to sell their vote in order to make ends meet. According to Chourik, everyone in Rostov would prefer to receive an envelope with a few roubles instead of posters and leaflets. He will vote nevertheless, and at eight o'clock in the morning, in order to please Kola. Considering myself to be only half-Soviet – my convoy is scheduled to leave on 15 March – I grumble a little. There is no good reason for getting up so early on a Sunday morning. Klava, though, thinks it a mere formality lasting only a few minutes, after which we shall be able to go back to bed. Some chance! The queue in front of the polling station is like that in front of a foodstore. Each 'agitator' has dragged his or her flock out of bed at sunrise, and everyone waits before putting in the bin their voting slip – which most people don't even bother to read.

There are at least six of us who go into the booth determined to strike out Ponomarev's name: Klava has invented this stratagem to avoid my gesture being noticed. She has persuaded her parents to imitate me and also Cathinka and Zeus. According to next day's *Molot*, 99.9 per cent of the electors at our polling station gave their votes to Ponomarev and not a single voting slip was cancelled. Kola declines all responsibility: he had no part in the count and had nothing to do with this fraud. He swears that he himself struck out Ponomarev's name in a gesture of solidarity with us, and because he didn't like the look of the candidate. We could have refused to take part in the rite, but it would have been dangerous, and what have we lost by it? One or two hours of Sunday rest. On the other hand, Kola will perhaps derive some benefit from it to help him make his way within the CPSU.

At the beginning of March Kostia arrives from Austria weighed down with presents at the same time as Vassia and Volodia get back from Germany, and the whole clan of Mietchotkians are reunited. With me Volodia finds it amusing to make fun of the Poles, not a very funny subject at the best of times but which just now really saddens me. He tells me that my 'Polaks' are worthless as soldiers, and cites as an example the Warsaw insurrection in August–September 1944. At that moment the Soviet Army was not in a position to cross the Vistula. On this point, Volodia is certain. He had to drop endless bombs to protect the bridgehead that Tchouikov had stupidly established much further to the south of Warsaw, which, having suffered heavy losses, proved useless at the time of the big offensive of January 1945. 'My Polaks' picked a bad moment for their insurrection for they were not strong enough to rout the Germans on their own nor could they be helped from the outside. The 'good' Volodia finds it funny, a good joke, and fails to take into account the fact that these 'Polaks' fought against our common enemy and, of more serious personal concern to me, that my own family may have disappeared beneath the rubble of Warsaw.

I lack the information to argue with him and in any case, I like him only when he is singing, which he does very well, not when he philosophizes. In my own mind, however, I had long since imagined an escape for my mother and sister that involved their transfer from Lodz to Warsaw. I had already mourned my father; since he was already a sick old man unable to face up to the Nazi persecution and the severe hardships of war, death would have been a deliverance for him and would have spared him further painful sufferings. My mother, in my view, might have quit Lodz, where she was politically marked, either to rejoin her parents in Warsaw or my brother Alexander in Pomerania. Of course I hadn't any information to substantiate my conjecture, but I had been convinced for several years that it had in fact happened.

Listening to Volodia's mockery on 'Polaks', I had yet other reasons to think of my mother: firstly because she had foreseen this tragic episode in Warsaw and told me that the Poles, in difficult moments of their history have always shown proof of heroic bursts of combative energy; next, because she detested the megalomaniac and contemptuous attitudes of a very large number of Poles towards Russians – the legacy of Polish hostility to czarist oppression. It was under my mother's influence that in 1939, while I was marching half-asleep across a Poland blitzed by the Luftwaffe, I dreamed of Soviet aid, to help us certainly, but also to put an end to these unbearable old disputes. As for the Warsaw insurrection, I haven't enough information in Rostov to discuss it with Volodia, but the idea does cross my mind that the Soviet Union has missed here an historic opportunity to totally transform its image in Poland. It would certainly have paid off as the Poles had indeed misjudged the military situation and had overestimated their strength. With regard to questions of strategy I trust Volodia almost as much as Vassia, since both of them have Cossack warrior blood and they inherit instincts passed down through three centuries of fighting experience.

I leave Volodia and let him get on with impressing Klava with his anecdotes about the experiences of a 'good' soldier. At the end of the day he doesn't say anything really malicious about the Poles: he explains that they are shrewder than the Russians in commercial matters, and atone for stealing German cattle – herds of them are brought across their territory – by putting a few bottles of vodka and some horns into the convoy trucks – evidence that the missing beasts have died en route. Perhaps it gives Klava the desire to join me in this curious country where the people are crafty in everyday matters but inept in war. After all, she has already seen plenty of warriors on the banks of the Don.

'You will have to explain to them what we are like in reality,' Klava says to me as we leave the cinema after having seen *The Star of the North*, an American film on the war in the Soviet Union. It was first shown in 1944, and the audience had howled with laughter then, just as they did on this occasion. But I find it interesting because of its stars (Erich von Stroheim and Dana Andrews), and also, a curious coincidence this, because two of its protagonists are a student named Klava and an airman named Kola. They really know how to choose charming names in Hollywood. Admittedly the plot is improbable and mawkish; it tells the story of the recapture of the village 'The Star of the North' by Soviet partisans in the very earliest phase of the war. Interestingly, it reveals one of the essential elements of the German drive to the East: on this front the Wehrmacht committed atrocities from the beginning of the occupation and the Soviets accordingly responded with a fight to the death.

It isn't the description that the Americans give of our partisans' exploits which makes the Rostov audience laugh, but rather the Hollywood vision of daily life in the USSR. In the village, 'The Star of the North', the people are all dressed in silk and invariably have a balalaika to hand, ready to dance at any appropriate – or inappropriate – moment. They are cared for on the spot in a modern hospital, managed by a 'great consultant' who is so famous that even the German major (played by Erich van Stroheim) defers to him. At the end, the great Russian doctor will kill the German major, who reveres medical science but has no respect for Russian children. (He stole their blood for wounded Wehrmacht soldiers, and the poor kids die as a result.)

I offer tentative defence of *The Star of the North*, reminding Klava that even Soviet films are not noted for their realism. Hasn't a film been released recently whose hero was a *woman* government minister? 'Ah but that's a projection towards the future. I might one day become a minister myself, whereas with the Americans it is a matter of crass ignorance of our present reality,' Klava insists. For her I am already mentally moving away from Soviet people and will soon have to explain things to them.

In fact Klava doesn't aspire to be a government minister. But, like all our friends she is annoyed when Soviet citizens are depicted as prosperous and rather frivolous people with their balalaikas; neither does she like the idea that foreigners should see their poverty or their sadness. When a delegation from the West came to visit her institute she saw nothing wrong in the fact that the most poorly dressed students were requested to absent themselves. 'Poverty is not a fault, certainly, but there is nothing in it to boast about.' Nor does she expect me to tell that in a Rostov whose population is half-starving,

bacon and eggs were served to all the wounded and sick patients in a
city hospital when Lady Churchill arrived on an official tour. What
must I tell them over there then, in that world on the other side of
the River Don which shows us so little understanding? 'Find the
means of telling them that we have suffered a great deal and that we
would be happy to improve our living standards, extend our
education and broaden our culture, and to live in peace. That's the
truth and you know it better than anyone,' – she says, half-playful,
half-serious. 'You are my personal ambassador abroad and, when I
become an architect, I shall come myself and build our private
embassy. It will have at least 56 square metres and two wash-hand
basins, no, one will do, but we shall have a separate kitchen and a
shower with hot water, like they have in a *bania*.' I agree with her,
let's dream together, the war hasn't left me with much time to play.

The period of waiting for my convoy offers Klava the opportunity to
fulfil a wish that she had first expressed at the time of our courtship.
During the theatre interval, I point out to her, Oleg: the room-mate
who denounced me to the NKVD in Yerevan. Klava promptly
disappears, asking me to excuse her. The next thing I know Oleg is
collapsing in a heap on the floor; those standing by rush to his aid,
confusion intervenes. It is impossible to say at a distance what has
happened. Klava comes back with a perky air and announces to me:
'We have settled accounts with him, let's go to our seats.'

I learn from some people beside me, before the curtain rises, that a
man has just been stabbed in the genitals. A tall tale: an Austrian
shoe (a present from Kostia), even a pointed one, is not a dagger.
Always this Russian habit of exaggerating! I could have told them
that this man would recover from the blow a lot quicker than I
would from my time in prison and the camps. Once at home,
however, I criticize Klava. Why take such risks in striking this
informer? There was no risk she maintains, he didn't even see her
face because she was so quick. If all the Olegs in the USSR received
from time to time a few kicks in the balls, life would be better all

370

round and there would be less arbitrariness. It is a distinctively Cossack style of reasoning, not in the least dialectical; Chourik will have to explain it to her after I am gone. As for me, despite my criticisms I am not too unhappy about the event at all.

On the eve of my departure, fixed for 15 March, Klava and I have to arrange the annulment of our marriage at the city hall. The clerk who deals with us doesn't take long to deal with Klava's papers: a long and narrow stamp saying *annulirovano* is placed over the stamp which, in July 1944 'registered' our marriage. Klava says nothing but her face expresses surprise or disappointment. She would never have believed that things could be sorted out so easily, without a single question, without the least inquiry. She doesn't close her passport and continues to stare at the cancelled page as if to draw the clerk's attention to the fact that the new stamp doesn't entirely cover the previous one, which is much larger and contains all my civilian details.

Next, the clerk tries to seize my passport and in exchange, give me a slip of paper certifying that my passport has been added to the dossier of our marriage annulment. Now this won't do at all for at the first identity check I shall end up in jail: our militia do not accept any old slip of paper, they require passports. The clerk goes off to consult with the office manager, who brings my passport back to me in person. 'We shall get it off you before you leave,' he says, as friendly as a prison gate.

In the street, the clerk runs after us. The poor woman has forgotten to stamp my passport and is filled with panic. A grave error: I am a husband without a wife! For the city hall administration, it is a disaster. This little incident revives our spirits. Until then we weren't too sure about just what to say, but now Klava begins to laugh at the frightened expression of the clerk and makes fun of me too: 'So, you thought to get away without a stamp, did you? Well, you were mistaken my lad, for stamp! stamp! she has given you two of them, one more than I have!' Two days later, upon learning from

Molot that on the same day, the title of 'People's Commissariat' was eliminated – they are now rebaptized 'ministries' – she sees all the comedy of the situation: 'It was definitely the day for stamps: they must have put an *annulirovano* on all of their passports as well.'

My convoy doesn't set out on time and I feel like someone who is outstaying his friends' invitation after having already said goodbye a thousand times. People who have taken my farewell visits seriously seem astonished to see me still around. They have even been generous with their advice about my forthcoming struggle in Poland for my country's independence and for its friendship with Russia. But their exclamations of surprise: 'So you're still here!' rather amuse me. It is indeed me, large as life; the railway authorities still haven't found a wagon for the 20 or so people awaiting repatriation from south Russia. The Polish 'hard-liners' have already gone back to Moscow, but we are still waiting.

I have said very little about these three Polish hard-liners – two men and one woman who formed a very supportive trio – because it would have taken too long to describe the misunderstandings which arose with them. From our first meeting, Klava took an instant dislike to them and, trusting to her Cossack instincts, announced that they were Chekists, and without culture. My impression, however, is that they had spent years in Siberia or in central Asia and had nothing to do with the NKVD. The first misunderstanding arose from Klava's insinuations. I didn't dare speak openly to them, nor to ask them for example to which part of Siberia they had been deported. No direct question was possible. They addressed me as *pan komsomolec*, which clearly showed that they were basing their opinion of me on my NKVD dossier, where I was still classified as a Komsomol member. In reality, since returning to Rostov in 1944, I had nothing to do with this prestigious organization. In short, we were delighted to talk in Polish together but our discussions were distorted by a reciprocal mistrust, based on the suspicion of each other's ultra-dogmatism. Obviously this didn't prevent us from joking about the incongruous aspects of Russian life, because Poles together would never deprive themselves of this pleasure. With regard to essential questions though, I never knew what they really thought about the USSR nor how they reconciled their experience on Soviet soil with their adherence to the Polish Workers' Party (the PPR), this party which preferred to call itself simply the party of the 'workers' as opposed to 'communist', while remaining unconditionally pro-Soviet.

The second misunderstanding: Klava imagined that these people were exerting pressure on me to return rapidly to Poland, when in fact they wished for nothing of the kind. In fact, our conversations reduced my *Reisefieber* (in the East to express the fever to be off, they always use the German expression). Clearly well informed, the hard-liners described life in Poland in a way that didn't correspond to how I had imagined things during the victory night in Gorky Park. Poland had been ruined by the war, it had lost one inhabitant in every five, yet despite this frightening carnage, certain basic determinants of its political life had remained unaltered. The shift to the left that was very clear in Western Europe had not occurred in Poland, and the new regime, supported by the protective power of the Soviet Army, devoted itself to outdoing the nationalists with protestations of patriotism. The keystone of the new ideology was to be the dramatic emphasis put on the value to Poland of her 'recovered territories', taken back from Germany (though not claimed for centuries), while alliance with the USSR was justified first and foremost by the need to defend these new borders. For the hard-liners, '*raison d'Etat*', and our 'historic rights' counted above everything, and they proudly showed me certain publications of the PPR which quoted from *Rota*, an anti-German right-wing hymn. It was a psychological mistake, because I have never been patriotic and I will neither sing the *Rota* in Poland nor pan-Slavic hymns in the USSR.

In Poland, geography and history distort all debate. Even before thinking of how to rebuild their home, the country's inhabitants want to know whether they are going to be invaded from the west (by the Germans) or from the east (by the Russians), or by both at once – the memory of the German–Soviet Pact is still in everyone's mind. Using a few German provinces as fodder to reassure those who most mistrust the Russians (this includes the majority of socialists) would not do the trick. The latter demanded secure frontiers to the east and never, despite the advice of Churchill, Roosevelt and de Gaulle, did they accept giving up their pre-1939 territories to the east, inhabited in the main by Ukrainians and Byelorussians, which had once again become Soviet after Yalta. During the German occupation, the communists were banished from the Polish underground, not on account of their revolutionary programme, but because they sided with the USSR – and in fact with all the leaders of the Grand Alliance – in this frontier dispute. It was also one of the major reasons for popular mistrust of the new government.

Frankly, my dear Klava is completely mistaken in believing that my meetings with the hard-liners could hasten my departure. No one is in a hurry to return to a country that is riven apart by civil war. In fact, without its being clear in my mind, I have a premonition that I shall not remain in Poland. Although hostile to the nationalists and to their Catholic-patriotic culture, I don't trust the new regime either. And it isn't my time in the Gulag which excites my rancour; I have got beyond this stage and, without being a Christian, am capable of forgiving. The mistrust I feel towards the USSR is nourished by my everyday experience in the rather favourable circumstances of my life in Rostov. For let us speak the truth: Stalin writes letters of thanks in honeyed tones to the peasants for their donations, knowing full well that their savings have been extorted from them, in the same way that the state extorts from us our 'voluntary' subscriptions for a state loan. And the rigged elections? And our 10 voting slips, which failed to be included in the count? And the lies about salaries and prices? What good does it do to add to the examples? For seven years the leaders of this country have done their best to convince me, at every opportunity, that they don't give a damn for their own people. After all that, I cannot in all honesty stand in Poland as guarantor of their good faith and ask my compatriots to trust Soviet promises not to interfere in Polish internal affairs.

The Poles in Rostov hope that thanks to the wealth of the recovered territories, there will be a rapid reconstruction of the country, which will give birth to a Polish government enjoying genuinely popular support. The new Poland will be at the same time a loyal but independent ally of the USSR. This seems to me to be a fragile hope but I decide to keep an open mind until I am able to form an on-the-spot opinion. I would be the first to rejoice at such a happy ending: Klava could then come and join me and construct 'our embassy'. (Nothing went according to this optimistic scenario however, and, three years later, I left Poland, which had been brought to heel and integrated into the socialist bloc in spite of all the preceding promises.)

When you're kept waiting for your train for a whole month, you go out gladly. Klava and I go out very often: mainly to the cinema, despite my dissatisfaction with this sector of Soviet cultural life.

As films are considered to be so important by the CPSU, each cinema in Rostov changes its programme at least once a week. Logically therefore, Soviet studios would have had to produce at least 210 films during the four war years to enable this to be done. In fact they produced only 30 and so the programming of our cinemas is a carousel on which each film turns around and comes back at least seven times. It is said that this was due to the fact that no feature film could be released without Stalin's personal approval. In wartime he is too busy to view films. Later, at the Twentieth Party Congress, Krushchev will accuse our supreme commander-in-chief of having followed the conduct of military operations on a globe instead of on staff field maps, but that by no means proves that he had a lot of free time for private showings. It might even have kept him busier still.

Be that as it may, my quarrel with the Soviet cinema isn't simply nostalgia for Greta Garbo or Marlene Dietrich, even though I miss them enormously, but rather from the fact that I don't like to see the same films seven times in four years.

These films, from *Zoia* to *Rainbow* remind us that we have come a long way after a great deal of suffering, but they no longer correspond to reality. It is the old problem with the time-lag in our film industry: in Kislovodsk, in 1942, when half of the Soviet Union was already occupied by the Germans, I myself presented films to my squadron which showed that no enemy could ever cross Soviet frontiers. The public became used to making their own connections: 'This is what we were supposed to think yesterday.' Just before our troops entered Germany, *Pravda* had given Ilya Ehrenbourg a friendly reprimand for his simplistic anti-German judgements ('Comrade Ehrenbourg Simplifies' was the title of the article) and, since then, we have been advised to make a distinction between 'good' and 'evil' Germans just as we do with other peoples. In fact the 'good' Germans are conspicuously absent from the films except for defeated marshals and generals of the Wehrmacht who change sides after having been sent to prisoners' camps. Even so, we are able to situate these old films in their original context, and wait patiently for new ones, realizing the slowness of 'Mosfilm' and the fact that Stalin doesn't have the time to give them distribution permits. At the beginning of April 1946, a new feature film plunges us into a state of total perplexity.

It is a recent film for it opens with the parade of German POWs in Moscow on 22 June 1944; they have been brought there directly from the front to allow Muscovites, on this third anniversary of the Nazi invasion, to see the vanquished conquerors close-up. Two kindly Soviet women notice, in the column of ragged prisoners, a soldier wearing glasses, an intellectual advanced in age, and they take pity on him: 'That fellow there is surely not an evil sort.' 'You're right,' the other replies, 'he's probably a decent man who was forcibly enlisted.'

The sequel, in flashback, shows the real personality of this intellectual, who likes to read Goethe in his splendid library and listens to *lieder* sung by his wife, an overfed Valkyrie, before torturing, like any good, sadistic Nazi, Soviet women deportees. The cruelty of this individual has no limits and you need a strong stomach to watch the sequences in which he goes to work on his victims. Klava, who is usually self-possessed, can't stop sobbing and finds certain images unbearable. But it is the moral of this film that particularly intrigues us, for it tends to show that there are no 'good' Germans, as though the old line has come back.

Chourik makes some rapid calculations to establish that after all, between July 1944 and January 1945 – the date of the article 'Comrade Ehrenbourg Simplifies' – Mosfilm has had the time to release this final contribution to the 'Kill him!' genre. Not content with a single hypothesis, Chourik puts forward a second, which takes into account Stalin's disappointment – and ours as well – at the absence of any popular resistance movement in Germany at the end of the war. With this in mind, and in order to avoid massacres, Stalin gave the order to attenuate the anti-German propaganda at the moment that Soviet troops were entering Germany, but he had also authorized the release of this film so as to invite us not to trust appearances, to be ready to expose the German beasts, who are notoriously capable of assuming new disguises.

That seems plausible enough, if rather depressing. In Kislovodsk, when we awoke the inhabitants at seven o'clock in the morning singing, 'We are fighting for the world of enlightenment' and the Nazis for the 'kingdom of darkness', the situation was simple and clear. Each step forward made by our camp was supposed to roll back the 'infernal night' brought on by the adversary and, in this triumph of good over evil, there was room for Germans on the side of the good. In practice, however, neither our victories nor those of our allies allowed the Germans to emerge from the 'realm of shadows and darkness'.

Klava listens to us, extremely distraught. This film about a sadistic intellectual seems to have been made deliberately to undermine her confidence in the role of culture for moral progress and the improvement of humanity. In it we are shown a German couple whose library had more books than all the Cossacks of the

Don ever possessed, and who, nevertheless, were more monstrous than the worst of them. Klava rates Schiller above Tolstoy (despite the role that the latter's *Anna Karenina* played in our personal history), and she has always found it hard to understand that the people which gave birth to Marx and Schiller, to Engels and Heine, to Hegel and Thomas Mann, had not possessed sufficient cultural antibodies to arm itself against 'the brown plague'. What remedy, she would like to know, can help cleanse it of its chauvinistic and racist poison?

No one is in a hurry to reply to her. Chourik will repeat yet again that after the defeat, the German proletarians will carry forward once more the torch of the class struggle against those who are responsible for their misfortune, and once again, I side with him. Both of us are aware, however, that in this matter there is something which exceeds our understanding and doesn't fit at all with the facts as we know them. Furthermore, if, according to Stalin, the Treaty of Versailles had facilitated Hitler's rise to power in 1933, isn't it illusory to want to cure the German illness by amputating territories much vaster than those seized after the First World War?

In Kislovodosk, militarily speaking, we were in the shit, but our morale was better, the situation more promising. Now everything seems to be foundering in a confusion without principles. Already, in February, after the famous elections to the Supreme Soviet, Stalin has been quoted in an interview as saying that capitalism remains based on the struggle for markets and that this will inevitably produce new wars. Churchill evidently deduced from it that the Soviet Union covets the markets of the capitalists, and replied with a speech at Fulton of which our only knowledge is that it prompted a run on the foodstores in Rostov. All of this is worrying. We sense that the Grand Alliance is in the process of falling apart even before the question of the Germans is settled, let alone that of the Japanese who have just had the unique privilege of seeing two of their cities destroyed by atomic bombs, the first ever to be dropped in wartime.

*

Klava still hasn't come to terms with this story about the German who read Goethe, and tortured Russian women. She counts upon my mother to explain to her the real effects of culture upon the behaviour of men. Chourik upset her in maintaining that there are more books which incite hatred than works which disarm it. 'At bottom, he has remained a soldier at heart, and had he not had a leg amputated he would be just like your friend Vassia.' She maintains that only a really intelligent woman like my mother will know what might be the best protection against men becoming wild animals. My answers have no value in her eyes because, even if she doesn't explicitly say so, she suspects me of having been contaminated by my wartime experiences. In my mother, however, she has full confidence. The evening before I leave she speaks to me about her endlessly, advises me on how I am to describe her daughter-in-law to her (dissimulating her little weaknesses) and she begs me to ask her (Klava's) questions, about life, culture, socialism.

I am grateful to Klava for prolonging my mother's existence in my mind even though I feel certain that she is dead. For had she been still alive she would have found me. The rest of my family, my brothers and my sister, or my friends, or my teacher Wegner, are perhaps waiting for my return without taking any steps to locate me, but my mother would have shifted heaven and earth to find her only son, whom she had hoped to make her spiritual heir. My mother's silence is less a portent than a confirmation: her presentiment in Radom had been correct – we shall never see each other again. But I am in no haste to discover the truth and, by listening to Klava talk about my mother, I almost end up dreaming that our reunion will in fact take place.

For many people, the war develops an unconscious refusal to accept the harsh fact of reality. In my case there is perhaps an additional reason to forget: I feel guilty for having, in 1939, abandoned my mother, as if I believed that the war would resolve all our problems, quickly and thoroughly, without the need of our having to live them through together.

What's done is done. During my crossing of the frozen Bug, I imagined an altogether different return to Poland; I hoped to find my family again, spared by the tragedy, and a country that had shed its outdated ideas. For Klava's sake, I prefer to appear relaxed, and she is calm too, much more so than during the previous winter. She is a strong woman, who regrets nothing and is afraid of nothing; she wants to accompany me to the station alone, with Kola perhaps, but without our other friends.

It is a beautiful late afternoon in April and the passengers of my *tieplouchka* are settling themselves down on their straw mattresses, under the supervision of a young fair-haired woman in military uniform, surely a Chekist, who takes their passports and assigns a place to each of them. Almost all of them are Jews, four families with grandparents and grandchildren. They know each other from having shared these years of exile together, and they speak Yiddish much better than Russian. As for me I stay with Klava and Kola on the platform. I have time enough to make the acquaintance of those who will share my last Russian journey. We quietly promise to write to each other every day and, during exam times, at least three times a week. Klava is wearing her white linen shirt, because it is too warm for her velvet dress and, as on the eve of our marriage, she is rehearsing a story for her parents who still haven't understood that I am leaving for a long time. Kola, very elegant in his Austrian suit (a present from Kostia), announces to me in high spirits that this summer he is going to go to Sotchi; he too is going to travel. Suddenly, Klava throws herself in my arms, crying, and Kola can no longer contain himself either; both of them have noticed that the train is about to leave. We had promised each other not to cry, because we are going to see each other again; the war is over, it is neither 1939 nor 1941, we have won, we are going to be happy, we shall only be apart a short time. 'You're right, it won't be long,' Klava says and starts to cry.

My neighbour to the left has a limp, and almost no baggage. He is a disabled veteran of the war in Spain but, apart from this episode of his life, I shall learn nothing further about him. Of a taciturn or mistrustful nature, he will not talk with anyone, particularly not with my neighbour to the right, our fair-haired military escort. She is not very talkative either during the early part of our journey but she has placed her mattress very close to mine, even though our *tieplouchka* is neither full nor short of space.

Until nightfall I chat away mainly with the heads of the four Jewish families who seem to take me for some sort of authority and ask me a great many questions about our destination. Natives of a frontier region in Galicia which is no longer Polish, they have heard it said that they will automatically be brought to the territories taken from the Germans and that they will no longer have the right to change their place of residence. This by no means appeals to them: they have no wish to live in houses belonging to the Germans, for there is every chance that one day the Germans will come back to dislodge them. They explain all this with great circumspection even if, in our *tieplouchka*, they are sheltered from danger, already having one foot out of the USSR. You might have said that anguish had become second nature to them, to such a degree have they internalized fear of the authorities and, obviously, of the Germans.

I do my best to dispel it: Poland is a free country and everyone can move about as they like; if they choose to set themselves up in the provinces recaptured from Germany, they have nothing to fear from the Germans either, for the world has changed and the *Drang nach Osten* will never be repeated; Nazism is dead for ever. In short, I serve up to them four-fifths of the theories of the 'hard-liners', omitting only to dwell on Stalin's support for the safeguarding of Polish frontiers because I suspect that they won't find it particularly reassuring.

They listen attentively to everything but being the early-to-bed, they don't prolong the conversation. To get to my mattress I brush lightly against that of my fair-haired neighbour, who doesn't even give me time to apologize: her mouth is already pressed on mine, her arms draw me towards her warm body. In all my life I have never experienced such a passionate embrace from a woman whose name I don't even know, and without me having shown the slightest interest in her. Admittedly this strange circumstance is not disagreeable, but what lends the situation a special spiciness is the fact that this woman is a Chekist. Sure enough, Vassia's theory on love-revenge immediately springs to mind and I tell myself that I have been presented with a golden opportunity, through this woman, to take my revenge on Captains Strel and Abak, on the moustachioed colonel of the Volgalag, on the entire NKVD. It is nature that has determined it so: the Chekist is underneath me, half in raptures, and it is I who am the master. Our respective positions illustrate beyond anything I could ever have imagined, the 'historic' turning point of my fate: in 1940, in an identical *tieplouchka*, the Chekists with the blue peaked caps deported me to Siberia under close guard; in 1946, on the return journey, it is one of their number who is squirming in my arms.

Since, however, I am not 'sex starved', as Vassia might put it, I disengage myself from the embrace of the ardent blonde: let's talk first about her functions, her rank within the evil NKVD, that will add a piquant edge to my revenge. She recovers her normal breathing rhythm but doesn't understand: 'Is it because of the girl who was crying at the station?' she asks, as if to recall to me my duty of fidelity towards Klava. 'And I suppose you sleep with just about anyone?' A clumsy question. Insulted by it, she pushes me away and, seizing her cue, launches into a long catalogue of complaints arising from her experiences as a military woman bundled about in a man's world like a small boat, anchorless in the storm. So much for my revenge. What tears there are on this woman's face, tensed with sorrow: she doesn't know what men want, they run after her then they reject her; some have humiliated her, raped her even, others have merely taken advantage of her; all of them have abandoned her to her infinite solitude. She flatly denies being a Chekist, she is only a *sanitarka* and escorts those who are being repatriated on behalf of the Soviet Army medical services. 'Why don't you go back home? The war is over, you will soon find yourself a *moujik*.' 'Where is

382

home? Everything was destroyed and my family were killed or else died of hunger. In the army, at least, you get enough to eat.'

Were we a privileged group in Rostov then, young people with projects, who had come through the war suffering less than the rest? But can you believe a girl who gives herself to you without even saying a word? 'What's your name?' I still don't know it. 'Cathia,' she says as if it were quite natural. Just think of that now: has destiny arranged things so that I should be unfaithful to Klava with a Cathinka? 'Good night,' and I turn my back on her. 'Are you going to sleep?' she asks, astonished, as though it were the very last thing to do in the middle of the night in a *tieplouchka* full of people.

No doubt she will make out a report to her bosses in the NKVD, to the effect that I am impotent; one falsehood more in their dossier on me. The uniformed blonde ends up going to sleep too, but she gets up before me and, when I waken, she presents me with some tea, and hot water for a shave. Taking advantage of her familiarity with the stations, she regularly goes off somewhere at each of our stops to fetch me something that will make my journey more comfortable. On her small alcohol stove she even makes me some omelettes. A mistress, even a wife, would probably not have shown proof of such devotion and yet receive nothing in return. All the passengers in the *tieplouchka* imagine they are witnessing an idyll, whereas nothing happens between myself and the woman; even our conversations are anodyne. Why then all this display of kindness? If it had been in order to write a report, she would have questioned me about Klava, my friends, the other Cathinka, but she simply smiles at me like a contented lover. Is it in order to convince me, then, that she isn't a Chekist and that she had told me the truth about her job, her life?

In Przemysl, a frontier town, our *tieplouchka* is detached from the Soviet train, and its destination no longer interests me because I am going to leave directly on my own for Lodz. Cathia meets up with me once again in the station and in a moving voice asks me a simple favour: 'Don't think badly of me, and don't forget me.'

And, it's true, I still remember her! With time this unusual episode has taken on an even greater significance than it had for me in the course of this 48-hour journey between Rostov and Przemysl. It recalls to me that at the end of the day I was lucky in Russia: having arrived there at the age of fifteen and a half, I left it seven years later, enriched by an unforeseeable and irreplaceable experience which will serve me as capital for the rest of my life. Thanks to my Russian friends, I am among those who, as Klava put it, 'know the truth', their truth, sorrows endured and hopes disappointed. The fair-haired Cathia on the train will have been like a messenger (just like the Siberian redhead, Liuba, a few years before, whom I hadn't trusted either) sent to me to make sure I have understood, one last time, how much her country has suffered – and 'so that I shouldn't forget'.